THE SCIENCES AND THEOLOGY
IN THE TWENTIETH CENTURY

THE SCIENCES
and
THEOLOGY
in the
TWENTIETH CENTURY

edited by

A. R. PEACOCKE
Dean of Clare College, Cambridge
England

UNIVERSITY OF NOTRE DAME PRESS

NOTRE DAME, INDIANA

University of Notre Dame Press edition 1981
Published by arrangement with
Oriel Press Ltd.

Copyright © 1981 Board of Management
of the Foster & Wills Scholarships
Oxford University, England

Set in Plantin by
Knight & Foster, Leeds.

Library of Congress Cataloging in Publication Data

Peacocke, A. R. (Arthur Robert)
    The sciences and theology in the twentieth
century.

    Papers from the Oxford International Symposium,
held at Christ Church College in Sept. 1979.
    Includes bibliographical references and index.
    1. Religion and science — 1946-   —Congresses.
I. Oxford International Symposium (1979: Christ
Church College) II. Title.
BL240.2.P35 1981   261.5'5   81-14771
ISBN 0-268-01704-2   AACR2

Printed in the United States of America

CONTENTS

Preface

The continuous dialogue between sciences and theology which for the most part has enjoyed the ring unmolested, in recent years seems to have been joined by a third-party deeply suspicious of both primary contenders. The public awareness of social responsibility, its associated environmental concerns and fear of over-burdening technological pressures on human values no longer accepts without question the priesthood of the scientist nor the dogma of human progress being identified with solely materialistic scientific research. Within science itself, it has to be admitted that the implications of some of its more recently acquired techniques, especially in genetics and molecular biology, call for the most careful appraisal. Anxieties at the present are only matched by anxieties over the moral and ethical issues which scientific research in the near future could bring.

This volume has been prepared as an interdisciplinary review in which theological, scientific, philosophical and sociological strands are brought together, and it arises out of meetings of international scholars at the Oxford International Symposium held at Christ Church in September 1979.

These Symposia were brought into being as a part of the memorial to the late Michael Foster, who himself was many years a Tutor in Philosophy at Christ Church and concerned himself deeply with some issues of science and Christianity. After his death in 1959, through the generosity initially of his friends, a memorial scholarship bearing his name, was endowed to allow a young German scholar to study in Oxford for two years. This was augmented subsequently by a further benefaction in memory of the late Michael Wills while the German Academic Exchange Service responded by making it possible for young Oxford graduates to undertake periods of study at German Universities. The arrangements were placed in the hands of the Board of Management of the Foster-Wills Committee and, following the visit of Chancellor Brandt to Oxford in 1970, were further extended to

vii

initiate the Oxford International Symposia. These have been held annually since 1972, with their subject matter broadly alternating between the arts and the sciences and in an interdisciplinary style. Each Symposium has provided the basis for the publication of a book, proceeds from which are devoted to the Foster-Wills Scholarship Fund. These Symposia are most generously supported by the Kulturabteilung of the German Foreign Ministry and by the good offices of the German Academic Exchange Service.

During the present Symposium, the participants and guests were entertained at dinner in the delightful surroundings of Oriel College and were privileged to have the company, sadly for the last time before retirement, of Herr Dr. Hubertus Scheibe, Secretary-General of the German Academic Exchange Service, and Frau Scheibe. The contribution made for many years by Dr. Scheibe to Anglo-German academic cooperation in the Oxford connection and in many other ways will always be remembered with much gratitude.

The Symposium once again was privileged to hold its meetings in Christ Church and thanks are extended to the Dean and Governing Body. The overall arrangements owe much to Herr Eschbach, Commander K. Cook and many others. The index was prepared by J. P. Kent.

P. W. Kent
Van Mildert College
Durham

Introduction[1]

A. R. Peacocke
Clare College, Cambridge, U.K.

IN 1976 I was fortunate enough to be present at Christ Church, Oxford, at one of the predecessors — a scientific one — of this Symposium. It occurred to me then that the flexibility with respect to the topics with which this series of distinguished Symposia are concerned, and the support it can command from the sources outlined in the Preface, afforded the ideal situation for bringing together that small, but increasing, body of thinkers in various disciplines who were concerning themselves, from the standpoint of their different kinds of expertise, with the relationship between the sciences and theology in the twentieth century. Moreover the regular Oxford location of these Symposia also had a particular pertinence, because it was at Christ Church that Michael Foster made his seminal contribution[2] to the theology-science dialogue in his analysis of the role of Christian theological attitudes in providing a fertile soil for the growth of the scientific attitude in the seventeenth century. It was particularly fortunate that it was Dr. P. W. Kent who had been acting as the convenor of these Symposia, for I knew his own personal interests also lie *inter alia* in this field. He, and his associated committees, responded warmly to the suggestion that such might be the topic of one of the Oxford International Symposia and I was furthermore fortunate in enlisting the enthusiastic support of Professor Mary Hesse who makes a retrospective contribution at the end of this volume.

I think it is true to say that this 1979 Symposium represented one of the first times that distinguished scholars who are interested in this theme have been brought together at an international level under academic auspices. I make the latter proviso because the World Council of Churches has been very active in catalysing interchange of ideas in this area, both amongst groups of experts and at a more lay level, as in its conference on "Faith, Science, and the Future" held in July, 1979, at the Massachusetts Institute of Technology in Cambridge, Massachusetts. At this Oxford Symposium we had no obligation to report back specifically to member churches, or to any other bodies, and Professor Hesse and I were able to think out a sequence of conference themes in some kind of rational order and to see that speakers were invited accordingly. We were, I think, fortunate in the response we received.

The significant role played by the Christian faith in the creative, initial phase of the natural sciences in their development in Europe is now widely recognised:[3] how Kepler drew upon a mediaeval Christian mysticism, how Giordo Bruno was a part of a Christian revitalization of classical humanism, and how, in seventeenth-century England, the new "natural philosophers" were devoutly motivated to read the "Book of Nature", which they regarded as written by God, alongside Holy Scripture. But for the last two centuries, and at least until recent decades, there has been an increasing alienation between those engaged in the scientific and theological enterprises, with a *modus vivendi* which amounted to little more than what Dr Habgood has called "an uneasy truce" between science and faith.

But now in recent years I begin to detect new tracks that are being made across the no-man's land separating these two armies, for changes have occurred in the mood of both scientists and theologians. Scientists no longer command the adulatory respect that they did perhaps twenty years or so ago for being able to 'deliver the goods', for the 'goods' that they deliver turn out to be a very mixed bag. We are all only too familiar with the cluster of ecological and human problems generated by modern industrial, biological and medical technology — the offspring of the natural sciences. Scientists across the whole spectrum of their activity have all come face to face with baffling ethical problems and the possibly dire social consequences of, at least some, of their apparently 'pure' research and have become more willing to explore them with others, even theologians! Developments in the philosophy of science have also served to modify the hegemony which science previously commanded, as some of the contributions to this volume remind us.

Changes have also occurred in theology: for myself I notice that there is an increasing awareness not only among Christian theologians, but also among believers in general that, if God is in fact believed in as the all-encompassing Reality that Christian faith proclaims, then that Reality is to be experienced in and through our actual lives as biological organisms who are persons, part of nature and living in society. So knowledge of nature and of society can never be irrelevant, to say the least, to our experience of God, if God is He whom the faith affirms. Secondly, the neo-Barthian reliance on the pure Word of God available through the Scriptures has come to be seen by many as a non-viable route. For the further it takes us away from the presumed fallibilities of our natural minds to the supposed divine word in Scripture (or even in the Tradition), the closer it brings us to the question "How can we know that these Scriptures, or this Tradition, is transmitting to us the genuine Word of God?" — and that immediately opens the door to the kind of critical and empirical enquiries which constitute much of modern theology and religious studies. For Christian theology, there can certainly now be no retreat into the citadel, and science and Christian theology cannot avoid encountering each other and thinking anew what kind of inter-relationship they might have today.

The supposed objectivity of science in discovering features of the 'real' world does not go unquestioned today — for example by those who stress the role of the 'interests' of society in determining the role of science and the activity of scientists, and also by those who see the 'truth' of natural science as success in prediction and control. A not dissimilar questioning of the objectivity of religious affirmations is more familar, though scarcely less critical of its truth claims, if we allow a functionalist -anthropological account of religion in society to be exhaustive and adequate — or accept apparently reductionist definitions of religion, such as that of Spiro, as: 'a cultural system consisting of culturally patterned interaction with culturally post-ulated super-human beings'.[5]

But acute and pertinent as these philosophical and sociological critiques of scientific knowledge undoubtedly are, they do not seem at the moment to budge the great majority of scientists (except perhaps particle physicists and cosmologists) from a sceptical and qualified realism, according to which their models and hypotheses are regarded as 'candidates for reality' — that is models of, hypotheses about, a real, but only imperfectly known, world to which the models approx-imate and the hypotheses genuinely refer. Indeed, from my own experience of doing scientific research, I do not think scientists could go on unless they held such a belief. A sceptical and qualified realism is in fact the working assumption of practical scientists and this is something I think cannot be lightly set aside.

In a not dissimilar manner, Christians, indeed all religious believ-ers, also regard themselves as making assertions about a reality which man can and does encounter. But for them, too, the terms which describe the reality to which they are committed are not, *should* not in my view, be regarded as fixed and irreformable with respect to their content and conceptual resources, even if their reference remains unchanged (as with references to 'electrons' by physicists who nevertheless change their understanding of that to which they are referring). Again I do not think believers could go on with the life of faith unless there was at least this degree of belief in the reality of that to which they are committed. However we would be unrealistic, if I may dare use the word, if we did not recognise that the whole question of realism is a very hotly debated topic in current philosophy.[6]

Interestingly, anthropologists — certainly those of a more 'structuralist' mould — increasingly draw parallels between scientific and religious mythological thinking (for example, R. Horton[7] on African traditional thought and its relations to Western science). There seems to be an increasing convergence in the roles and in the theoretical structure assigned by anthropologists both to science in Western societies and to religious cosmological myths in all human societies, for these latter are symbolic narratives which purport to describe an otherwise indescribable and inaccessible transcendent order. Such anthropologists make a *prima facie* case for attributing a similarity in *intention* to religious and scientific cosmologies. Both attempt to take into account as much of the 'data' of the observed universe as possible and both use criteria of simplicity, comprehensiveness, elegance, and plausibility. Both direct themselves to the 'way things are', not only by developing cosmogonies, accounts of the origin of the universe, but also in relation to nearer-at-hand experiences of biological and inorganic nature. So a social anthropological viewpoint serves to make explicit an intention which is common to both the religious and scientific enterprises and which can still be discerned today even in their present sophisticated forms — namely, their search for *intelligibility*, for what makes the most coherent sense of the experimental data with which they are each respectively concerned. What proves to be intelligible is applied, in science, to prediction and control and, in theology, to provide moral purpose and personal meaning and to enable human beings to steer their path from birth to death.

Whether or not, and to what extent, this common intention to seek intelligibility in human life and its surroundings gives rise to any mutual modification of the one enterprise by the other is the question that underlies this volume. Science has a long history of shaking off[8] theological shackles and theology too has, under Barth's influence, claimed its own kind of autonomy. But, we need to ask, can and should this cool and distant relationship persist? I have suggested that the undermining of both ivory towers has generated cracks in each through which they might at least be willing to peer at each other.

More positively, I think theology has to consider how its propositions can be taken seriously, how they may be made coherently relatable to the world in which man finds himself — and today that world, which affords the context in which he seeks intelligibility and personal meaning, is pre-eminently a world described in the terms of the natural sciences as the best-authenticated answers to questions men have always asked about it: What is there? What goes on? How does it change? Why does it change?

So I see cogent reasons why the traditional affirmations of Christian theology (*e.g.*, concerning creation, the nature of man, salvation and hope) must be related, even re-cast, if Christian theology is not to operate in an intellectual vacuum, indeed, in a cultural ghetto. The nature and mode of this relating is explored in this volume — and even, though to a lesser extent, the other almost unthinkable possibility that some urge, of whether or not the map of scientific knowledge might not at least require a new frame and new reference points when the character of the scientific enterprise is related to the wider concerns to which the theological enterprise seeks to respond. Perhaps what we are basically seeking is a new 'theology of nature', rather than a revamped 'natural theology' inexorably doomed to failure in attempting to read off, as it were, the nature and the attributes of the deity from the natural world. But since reflection on that natural world, as described by the sciences, may well engender specific and appropriate styles of theologising, perhaps the funeral rites on natural theology ought not to be prematurely inaugurated.

It is not surprising that the ways of relating modern science to the Christian faith are so variegated and numerous. For there is, in the churches today, both a plurality of ways in which faith is regarded and of how God's relation to he world is conceived; and there is also a wide range of scientific activity with respect to its methodology, to its subject matter (which includes man and human behaviour) and to its relation to society. We clearly need at least a bi-axial grid (possibilities of another dimension will be mooted later) on which to map the possibilities and it will not be easy to choose the parameters to constitute the variables of each axis. Let me tentatively identify some of the possible loci of proposed interactions on this two-dimensional grid.[9]

(i) *Science and theology are concerned with two distinct realms:* the natural/supernatural; the spatio-temporal/the eternal (*cf.* Karl Heim's[10] 'spaces'); the order of nature/the realm of faith; the natural (or physical)/the historical; the physical-and-biological/mind-and-spirit. Reality is conceived of as existing in two orders, a duality, both operating in our world.

(ii) *Science and theology are interacting approaches to the same reality.* Thus each may modify the other. This has been the view I have tended to take so far in this introduction (indeed the 'grid' metaphor implies it) but, although it is widely held by many who otherwise differ markedly in their theologies, it has been strongly resisted. Moreover the modifications required in theological affirmations and the attitudes to science that proceed from it are manifold.[11]

(iii) *Science and theology are two distinct non-interacting approaches to the same reality.* Thus science may be conceived of as dealing with observable qualities (prediction and control?); but theology with ultimate goals and forms of understanding. Or, as popular apologetic has often put it, science seeks to answer the question 'how?' and theology the question 'why?'.

(iv) *Science and theology constitute two different language systems.* The assignment of science and theology to two distinct 'language games' or 'forms of life' in the late-Wittgensteinian manner would license little or no communications between them, for each would then have logical pre-conditions of use such that the one could have no bearing on the other.

(v) *Science and theology are generated by quite different attitudes* in their practitioners — science that of objectivity and logical neutrality, theology that of personal involvement and commitment.

(vi) *Science and theology are both subservient to their objects and can only be defined in relation to them.* Both are confessional enterprises (science has "faith" in the intelligibility of nature, and in the orderliness of the universe; theology in God). Both are intellectual disciplines shaped by their object (nature or God) to which they direct their attention. Both include a confessional and a rational factor. For those who take this view, theology is also one of the 'sciences'.[12]

(vii) *Science and theology may be integrated.* Many advances in the natural and human sciences prove to be consonant, on this view, with Christian perspectives enshrined in the Bible and the writings of the Fathers. This varies from a reasonable, and *prima facie*, legitimate utilisation of scientific notions (*e.g.*, 'open systems' by Moltman;[13] 'systems theory' by Pannenberg;[14] 'information processes' by Bowker[15]) to illuminate Christian insights, with an admittedly conscious extension and extrapolation of them; to an attempt[16] to interpret the 'Word made flesh' of Christian theology as an adumbration of the translation of the genetic *code* (a 'word') of nucleic acids into *proteins* (equals 'flesh'). This latter goes beyond the bound of legitimate extrapolation, and of plausibility, we instinctively feel — but what are

xiv

our criteria here?

(viii) *Science generates a metaphysic in terms of which theology is then formulated.* This metaphysic develops either from the content of contemporary science (Whitehead's metaphysics forming the basis of process theology) or from a philosophy of science itself (those of Einstein and Polanyi forming the basis of Torrance's[12] 'theological science').

So here are eight putative locations on the two-dimensionsal science-theology grid. But already I have some unease about it. Firstly, have we not too readily presumed we agree about the epistemological status of science and theology in this mapping? And, secondly, have we not left out a third dimension? Ought not our two axes rather to be the epistemology of science and the epistemology of religion, and should not a third axis, namely, the sociology of knowledge, also be introduced to provide points from which *both* may be viewed? Whether such a viewing by sociology constitutes a 'looking down' on science and theology from a higher vantage point of enhanced clarity or whether a 'looking upwards' from the lower darkness of a Nibelheim to the light above, it is premature to judge. But what is already clear is that the sociological critique, however unpalatable to both scientists and theologians, can only be ignored at the peril of irrelevance of the whole exercise.

It was with such considerations in mind that there was developed the sequence of this volume, which corresponds broadly to that of the Symposium itself.

The volume begins (Part I) with contributions which are concerned with the nature of the broad relation between theology and the sciences today: questions addressed to scientists by the theologian *W. Pannenberg;* an analysis by *E. McMullin* of how scientific cosmology has been and should be related to theology, in particular to the doctrine of creation; and an analysis by *P. Hefner* of a 'risky' relationship between science and theology evidenced in the *is/ought* distinction and its application, and mis-application, in the intense debate on sociobiology.

Part II is concerned with some particular issues and modes of interaction between theology and science which concern the perennial themes of nature, man and God. *T. F. Torrance* stresses the order of the natural world as being both divine in origin and contingent in character and analyses what this involves for theology and for science, both of which "have a stake" in the conjunction of these two features of the world. *J. Bowker* takes up the theme of teleonomy in nature, rather than teleology, in relation to the doctrine of creation and, in particular, to the origin of life and the anthropic principle (which McMullin had also examined for its possible theological import). *S. Daecke* then reviews the theological attitudes to nature that, stemming from biblical exegesis, have until recently prevailed in German theology, much of which has made, so he argues, a sharp distinction between a holy God and profane nature; he goes on to survey the ecumenical studies of this relation and some British and American evolutionary and sacramental theologies of nature, as well as those of Teilhard de Chardin. *R. Schlegel* concludes Part II with an account of the 'return of man' in quantum physics which he argues contributes to a rehabilitation of the significance of personal encounter with the world as formative both of personhood itself and as a source of a genuine awareness of God.

Because the intellectual issues between science and theology are of such a kind that they cannot be pursued without philosophical analysis, Part III turns to epistemological questions. Actually, the first contribution in this section, by *R. Alves*, is a strong plea for a new emphasis on the "truth" that comes from action rather than from contemplation and objective cognition; and he urges that religion is primarily located in the context of the former and science in that of the latter. In the next contribution, *R. Swinburne* seems to support Alves' contention by arguing for the evidential value of religious experience, enunciating a 'Principle of Credulity', nevertheless by employing a mode of argumentation which perhaps places it, rather, in Alves' category of "contemplation and objective cognition". That such distinctions are hazardous and can be overdrawn for the historian of science is one of the main themes of the account by *J. Ravetz* of the "varieties of scientific experience" which involve more elements of 'illumination', involvement, tradition, 'wisdom', and intuition than are usually allowed and so, he concludes, the boundaries between 'science' and 'religion' and between their sources of knowledge are conditioned by the cultural environment — thereby providing a suitable prelude to the theme of Part IV.

For this fourth part is devoted to an area of discourse which has become, as we have hinted, at least as important as the philosophical in recent decades in any account of relationships between disciplines: namely, in this context, the sociological critique of both science and theology. It begins with an account by *N. Lash* of the characterisation of religious and theological discourse as 'ideological' in both the Marxist tradition and in non-Marxist sociology and then reflects on the response of theologians to these critiques and on the supposed distinction between 'science' (which can include 'theological science') and 'ideology' (which can include, some would say, religion). The paper of *D. Martin* compares the "different maps of the same ground' — those of the sociologist and theologian — when he elaborates the perspective of a sociologist on some "ordinary working religious sentences" that refer, through the power of signs and images, to the basic spiritual relations of: transition; incorporation and solidarity; and limitation and contingency — and transcendence over them. He concludes that "nothing a sociologist might tell us about the social reality of the various transitions where they come into play ... could conceivably bear on the realities to which signs claim to refer". *M. Rudwick*, in taking "another look at the historical relation of science and religion" and in giving a not unsympathetic account of the 'strong programme' in the sociology of natural-scientific knowledge, also finds it incumbent upon himself to refer to a particular 'reality'. It is the externality of the natural world which has constraining and differentiating effects on the construction of claimed 'knowledge', and serious consideration of these effects Rudwick urges upon the sociologists of science. He goes on to insist that sociologists of religion equally cannot exclude the possibility that religious 'knowledge', like scientific, is constrained by an externality that, in this case, is characterised in theistic terms. The last contribution in this section, by *E. Barker*, takes a step back, as it were, from the debate and reports a sociological study of the ways in which science, in a so-called 'age of science', actually affects the theological beliefs of contemporary society — and thereby provides a salutary corrective to any inflated presumptions that might be possessed by those engaged in the intellectual dialogue represented in this book concerning the extent to which their analyses had yet been taken seriously by their contemporaries. The volume ends with a retrospective survey by my co-chairman at the Symposium, Professor Mary Hesse, together with a few comments on that survey by some of the authors.

REFERENCES AND NOTES

1. Some of the material in the first part of this introduction is developed more fully in: Peacocke, A. R., *Creation and the World of Science* (Oxford, Clarendon Press, 1979), chap. I, 'The Two Books'.
2. Foster, M., "The Christian Doctrine of Creation and the Rise of Modern Natural Science", *Mind*, 43 (1934) 446–68.
3. Though how *definitive* it was is highly disputed among historians of science.
4. Habgood, J., "The Uneasy Truce between Science and Religion", in *Soundings*, ed. Vidler, A. R. (Cambridge, Cambridge University Press, 1963), pp. 21–41.

5. Spiro, M. E., "Religion and the Irrational", in *Symposium on New Approaches to the Study of Religion*, ed. Helin, J. (Washington, University of Washington Press, 1964), p.103.

6. For references, see ref. 1, p. 21, *n* 37.

7. Horton, R., "African Traditional Thought and Western Science", in *Rationality*, ed. Wilson, B. R. (Oxford, Blackwell, 1970), pp. 131–171.

8. Or, at least, of appearing to do so — the historical reality is more complex, see chapter 11 by J. R. Ravetz, this volume.

9. The following section is partly indebted to the deliberations at the World Council of Churches Conference on "Faith, Science and the Future", Cambridge, Mass., 1979, that took place in Section I on "Nature of Science and Nature of Faith", of whose report-drafting committee the author was a member. (This report has now been published as *Faith and Science in an Unjust World*, Vol. 2 (Reports and Recommendations), ed. Abrecht, P. (Geneva, World Council of Churches, 1980).

10. Heim, K., *The Transformation of the Scientific World-View* (London, SCM Press, 1953).

11. I have demurred from describing this possible relation as being that of the 'complementarity' of science and theology because I think the use of this term in this context is ambiguous. It may apply, as in physics, to the two descriptions (*e.g.*, 'particle' and 'wave') of the same purported reality (*e.g.*, an electron) in the same realm of discourse (physics) *or* it may refer to the relation between the knowledge of two kinds of reality, the subject of two realms of discourse.

12. *E.g.*, Torrance, T.F., *Theological Science* (Oxford, Oxford University Press, 1969).

13. Moltmann, J., "Creation and Redemption', in *Creation, Christ and Culture*, ed. McKinney, R. W. A. (Edinburgh, T. & T. Clark, 1976), pp. 124–5, 130, 131.

14. Pannenberg, W., *Theology and the Philosophy of Science*, Eng. transl. McDonagh, F. (London, Darton, Longman & Todd, 1976), pp. 131–2, 143, 152.

15. Bowker, J., *The Sense of God* (Oxford, Clarendon Press, 1973) and *The Religious Imagination and the Sense of God* (Oxford, Clarendon Press, 1978).

16. Ninan, C. A., *Scientific Foundations of Faith — DNA and Christian mystery* (Trivandrum, 1979).

Part I

THEOLOGY AND THE SCIENCES TODAY

Chapter 1

THEOLOGICAL QUESTIONS TO SCIENTISTS

Wolfhart Pannenberg
Ökumenisches Institut, Universität München, West Germany

IN THEIR DISCUSSIONS with theologians, few scientists seem motivated primarily by theoretical questions. There is rarely much desire for the help of theologians in explaining the world of nature, but rather a widespread awareness that science alone is not sufficient in order to cope with the consequences and side effects of scientific discoveries, especially in their technological application. Frightened first by the development of nuclear weapons and later on by the threat of ecological disaster and by the dangers involved in modern biochemical techniques, a sense of responsibility for the application of their work has led many scientists to look for moral resources that could be mustered in order to prevent or at least to reduce the extent of fatal abuse of the possibilities provided by scientific discoveries. At this point, then, the churches are appreciated once more as moral agencies that should help the human society in responsibly dealing with the potential of science and technology.

The churches should certainly not refuse to face their particular responsibilities in these matters, and theology may be of some assistance here. But in modern society, the moral authority of the churches and of their theologies is limited. It has been seriously weakened, because the underlying religious interpretation of reality is no longer taken as universally valid, but as a matter of private preference, if not as superstition.

This situation has been brought about — not primarily, perhaps, but — to a large extent by what has been called the "warfare" of science with theology. According to public opinion in our Western culture, this war was lost by Christian apologetics. This does not necessarily mean that the issues have been solved to everybody's satisfaction. On the side of Christian theology, there was certainly a lot of bad apologetics involved, especially in the long struggle against the principles of continuity and evolution in natural processes. But there were also important issues at stake. On the side of the scientific

3

culture, a sort of overkill was achieved, when scientific inquiry was declared independent of any association with religion. That amounted, of course, to denying religion its claim on the reality of nature.

It could offer little comfort, in this situation, that some religious interpretation of the findings of science was regarded as compatible with science in terms of a private and optional belief. Even when many scientists personally continued to hold and develop religious views of their work, that did not alter the fact that in the area of public discourse religious assertions were considered superfluous with regard to human knowledge of the natural world. This meant that religion does not make any difference to the scientific description of the reality of nature and the logical implication was that religion has no legitimate claim on reality to the effect that the reality of nature could be fully understood without the God of religious faith. Considering the seriousness of this blow to religious truth claims, it would seem appropriate if the renewed interest of scientists in religion and especially in a dialogue with Christian theology were accompanied by some sense of surprise that Christianity is still around. Perhaps it survived only by temporarily separating the outlook of faith from the rational and scientific investigation and description of the natural world. But such an attitude cannot be continued forever, because it is profoundly unacceptable on theological grounds.

If the God of the Bible is creator of the universe, then it is not possible to understand fully or even appropriately the processes of nature without any reference to that God. If, on the contrary, nature can be appropriately understood without reference to the God of the Bible, then that God cannot be the creator of the universe, and consequently he could not be truly God and could not be trusted as a source of moral teaching either. To be sure, the reality of God is not incompatible with all forms of abstract knowledge concerning the regularities of natural processes, a knowledge that abstracts from the concreteness of physical reality and therefore may also abstract from the presence of God in his creation. But neither should such abstract knowledge of regularities claim full and exclusive competence regarding the explanation of nature and, if it does so, the reality of God is thereby denied by implication. The so-called methodological atheism of modern science is far from pure innocence. It is a highly ambiguous phenomenon. And yet its very possibility can be regarded as based on the unfailing faithfulness of the creator God to his creation, providing it with the unviolable regularities of natural processes that themselves become the basis of individual and more precarious and transitory

4

natural systems — from stars, mountains and valleys and oceans to the wonders of plants and animal life, resulting in the rise of the human species.

The abstract investigation of the regularities underlying the emergence of these natural forms need not separate them from their natural context in the creation of God and thus from God himself. But in fact there has been a strong tendency in modern science towards such a separation by putting the knowledge of the abstract regularities of nature to the use of man for whatever purposes he thinks fit. In particular, the abstract character of modern sciences allows the results to be at the disposal of human groups and societies and to serve the most diverse aims. The desire of using scientific research for ever extended domination and exploitation of natural resources has deeply influenced the direction of research iteself. Modern experimental science not simply observes the natural processes, but invades them and thus does not leave the change of the natural environment to technological application, but starts itself on that line by its experimentational techniques.

That modern science so easily lends itself to abuse cannot be prevented in principle. It is one of the risks involved in the abstract study of the regularities that are either inherent in nature itself or can be imposed on natural processes. This risk cannot be met on the level of scientific description itself, but first on the level of philosophical reflection on the work of science. It is on this level that the abstract form of scientific description must be considered with special attention to what it is "abstracted from" and what is methodically disregarded in the abstract formulas of science. It is on this level, then, that theologians should address their questions to scientists since God the creator and the nature of things as creatures belong to those aspects of reality that are abstracted from in the mathematical language of science.

There are five such questions that will be raised in the rest of this paper. They have been selected, because all of them seem to be of particular importance in the dialogue between natural science and theology, since the answers given to each of these questions will significantly contribute to any decision concerning the compatibility of modern science with faith in the Biblical God as creator and redeemer of humankind and of his entire creation.

The *first* and most fundamental of these questions runs like this: Is it conceivable, in view of the importance of contingency in natural processes, to revise the principle of inertia or at least its interpretation? The introduction of this principle in modern science played a major role in depriving God of his function in the conservation of nature and in finally rendering him an unnecessary hypothesis in the understanding of natural processes. Closely connected is the *second* question: Is the reality of nature to be understood as contingent and natural processes as irreversible? This question aims at the historical character of reality — not only of human history, but also of nature — that seems to be specifically related to the Biblical idea of God. The *third* question is also related to the Biblical perspectives of created existence and this time especially of life: Is there any equivalent in modern biology to the Biblical notion of the Divine Spirit as origin of life that transcends the limits of the organism? While historicity indicates the general character of reality in the perspective of Biblical faith, the Divine Spirit, at the same time immanent in creation and yet transcending the creature, constitutes its living reality in its relation to an ecstatic beyond of self-giving and satisfaction. Since this includes the hope for resurrection and eternal life, the next, *fourth* question refers to the relation between time and eternity: Is there conceivable any positive relation between the concept of eternity and that of the spatio-temporal structure of the physical universe? This is one of the most neglected, but also one of the most important questions in the dialogue between theology and science. It is unavoidable, if the reality of God is to be related in a positive way to the mathematical structure of the spatio-temporal world of nature. It will prove indispensable also in approaching what is perhaps the most difficult, *fifth* question in the dialogue between theology and modern science — the question of eschatology: Is the Christian affirmation of an imminent end of this world, that in some way invades the present even now, somehow reconcilable with scientific extrapolations of the continuing existence of the universe for at least several billion years ahead? Even to ask this question in a way that does not simply reduce the Bibical language to metaphor, or dismiss it as mythological, is extremely difficult. But this difficulty already arises with the third question regarding the Spirit. And from the beginning of such a discourse it lurks behind the very term "God". It is only the exploration of the function of "Spirit", connected with a redefinition of that term, and a clarification of the interrelation between time and eternity and finally the issue of eschatology that possibly can explain the meaning of the term "God" so that this term itself — in its Biblical concreteness — can be understood in its importance to the world of nature. The first two questions simply provide a starting point for such an exploration, but of such a kind that perhaps it could prevent theologians and scientists talking on different levels which remain unrelated, so that from the outset any agreement in terminology is reduced to mere equivocities of language.

I

Is it conceivable, in view of the importance of contingency in natural processes to revise the principle of inertia or at least its interpretation? The crucial importance of this question in the dialogue between science and theology is generally under-estimated. Perhaps this is so, because under the impact of deism the relation between God and the world was reduced to the *origin* of the world and especially of our planetary system. But as early as in the 14th century the question of the *conservation* of finite reality had become more prominent in the discussion on the indispensability of a first cause regarding the interpretation of nature. William Ockham rejected the view of the 13th century that in the order of existence the assumption of a first cause is necessary. He argued that in the sequence of generations it is quite natural that the later generation is alive while the former generations are already dead. In order that a new generation take rise, the continuing existence of a first forefather is not required. In the same way, there is no first cause nor is its continuing existence required in order to account for the continuous rise of new beings in the world. If it were only for this reason, the chain of natural causes could be traced back *in infinitum*. But the need for *preservation* of what came into existence led Ockham to a different conclusion. If continued existence is not self-explanatory, but requires the continued activity of the cause that gave origin to the creature, then without the continued existence and activity of a first cause all its effects would vanish whatever the mediation of their origin may be. Therefore, in Ockham's view, God was still indispensable in the explanation of the physical world, because without him no finite reality could persist. This was changed, however, when in the 17th century the principle of inertia was introduced in modern physics. It ascribed an innate potential of persistence to any physical reality, be it in a state of rest or in a state of motion, unless it is disturbed by some other force. The far reaching impact of this principle on the relation of physical reality to God went largely unnoticed until recently. The philosopher Hans Blumenberg, in an article published in 1970, demonstrated in some detail that the introduction of the principle of inertia in 17th century physics was to replace the dependence of physical reality on God's activity of continuous creation by the idea of self-preservation, an idea that presumably was derived from Stoic traditions.[1] Interestingly enough, Descartes considered the principle of inertia still to be in need of some deeper foundation. He traced it back to the immutability of God in his dealings with his creation. Since Descartes still believed that everything created in each moment of its existence depended on the continuous activity of the creator, on his *creatio continua*,[2] only the immutability of the creator could account for the stability in the order of creation, the basic manifestation of which is to be found in the tendency of everything to persevere in the status once acquired unless disturbed by other forces.[3] Later on, Isaac Newton was content to use the principle of inertia in his *Principia Naturae* (1687) without explicit reference to God (Def. 3 and 4), but Spinoza was the first to identify the essence of things with their perseverance in being, and thus he provided a metaphysical foundation for the emancipation of nature from its dependence on divine conservation, on a continuous concursus of a transcendent God[4] The emancipation from the creator God entailed in the principle of inertia did not only apply to individual natural bodies and beings which at the same time continued to undergo influences from outside themselves. Even more serious was the consequence that the system of the natural universe had to be conceived now as an interplay between finite bodies and forces without further need for recourse to God. When, almost 100 years after Spinoza, Immanuel Kant again used the contingency of all finite reality as a starting point for developing his idea of God, he found himself confined to the puzzlement such contingency presents to human reason, because he could no longer claim a direct dependence of contingent reality on God for its preservation.[5] Christian apologetics, on the other side, as soon as it accepted the new basis of natural philosophy provided by the principle of inertia, was now left to the unfortunate strategy of looking for gaps in the continuity of natural processes, if it wanted to preserve certain occasions for divine interference in the natural world.

But perhaps the principle of inertia or of self-persistence is in fact not as self-evident as it has been believed to be. If the stuff of the universe is finally made up of events rather than of solid bodies and if the latter are already the products of the regularities of events, then their inertia or self-persistence is no more self-evident than any other natural regularity. The "atomic" view of time and the awareness of the contingency of temporal sequence, that kept Descartes from taking inertia as a self-evident principle and led him to seek its basis in the invariable faithfulness of the creator, may be, after all, closer to the views of modern science than the opposite view of Spinoza is.

Perhaps after three centuries the conclusion from physical phenomena to an action of God does no longer go so smoothly as at the time of Descartes. But if it depends on a combination of contingent conditions, the phenomenon of inertia or persistence may tacitly imply the framework of a field of force to provide the conditions for such a phenomenon to exist.[6]

II

The second question squarely faces the issue of contingency and regularities of nature in its general form: Is the reality of nature to be understood as contingent and natural processes as irreversible? The combination of the two parts of the question suggests that irreversibility is related to contingency and may be rooted in it. In order to explain this, a number of steps is necessary, before the impact of the issue on a theological view of the historicity of nature can become apparent.

First of all, contingent conditions are required for any formula of natural law to be applied, initial conditions as well as boundary conditions. They are contingent at least in view of the particular formula of law under consideration in that they cannot be derived from it.

Secondly, the regularity itself which is described by a formula of natural law, can be considered as contingent, because its pattern represents a repeatable sequence of events, a sequence, however, that as a temporal sequence must have taken place for a first time before being repeated and before becoming a *regular* sequence.[7] The mathematical formula of a natural law may be valid without regard to time. The physical regularity that is described by such a formula is not independent of time and of temporal sequence. But it is only that physical regularity that makes the mathematical formula a law of nature. This suggests that laws of nature are not eternal nor atemporal, because the field of their applicaion, the regularities of natural process, originates in the course of time. Thus it also becomes understandable that new patterns of regularity emerging in the sequence of time constitute a field of application for a new set of natural laws in such a way that "the laws governing matter in a higher level of organization can never be entirely deduced from the properties of the lower levels".[8]

Thirdly, if this consideration applies to all natural regularities in temporal sequences, it leads to a general thesis on irreversibility in natural processes. This irreversibility which is ultimately based on the irreversibility of time, does not preclude the emergence of repeatable patterns of temporal sequence, but such an emergence itself becomes a contingent event. The regularity as such and taken by itself, therefore, is only an abstraction, abstracted from the contingent process and context of its emergence, and therefore its explanatory potential is necessarily limited.

The irreversiblity in natural processes is often argued for on different grounds, especially in relation to the law of entropy. This has been also applied to cosmology and contributed to relativistic models of the universe such as the "big bang" theory. But the ultimate basis of irreversibility may rather be looked for as C. F. v. Weizsäcker suggests,[9] in the irreversibility of time. Here, then, contingency and irreversibility may have their common root.

The theological interest in such considerations is due to the Biblical understanding of reality as historical. It is intimately related to the Biblical understanding of God the creator who acts freely and unrestrictedly not only in laying the foundations of the universe, but also in the subsequent course of events. This "continuous creation" is basically characterized by contingency, because future acts of God cannot be deduced from the former course of events. And yet there emerge regularities and persistent forms of created reality giving expression to the faithfulness and identity of God in affirming the world that he created. The continuity of this "continuous creation" can be characterized as a "historical continuity", the continuity of a history that God is engaged in with his creation. This historical continuity adds to the continuity that is expressed in the regularities of natural processes: While the description of those regularities in form of "natural laws" abstracts from the contingent conditions of their occurrence, historical continuity comprises the contingency of events together with the emergence of regularities. Thus the category of history provides a more comprehensive description of the continuous process of nature. But, on the other hand, the continuity of that history in its Biblical conception seems to be placed outside the created process, i.e. within God himself. Thus we have to look whether this continuity also manifests itself inside the process of nature. This leads to the third question, which is concerned with the Spirit of God.

III

Is there any equivalent in modern biology to the Biblical notion of the Divine Spirit as origin of life that transcends the limit of the organism? The question is focused on the phenomenon of life, because in the Biblical writings the work of the Spirit is specifically related to life. But it also relates to the created world in its entirety, as the initial words in the book of Genesis indicate.

In the Biblical traditions, life is not considered as a function of the organism. This constitutes the basic difference from the view of modern biology.[10] The life-giving power is seen as an agent that influences the organism from the outside. When it is called "spirit", one must not think of consciousness and intelligence in the first place. The Spirit is rather a mysterious reality, comparable to the wind (John 3,8). When God breathes it into the creature which he had built before, it comes alive (Gen. 2,7). Thus the human person has a life in himself or herself, but only a limited share of it. In the event of death "the dust returns to the earth as it was, and the Spirit returns to God who gave it" (Eccl. 12,7). Further, this view of life as originating from a transcendent source, is an indispensable presupposition for the hope in a resurrection to a new life beyond death. Only if the source of life transcends the organism, is it conceivable that the individual be given a new life that is no longer separate from the Divine Spirit, the source of life, but permanently united with it as a "spiritual body" (1. Cor. 15,42 sqq.).

These Biblical conceptions quite obviously belong to a different universe of discourse than what modern biology has to tell about life and its origin. But these Biblical conceptions cannot easily be dismissed as transient with the culture of their time, because they possess far reaching importance for basic affirmations of the Christian faith. If they are to be taken as carrying an important truth, however, it must somehow also be present, if only in oblique form, in modern biological descriptions of life.

Now the living organism, in the view of modern biology, is not a closed system. It transcends itself by inhabiting a territory within an appropriate environment, and it literally lives "on" that environment. In its drives it relates to a future that transforms its own status of life, and sexuality is a particularly powerful manifestation of the ecstatic nature of life.

If one tries to develop a synthetic account of these phenomena, one may be led in a direction similar to that of M. Polanyi's explanation of individual morphogenesis on the assumption of a "morphogenetic field" that comprises all the boundary conditions of individual development.[11] Polanyi himself did not shy away from expanding that notion in conceiving the idea of a phylogenetic field that governs the process of evolution and in the perspective of which the individual organisms are to be considered as singularizations. He says that "the evidence provided by the various branches of biology (including psychology)" seems "to cry out for the acknowledgement of a field as the agent of biotic performances".[12] At this point Polanyi's thought meets with the vision of Teilhard de Chardin who envisaged Point Omega at work in the process of evolution as the power of the Divine Spirit, although he did not use the field concept in describing the efficacy of that power in the way Polanyi did.[13] To the theologian, the description of the evolution of life in terms of a generalized field theory is extremely suggestive, because it seems to offer a modern language that possibly could express the Biblical idea of the Divine Spirit as the power of life that transcends the living organism and at the same time is intimately present in the individual. In the perspective of such a field theory of life, one may follow Polanyi's "logic of achievement" in the sequence of emergent forms of life and in his final vision of a "cosmic field which called forth all these centres by offering them a short-lived, limited, hazardous opportunity for making some progress of their own towards an unthinkable consummation".[14] But it is not by chance that Polanyi calls that consummation "unthinkable", because neither the eschatological presence of God's kingdom nor the Christian hope for the new life of a resurrection of the dead is imaginable as just another stage in the temporal sequence of the evolutionary process. It adds another dimension, the transfiguration of the temporal by the presence of the eternal.

IV

Is there conceivable any positive relation between the concept of eternity and the spatio-temporal structure of the physical universe? As I said before, this is one of the most arduous, but also one of the most important questions in the dialogue between theology and natural science. If eternity means the Divine mode of being, then it is directly concerned with the question of how the reality of God is related to the spatio-temporal universe. Without an answer to the question regarding time and eternity, the relation of God to this world remains inconceivable.

Now eternity has been interpreted traditionally as timelessness, and in this interpretation its relation to time appears to be purely negative. But this contradicts the Christian hope for resurrection, because that hope does not aim at a completely different life, replacing the present one. It aims rather at a transformation of this present life so as to let it participate in the divine glory. Salvation cannot mean pure negation and annihilation of this present life, of this creation of God. Therefore, in a Christian perspective time and eternity must have some positive relation, as is also implied in the doctrine of the incarnation, since that means a togetherness of the human and of the Divine in the person and life of Jesus Christ.

The notion of eternity certainly means unlimited presence. But this need not exclude the temporal that came into existence once and passes again into non-existence. The positive relation of the temporal to the eternal could mean that in the perspective of the eternal the temporal does not pass away, although in relation to other spatio-temporal entities it does do so. On the basis of this it is also conceivable that the lasting presence of the temporal before the eternal God may become the experience of the temporal itself, so that it experiences itself as it stands in the presence of God, vanishing in its contradiction to God or transformed in participation in his glory.

Such an inclusive interpretation of eternity in relation to temporal reality, however, requires a systematic way of relating the extensions of time and space to a conceptual model of eternity. Such a model should be mathematical in character in order to comprise the mathematical structures of space and time. A German mathematician, Günter Ewald of the university of Bochum, is developing such a model. It is based again on the notion of a field much as the theory of relativity conceives of the spatio-temporal universe as a single field. According to Ewald, this notion can be further expanded so as to include beyond the real numbers also the complex numbers. Since in the level of complex numbers no linear sequence occurs, the transition from complex numbers to real numbers can be interpreted as transition into spatio-temporal existence, and generally the field of complex numbers in its relation to real numbers can provide a model of the relation of eternity to spatio-temporal events. It remains to be seen how far the explanatory power of this model goes. Does it explain not only the transition from the eternal to temporal existence, but also the manifestation of the eternal within the temporal sequence? According to Christian doctrine, such a manifestation of the eternal within temporal reality will occur in its fullness in the eschaton, but by anticipation it occurred in the midst of the ongoing sequence of events in the resurrection of Jesus. This event persuaded the Christian community that the eternal Logos was incarnate in Jesus. The entire problem of miracles is related to the question of the anticipatory presence of the eschatological consummation. But there are also other and more ordinary modes of an anticipatory presence of the eternal in time. According to the Christian doctrine that the Divine Logos had an important part even in the creation of the world, in every creature the logical structure should somehow be present that became manifest in the person and history of Jesus Christ. Just as Jesus' identity as the son of God is to be finally confirmed in his eschatological parousia, so the essence of all things is presently realized only by anticipation and will be finally revealed in the ultimate future where the temporal will be reconstituted in the presence of the eternal. This is but one aspect of how every creature bears the imprint of the Logos. There seems to be, however, a tendency towards increasing participation in the Divine Spirit and Logos in the course of the evolution of creatures, approximating the eschatological presence of the eternal in the temporal. The human mind is distinguished by a unique degree of openness to the presence of the eternal which is expressed in the experience of an amplified presence that overlaps, although in a limited way, past and future events. The participation of the human mind in the eternal Logos through the ecstatic power of the Spirit may also account for the possibility and specific character of human knowledge of the created world.

In a trinitarian perspective, the work of the Logos and that of the Spirit in the creation of the world belong closely together. Can this still be expressed in a language that takes account of modern science? If the suggestion of C.F. v. Weizsäcker[15] is followed that the ancient philosophical logos doctrine could be reformulated in terms of the modern information theory, then it does not seem completely inconceivable that a field theory of information could do justice to the cooperation of Logos and Spirit in the creation of the world.

V

The last question, the question of eschatology, was already touched upon in connection with the work of the Spirit and with the transfiguring presence of the eternal in the temporal. But it needs to be raised in its own right, because it points to one of the most obvious conflicts between a worldview based on modern science and the Christian faith: Is the Christian affirmation of an imminent end of this world that in some way invades the present even now, reconcilable with scientific

14

extrapolations of the continuing existence of the universe for billions of years ahead? To this question there are no easy solutions. Scientific predictions that in some comfortably distant future the conditions for life will no longer continue on our planet, are hardly comparable to Biblical eschatology. On the other hand, some people are always too ready to expunge from the religious traditions elements that seem to make no sense to one period in the development of scientific insight. Perhaps one should rather accept a conflict in such an important issue, accept it as a challenge to the human mind to penetrate deeper still into the complexities of human experience and awareness. It does not seem unreasonable to expect that a detailed exploration of the issues involved in the question concerning time and eternity may lead one day to more satisfactory ways of including the Biblical eschatology in an interpretation of the natural world that takes appropriate account of modern science.

REFERENCES AND NOTES

1. Blumenberg, H., *Selbsterhaltung und Beharrung — Zur Konstitution der neuzeitlichen Rationalität*. Abhandlungen der Mainzer Akademie der Wissenschaften und der Literatur, geistes- und sozialwissenschaftliche Klasse, Jg. 1969 Nr. 11 (Mainz, 1970), pp. 333-383. Reprinted in *Subjektivität und Selbsterhaltung, Beiträge zur Diagnose der Moderne*, ed. Ebeling, H. (Frankfurt, Suhrkamp, 1976), pp. 144-207.

2. Blumenberg, *loc. cit.*, ed. Ebeling, H., pp. 182 ff.

3. Descartes, Princ. II, 36 and 37, Tannery VIII/1, 1964, 61 ff.

4. Blumenberg, *loc. cit.*, p. 185 sqq.

5. Kant, I., *Der einzig mögliche Beweisgrund für eine Demonstration des Daseins Gottes* (1763); compare the commentary of Redmann, H. G. *Gott und Welt: Die Schöpfungstheologie der vorkritischen Periode Kants* (Göttingen, Vandenhoeck und Ruprecht, 1962), p. 142 ff. See also 98 ff.

6. Weizsäcker, C. F. v., *(Die Einheit der Natur* (München, C. Hanser, 1970), p.364) calls the principle of inertia "eine Folge der Wirkung des Universums auf das einzelne Urobjekt". This corresponds to the view of A. Einstein (in his preface to Max Jammer's *Concepts of Space*, 1954) that Newton introduced his concept of absolute space "als selbständige Ursache des Trägheitsverhältnis der Körper" in order to secure "dem klassischen Trägheitsprinzip (und damit dem klassischen Bewegungsgesetz) einen exakten Sinn". According to Einstein, the concept of absolute space (or its amplification to that of an "inertial system" including time) could only be overcome when "der Begriff des körperlichen Objektes als Fundamentalbegriff der Physik allmählich durch den des Feldes ersetzt wurde", since then "die Einführung eines *selbständigen* Raumes" is no longer necessary. Einstein concludes: "Eine andere Möglichkeit für die Überwindung des Inertialsystems als den über die Feldtheorie hat bis jetzt noemand gefunden".

7. Pannenberg, W., *Kontingenz und Naturgesetz* in Muller, A. M. K. and Pannenberg, W., *Erwägungen zu einer Theologie de Natur* (Gütersloh, G. Mohn, 1970) p. 34 ff., esp. 65 ff.

8. Peacocke, A. R., *Science and the Christian Experiment* (London, Oxford University Press, 1971), p. 87.
9. Weizsäcker, C. F. v., *Die Einheit der Natur* (München, C. Hanser, 1971), p. 239 ff.
10. More detail on this argument is given in my article "The Doctrine of the Spirit and the Task of a Theology of Nature" in *Theology* LXXV (1972) 8-21.
11. Polanyi, M., *Personal Knowledge: Towards a Post-Critical Philosophy* (London, Routledge & Kegan Paul, 1958, 2nd ed. 1962), p. 356.
12. *Loc. cit.*, p. 402 cf. for the generalized field concept pp. 398 ff.
13. See my discussion of Teilhard's views on energy, "Geist und Energie. Zur Phänomenologie Teilhard de Chardin", in *Acta Teilhardiana* VIII (München, 1971), pp. 5-12.
14. Polanyi, M., *loc. cit.*, p. 405. Polanyi's use of the field concept should not be mistaken as just another form of vitalism. It is rather opposed to the vitalist assumption of a finalistic principle working within the organism like the Aristotelian entelechy. Contrary to this, the field concept involves no finality, nor does it dwell in the organism as some occult quality distinct from its more ordinary aspects open to physical description. The field concept rather offers an integrative framework for a comprehensive description of all aspects of organic life including its interaction with its ecological context.
15. Weizsäcker, C. F. v., *Die Einheit der Natur* (1970), pp. 343 ff.

Chapter 2

HOW SHOULD COSMOLOGY RELATE TO THEOLOGY?

Ernan McMullin
History & Philosophy of Science Program, University of Notre Dame, Indiana, U.S.A.

IS THEOLOGY relevant to cosmology? Is cosmology relevant to theology? Scientists today would be emphatic in their negative answer to the first of these questions. Theologians would be more hesitant about the second, but most would probably lean in the negative direction. Yet the Old Testament opened with a detailed cosmogony, one which served to define some of the basic beliefs about God and His world that informed later books of the Bible. The writers of those books would have answered the two questions above with a straightforward affirmative, it would seem, though the questions themselves would have to be phrased rather differently in order to be understood in those centuries before the enterprises of either theology or cosmology had taken shape.

Where does the issue stand today? If cosmology be defined as a unified scientific treatment of the origins and structures of the physical universe taken as a whole, then it might be said to be only half a century old. The Newtonian universe offered little foothold for the cosmologist; the distribution of matter through its dual infinities of space and time appeared to all intents and purposes random. Though one could speculate as to how dust clouds might coalesce to form stars and planetary systems, there was no way to account for the light of these stars nor to discover their composition. And the elements of which the primordial dust-clouds were composed had to be taken as a given, their properties and relative abundance entirely a matter of contingency.

What made cosmology possible was the combination of the two principal advances in physical theory of our century, the general theory of relativity and the quantum theory of matter, and the discovery by Hubble in 1929 of the galactic red-shift, the simplest interpretation of which was a general recession of the galaxies from a single origin. In its early days, the new cosmology was often attacked as unduly speculative, as "unscientific." The idealizations it was forced to use appeared likely to prove empirically unfounded, and there did not seem to be any satisfactory way to select between the multiplicity of models proposed by different investigators. The growth of the new observational science of radio-astronomy provided, however, an enormous array of new evidence that optical telescopes could never have revealed. And the growing sophistication of the theoretical models of large-scale relativistic effects as well as of the quantum processes by which the cosmic constituents were originally formed, eventually permitted a degree of testing that the sceptics of the 1930's had not foreseen. The discovery in 1965 of the 3°K radiation permeating the universe, which the "Big Bang" model had predicted and which it identified as the last trace of the initial explosion from which the galactic expansion began, seemed to bring cosmology finally into the circle of the respectably predictive sciences. Not that debate about its "scientific" status has ended. But it has now a fairly secure position and an extraordinary rate of theoretical advance which makes it one of the most attractive fields today for young researchers trying to decide where to place their efforts.

Our concern in this essay is with the implications, if any, of this new science for Christian theology. Are the two entirely unrelated? Or does Christian belief have a "cosmic" component that would make cosmological discoveries potentially relevant to it? This is by no means a new issue, so that before we go on to some contemporary case-studies, it will be of interest to recall in some detail the occasions on which this battle was first joined.

I

Augustine and Galileo
The Manichaeans of the fourth century had their own dualist cosmogony, a quite elaborate story of how our universe of discord took its origin and present form from a strife between the Father of Light and the Archons of Darkness. Though the details of the cosmogony may seem rather fantastic to us (the vegetation of the earth originated, for example, from the semen of the Archons lusting after the Twelve Virgins of the sky who are made visible in the constellations), the Manichaeans claimed that their doctrine was based on reason and understanding rather than demanding acceptance on faith. Though Jesus (not as a historic personage but as a purely divine being) was assigned a role in their salvation story, they rejected the Old Testament as a tissue of fables. In particular, they challenged the *Genesis*

account of creation and found many inconsistencies in it (in its use of
the notion of "day," for example).

One of the things that had originally attracted Augustine to Man-
ichaeism was its stress on rationality, so that after he became a
Christian, it is not surprising that he should have thought it so
important to provide an acceptably "rational" construal of the Biblical cosmogony. His first attempt at a commentary on *Genesis* he left
unfinished, perhaps because of the difficulties he was encountering.
But in 415 A.D., he completed an elaborate work in twelve books,
the *De Genesi ad litteram*, in which he attempted to weave the best of
the scientific knowledge of his day into the *Genesis* cosmogony in
order to provide a single consistent account. In order to do this, he was
forced to take the latter metaphorically in some of its details, in its
division of the work of creation into six days, for example. The
resulting hermeneutic problem he wrestled with again and again
throughout the work. How is one to decide when an expression is
metaphorical, without compromising the absolute authority of the
literal reading of God's Word?

A first response would be to say that a literal interpretation is to be
adopted unless there is reason to suppose that the passage is to be read
metaphorically. What sort of reason? The testimony of language, of
context, of parallel passage. But suppose there is an apparent conflict
between the literal reading and a proposition believed to be true on
everyday or on "scientific" grounds? Is this enough to ensure that the
Biblical passage must be taken to be metaphorical? This is a crucial
issue in the defence of *Genesis* against Manichaean criticism. Augustine's theory of knowledge led him to give maximum weight to the
literal reading unless one could establish beyond all doubt the necessity of adopting an alternative metaphorical reading. And one way to
do that (he notes) is to show that the literal reading leads to conflict
with a demonstrated truth:

> But, someone may say, why does what is written in our Bible: "He who
> stretches out the heavens like a curtain (lit.: skin hanging)" not con-
> tradict those who attribute spherical shape to the heavens? If what these
> latter said were to be false, then it would indeed be in contradiction.
> For that is true which rests on divine authority rather than that which
> proceeds from human weakness. But if on the other hand they can
> prove their claim with such evidence (*documenta*) that it is placed
> beyond any doubt, then it must be demonstrated that our speaking of a
> curtain does not in fact conflict with their true assertion. Otherwise,
> there would be a contradiction even with those other passages in
> Scripture where the heavens are said to be suspended like a dome.[1]

In passages such as this one, Augustine is making use of a principle which we shall call the relevance-of-theology-to-cosmology principle (relevance principle) in one of its strongest forms. (The only stronger form would make Scripture the primary document in the constructing of a cosmology). He presumes that the Scriptures contain a cosmology whose claim on our assent is that of Scripture itself. His reasoning is simple: since references of a cosmological sort are frequent in Scripture, and since the literal sense of Scripture is to be adopted except in passages where a non-literal sense can be conclusively shown to be required, one must presume that the cosmology implicit in Scripture has, on the whole, the warrant of Scripture itself. And so he discusses the challenges to this cosmology: can there be waters above the firmament? is air to be equated with the "heavens?" do stars differ from one another in glory (brightness)? what is meant by saying that everything was disposed by measure, number and weight? could the whole earth have been watered from a single spring? was there death and suffering in the animal world before the fall of man? and so on.

To those, then, who would try to make use of cosmology to undermine belief in Scripture generally, his response is:

> We must show our Scriptures not to be in conflict with whatever [our critics] can demonstrate about the nature of things from reliable sources (*veracia documenta*), but whatever in their books they put forward as contradicting the Scriptures, that is, the Catholic faith, we should either by some means show, or else unhesitatingly believe, to be most false.[2]

From our vantage-point, this hermeneutic principle seems an extraordinarily precarious one. It gives no status to the claims of natural knowledge unless these can be said to be *demonstrated*. If they are only probable, the literal reading of the Biblical text takes precedence over them, unless for literary or other internal reasons one has conclusive reason to suppose that the literal interpretation ought *not* be taken. Augustine is led to this strong version of the relevance principle by his theory of illumination which made the "lightest" word of God a better witness to truth than the "heaviest" word of man, except when this latter is a demonstrated claim (i.e., science proper). Since science too comes from God and since there can be no inconsistency between the two truths, in this latter event the conflict has to be dissolved by whatever means one can find, for instance by showing that the Scriptural passage in question is figurative or has not been understood aright.

But there is a second and very different tendency at work in Augustine also. He is very critical of those Christians who turn to the Scriptures for answers to every cosmological question:

> It is often asked what is to be believed about the form and shape of the heavens according to the Scriptures. Many dispute much about such issues, which the Biblical authors, in their greater wisdom, have left aside as of no relevance to those who would learn about a blessed life ... What is it to me whether the heavens like a sphere surround the earth which is balanced as a mass at the centre of the universe, or whether they cover the earth as would a disc placed over it? ... As far as the form of the heavens is concerned, it can be said in brief that the Biblical authors knew where the truth lay. But the Spirit of God, who spoke through them, did not wish to teach men things of no relevance to their salvation.[3]

This last remark appears, however, to clash with the relevance principle. Why should a knowledge of cosmology be thought to be relevant to salvation? Why should it matter to the believer whether there are waters above the firmament or not? To those who ask him how the heavens can properly be called a "firmament," since the stars orbit in circles around the poles, Augustine responds that it would take "many subtle and laborious reasonings" to discover the truth about the motion or rest of the heavens, but that such an inquiry is of no concern to someone like himself whose care it is to instruct people in matters necessary for salvation.[4] But if cosmology is *not* relevant to salvation, why should it be supposed that cosmological details in the Scriptures are to be taken as literal truth-claims?

Augustine's answer would undoubtedly be that they are covered by the warrant that the literal sense of Scripture possesses, and that one cannot require relevance to the salvation message of every passage for which this is to hold. The details of Israel's history with which the Old Testament abounds lack such relevance, yet they must (he would insist) be taken to be historically accurate. The main target of Augustine's criticism is the Christian who claims the sanction of Scripture for his speculations concerning such topics (he says) as the orbits of the sun and moon, the distance of the stars, the nature of animals, fruits, stones, while not troubling to ascertain whether these speculations run counter to demonstrated truths in the natural order. All that critics of the Bible need do in such a case is to show that such a conflict exists in order to undermine the Bible's authority in regard to far more important things like the resurrection of the dead.[5]

This is epistemologically muddy ground, to say the least. Anything short of demonstration on the "scientific side" does not count apparently as an epistemic challenge to a theological claim. And even though Augustine is critical of those who would make use of the Scriptures for purposes remote from their end as salvation-message, in practice his objection against those who invoke them in matters cosmological seems to arise only when conflict with an established truth results.

The reader may already have encountered the passages from Augustine quoted above. All of them are referred to in Galileo's *Letter to the Grand Duchess Christina* (1615), in which Galileo attempted to lay out in a more systematic way the principle governing the relationship of cosmology and Scripture.[6] It was a matter of the utmost urgency to him to find a way to insulate Copernican astronomy from theological critics who based their objections on phrases in the Old Testament which, taken literally, implied that the sun moved or that the earth stood still. He was not concerned with *Genesis*, with questions of origins or the nature of man, where the case for the epistemic relevance of the Scripture texts and themes was much stronger. His question was about the background of cosmic beliefs implicit in the ways of speaking of the ancient authors, rather than about apparently direct cosmological teachings of the kind one finds in *Genesis*.

Not surprisingly, the same sort of ambivalence we have noted in Augustine reappears in Galileo's account, but now much more strongly accentuated. Indeed, it might be said that he enunciates two quite different, and mutually inconsistent principles, one of them the Augustinian version of the relevance principle and the other, a principle of cosmological neutrality akin to the one we have seen Augustine hinting at ("The Spirit of God did not wish to teach men things of no relevance to their salvation"), but now much more explicitly formulated and defended.

First, he paraphrases Augustine:[7]

> In the books of the sages of this world there are contained some physical truths which are soundly demonstrated, and others that are merely stated; as to the former, it is the office of wise divines to show that they do not contradict the holy Scriptures. As to the propositions which are stated but are not rigorously demonstrated, anything contrary to the Bible involved by them must be held undoubtedly false and should be proved so by every possible means.[8]

This kind of distinction between two sorts of physical claim, one of which has "previously been made certain by manifest sense and neccessary demonstration"[9] or has been "rigorously demonstrated," and the other which "has been stated but not rigorously demonstrated," [10] he goes on to amplify:

> Among physical propositions there are some with regard to which all human science and reason cannot supply more than a plausible opinion and a probable conjecture in place of a sure and demonstrated knowledge; for example, whether the stars are animate. Then there are other propositions of which we have (or may confidently expect) positive assurances through experiments, long observation, and rigorous demonstration; for example, whether or not the earth and heavens move, and whether or not the heavens are spherical. As to the first sort of propositions, I have no doubt that where human reasoning cannot reach — and where consequently we can have no science but only opinion and faith — it is necessary in piety to comply absolutely with the strict sense of Scripture.[11]

But now the distinction is beginning to shift. It is no longer quite the Augustinian one between cases of strictly demonstrated knowledge (to which epistemic priority is given over apparently conflicting readings of Scriptural passages) and those of merely probable or likely knowledge-claims (which are to be overridden in the case of conflict). Now it sounds like one between that which can in principle be demonstrated physically (even though it may not yet have been), and that to which human reasoning in principle cannot reach. It is a much weaker claim, theologically speaking, to attribute relevance to the Scriptural passages in contexts where science could not in principle reach, than to give it authority in every context other than one in which a contrary point has already been strictly demonstrated. Yet this latter, much stronger, version of the relevance principle is also found throughout the *Letter*, especially in those passages where allusion is made to Augustine or other patristic authorities.

But Galileo's ambivalence is even more marked than this. In a number of passages, he argues for a principle of neutrality in regard to Scripture (theology as neutral in regard to cosmology), here again relying on the hints in Augustine's text. After quoting a passage to which we have already referred, where Augustine asserts the irrelevance to the central issue of salvation, of questions such as the one posed him as to whether the heavens move, Galileo concludes:

23

> It follows that since the Holy Ghost did not intend to teach us whether heaven moves or stands still ... so much the less was it intended to settle for us any other conclusion of the same kind ... Now if the Holy Spirit has purposely neglected to teach us propositions of this sort as irrelevant to the highest goal (that is, our salvation), how can anyone affirm that it is obligatory to take sides on them?[12]

He gives several arguments why the manner of speaking regarding cosmological matters in Scripture ought not be assumed to be literal in intent, unless this can be expressly shown, i.e., the onus is on those who claim the literal sense, instead of the other way around. First, there are many clear cases where it would be generally agreed that the Bible speaks metaphorically (as when it attributes human features to God). Second, the writers of the Bible had to "accommodate themselves to the capacity of the common people"; on abstruse physical issues it would have led to confusion in the minds of the intended readers if the text had been written in order to instruct them also on the physical nature of the universe, such confusion indeed that the original salvation purpose of the texts would have been defeated.[13] Third, the aim of the Bible was to teach us how to attain to salvation, and a knowledge of cosmological matters in no way pertains to this. Thus, the Bible ought not be called on, save in matters "which concern salvation and the establishment of our Faith."[14]

The implication of this neutrality principle is that the descriptions of physical phenomena found in the Bible have *no* cosmological bearing; they testify only to the common mode of speech at the time of composition. Only where the topic bears on the salvation-message ought the Scriptures be taken to have any cosmological relevance. Is this ever the case? Galileo does not say, but might well have allowed the *Genesis* account of origins to qualify because there the intent of conveying something about the origins of the cosmos seems to be explicit. Whereas in passing phrases about the sun standing still or the like, it did not seem that the writer intended a truth of a cosmological sort to be communicated.

The reader will have noted that the consequences of the two principles Galileo clearly enunciates in the *Letter* are completely different where the Copernican issue is concerned. If the *relevance* principle is correct, then he will have to *demonstrate* the Copernican claim beyond all cavil. Otherwise, the anti-Copernican tenor of the various Old Testament passages that mention the movement of the sun or the stillness of the earth will have to be given full weight. A merely probable physical theory or well-supported hypothesis will not suffice. On the other hand, if the neutrality principle be adopted, then these Scripture passages are irrelevant to the issue, and the question of the earth's motion will be decided by the scientific theory above. The question of whether the theory is *demonstrated* or not will not enter into the discussion; the theologian will not be put in a position (as he is under the relevance principle) where he has to assess the strength of the *scientist's* argument before he can decide whether or not the Scriptures may be invoked.

We shall not speculate here about the effects of this ambiguity on the way the *Dialogo* was constructed and on the way it was received by its readers. This is a matter for another occasion. Our purpose in opening a paper on the interrelations of cosmology and theology with this lengthy historical discussion is not a merely antiquarian one. The issue at odds between Galileo and his opponents is no longer debated today. Pope Leo XIII in his encyclical *Providentissimus Deus* (1893) enunciated a principle of Scriptural interpretation very like the neutrality principle defended by Galileo. Though there are still some fundamentalist Christians who would propose something like Augustine's relevance principle, the vast majority of Christian believers today would not allow any sort of cosmological relevance to those phrases in Scripture where the authors seem to be simply following the manner of speech of the day in regard to some common physical phenomenon.

But the debate is not *really* over. It has only shifted to a different ground. Are there *any* Biblical passages (or more broadly, Christian teachings) whose cosmological relevance the Christian has got to take seriously? Or is the Christian message entirely neutral in regard to the positions one adopts in regard to the origins and nature of the world? This is not a simple matter, and we shall see that something of the old ambivalence between a "relevance" and a "neutrality" principle still manifests itself in recent debates. It would be generally agreed that the Christian is committed to certain beliefs about human freedom and responsibility, and that these may interact with scientific theories, such as Freud's theory of psychoanalysis, or Wilson's sociobiology, for example. But what of the cosmos beyond man? Does Christian belief impose any constraints on (or, in a different idiom, give any guidance to) cosmological speculation?

II

The Issue an Epistemological One
One final preliminary comment may be worth some emphasis. The

question of how science and religion should interrelate is not primarily either a scientific or a theological one. Nor is it primarily historical or sociological, though one will surely want to know much about the historical relations of the two, as well as about the sociological issues these relations raise, before coming to any conclusions. The question is primarily an *epistemological* one about how two different sorts of claim to knowledge are to be related. In discussing it, it is important to be sensitive to the complexities of the properly scientific and properly theological issues involved. It is also important to be aware of the historical records and the relevant sociological observations and of what may be learned from them. But in the end, the question itself is a characteristically epistemological one, one of great complexity.

This is not to say that the philosopher is necessarily the person best qualified to discuss it. The context will indicate the degree of expertise required in these other areas, and it may well be that a scientist or historian sensitive to the issues may contribute most to some aspects of the topic. But when they do, they are contributing to a problem which is basically one about the nature of knowledge. And this is not a matter of science nor of theology, let alone of history or of sociology.

The discussions of Augustine and Galileo above indicates that there are three different very general questions involved:

1. What is the status of scientific claims about the cosmos?
2. Under what circumstances (if any) is the Biblical narrative to be given cosmological weight?
3. In formulating a single world-view, what relative weight is to be attached to science and to theology in matters cosmological? What sorts of logical relations (if any) hold between them?

The first of these gave Augustine and Galileo considerable trouble. Augustine thought of science as aiming for "necessary demonstration"; anything which fell short of that was something less than (or even other than) science. One can find two different conceptions of science in Galileo's work. The classical demonstrative ideal still pervades much of his mechanics, whereas the beginnings of a retroductive (hypothetical) mode of reasoning, not admitting of conclusive demonstration, can be seen especially in his discussions of the distant (comets, sunspots, the lunar surface) and the very small.[15] And so it was still possible for him to concede something like the Augustinian relevance principle, i.e., to require *demonstrative* status in the scientific claim under investigation before taking it seriously as a competitor of a putative theological claim. Yet he was also coming to

26

realize, through the exigencies of his own scientific work in new domains to which classical demonstration might never reach, that the demand for strict demonstration might be inappropriate, that a weaker sort of warrant might very well still qualify as properly "scientific." Galileo himself never quite resolved this ambiguity; for that matter, neither did any other scientist of the century that followed. But it was obviously critical in any assessment of the Augustinian form of the relevance principle. One can see the same issue reappearing today when supporters of the literal interpretation of *Genesis* characterize the theory of evolution as being "only" a theory, and argue that as long as this is so, the issue between the evolutionary and the special creation accounts must remain at the very least an open one.

The second question above would be currently the most debated one. In recent discussions of "internal" versus "external" history of science, it has been generally assumed that theological influences on the past development of science must be treated as intrusions, as being in need of special historical explanation.[16] Even those historical sociologists who argue that rational and non-rational factors in the history of science ought to be regarded as equally in need of explanation (the "symmetry principle") appear to place theology automatically on the "non-rational" side. The undoubted influence of theological considerations on scientists like Galileo, Descartes, Newton, Faraday, is presumed to be explainable in non-epistemic terms by invoking political motives, a trait of character, a perculiarity in cultural milieu. The fact that such considerations rarely seem to affect scientific inquiry today is taken to confirm the presumption that from a strictly scientific viewpoint they never ought to have done so.

What sort of knowledge-claim, if any, does religion make? This is one of the most controverted topics in contemporary philosophy of religion. We are concerned here only with cosmological knowledge, warranted assertions about the nature of the physical world around us. Can religion, specifically Christian religion, lay claim to any knowledge of this sort on the basis of Revelation? Obviously, this question is posed from the point of view of the Christian believer; for others, the answer would be a simple negative. But what is the believer to say? And how is he to back up his response? What strategies are open to him in arriving at an answer to this question? It may well be that his response will be negative, but his reason for this cannot be the implicitly positivist one that seems to underlie so much of the recent treatment of this topic, namely that religious belief can never in principle serve as rational grounds for holding some view about the nature of the world. The Judaeo-Christian concept of Revelation implies, for example, at least the *possibility* of a knowledge that the Creator could pass on.

Suppose that one does defend the claim that Revelation contains cosmological implications that must be taken seriously. This brings us to the third question posed above. What sort of weight is to be given to these implications? What kind of assurance can one have of their truth? In particular, what relative weight do they have in relation to scientific theories? If the two conflict or seem to conflict (the Augustine-Galileo case), what is to be done? Where they do not conflict, can one be used to support the other? For example, would it be proper for a Jewish or Christian believer in creation to allow this belief to sway his choice between the big-bang and the continuous-creation models in cosmology? Or must science be insulated in principle against the intrusion of such "outside" beliefs? These questions serve to introduce the first of the illustrative cases we have chosen in order to give concrete form to these rather abstract epistemological issues. History here as elsewhere may furnish the best means of deciding which among many epistemological "possibles" has in fact been realized. Revelation *might*, in principle, contain knowledge of serious cosmological import; one strategy we can surely adopt is to ask whether it seems to have done so.[17]

III

Cosmology and Creation

If there was any one cosmological assertion which Jew, Christian and Moslem alike might have agreed on as a theological "given" in the early medieval period, it was surely that the universe has a beginning in time. That seemed the very least one could infer from the *Genesis* story of the creation. Augustine, willing (as we have seen) to take the road of metaphor to avoid conflict with a demonstrated truth, was at some pains to show that no such conflict was involved here. Creation (he argues) is a single timeless act, through which time itself (as well as the changing things of which time is the measure) comes to be. He pokes fun at the idea that there was a long period of time during which God was waiting for the propitious moment at which to bring the universe to be.[18] To his mind, such an idea betrays a complete lack of understanding of what time is.

The rediscovery of Aristotle, first in Islam and then from 1200 onward in the Latin West, introduced a challenge to the creation doctrine. Aristotle had argued strongly that neither matter nor time (the measure of matter's motion) could have a beginning. This rapidly became a focal point in the controversy over the acceptability of Aristotelian physics to the believer. The confrontation between a "pagan" cosmology and Christian theology brought about the most serious intellectual crisis the church had faced in almost a thousand years. The condemnation in 1277 by the bishops of France of numerous theses drawn from that cosmology did not end the crisis. Its aftermath can be seen, for example, in the nominalist-Thomist dispute of the following century, when the proper relation of physics and theology was still one of the main points at issue.

Throughout the debate, the discussion focussed mainly on whether the prior eternity of the world had been properly demonstrated.[19] Maimonides (following the same principle as that earlier enunciated by Augustine) declared that if it *were* demonstrated, the passages in *Genesis* and elsewhere where a temporal beginning of the universe seemed to be taught would have to be interpreted allegorically. He saw no difficulty in this, provided that one did not adopt a version of Aristotle's physics that would entirely exclude God's intervention in the universe. There could be no surrender, he insisted, on *this* point. He did not believe that the eternity of the world *had* been satisfactorily demonstrated, however, and thought it to be an open question philosophically, with a somewhat better case in favour of a temporal beginning.

For the Christian writers, matters could not be so simple. The Fourth Lateran Council (1215) had defined it as a doctrine of faith that the universe had a beginning in time. So the second Augustinian alternative (a metaphorical interpretation of the conflicting Scriptural passages) was not open to them. They had to attack the Aristotelian position. Some (like Bonaventure) argued that this position was not only false, but that its contradictory (the origin of the universe in time) could be philosophically demonstrated. A good deal of ingenuity went into alleged proofs of this sort. Aquinas did not believe that *either* side of the debate could be demonstrated; in fact, he thought he could show conclusively that *neither* position could be demonstrated philosophically. While the Christian Averroist followers of Aristotle, like Siger, were in the uncomfortable position of holding that Aristotle's demonstration of the world's eternity was valid, while allowing that the opposite doctrine had nevertheless to be given precedence over it on religious grounds (thus giving their opponents the opportunity to reproach them, unfairly, it would now seem, with a doctrine of "double truth").

29

With the coming of the "new science" in the seventeenth century, the terms of the debate changed. Newton's mechanics appeared to allow for a compromise position. The absolutes of space and time were without beginning, but were also without content. Creation meant that God brought matter to be within the confines of space at a finite time in the past. And the numerous traces of historical development on the earth's surface, and the later discovery of the second law of thermodynamics, made the Aristotelian notion of a cosmos that had always been and always been more or less as it is now, seem quite implausible. But was space eternal and if so, how did it relate to the eternity of God? Leibniz criticized Newton on this score, and there were many who believed that the Newtonian universe could not ultimately be reconciled with the Biblical cosmos. There was, however, as we have already noted in our introduction above, no unified theory of matter, space, and time, no cosmology proper, which would allow answers to be given to questions about the cosmos as a whole.

The General Theory of Relativity combined with the discovery of the galactic red-shift led Lemaitre to postulate an expanding model of the universe, what Gamow later called the "Big Bang" model. The current version of this model postulates a singularity somewhere between ten and twenty billion years ago, from which this expansion of the universe began. For the first time, then, physical science was led to assert on its own resources something that sounded like a beginning of time. No wonder that scientists and non-scientists alike came to speak of this horizon-event as "the Creation," and of the time since it occurred as "the age of the universe."

The potential relevance of this to the age-old theological issue was perceived by believers and non-believers alike. Two illustrations will have to suffice. In 1951, Pope Pius XII in a widely-publicized allocution to the Pontifical Academy of Sciences in Rome spoke of the implications of the new cosmology for Christian belief.[20] He praised scientists for their unveiling of the secrets of nature; in "the language of figures, formulas, and discoveries," they were in effect disclosing "the harmony beyond words of the work of an all-wise God." Indeed, it might seem as though, in the light of recent discovery, "God were waiting behind every door opened by science." The new discoveries, if taken as "the basis for rational speculations" afford a "greater certainty" to the conclusions of the philosophers. Preeminent among these is the claim of God's existence. Thus:

> If the primitive experience of the ancients could provide human reason with sufficient arguments to demonstrate the existence of God, then,

30

with the expanding and deepening of the field of man's experiments, the mark of the Eternal One is discernible in the visible world in ever more striking and clearer light.[21]

Pope Pius was not concerned with the thirteenth-century issue of how to *reconcile* the findings of science with Christian theology. Rather, he was attempting, much more boldy, to use these findings to strengthen the "classical proofs" (as he calls them) of the existence of God. They do so, he argued, in three ways. First, they bring masses of new evidence for the *mutability* of the cosmos at all levels, thus supporting Aquinas' First Way which requires a Mover itself unmoved, to account for the pervasive feature of becoming in the world. Second, science shows a *direction* to these transformations, an irreversibility. Thermodynamics indicates that the cosmos is inexorably moving towards a cessation of material processes:

> This unavoidable fate, from which only hypotheses — sometimes unduly gratuitous, such as that of continued supplementary creation — have endeavored to save the universe, but which instead stands out clearly from positive scientific experience, postulates eloquently the existence of a Necessary Being.[22]

Finally, the fact that "everything seems to indicate that the universe has in finite times a mighty beginning" would lead the unprejudiced scientific mind, "weighing this problem calmly" to "break through the circle of completely independent matter" to "ascend to a creating Spirit."[13] When the scientist asks how matter reached the initial state or what went before it, he seeks "in vain an answer in natural science" which finds all this an "insoluble enigma." But the same sort of clear and critical look that characterizes scientific inquiry ought to bring the scientist to see the universe as the "work of creative omnipotence, whose power set in motion by the mighty *Fiat* pronounced billions of years ago by the Creating Spirit, spread out over the universe."[24]

The Pope continues:

> It is quite true that the facts established up to the present time are not an absolute proof of creation in time, as are the proofs drawn from metaphysics and Revelation in what concerns simple creation, or those founded on Revelation if there be question of creation in time.

So that cosmology must be developed further before it "can provide

31

a sure foundation for arguments which of themselves are outside the natural sciences." But it can already testify to both a beginning in, and an end of, the cosmos, thus confirming its contingency and the need to postulate for it a Creator.

A great deal could be said about the epistemological assumptions that underlie this discourse, its contrasting of "hypothesis" with "positive scientific experience" (almost in the words of Bellarmine as he rejected the Copernican claim), its interweaving of scientific theory and metaphysical reasoning, its linking of the "Big Bang" cosmological model with Aquinas' contingency argument for the existence of God. And something might be said too about the theological assertion that there is an "absolute proof" from Revelation that the universe has a beginning in time. But we shall forgo a commentary and return to some of these points later.

Sufficient for the moment to recall that the Pope's speech, as one might have expected, elicited a heated reaction from many scientists, although there were some (like Sir Edmund Whittaker, a member of the Pontifical Academy, whose comment that the Big Bang may "perhaps without impropriety" be referred to as "the Creation" is quoted with approval in the speech) who supported the line of argument it embodied. Gamow was particularly upset; he felt that the Big Bang model simply could not be utilized in this way to support the affirmation of a transcendent Creator. Even Lemaitre, himself a priest-member of the Pontifical Academy and the original proponent of the "primeval atom" hypothesis, was unhappy with the unqualified use of his hypothesis in this context.[25] The controversy died down in a short while, leaving (so far as one can see) little impress on natural theology, where arguments from contemporary cosmology still rarely appear.

This, then, was one sort of response a Christian believer might make to the new cosmology. At the other end of the spectrum was the reaction to the Big Bang model of Fred Hoyle. He has been assuredly its most vocal and most intransigent critic. He was prepared to admit that as a theory it was internally consistent and accounted for the data. But nonetheless, it was totally unacceptable to him, no matter what its theoretical virtues in other respects might be, because it rested on a time-singularity beyond which the history of the universe could not be traced. He found it unpalatable "on scientific grounds" because the Big Bang is "an irrational process that cannot be described in scientific terms." It was unacceptable on "philosophical grounds" because the process lay in principle beyond the reach of observation.[26]

And so he adopted an alternative model, which had first been formulated in 1948 by Bondi and Gold. In it outward expansion of the galaxies is "balanced" by the appearance *de novo* of hydrogen atoms at a constant slow rate throughout space. This violation of the local conservation laws, as well as the troubling unobservability in principle of the process of hydrogen "creation" on which the model depends, made the steady-state (or "continuous creation") model unacceptable, however, to most cosmologists. Hoyle's defence was that conservation on the cosmic scale could still be maintained and that the hydrogen "creation" (unlike the Big Bang) could be represented by mathematical equations whose consequences can be worked out and compared with observation.[27] To which his critics could, of course, easily respond that the Big Bang can be equally well represented by equations, whose consequences could, ultimately, be tested. Hoyle thought that the continuous hydrogen creation could somehow be understood in terms of the agency of the rest of the universe. But there was no agency, or at least none that he could admit, that could be responsible for the Big Bang.[28]

For twenty years, the struggle between the two sides went on, a rather unequal one since the great majority of cosmologists were on the Big Bang side. As new data came in, and the steady-state hypothesis and the large-scale homogeneities it presupposed came under sharper and sharper attack, Hoyle held out as long as he could. With the discovery of the 3°K radiation in 1965 (which his model did not seem able to handle), he eventually came to concede that a new model would have to be found. And find one he did, one with even more troublesome features built into it than the earlier one. Galactic red-shifts are explained by a steady increase in the masses of elementary particles over time, galactic distances remaining constant. The model does have a singularity in the past when all particle masses were zero. But this singularity was not a beginning, because there was a prior cosmic state of negative masses. And the requisite homogeneity over space (against which there is now quite considerable evidence) he hopes may ultimately be found on a scale much larger than that of galactic clusters. The details need not concern us further. But his tenacity is surely worthy of note. He still maintains that the Big Bang, no matter what its successes, simply *cannot* be a good scientific theory. Under no circumstances ought anything that sounds like a cosmic beginning be acquiesced in by the scientist.[29]

Why is he so adamant? Are his philosophical reasons sufficient to explain such reluctance? Since he never specifies these in anything other than an offhand way, it is hard to be sure. But it is surely significant that the brief remarks he makes on the unacceptability of

THE SCIENCES AND THEOLOGY

the notion of cosmic beginning are dotted with expressions like 'I believe' and 'I prefer.'[30] Can his strenuously negative views on Christianity, which he feels it appropriate to introduce at some length into several of his books on cosmology,[31] be in part responsible for the vehemence of his opposition to the Big Bang view, which he (like so many believers on the other side) associates with the Christian doctrine of creation? The earlier generation of cosmologists in Britain, Eddington, Milne, Jeans, all explicitly associated their science with their belief in a Creator, so that cosmology, at the time Hoyle came to the forefront in British cosmology, had the reputation of being somehow almost on the fringe between science and religion. Hoyle reacted strongly to this, and tried from the beginning to separate the two in every way he could. Among cosmologists he has been distinguished on the one hand for his unyielding opposition over the last three decades to models of the Big Bang sort and on the other for the explicitness with which he introduces attacks on Christian religious belief into his cosmological works. It does not seem unreasonable to see the conjunction as significant, and thus to present him as our most colourful example of the potential relevance of *anti*-religious views in the choice of cosmological models. We shall discover some other examples shortly.

Having seen these two very different responses to the Big Bang model, let us now formulate in a more systematic way some of the questions that need to be answered. How is one to know, first of all, that the Big Bang was not preceded by a Big Squeeze? Could there not have been (as far as cosmological knowledge is concerned) an earlier series of expansions and contractions, for example? Such models are presently being studied. Even though a Big Squeeze would destroy all traces of the history that preceded it, some general features of the prior sequence (the period of its cycle, for example) might possibly be inferred. Though one might prefer to speak of the universe that preceded the Big Bang as a "different" universe, there would still be a perfectly legitimate sense in which, because it provided the "materials" for the next stage, it could be called the "same" universe as ours.

In a useful review of recent cosmology, Virginia Trimble takes for granted that in a cyclic repetition each successive cycle would constitute a different universe. She remarks:

> The question: What happened before the Big Bang? belongs to the realm of pure speculation (philosophy?) rather than that of physics. It is rather like putting a car into a steel blast furnace and asking [of] the trickle of molten metal that comes out whether it was a Pinto or VW before.[32]

34

Of course, one might ask instead whether it was a Pinto or a Cadillac; a mass-measurement could suffice to answer this. Cosmologists who postulate a contraction preceding the Big Bang are not indulging in "pure speculation" (or philosophy either!), but are assuming that certain parameters remain invariant (total mass, for example) or are continuously traceable throughout (radius, volume, rate of change in size).[33] Even if the progress of cosmology leads us to opt for the "open" rather than the "closed" expanding model, i.e., one which puts our present universe in a state of indefinite future expansion rather than in a finite stage of expansion to be followed by a contraction,[34] this could hardly be said to rule out the possibility of a preceding stage of matter, to which we simply have no access through the singularity.

The Big Bang cannot automatically be assumed, therefore, to be either the beginning of time or of the universe, nor can one take for granted that the lapse of time since it occurred is the "age" of the universe. There is a further complication about this latter assumption, as Milne pointed out long ago.[35] Even if one takes the Big Bang to be the event from which the age of the universe is to be counted, this "age" may come out either as finite or as infinite, depending on the choice of physical process on which to base the time-scale.[36] If this latter is based on a cyclic process (solar years, atomic pulses), so that one is counting cycles, the age will come out as finite. If, however, it is based on a continuous process like the cosmic expansion itself, it *could* come out as infinite. So that the question so much debated in the Middle Ages, about the finitude or infinity of past time, cannot be answered in absolute terms.

Even the question: did the universe have a beginning? is not quite as well-defined as it looks. On one time-scale, the Big Bang is estimated to have taken place somewhere of the order of twenty billion years ago; on the other, the same event could come out as being at an infinite time in the past. Would one speak of a "beginning" in this latter case? Obviously, much more precision about the notions of "beginning," of a "first moment," and of time-measurement generally, would be needed in order to answer this. These are questions that medieval natural philosophers would have delighted in, and had already to some small extent anticipated.[37]

One is led to ask, then, whether there *is*, indeed, an "absolute proof of creation in time" based on Revelation, of the sort assumed by Pope Pius in his speech. Proof, we have learned from Augustine and Galileo, must take account of the determinations of the scientist in debates concerning the literal intent of phrases such as "In the begin-

35

ning." And following the second of the Augustine-Galileo principles, one must ask what the likely intent of the *Genesis* passages would be. They certainly underline the dependence of the universe on a Creator; they bring out God's special care for man (whose temporal history *is* assuredly finite). But do they specifically indicate a first moment in time in the technical sense of the modern cosmologist? Do they commit one to supposing that in a time-scale based on a cyclic physical process (the sort of scale the Biblical authors would have been likely to assume), one can count backwards to a privileged "singularity," a unique "moment of Creation"? Was this part of the point the author of *Genesis* must be supposed to have been making? Is it plausible that a literal intent of this sort would have been relevant to the theological task at hand? These questions raise much broader issues about the nature of Biblical inspiration, about the sense in which one is to speak of *Genesis* as "Revelation." These are not the issues with which we are concerned here. And they are ones on which contemporary Christian theology is deeply divided. Our point was the simple one that the progress of cosmology adds some new dimensions to the long-debated question about whether (and in what sense) the *Genesis* story commits the Christian to the acceptance of a cosmic "beginning."

The argument of this section up to this point can be summarized under two conclusions. First, the Big Bang (if it occurred) need not have constituted a strict "beginning in time." Second, it is debatable whether the *Genesis* story ought be taken to refer literally to such a beginning either. Now let us move to the other side of the issue. Is there any compelling reason why the Big Bang might *not* have constituted such a beginning (assuming, for the moment, some simple cyclic measure of time)? Mario Bunge asserts that science requires a "genetic principle" which would exclude such "irrational and untestable notions" as that of an absolute beginning of the universe.[38] E. H. Hutten makes a similar claim: the notion of a first event makes no sense (he says) because one can always ask: "What happened before?"[39] The most determined opposition to the idea of a cosmic "beginning" comes, of course, from Marxist-Leninist writers who claim that the notion of an absolute beginning is fundamentally incompatible with the principles of dialectical materialism.

This has led Soviet cosmologists to view the Big Bang model with suspicion, and on occasion to reject it outright. In a book published in 1956, V. I. Sviderskii rejected both the Big Bang and the steady state models (the only major theoretical altenatives available at the time), noting about the former that it was an "unscientific popish conclusion";[40] later at a conference on cosmology held in 1964, he asserted that the problem of cosmic beginnings "is in the competence first of all of philosophy, and not cosmology, as some people maintain."[41] The leading Soviet astrophysicist of the day, V. A. Ambartsumian, declared in 1959 that the advances of science "irrefutably attest to the truth and fruitfulness of dialectical materialism" as well as "convincingly demonstrating the complete unsoundness of idealism and agnosticism, and the reactionariness of the religious world-view."[42] Throughout the 1950's and early 1960's, he continued to criticize the homogeneity principles used in deriving the Big Bang model, arguing for extreme inhomogeneity on the cosmic scale (an attempt that he ultimately had to abandon as the evidence for homogeneity grew). He questioned (and still questions) the validity of cosmological reasoning at the cosmic level, on the grounds that according to the principles of dialectical materialism one would expect qualitatively new properties to be found at the level of the universe as a whole, properties which could not be predicted from a limited study of the lower levels. And he rejected (and still rejects) the Big Bang model when it is taken to imply absolute beginning, both on the grounds that a previous period of contraction cannot be excluded and also that such a beginning is philosophically inadmissible. He no longer asserts that defenders of the Big Bang model are inspired by epistemological idealism or by a religious world-view. But he is emphatic that the notion of an "age" of the universe contains so many implicit assumptions that it is virtually useless.

There can be no doubt that challenges of this sort are healthy for science; Ambartsumian's unsparing criticisms of the Big Bang model, especially of the assumptions it makes concerning the interpretation of the Hubble constant, have been beneficial because they have forced proponents of this model to make explicit their theoretical assumptions. Whether this has helped his own work is another matter. He claims that dialectical materialism is warranted, in part at least, by its success in guiding scientific theorizing into fruitful directions. It is arguable whether it has done so in his case, arguable too whether this would in the end be allowed to count against it.

This raises a complicated question concerning the kind of warrant that underlies the dialectical materialism which is so often appealed to in Soviet science, most especially in cosmology. Does it rest broadly on science (as is often alleged; this would make it potentially open to long-term refutation)? Is it properly philosophical? Does it rest in part on an appeal to the authority of the Party? The analogy to the appeal to the authority of the Church on the part of Christians has not escaped the notice of commentators, but as one of these[43] has pointed out in some detail an important difference is that there is an elaborate theory on the Christian side relating God, faith, reason, tradition, and the believing community, whereas a corresponding theory of warrant is almost entirely lacking on the Soviet side.

Returning to the claim that an absolute beginning is excluded by the laws of physics, one is reminded of Aristotle's argument for a very similar position. The real question here, however, is the applicability of these laws to the sort of singularity the model postulates. Hawking is insistent that the laws of "normal" physics ought *not* be expected to apply to a singularity, especially not a singularity which comprises the entire universe.[44] (Ambartsumian's notion of qualitatively distinct levels might also suggest something of this sort). A genetic principle which tells the scientist he ought always seek for an explanation of a particular state by looking to an earlier state, or a conservation principle which directs scientists to try every other alternative before admitting that conservation of a particular sort fails, are in the first instance methodological prescriptions of a highly successful kind. Scientists ought not assume that the Big Bang had no antecedent; they ought to do whatever they can to establish a law-like succession. But this is not to say that there *must* be an antecedent, that the success of these principles demonstrates that an absolute beginning is impossible. This is a metaphysical claim, and it would require more on its behalf than a mere inductive appeal to the success up to this point of the genetic and conservation principles. If it be taken to rest on the metaphysics of dialectical materialism, Kant's warnings of the dangers of applying metaphysical principles rooted in a limited experience to the making of judgements about the cosmos and its beginnings, are surely appropriate.

Our conclusions are, first, that the Big Bang model does not entitle one to infer an absolute beginning of time, second, that there is nothing scientifically or philosophically inadmissible about the supposition that an absolute beginning *might* have occurred (though on methodological grounds such a beginning ought be conceded only if all of the familiar sorts of continuity could be excluded), and third, that if an absolute cosmic beginning *did* occur, it could look something like the horizon-event described in the Big Bang theory. This brings us to a last set of questions.

Suppose this horizon-event *were* to be an absolute cosmic beginning. Let us lay aside for the moment our hesitations about the notion of "beginning." Could that event then be called "the Creation"? Creation is the act of a creator. A spontaneous uncaused beginning would not, strictly speaking, be a "creation;" it would be an absolute coming-to-be, nothing more.[45] Though the term has come to be used more loosely in physics (as in "pair-creation"), it is in its origins an explanatory, and not just a descriptive term.[46] To describe the horizon-event as "the Creation" is to explain it implicitly in terms of a creative cause, a cause presumably outside the time-sequence, since its action brings to be even the conditions for physical time itself to begin. Clearly, such an explanation is not a scientific one; of itself, science could not establish a sufficiently strong principle of causality. Could philosophy do so? Until Hume's time, it was generally supposed that it could, but the critiques of Hume and even more of Kant, made philosophers wary of what has come to be called the "cosmological argument." The issues involved are too large for us to embark upon them here.[47]

Does the Big Bang model have any special relevance to this sort of argument? If the universe began at a point of time, would this give stronger support to the claim that a Creator is needed than if the universe always existed? Aquinas argued that in a sense it would, even though he was insistent that a universe which had always existed *would* equally need a Creator to sustain it. But creation in time rather than from eternity makes the work of God's power more evident, Aquinas says, because an agent displays the more power in acting, the more removed from act is the potency acted upon. And in creation in time there is no potency of any kind to work on. This of itself immediately shows the infinity of the power required to summon a universe into act.[48] Looking at this from another point of view, one might say that an eternally existing universe seems a more plausible candidate for self-sufficiency than one which comes to be.

But the difficulties about the notion of an "absolute beginning" in time, noted above, warn us to proceed carefully in this domain. And the objections brought by Kant against cosmological arguments generally have to be met. What one *could* readily say, however, is that if the universe began in time through the act of a Creator, from our vantage point it would look something like the Big Bang that cosmologists are now talking about. What one cannot say is, first, that the Christian doctrine of creation "supports" the Big Bang model, or second, that the Big Bang model "supports" the Christian doctrine of creation.

We have seen some specific objections to regarding either of these as valid inferences. Even if 'support' be taken in a much weaker sense than 'imply,' it would be risky to say that the Christian doctrine of creation would lean one to a Big Bang type of model among the cosmological alternatives that have been proposed in late years. It

39

would be even more risky to assert that the success of the Big Bang model "warrants something like," or "gives strong support to," the Christian doctrine of creation. Something much weaker in the way of a logical relation is indicated in both cases. We shall return to this in the final section below.

IV

The Anthropic Principle[49]

One of the liveliest debates in fourteenth-century philosophy focussed on the question: are the principles of physics necessary (as the Aristotelians maintained) or are they contingent (as the nominalists insisted). Might the universe have been other than it is? The Aristotelian view was that physics is a demonstrative science based on intrinsically evident principles. Contingency requires further explanation; if at the cosmological level one finds something that might have been other than it is, then one has to *explain* why it has taken the form it did. Whereas something that is necessary requires no further explanation, and can thus be properly regarded as a scientific principle. The nominalist-voluntarist objection to this was that it limited God's freedom of choice; if God is free, then the universe might not only not have been, but it might have been of a quite different kind, operating in a different manner. To the charge that this left unexplained contingency at the heart of physics, the fourteenth-century nominalists' response was two-fold. First, they argued that a demonstrative science of nature is an illusory goal; some kind of likelihood is the best one can achieve. Second, the contingencies of the world *can* be explained, "explained" in a different sense admittedly than the Aristotelian would be willing to concede, it terms of God's will. The world is the way it is, not because it had to be so, but because God willed that it should be so.

A strikingly similar debate goes on around recent cosmological results. In the Newtonian universe, contingency abounded.[50] It was plausible to argue, as Kant did, that the basic laws of Newtonian physics could not be other than they are. But the infinite universe of stars going in all directions was full of things that "could have been otherwise." The unification brought about in recent cosmology has revived the older question again. In an evolutionary universe each stage is explained by an earlier one. But when one gets back to the Big Bang, what should one expect? A state that could not have been otherwise? An entirely structureless entity? To put it in older terms,

40

how can the Many come from One, unless there is some multiplicity latent already in the One? And if there is, how is *it* to be explained?

Coming at this from another angle, how is one to decide whether a particular feature of the universe is necessary or contingent, since we have only one universe, and thus cannot fall back on the simplest way to test a claim to necessity, i.e., that it occur in all cases? The argument for necessity will have to be a *theoretical* one. But such arguments are difficult to construct and notoriously open to self-deception. The scientist is caught at this point. The case for necessity makes him uneasy; yet settling for contingency leaves him dissatisfied. If, so far as one can see, something *could* have been otherwise, it seems fair to expect an answer to the question: well, then, why *is* it this way? Is there a limit to structural explanation, a point at which any further question (like: why is the proton/electron mass-ratio what it is?) is illegitimate? And is there a similar point beyond which genetic explanation cannot be carried, when we get back to a first state that just *was* that way?

In 1973, Collins and Hawking constructed a particularly teasing variant of the old question.[51] The universe is now known to have a very high degree of isotropy; this is no longer the simplification assumed for the sake of a first calculation that it was in the first cosmological models of the thirties. What initial conditions would have allowed such isotropy to develop? It turns out that hardly any of the (so far as is known) possible initial conditions would have done so. It appears to be extremely difficult to construct a plausible genesis for the observed isotropy. It is not only contingent; worse, it is extremely improbable, "improbable," that is, in the sense, that isotropy is produced only by an extremely small fraction of all the permitted ways in which a universe obeying the equations of general relativity might develop.[52]

A more detailed recent study by Carr and Rees suggests that the scales of most natural structures (the Universe itself, galaxies, stars, planets, organisms and atoms) are largely determined by two basic physical constants, the electromagnetic and the gravitational fine-structure constants.[53] This inevitably leads the scientist to ask why *these* constants (as well as the two other constants needed to specify structures at the sub-atomic level, the weak and strong interaction coupling constants) have the magnitudes they do. Carr and Rees show, on the basis of plausible and very ingenious arguments, that if these constants were not to lie within a fairly narrow range around the values they are known to have, life as we know it would be unlikely to develop in the universe. (1) Supernovae (on which the production of

41

the heavy elements needed for life appears to depend) would not appear. (2) The cosmic production of helium would be either 100% (in which case there would, for example, be no water) or 0% (in which case once again, supernovae would probably not develop). (3) Galaxies and stars would be unable to form through gravitational condensation. (4) The lifetimes of planetary systems would probably not be long enough for complex organisms to develop through evolutionary modification. (5) Carbon would not form in the quantities needed for carbon-based life.

The appeal to what Carter has called[54] the "anthropic principle" in this case takes a slightly different form than in the original isotropy argument, where the isotropic outcome is asserted to be exceedingly improbable on the basis of accepted current physical theory. Carr and Rees, on the other hand, note that present theory has nothing to say about how likely it would be that the cosmical constants might have other values. They leave open the possibility that later theory may disclose further constraints on their values, that it might even show that they *have* to be what they are. Their conclusion is worth quoting at length:

> The possibility of life evolving in the universe is contingent on the values of a few basic physical constants, and is in some respects remarkably sensitive to their numerical values. Indeed, the anthropic relations quoted above determine the order of magnitude of most of the interesting numbers in physics ... To what extent this lends support to the anthropic principle ... depends upon one's point of view. From a physical point of view, the anthropic "explanation" of the various coincidences in nature is unsatisfactory, in three respects. Firstly, it is entirely *post hoc*: it has not yet been used to *predict* any feature of the universe ... Secondly, the principle is based on what may transpire to be an unduly anthropocentric concept of "an observer." The arguments invoked in this article assume that life requires (1) elements heavier than hydrogen and helium, (2) water, (3) galaxies, and (4) special types of stars and planets. It is conceivable that some form of intelligence could exist without all of these features. Thirdly, the anthropic principle does not explain the *exact* values of the various coupling constants and mass-ratios, only their orders of magnitude ... On the other hand, there is no doubt that nature does exhibit a number of remarkable coincidences and these do warrant *some* explanation. The anthropic explanation is presently the only candidate and it cannot be denied that the discovery of every extra anthropic coincidence in some sense increases the *post hoc* evidence for it.[55]

But in what sense *is* this an explanation? One might call upon the isotropy of the universe, its age and size,[56] the magnitude of the basic constants, in a causal account of how life originated. This would be a hypothetical explanation of the conventional sort. But the order may not be reversed. Even if one can show that life could have originated *only* if these same causal conditions were fulfilled, so that the logical implication works in *both* directions, it would not be permissible to explain the causal conditions in terms of the effect. Even if lunar craters were to be caused only by meteorite impact, the lunar craters would not serve to explain *why* meteorites fall on the moon. The presence of observers in a universe may allow one to predict that that universe is isotropic. But when isotropy is said to be only one among a large number of possible universe-states, and one goes on to ask why it (and not one of the other states) should be the case, one cannot invoke as explanation the presumably at least equally improbable presence in it of observers. The question rather is: Why should the *joint* state, observers plus isotropy, have occurred in the first place?

One might simply respond: This is where explanation ends, and all explanation has to end somewhere. But scientists like to push as far as their methodologies will allow. One way to construe the anthropic principle as a proper *explanation*, Carr and Rees suggest, is to suppose that many "possible" universes (i.e., universes not excluded by physical laws) do, in fact, come to be in some sort of parallel way.[57] Trimble speculates that such universes might be "imbedded in five (or higher) dimensional space, existing simultaneously, from the point of view of a five (or higher) dimensional observer."[58] In this case, one would not need to ask: Why is this particular universe (rather than one of the many other possible universes) realized? They are all, in some sense, "there." And, of course, that *we* should be in the isotropic type of universe, rather than in one of the much more numerous non-isotropic ones, can be explained in terms of the considerations advanced in support of the anthropic principle.

But does this mean that the isotropy and the values of the basic physical constants in this particular universe would be *explained* by the presence of man in it? Not in any proper sense of the term, 'explain.' The anthropic principle would tell us to *expect* these physical features, once we know that this is the universe that has man in it. But to expect them, given the presence of man, is not the same as to explain why they occur in the first place. That would have to come from a broader theory of how the "possible" universes diversify, develop, and so on. There is also some question about the scientific meaningfulness of a many-universe postulate where the universes are

43

not in causal connection with one another. But even if this be left aside, it does not appear that this speculative postulate suffices to make the anthropic principle a properly explanatory one. "Why is this particular universe isotropic? Because it has man in it" does not of itself work as explanation, not even in the "many-universe" supposition.

Why, then, have so many scientists taken the anthropic principle to constitute an explanation? Carr and Rees remark that even if the isotropy and other anthropic features of our universe could be explained in terms of some more general physical theory, "it would still be remarkable that those relationships which were dictated by physical theory happened also to be those propitious for life."[59] But why should this be remarkable? Only if the presence of man is somehow signficant in its own right, so that the physics can be construed as a means to bring man to be. For the anthropic principle to function as explanation, the anthropic features of the universe must be explainable by their connection with human origins: "The universe is isotropic in order than man should be." But this is not the explanation-pattern of physics and chemistry. Rather, it is teleological in form.

If the universe is taken to be the work of a Creator who wills that conscious life should develop in it, then the presence of such life would in this sense "explain" the co-presence in the universe of whatever physical features are necessary as means to that end. In the traditional Christian perspective, the act of Divine Creation has man as its focus; the story of man's flawed freedom and of his redemption by Christ separates his destiny from that of all other created beings. What would from another perspective appear as an impossibly anthropocentric assertion, from the Christian point of view becomes a crucial element in the "good news" conveyed by the person, words, and deeds of Christ.

Belief in God as Creator and in the centrality of man could therefore make the anthropic principle function as properly explanatory. "Why is the universe istropic? Because it had to be so for the Creator's purpose in creating it to be accomplished." This is not a scientific explanation, of course, nor could it ever be transformed into one. As a theological explanation, it rest on two premises.

First is the theological one that man is in some privileged sense the goal of God's creative act. The *Genesis* story, the long history of Israel's struggle, the mission of Christ, all seem to bear testimony to a special relationship between mankind and the Creator. Despite the stress in even the earliest Hebrew thought on the distance between creature and Creator, on the humanly incomprehensible powers and nature of a Being on whom the universe depends for all that it is, there was also the resolute belief in His care for His chosen people. The Christian doctrines of Incarnation and Redemption claim a much more intimate involvement of God in human history. It would seem safe to say that these doctrines represent mankind as God's special concern. The first premiss appears then to be reasonably secure from the Christian standpoint.

But the second is not. The inference from the presence in the universe of a man-like being to the *necessity* that this universe should be isotropic etc., is an extremely speculative one, as Carr and Rees emphasize. Recall the sort of objection that the voluntarist theologians of the thirteenth century raised against very similar inferences in the Aristotelian natural philosophy of the day. It may well be possible to construct a plausible theoretical account relating cosmic isotropy, say, with the appearance of man. But this of itself is assuredly not enough to warrant the claim that God could *only* have produced a being sufficiently manlike to satisfy His cosmic purposes in an isotropic universe of a certain size, age, and so forth. Thus, the status of the anthropic principle as explanation even in the most favourable case, i.e., the Christian cosmic perspective, is dubious.

Two final reflections. Whatever the *explanatory* value of the anthropic principle, it ought to be clear that the presence of "anthropic" features in the universe cannot properly be used as *argument* for the Christian doctrine of a Creator. Such a reasoning would have some affinity with the teleological arguments from order and design so popular in the seventeenth and eighteenth centuries: "The anthropic features of the universe are of themselves very 'improbable.' Their occurrence is most easily explained by supposing the universe to be the work of a Creator, part of whose purpose in creating the universe is to have man develop through natural evolutionary process." Once again, we encounter familiar Kantian objections, as we did in the case of the "cosmological" argument of the previous section. But in addition, there is the difficulty in showing the anthropic features to be "improbable." Though present theory may represent these features as occurring only in one, or a small number, of the many "possible" universes, it is quite conceivable (a point made by Carr and Rees) that later theory might show such features to occur in all, or nearly all, possible unverses, and thus in that sense to be quasi-necessary. The force of the anthropic principle in this context depends on the theorists' success in showing the anthropic features to be "improbable." And this is highly vulnerable to theory-change, as well as to conceptual difficulties in the modal notions of 'possible' and 'probable' used in the proof.

The theological premiss of man's centrality evokes one further question. Has this premiss been rendered less likely by the enormous increase in the size and age scales of the universe? In a recent book, Roland Puccetti strongly argues an affirmative answer to this.[60] Indeed, he takes the rebuttal (as he sees it) of this premiss by recent cosmology to be a direct challenge to Christian belief. This topic would take us too far afield on this occasion. Nevertheless, a brief statement of Puccetti's case may be illuminating.

His claim is that "the prospect of extraterrestrial intelligence ... generates a profound suspicion that terrestrial faiths are no more than that." It is not primarily the immensity of the universe that he takes to undercut the Christian assertion of man's significance in the plan of Creation. Rather, it is the discovery that conscious life has developed, and is developing, in hundreds of millions of different locations in the universe. Relying on the abundant recent literature regarding extraterrestrial intelligence, he makes predictive use of the theory of evolution to conclude that life is likely to develop, given sufficient time, on any "habitable" planet. He is aware that many evolutionary theorists are sceptical of the methodology underlying this argument, but feels called on to "formulate a firm stand" against such a "pessimistic view."[62]

He gives four reasons why this "discovery" ought to pose a challenge for Christianity. First, one would expect that the Bible would contain some reference to extraterrestrials, if indeed it be Divine in origin. Yet nothing is said of them, even though they would have to be part of the scheme of salvation. Second, the particularity of all world religions, East and West, becomes quite scandalous in the face of this cosmic universality of persons. How could the news of Christ's coming be spread to all the galaxies? And how otherwise (in the Christian view) could these extraterrestrials be saved? Third, if instead one supposes an Incarnation on every inhabited planet, it might involve God in as many as 10^{18} different cosmic interventions as a bodily person. Perhaps 10^9 of these might have to be "at the same time".[63] But nothing properly called a *person* can be in more than one place at the same time. Nor can even God be two distinct corporeal persons at once.[64] Fourth, belief in union with Christ in the afterlife runs into the difficulty: what if there are 10^{18} species of resurrected persons, and therefore 10^{18} Christs? Pucetti's intent is to show that the Christian doctrine of Incarnation makes no sense in the new cosmic context.

But if this is his aim, a much more serious and theologically literate argument would be required. And we still have not the least idea how to estimate the likely frequency of intelligent life elsewhere in the Universe. The basic argument is that the number of inhabitable planets is so unimaginably great that it is unthinkable that an admittedly natural phenomenon, such as the life we know on earth, would not have originated millions of times elsewhere. The argument is a weak one because we know so little as yet about factors that may have served as necessary conditions in the long four-billion-year development of the only instance of life we know of, that here on earth. It is quite possible that conscious life *has* developed in many other locations, but we must be wary of attaching even the roughest numerical estimate to this speculation.

Nevertheless, Puccetti's objections do point up the necessity for Christians, and indeed for religious believers generally, to give this new cosmic context of thought the attention it deserves. The discovery of new lands during the Renaissance forced Christians to rethink some of their particularistic beliefs about membership in the visible Church as the only means of salvation. This challenge to particularism continues today, as East and West become more aware of their differences in values and religious beliefs. Puccetti is quite right to assume that a religion which is unable to find a place for extraterrestrial persons in its view of the relations between God and the universe could find it increasingly difficult to command man's assent in times to come.

V

Conclusion
These case-studies in the interaction of theology and cosmology in our own century may help us now to sum up on the question with which this essay opened. Is the relation one of neutrality or one of relevance? And if the latter, in what sort of terms can it be described? In favour of neutrality is the Galilean argument that the Scriptures could not have been written with cosmological instruction in mind. The consensus of modern Biblical scholarship would tend to support this claim. Some of the more fundamentalist Protestant groups would still see *Genesis* as special revelation from God of the actual historical and scientific details of the formation of the universe. But a majority of theologians would probably agree that its literary form alone excludes any such literal reading. And nearly all theologians would say that the passing phrases dotted throughout the Bible where physical phenomena are

47

alluded to like the "sun standing still" (which gave Galileo so much trouble) testify to nothing more than the common usage at the time the particular writing was composed.

Would this imply that no conflict between Christian belief and the contents of science could arise? As already noted above, there are (and will always be) some beliefs regarding the nature of man on which Christians cannot compromise. They are crucial not because they are directly revealed in the Scriptures, but because they are presuppositions of the meaningfulness of the Christian enterprise generally. Such would be the belief in human freedom and its correlative, individual moral responsibility. What about belief in resurrection? Does it commit the Christian to some form of dualistic theory of man? Many would say so, and certainly the two notions have been closely linked in the Christian theological tradition. But many theologians today would insist on the distinction between the Greek belief in a (natural) immortality of the soul and the Christian belief in a non-natural resurrection of the whole person. The Christian promise, in their view, in no way depends on the dualist's ability to separate soul and body. Nor ought the Christian in consequence require a miraculous Divine intervention to bring the first (and presumably each later) man to be.

But these are not issues for cosmology (although the notion of evolution implicit in the last one does touch on cosmology). Has Christianity given up any sort of cosmic claim? Ought the cosmological issues we discussed above be dismissed by the Christian as distraction, as irrelevant in principle to the Christian task, which is in the immediate order of action, not the objective order of contemplation?[65] Our century has seen a progressive heightening of Christian sensitivity to the victims of poverty, injustice, prejudice, and a correlative loss of interest in speculative theological issues. Does this suggest that the Christian must finally set aside the cosmological and ontological concerns that (so critics allege) trace back to Greek philosophy rather than to the Bible?

It may be instructive to glance for a moment at that more-or-less modern phenomenon, science-fiction. Judging by its popularity, it must set up some sort of deep resonance in the contemporary Western imagination. It is quite striking to note how constantly theological or quasi-theological themes recur in it. Some of the most memorable recent works in the genre, Frank Herbert's *Dune*, and Arthur Clark's *2001: Space Odyssey*, for example, press byond the terrestrial confines of the regular novel to pose theological questions on a cosmic scale. Since so much science-fiction is concerned with regions of the cosmos beyond the earth, this is perhaps not surprising. But what *is* striking is that so many of these authors not only explore speculative answers to properly theological questions but that they by implication intend these answers to illuminate man's terrestrial quest for meaning. Clark, Herbert, Walter Miller, and the rest, seem to be saying that man's ineliminable questions about the purpose of human existence must not be restricted to the terrestrial stage only, if truthful answers are sought. If science-fiction be any guide to the popular imagination, it is clear that questions about the implications of cosmology for theology (and vice versa) have by no means evaporated, as an inspection of contemporary writing in theology might have led one to believe.

Judaism, Christianity, Islam, all speak of a *Creator*, of a being who is totally responsible for *all* that is. As religions they are not just moral codes; they make a *cosmic* claim. Though they focus on the story of man in terrestrial history, they imply quite clearly that this story cannot be told in isolation or it will be distorted. It is a bold, many have always said, presumptuous, claim. But it cannot be diminished, or reduced to a this-worldly set of maxims about social justice, peace, and the rest, without compromising its basic character. For better or for worse, faith in a transcendent Creator commits one to a larger story than even the already-large story of man's Fall, Redemption and ultimate destiny.

But how much do we know of that larger story? Must the Christian return to some strong form of relevance principle relating cosmology and theology? Clearly not, since the Scriptures have nothing specific to say of the larger story, and (as we have seen) are in any event not to be taken to have a directly cosmological intent. Is there some weaker form of the principle? Is it legitimate to speak of "logical implications" of one for the other?

The difficulties in the way of this, as we saw first in the discussion of Augustine and Galileo, and then in the review of recent cosmology, are twofold. First, there is the problematic nature of the *scientific* knowledge involved. Though Augustine's demand for demonstration would not be regarded as epistemologically appropriate today, there is no agreement as to what truth-status *ought* to be assigned to well-supported scientific theory and most especially to the speculative theories of the cosmologist. One of the reasons why we argued above against drawing any direct implications from the Big Bang model or from the authropic principle is the tentative nature of the scientific theorizing involved in them. To draw a logical implication from them for theological belief would obviously be hazardous on these grounds alone.

Nevertheless, there are highly-supported theories which some *have* argued to be relevant to the Christian view of the world. Notable among these is the theory of evolution, which Teilhard de Chardin, in a series of controversial writings, argued to be a "light" for the Christian theologian. His view was that evolution allows one to understand first the modality of Divine action in the cosmos, no longer the series of miraculous interventions that the literal understanding of *Genesis* seemed to suggest, and second, the scope of the Incarnation and Redemption, which are no longer to be restricted to the human soul as though it were an alien imported entity. They must now be taken to have broader implications for the web of organisms and pre-organisms that find their apex in man, as man does in Christ. The debate surrounding the work of Teilhard is an index of how controversial these themes are, for the theologian no less than for the scientists.[66] But it seems safe to say that the Christian account of man's origins and of God's work in creation surely cannot disregard the theory of evolution, and indeed may be said to be illuminated by it.

The second difficulty in the way of maintaining relations of implication between cosmology and theology lies on the side of theology. The theological affirmation in the cosmic domain has proved no less problematic than the scientific one. Augustine and Galileo struggled with the issues of Biblical interpretation in matters cosmological. Modern theologians ask whether the *Genesis* story commits the believer to a cosmic beginning in time, and if so, how that is to be defined. Neither the Bible nor the theology derivative from it offers any simple fixed beliefs in matters as complex as this. Nowhere has the development of doctrine of which Newman spoke been more evident than in this domain.

This is one reason why the implication relationship proposed by Wolfhart Pannenberg[67] seems too strong. He argues, for instance, that the introduction of the principle of inertia in seventeenth-century mechanics rendered superfluous the continuous efficacy of a First Cause, thus reducing the theological claim to one about origins, at best. This led Christians to deism and to the "God of the gaps." Must one not, then, re-evaluate the validity of the principle of inertia from the Christian standpoint, or at least see whether there is not some interpretation of post-Newtonian mechanics which would allow one once again to introduce explicit reference to God's conserving action? Pannenberg argues further that in the Biblical view the Spirit of God is the origin of life. Only if life somehow trancends the organism is the promise of future life meaningful. Must not these Biblical affirmations be present in an implicit form in modern biology if it is to retain our confidence?

There are two ways in which these, and other suggestions Pannenberg makes, might be interpreted. One would be to take him as saying that Christian faith is specific enough in its affirmations in these areas to lead to a critique of the scientific theories involved. For the reasons earlier given, this appears rash. Furthermore, it leads to an epistemological tangle about the status of such a critique, and about the propriety of making use of it in science as a criterion of theory-appraisal. Here the stubbornness of Newton in adhering on part-theological grounds to a version of the principle of inertia which represented matter as a wholly inert principle, with "active principles" affecting it only "from the outside" ought to be recalled. Despite the obvious implication of his own gravitational theory, he continued for several decades, without success, to find a locus of these "active principles" which would (from his point of view) better satisfy the theological demand that matter have no activity in its own right. All activity, he thought, must be seen to come from the conserving action of God. Later Newtonians gave up the attempt, and by Kant's time, the *essence* of matter could be taken to be the active force it exerts. The moral of this well-known story[68] seems clear. It would certainly lead one to treat with caution the suggestion that the Biblical view of creation ought to lead us to question the classical principle of inertia.

But there is a weaker sense in which Pannenberg may simply be asking us to look harder at the theories of physics and biology, not to alter them, but to find interpretations that will be maximally acceptable from the Christian standpoint. This would be to take theology not as an autonomous source of logical implication capable of affecting scientific theory-appraisal, but as one element in the constructing of a broader world view. The aim could be consonance rather than direct implication.

The solution to our problems must in the end lie in this direction. There are two extremes to be avoided. First is the positivist one which would restrict the label, 'knowledge,' to science only, and reject on principle any cognitive claim on the part of theology. At the other extreme is the construal of the Biblical world-view which would make it sufficiently specific and assured in its cosmological assertions to render it a proper resource for the scientist concerned to construct the most general theories of physics, biology, and cosmology. The argument of this essay has focussed mainly on the second of these, and has raised some serious objections in its regard.

51

Is there an intermediate position? The answer is not a simple one, and only the materials for it have been presented here. The Christian cannot separate his science from his theology as though they were in principle incapable of interrelation. On the other hand, he has learned to distrust the simpler pathways from one to the other. He has to aim at some sort of coherence of world-view, a coherence to which science and theology, and indeed many other sorts of human construction like history, politics, and literature, must contribute. He may, indeed, *must* strive to make his theology and his cosmology consonant in the contributions they make to this world-view. But this consonance (as history shows) is a tentative relation, constantly under scrutiny, in constant slight shift. Questions of this sort will still be put: "is it proper for a cosmologist who is also a Christian to allow adherence to the Biblical view of creation to affect his choice between say, the Big Bang theory and the steady state theory?" Answers to questions such as this one may not be hard to reach in some cases. But the long trail we have followed in this essay will have been worthwhile if we have convinced the reader how very difficult such questions may sometimes be, and how far beyond our present reach a definitive general answer to them lies.

REFERENCES AND NOTES

1. *De Genesi ad litteram*, II, 9. The translation is mine. It is to be regretted that no English translation of this work, which so heavily influenced early medieval cosmogonic thought, has yet appeared.
2. *Op. cit.*, I, 21.
3. *Op. cit.*, II, 9.
4. *Op. cit.*, II, 10.
5. *Op. cit.*, I, 19.
6. Translated by Stillman Drake in *Discoveries and Opinions of Galileo* (New York, 1957).
7. Galileo is not always accurate in his citation of Augustine's text. This was not unusual practice in his day. In a few cases, he does alter the sense somewhat. In the section cited here, for example, he first gives a text from Augustine, and then paraphrases it in the words cited in our text above. The text is the one we have translated at reference 2 above. The opening words of the quotation are: "Hoc indubitanter tenendum est, ut quidquid sapientes huius mundi de natura rerum veraciter demonstrare potuerint . . ." But Augustine did not say that "it had to be held as indubitable"; he *might* have said something like this, but no such phrase occurs in his text. Nor did he speak of the "sages of this world" (the phrase that Galileo repeats, and emphasizes in his own paraphrase of the text); Augustine is talking about those opponents of his (the Manichaeans) who "calumniate the Scriptures". And he spoke not just of "demonstration", but of demonstration "by means of reliable authorities" (*documenta*, evidences, sources), a phrase Galileo omits. When Drake (*op. cit.*, p 198) translates a later passage from the same chapter of Augustine (the one at reference 1 above), he renders 'probare

documentis' as 'prove by experiences'. Galileo no doubt would have *liked* to read it this way, but that was not what either Augustine, or Galileo quoting him, actually said.

8. *Op. cit.*, p. 194.
9. *Op. cit.*, p. 186
10. *Op. cit.*, p. 194.
11. *Op. cit.*, p. 197. A similar distinction occurs on p. 199.
12. *Op. cit.*, p.185.
13. *Op. cit.*, p. 182.
14. *Op. cit.*, pp. 188-9.
15. See McMullin, E., "The conception of science in Galileo's work", *New Perspectives on Galileo*, ed. Butts, R. and Pitt, J. (Dordrecht, 1978), pp. 209-257.
16. This is the approach advocated by Kuhn and Lakatos, in particular; it is exemplified in the work of such major historians of seventeenth-century science as A. R. Hall and A. Koyré. It is challenged by L. Laudan (*Progress and Its Problems* (Berkeley, 1977) chapter 2), who attempts to broaden the criteria for what would count as "rational" influences on the development of science, while still retaining a very broad requirement (involving problem-solving efficacy) which all such influences would have to satisfy in order to count as "rational". See McMullin, E., "How Do Controversies End In Science?", to appear in *The Closure of Controversy in Science and Ethics*, ed. Caplan, A. and Engelhardt, T.
17. To do this properly would mean turning to "completed" stories from the past history of science and asking how well the introduction of theological considerations into discussions about physical issues has served scientists like Newton and Faraday. What have we learned about it as an epistemic strategy? This is a complex question which is much broader than the scope of this essay, which deals only with recent cosmology.
18. How ironic, then, to find a recent writer of popular science, P. C. W. Davies, claiming that the view of space and time as "properties of the material world" is the product of modern science. The "biblical account of creation", according to him, took for granted that God had built "form into a pre-existing but uninteresting space and time", thus imagining God to have reigned "in an earlier phase of the cosmos and being motivated to cause the cosmos" (*Space and Time in the Modern Universe* (Cambridge, 1977), pp. 216-7). Ironic, because this latter view of creation was just the one that Augustine, the most influential of Christian writers on this topic, was concerned to reject. Doubly ironic because it is not unlike the view propounded by Newton, the view which dominated scientific thinking for two centuries.
19. For a good review of this controversy, see Massey, G., "The Eternity of the World: Maimonides and Aquinas", *American Philosophical Quarterly*, to appear.
20. A translation of the main part of the text will be found in the *Bulletin of the Atomic Scientists*, 8 (1952) 143-6, 165.
21. *Op. cit.*, p. 143.
22. *Op. cit.*, p. 145.
23. *Op. cit.*, pp. 145, 146.
24. *Loc. cit.*
25. The present writer was attending a graduate seminar with Lemaitre in 1951, and can recall very vividly Lemaitre storming into class on his return from the Academy meeting in Rome, his usual jocularity entirely missing. He was emphatic in his insistence that the Big Bang model was still very tentative, and further that one could not exclude the possibility of a previous cosmic stage of contraction. Lemaitre was not mentioned in the Pope's speech, though a member of the

THE SCIENCES AND THEOLOGY

Academy. It was said at the time that the principal author of the speech was Fr. Agostino Gemelli, a Franciscan priest-psychologist from Milan on whom Pope Pius frequently relied in matters scientific. Lemaitre's uneasiness may have been in part prompted by the fact that some Soviet critics of the Big Bang model claimed that it derived from the "idealism" of the Christian world-view (see below). Loren Graham notes that several of the Soviet delegates who were present at the Academy meeting when Pope Pius spoke, later reacted angrily in print to the theological implications the Pope had drawn, and Graham goes on to add on his own account: "If one were to take the [Pope's] comment seriously, such reaction would indeed be appropriate". *Science and Philosophy in the Soviet Union* (New York, 1972), p. 170.

26. *The Nature of the Universe*, rev. ed. (New York, 1960), p. 124.
27. *Loc. cit.*
28. "The objection to the concept of God as being outside the Universe is that nothing sensible can be made of it", Hoyle, F., *Ten Faces of the Universe* (San Francisco, 1977), p.6.
29. *Astronomy and Cosmology* (San Francisco, 1975), p. 684.
30. See Hoyle, F., *Ten Faces of the Universe*, chapter 6, for example. P. G. W. Davies assures us that the new cosmology (unlike the older religious world-views) "does not deal in beliefs but in facts. A model of the universe does not require faith, but a telescope" (*op cit.*, p. 201). Hoyle is perhaps the one who is most often reduced to expressions of belief, but this impoverished empiricist understanding of what theoretical statements amount to would be inapposite to describe the work of *any* cosmologist of today, or (one supposes) times to come.
31. *The Nature of the Universe*, chapter 7: "A Personal View"; *Ten Faces of the Universe*, chapter 1: "God's Universe". In the latter, he argues that the "nonsense words" of Christianity and the frustrations they evoke are responsible for the political troubles in Northern Ireland. In his veiw, this is basically a "religious quarrel" which could be settled by giving long jail sentences "to every priest and clergyman in Ireland" (p. 7). As a political analysis, this leaves something to be desired! But it is put forward perfectly seriously in a work on scientific cosmology; the strength of his negative feelings on the subject of Christianity could hardly have had better illustration.
32. "Cosmology: Man's Place in the Universe", *American Scientist*, 65 (1977) 76-86; see p. 78.
33. Hawking has, however, recently questioned whether even this sort of "information" could come through a singularity in the past. "Breakdown of Predictability in Gravitational Collapse", *Physical Review D*, 14 (1977) 2460-73.
34. Gott *et al.* argue in a recent paper that the evidence already favours the "open" model, which would mean that the universe would expand endlessly into a form of "heat-death" rather more thorough than that predicted by nineteenth-century thermodynamics. If the usual assumptions involved in constructing "Big Bang"-type models are made, the decisions about "open" or "closed" depends mainly on the average matter-density of the universe: is it high enough to cause a contraction to set in eventually? See "Will the Universe Expand Forever?", *Scientific American*, 236, 1 (1977) 34-40.
35. Milne, E. A., *Kinematic Relativity* (London, 1947).
36. See Misner, C., "Absolute Zero of Time", *Physical Review*, 186 (1969) 1328-33.
37. Massey (*op. cit*) points out the interesting fact that the article of faith laid down by the Lateran Council mentions a "first moment of time". This was, it might seem, a fortunate formulation since it is a question of *fact* whether there was a first moment or not. (The Big Bang, if not preceded by a period of contraction, would

54

have a "first moment", no matter which of Milne's time-scales were used). But if the Council had laid down only that the world had not existed from eternity, or that the stretch of past time is finite, or one of the other vaguer formulations in common use in this debate, the matter would no longer have been one of fact, but only of a convention of measurement, and the Council declaration would have been emptied of content by contemporary analyses of time-measurement.

38. Bunge, M., *Causality* (Cambridge, Mass., 1959), pp. 24, 240.
39. "Methodological Remarks Concerning Cosmology", *Monist*, 47 (1962) 104-15.
40. Sviderskii, V. I. *Filosofskoe znachnenie* ... (Leningrad, 1956), p. 262; quoted by Graham, *op. cit.*, p. 173.
41. *Filosofskie problemy* ..., ed. Dyshlevyi, P. S. and Petrov, A. Z. (Kiev, 1965), p. 267; quoted by Graham, p. 185.
42. "Nekotorye voprosy kosmogonicheskoi nauki", *Kommunist*, 8 (1959) 86; quoted by Graham, p. 156.
43. Blakeley, T. J., *Soviet Scholasticism* (Dordrecht, 1961).
44. "Black Holes and Thermodynamics", *Physical Review D*, 13 (1976) 191-7; "The Quantum Mechanics of Black Holes", *Scientific American*, 236, 1 (1977) 34-40.
45. Whether the coming-to-be of the H atoms in the steady-state model could be said to be strictly "uncaused", since it obeys statistical laws related to the state of the universe, is another question. And the use of the term 'creation' here (as in the "continuous creation model") also raises some questions. Hoyle had no objection to a multitude of small "creations", perhaps because no theological overtone was attached to this.
46. Bondi has argued that the steady-state model brought the "problem of creation" into "the scope of physical inquiry", by proposing a statisticsl law which the new appearances of matter in that model would follow (*Cosmology* (Cambridge, 1960), p. 140). Whether such a law *explains* the events in question depends in part on what one thinks of the DN model of explanation. But even if it did, it would be still misleading to assume that the problem solved was "the problem of creation".
47. See, for example, Rowe, W. L., *The Cosmological Argument* (Princeton, 1975); *Cosmological Arguments*, ed. Burrill, D. (New York, 1967); Kenny, A., *The Five Ways: St. Thomas Aquinas' Proofs of God's Existence* (London, 1969); Burrell, D. B., *Aquinas: God and Action* (Notre Dame, Ind., 1979).
48. *Summa contra Gentiles*, I, 44. See Massey, *op. cit.* In an interesting discussion of the question, "Does the universe need creating?", Charles Misner argues that whether or not the physicist's formula ultimately shows that the universe began from some sort of Big Bang, one would still have to say that God "blessed one formula in a creative act" and dismissed the other possible ones. The need to invoke a transcendent Creator (and not just the immanent one many scientists and theologians prefer) " is a reflection of a distinction I perceive between [the physicist's] conceptual, mathematical visualization of a possible universe, and the alternative state where there actually exists a space-time to be modeled", "Cosmology and Theology" in *Cosmology, History and Theology*, W. Yourgrau and A. D. Breck eds. (New York, 1977).
49. A first version of this section of the paper was presented at a symposium on cosmology at the XVI International Congress of Philosophy in Dusseldorf in 1978. The paper "Cosmology and the Philosopher", to appear in the *Proceedings* of that Congress (ed. A. Diemer, 1980) is complementary to the present paper, since it discusses the issues of relating cosmology not to theology but to philosophy. I am grateful to two of my fellow-panelists in Dusseldorf, Professors V. Weidemann and R. Sexl, for their help in delineating the conceptual issues associated with the "anthropic principle".

50. Later in the conference discussions at Oxford (1979), Professor Torrance argued that the Newtonian universe was a necessitarian one in which contingency was almost entirely absent, and that Einstein reintroduced contingency and spontaneity by his non-determinist and non-mechanist ideas, especially his ideas of time. To this, let me respond briefly as follows. 1) The Newtonian physical universe *was* a deterministic one, but then so was that of Einstein. It was quantum theory, not relativity theory, which challenged this determinism. Einstein, as is well known, advocated a return to a more deterministic theory. 2) The *order* of the Newtonian universe was in key respects a radically contingent one. There seemed to be no particular reason for the distribution of matter and motion in the universe, other than the decision of God that it be so. On the other hand, the universe of general relativity (especially as displayed in the cosmological models we have been discussing) is strongly interconnected in ways that limit contingency more and more.

51. "Why Is the Universe Isotropic?", *Astrophysical Journal*, 180 (1973) 317-334.

52. It should be emphasized that this inference is not generally admitted. Trimble, though she agrees that the universe is a "delicately balanced" one in regard to the possibility of the development of life, supports the earlier view that galactic formation is an expected development: "The matter of this [early] stage was not perfectly smooth but was concentrated in clumps . . . The cause of the clumps is not well understood, though they are not unexpected, since when the universe was very young, there had not yet been time for interactions and smoothing to have occurred across large distances. But they must have been there, because we see galaxies and clusters now" (*op. cit.*, p. 78). It is the explanatory force of this "must have been" that is at issue.

53. Carr, B. J. and Rees, M. J., "The Anthropic Principle and the Structure of the Physical World", *Nature*, 278 (1979) 605-612.

54. Carter, B., "Large number Coincidences and the Anthropic Principle in Cosmology", in *Confrontation of Cosmological Theory with Astronomical Data*, ed. Longair, M. S. (Dordrecht, 1974), pp. 291-298. Carter uses a similar argument to "explain" why gravity is so weak, by noting that stable stars (and hence planetary life) could not develop, were gravity to be a stronger force.

55. *Op. cit.*, p. 612.

56. Davies, *op. cit.*, section 7.3.

57. They give as an example the "many-worlds" interpretation of quantum mechanics suggested in 1957 by Everett, according to which, at each observation, the universe "branches" into many possible universes, each corresponding to one possible outcome of the observation. Because observation can occur only in a universe with observers, this example will not serve to illustrate the notion of a multiplicity of "possible" universes, in only one of which observers can exist.

58. *Op. cit.*, p. 85. Wheeler goes further and summons up an infinite ensemble of universes, most of them "stillborn", in the sense that the physical conditions prevailing in them would prevent the development within them of life; thus they could never become "aware of themselves" (*Gravitation*, eds., Misner, C. W., Thorne, K. S. and Wheeler, J. A. (New York, 1971), chapter 44). This way of putting the case raises even more difficult problems.

59. *Loc. cit.*

60. *Persons: A Study of Possible Moral Agents in the Universe* (New York, 1969). For an extended discussion of Puccetti's argument, see McMullin, E., "Persons in the Universe", *Zygon*, 15 (March), 1980.

61. *Op. cit.*, pp. 125-6.

62. *Op. cit.*, p. 95.

63. The Special Theory of Relativity would raise a question about the applicability of this phrase at the cosmic level.
64. This objection rests on the extended analysis of Strawson's notion of the person which occupies much of Puccetti's book. But even if one admits his conclusion that a human person cannot be in two places at once, does it follow that if God Incarnate is in two places at once, the term 'person' cannot be applied? The most that Puccetti shows is that a univocal Strawsonian notion of the person is inapplicable to Christ in the event that "He" is present in bodily fashion in more than one place at the same time. But then, theologians have always insisted on the analogical character of *all* language about God, the term 'person' included.
65. This was urged by one speaker, Rubem Alves, at the Oxford conference, where the first version of this paper was offered.
66. See, for example, McMullin, E., "Teilhard as a Philosopher", *Chicago Theological Seminary Register*, 60 (1964) 15-28.
67. "Theological Questions to Scientists", preceding paper in this volume, and at more length in his *Theology and the Philosophy of Science*, trans. McDonagh, F. (Philadelphia, 1976).
68. See "Matter and Activity in Later Natural Philosophy", Chapter 5 in McMullin, E., *Newton on Matter and Activity* (Notre Dame, 1978).

Chapter 3

IS/OUGHT: A RISKY RELATIONSHIP BETWEEN THEOLOGY AND SCIENCE

Philip Hefner
Lutheran School of Theology at Chicago, U.S.A.

I

THE PROBLEM of relating *is* and *ought* is that of reconciling, on the one hand, our sense of what is to be valued and what that value requires us to do with, on the other, the way things really are, with what we believe to be the objective character of reality. The identity of *is* (description) and *ought* (evaluation or prescription), or even the easy transition from one to the other has been challenged strongly by philosophers and theologians. The most important reasons for insisting that there is a gap between is and ought are these: (a) that there is no evaluation possible which does not include an element of personal preference or bias, and therefore it cannot claim to be pure description; and (b) simply to describe something is not to commend it or to render it an *ought*. The logic of these objections to a direct move from *is* to *ought* has been amply set forth in British and American philosophy since 1900, while Existentialists have described the tension within the human spirit that results from the basic gulf between what we know is objectively true and the will to act in accordance with that truth.

Theology has a great stake in discussions of the is/ought relationship, particularly as science enters that discussion. As I hope to show in this essay, theology claims that the religious symbols out of which it works embrace within themselves both the *is* and the *ought* and also an expression of how the two are unified. This claim is essential to the religious symbol and to theology. As science intensifies its claims to perform the same illumination and unification of *is* and *ought*, theology finds an increasingly urgent need to clarify its relation to science. In what follows, I shall describe the moves by which science today makes its claim to the *is/ought* territory. The reader will necessarily be disappointed if he seeks here a thorough critique of science's developing claims. Here I can only sketch the claims and allude to their

58

significance for Christian theology. Unless these claims of science are understood, no cogent critique is possible.

I.1. In some circles, it seems to be agreed that the dualism between *is* and *ought* is a dogma so firmly attested that it merits no further discussion. Efforts to reassess the relation between *is* and *ought* and to negotiate a transition from the one to the other are dismissed very simply as the "naturalistic fallacy," with a ritualistic reference to David Hume's *Treatise of Human Nature* and G. E. Moore's *Principia Ethica*. The state of things in this regard is not so simple, however. There seems to be a basic human sense that human knowledge and existence should be in touch with and live in accord with "the way things really are." There is a natural tendency not only to refer our knowledge and our action to "the way things really are," but to insist as well that knowledge and action be in harmony with the way things are.

I.2. This basic human tendency is spelled out on grounds that are scientific, philosophical, and theological. The scientific understanding views human beings as "part of the world of nature, of the world of natural living things: they share the characteristics common to other elements of the physical and biological universe and are affected by the characteristics of the whole natural system of which they are members."[1] The implications of this view are obvious — human beings must know the objective nature of the universe as fully and as clearly as possible; they must avail themselves of objective scientific information about the universe to which they belong. Further, they must live as fully as possible in accord with the world as they understand it. Such scientific considerations have sunk deeply into the consciousness of the race, and they provide compelling reasons to insist that our *oughts* be in touch with what really is. Our best, most objective knowledge of the world tells us that we are a part of the world-system — that constitutes an objective *is* — and that same knowledge illumines for us the natural requirements to which we must adapt in the world of which we are a part — that constitutes an objective *ought*.

I.3. Despite the considerable philosophical literature that underscores a supposed dichotomy between *is* and *ought*, the tradition of western philosophy is even more impressive in its concern for the unity of the two. We may go back to Aristotle's definition of the end of human beings as happiness, or flourishing. Thereby, he not only used as criterion a category that is open to empirical means of description (the *is*), but one that drives equally into the empirical realm to describe objectively what it is that sustains happiness or flourishing (the *ought*). Saint Thomas develops this view in a natural law doctrine. Spinoza also developed natural law theory, writing, *"good is that which all things seek after.* Hence this is the first precept of law, that *good is to be done and promoted, and evil is to be avoided.* All other precepts of the natural law are based upon this . . ."[2]

The Kantian and Existentialist traditions notwithstanding, modern philosophy continues to argue strongly for relating fact and value very closely. The Hegelian tradition, with its Marxist off-spring, has insisted that the *ought* is the dialectical fulfillment of what is — the tension between the two constituting not an impassible chasm, but rather an instance of the negation process which is itself the unfolding of what is.

British analytic philosophy, together with its American practitioners, has expended an impressive amount of energy on the *is/ought* question, out of which has come a discernible stream of thinkers who insist that the two belong together, that the transition from *is* to *ought* can indeed be negotiated by logical inference and deduction. To mention the names of Alisdair MacIntyre, Geoffrey Hunter, Max Black, G. E. M. Anscombe, Philippa Foot, Mary Midgley, J. R. Searle, and the like is to indicate the breadth of this stream of current thought.[3] It is perhaps more telling to mention the names of R. M. Hare and William Frankena,[4] firm defenders of non-naturalist moral philosophy, who nevertheless insist that although it may not be (in Frankena's words) "strictly according to logical Hoyle" to move from *is* to *ought*, it is certainly rational to do so.[5] And both men pick up an argument not dissimilar from Aristotle's. Hare writes, "most of us have a high regard for our survival, . . . and our pro-attitudes are fairly consistently related to these," and he concludes from this that evaluative (*ought*) words do indeed have descriptive (*is*) meanings.[6] Later in this discussion I shall return to these philosophers.

I.4. The Christian theological ground for the basic human tendency to hold *is* and *ought* together may be stated very simply: God is the creator and sustainer of all reality, and He holds things together in the patterns of meaning which He has also created. Being and obligation, *is* and *ought*, fact and value — all therefore have their origin and meaning in the same God. The foundational *ought* is always "Become what you are!", *"Sei was Du bist!"* And what we are is the creation of God. To be in relationship to God is in fact to be in conformity with the "way things really are," despite any appearances to the contrary.

PHILIP HEFNER

II

I have asserted that the transition from *is* to *ought* is a natural one for humans, since it is a deeply embedded conviction that the transition can and must be made. I also suggested that there are significant supporting beliefs for this conviction arising from science, philosophy, and Christian theology. Now I want to turn to each of these latter three — science, philosophy, and theology — and describe in more detail just how I understand their basic argument in moving from *is* to *ought*.

II.1. *Sociobiology as paradigm science, the "biologicization" of ethics.* We take our subtitle from the leading theoretician of the emerging science called sociobiology, Edward O. Wilson.[7] Sociobiology is defined as the "systematic study of the biological basis of all social behavior."[8] When I speak of science in this paper, I refer to this one science. I focus on this one science, because I believe that it is the most sophisticated hard science that deals with animal and human behaviour. It is the paradigmatic science that is relevant to the discussion of the *is/ought* relation, because of its striking (and even outrageous) claims to have related the most important activity of the human spirit to underlying observable dynamics of the evolutionary process. Even though it is a young enterprise and stands at the centre of a vigorous controversy in which its credibility as science is regularly challenged,[9] its thrust is fairly clear, and it has already received substantial, if critical, support in the philosophical community.

Several citations from Wilson may set the stage for understanding how sociobiology negotiates (according to its own canons) the transition from *is* to *ought:*

> Scientists and humanists should consider together the possibility that the time has come for ethics to be removed temporarily from the hands of the philosophers and biologicized.[10]
> Even if the problem were solved tomorrow [the problem of elaborating the developmental-genetic basis of L. Kohlberg's theory of the stages of the development of moral judgment], however, an important piece would still be missing. This is the *genetic evolution of ethics*. In the first chapter of this book I argued that ethical philosophers intuit the deontological canons of morality by consulting the emotive centres of their own hypothalamic-limbic system ... Only by interpreting the activity of the emotive centres as a biological adaptation can the meaning of the canons be deciphered.[11]

61

... innate censors and motivators exist in the brain that deeply and uconsciously affect our ethical premises; from these roots, morality evolved as instinct. If that perception is correct, science may soon be in a position to investigate the very origin and meaning of human values, from which all ethical pronouncements and much of political practice flow. Philosophers themselves, most of whom lack an evolutionary perspective, have not devoted much time to the problem. They examine the precepts of ethical systems with reference to their consequences and not their origins. Like everyone else, philosophers measure their personal emotional responses to various alternatives as though consulting a hidden oracle. That oracle resides in the deep emotional centres of the brain, most probably within the limbic system, a complex array of neurons and hormone-secreting cells located just beneath the "thinking" portion of the cerebral cortex. Human emotional responses and the more general ethical practices based on them have been programmed to a substantial degree by natural selection over thousands of generations. The challenge to science is to measure the tightness of the constraints caused by the programming, to find their source in the brain, and to decode their significance through the reconstruction of the evolutionary history of the mind ... Success will generate the ... dilemma, which can be stated as follows: Which of the censors and motivators should be obeyed and which ones might better be curtailed or sublimated?[12]

These quotations set forth with some force the sociobiological move from *is* to *ought*. Human behaviour is genetically conditioned, and that behaviour includes the activity of the human spirit refined through the process of natural selection as it engages in ethical reflection. Science can lay bare the dynamics and the structure of this behaviour, including in its descriptions the interplay between conditionedness and freedom, that is, the degree to which parameters have been prescribed for the behaviour as well as the extent to which that behaviour can exert itself on the basis of its own assessments and decisions.

The *is* which the sociobiologist examines possesses within itself, in other words, a very profound dimension of *oughts*. The evolutionary record itself exhibits the *oughts* which have been chosen in the past. Furthermore, sensitivity to the question of decision and of *ought* is itself an element of the *is* which the scientist describes, and the particular *ought* is itself an emergent from the selection process which reinforces the *ought*-decisions which have been the most adaptive. Intrinsic to the *is*ness of the evolutionary process is the activity of perceiving oughts and conforming to them. It is against this background, that these scientists consider it genuinely baffling to speak of a dichotomy between *is* and *ought*, let alone an unbridgeable chasm.

II.2. *The central problem in moral philosophy* — **is/ought.** Just as I focused upon sociobiology as the representative of the sciences, so I choose to restrict the discussion of philosophy to certain mainstream figures in the *is/ought* discussion in Britain and the United States.

II.2.1. There are a number of distinctly different arguments advanced by philosophers who are working to show the unity between *is* and *ought*. Perhaps the most widely shared argument is that which identifies *oughts* as the propensities that correspond to basic human needs. The bridge between *is* and *ought* consists in the fact that the *oughts* are values that arise in response to the needs which occur objectively in human nature. The needs are the descriptive, the *oughts* the evaluative elements.

That Anscombe, Foot, Midgely, Hunter, and MacIntyre advance the argument that *is* corresponds to needs to which our *oughts* correlate may be no surprise, since they resist throughout the separation of *is* and *ought*.[13] More striking perhaps is the appearance of R. M. Hare, William Frankena, and Alan Gewirth among this number.[14] The larger galaxy of names represents a line of argument which asserts that it is possible to move according to rules of logic from *is* to *ought*. The logical move is possible, flying in the face of the often reiterated maxim that "no set of descriptive statements can entail an evaluative statement without the addition of at least one evaluative premise,[15] simply because the needs which cry out for value-motivated response are themselves the initial premise of the argument. The demand for the *ought* is intrinsic to the need analytically, and not added unto it synthetically.

Hare and Frankena take exception to the suggestion that the distance between *is* and *ought* can be traversed with logic. Hare writes:

> . . .most of us have a high regard for our survival, and for such other things as I have mentioned, and our pro-attitudes are fairly consistently related to these. *It is not, indeed, logically necessary that they would be.* (Emphasis added).[16]

Given this proviso, Hare admits, in one of his more recent discussions of this question, that he has in fact provided an example of an "*is-ought* derivation," but one that does admit of exceptions.[17] Frankena sets forth a clear distinction between logicality and rationality. One moves from *is* to *ought* by the latter. He writes:

> . . .when a piece of practical reasoning seems reasonable and justified, there is present both a factual premise or reason and something that may be called an attitude, interest, or point of view . . . . one may rationally and justifiably, at least in principle, proceed to a normative conclusion, even if the inference is not according to *logical* Hoyle . . . . Normative discourse just *is* the appropriate discourse in which to express oneself when one is taking some conative point of view and apprehends facts relevant to it.[18]

Gewirth asserts a structure of *oughts* which are more than contingent or hypothetical, because they "logically must be granted by all agents, on pain of contradication."[19] Hence, these *oughts* have "an absolute status, since their validity is logically ineluctable within the whole context of their possible application."[20] They are not contingent on the agent's self-interested desires or on social institutions, but rather on logic. This I take to be an *is-ought* derivation that stands in a sort of first-cousin relationship to Foot, Anscombe, Midgley, *et al.*, in that it argues from facts to values according to logic, but the facts may be called needs only in a special sense, namely, in that they are prerequisites to action by agents.

II.2.2.   Consonant with the argument from needs is that of John Searle, in which he introduces the concept of "institutionalized facts."[21] The *oughts* or values are not intrinsic to human existence as needs, but rather intrinsic to the context or "institution" in which words are spoken and actions undertaken. Thus, in his example of promising, Searle argues the *ought* or value is intrinsic to the rules of the game in which promises are uttered, and not necessarily in the preferences of the one who makes the promise. One is born into the game, so to speak, and therefore no particular decision is required in order for one to play the game and adhere to its basic values.

II.2.3.   One of the most helpful recent philosophical moves from *is* to *ought* comes from Arthur Dyck, who has utilized the work of phenomenologists in philosophy and psychology.[22] Dyck argues that the *ought*, which he calls "moral requiredness," is given with percepts. The structure of the *ought* or requiredness is a "gap-induced requiredness." Examples of such requiredness in non-moral contexts are an unfinished melody or a defective sentence. Given with our factual experience is the incompleteness of the melody or sentence and also the sense that completion is required. Moral requiredness is a gap which we feel compels us to act so as to fill the gap in order to improve the situation. A claim is made upon us in the the moral experience in which we feel a duty or obligation to fill the gap.

Dyck sets down several criteria which the experience of gap-induced requiredness must fulfill: the requiredness must appear to be a true gap from an impersonal point of view; it must be an invariant gap, that is, one that would appear to any person in the same situation; it must, finally, demand that the self will an action of gap-closing — that is, it must be a genuine performative.

Dyck responds to the question how one determines that the experience of gap-induced requiredness is veridical rather than illusory with the assertion by the phenomenologists that there is a given sense of fittingness in the experience which reveals an objective rightness of the gap-closing act.[23] The work of the phenomenologists suggests that relativism in moral perception is relatively rare, since most variations in perspective are acutally due to the fact that different experiences are received. The psychological research data, Dyck argues, do not support the conclusion that in fully identical situations persons arrive at differing moral judgments. Rather, the data suggest that there is a tremendous variability in situations, with each small variation influencing the experience of gap-induced requiredness.[24]

II.2.4. A fourth group of philosophers may be identified as scientifically based philosophers like Stephen Pepper, May Leavenworth, and Abraham Edel.[25] These thinkers argue very much like E. O. Wilson. Values or *oughts* are adaptive responses to human needs which are correlated to the demands of the environment. Objective scientific description not only reveals values, therefore, in its descriptions, but it also contributes information about the strategies that will best meet those needs. These thinkers argue that the *is/ought* dichotomy rests upon a presupposed "set-apartness" of the human being against its environment. Edel specifically charges Bertrand Russell with this assumption that the "self is outside of, and apart from, the causally determined natural universe."[26] Edel and Leavenworth vigorously reject this view of the self. Not dissimilarly from Anscombe, they insist that biological, psychological, and sociological facts about the human evaluator and the environment are relevant to the evaluative judgment. The human evaluator is part of the world, not alienated from it.

II.2.5. The common thread running through all these philosophical arguments is the insistence that the givenness of human experience is not adequately described by the sort of fact/value dichotomy suggested by G. E. Moore. Nor is the naturalistic fallacy which Moore described a helpful concept in considering that experience. A holistic, non-dualistic concept of human beings in interrelationship with the world, their experience, and their judgment stands as the common emphasis of these philosophical schools.

II.3. *Judaism and Christianity* — **is** *and* **ought** *unified in the symbol.* We have spoken of the persisting human concern for the unity of our values with "the way things really are." Religion (and here I am speaking of Christianity first and also of Judaism) manifests this concern in its symbols. The symbol, as it has often been observed, performs three operations, all of which are necessary if the symbol is to be successful in its own terms: it brings to awareness an event of meaning; it projects that meaning into the objective realm, thereby identifying it with the "way things are"; it provides an image of activity which, if carried through, brings the agent into harmony with that objective order of meaning.[27] These operations, illumining and unifying *is* and *ought,* are fundamental and essential to religious symbols.

By virtue of its very nature, the religious symbol claims to be the unity of is and ought. The symbol qualifies as the *is,* since it represents the true or ultimate character and meaning of "the way things really are." The second operation, namely that of objectivizing the event of meaning that transpires in the symbol's coming to expression, by definition grants the symbol the status of fundamental being, the *is* in the sense that counts most. At the same time, the symbol stands as the law of what is, the profoundest *ought.* The symbol, by virtue of its expressing the indicative mode of what is, embodies as well the imperative of that same *is.* As Tillich and others have remarked, there is no imperative that can match in force the imperative which is but the obverse side of one's essential nature.[28]

The Hebrew-Jewish symbol of the covenant presents a good example of the essential nature of the religious symbol and its unifying of *is* and *ought.* The primal event of meaning is that certain tribes of people perceived themselves standing in a special relationship to God — He is their God, they are His people. Objectification takes place when this meaning is extrapolated as the generic characteristic of God and of human beings. It is God's nature to show *chesed,* mercy, to his people and to establish a covenant order with them, in which they share his love in the context of peoplehood and the possession of the land. In a correlative manner, it is said that the essential nature of humans is to be in the relationship of peace, *shalom*, within a covenant with God, fellow creatures, and the land.

Having set this forth as the foundational *is* or indicative, the symbol of the covenant points immediately and without any break in intelligibility to the imperative. To be human is to live in accord with the covenant of God, which is summarized in the life of *shalom*, oneness with the nation and with the land. To exist outside the covenant relationship of *shalom* is to be a "no-person." A person without a vital relation to the nation and the land and to God no longer exists.

The religious symbol thus qualifies, at least in the minds of its adherents, as one of those empirical bits of experience in which the oughtness is incarnated in the isness. The symbol satisfies Leavenworth's criterion, for example, in that it does "eliminate the artificial, sharp bifurcation made by antinaturalist philosophers between factual or descriptive discourse (statements about what *ought* to be)."[29] Paul Ricoeur has spoken of the symbol's functioning in his phrase, "the symbol gives rise to thought" — suggesting the symbol's power to engender reflection upon what is.[30] James Smurl has extended this in his statement, "the experience gives rise to the symbol; the symbol gives rise to thought, and thought gives rise to plans and procedures" — calling attention to the symbol's impetus for ethics, reflection on what ought to be.[31]

III

The question of the relation between *is* and *ought* takes on particular importance today, precisely because sociobiology has brought scientific theory and research to the point where it can provide relatively precise accounts of those features of human behaviour and of the world in which that behaviour transpires which philosophy has said are necessary if we are to have a solid grasp on the *is* which contains the *ought*. That is to say, a solid stream of opinion in contemporary philosophy has said that certain data of experience contain within themselves the *oughts* that comprise our values and guide our actions. Sociobiology has developed to the point where it can provide us, or at least it promises to provide us, with scientific, empirically verifiable accounts of the data of experience which philosophers have ruled necessary for knowledge of our basic values. Science, in other words, steps on the stage today and presents itself as a massive, trustworthy and generally accessible source of knowledge for discovering and understanding the values that humans live by, and it does so not by declaring philosophy wrong or misguided, but rather by providing exactly what philosophers have called for. This describes the point where sociobiology makes its impact on the *is/ought* problem today. Let us probe this contention in some detail.

III.1. *Is, Ought and Needs.*

III.1.1.   We have noted the philosophical opinion, widely held, that the experiential data that contain *oughts* within them are the experiences of needs. Hare writes: "We have the pro-attitudes that we have, and therefore call the things good which we do call good, because of their relevance to certain ends which are sometimes called 'fundamental human needs'."[32] Anscombe called at one point for a moratorium on moral philosophy until such time as a philosophical psychology was developed which could, among other things, provide and account "at least of what a human action is at all, and how its description as 'doing such-and-such' is affected by its motive and by the intention or intentions in it."[33] Philippa Foot epitomizes this insight in her argument that the practical implication of the use of moral terms is that virtues of *oughts* actually turn out to be needs.[34] Midgley elaborates the point at some length, suggesting "that, when we wonder whether something is good, common sense will naturally direct our attention to *wants*."[35] Our wants conflict, and so we need to have the full *facts* about our wants clearly before us if we are to order them into a system of reasonable priorities.

> If we say that something is good or bad for human beings, we must take our species' actual needs and wants as facts, as something given .... It is hard to see what would be meant by calling good something that is not in any way wanted or needed by any living creaure .... we have no option but to reason from the facts about human wants and needs.[36]

III.1.2.   We shall have to overlook, for the purposes of this discussion, the fluid, even careless use of the terms "needs" and "wants," as if they were synonyms. The important thing to notice is that sociobiology now provides or promises to provide a verifiable description of the wants and needs of living species and human beings. This description can supplement and deepen the descriptions of the needs and wants of human beings provided by the various social sciences. The descriptions of the sociobiologists range from the micro-genetic

68

level to the level of gross behaviour that is scrutinized by ethologists, anthropologists, and experimental psychology. These descriptions throw light not only on external behaviour, but also on feelings, desires and the like.

One example of such a description is the discussion in the sociobiological literature of altruism. Trivers, Dawkins, and Wilson (who rely also on the work of many others) have devoted attention to the genetic considerations that pertain to altruistic behaviour in living creatures, and their discussions throw light on natural selection of genes that produce the behaviour that could be called altruism.[37] These same scientists, together with ethologists and others have observed the gross behaviour of organisms and animals, up to and including the higher primates and humans.[38] Others have dealt with altruism on a still larger scale, as naturally selected in cultural evolution, and the relationship of the sociocultural and genetic factors in generating altruistic behaviour (Donald T. Campbell and Ralph W. Burhoe).[39] These studies include both detailed scientific research data and also breathtaking theoretical conceptualities. Sometimes these levels are combined, as when Solomon Katz, an anthropologist, recently described altruism in the context of the cultural phenomenon of grandmothers' relationship to grandchildren, in terms of cultural, psychological, and genetic dimensions.[40] We might also mention Gary Becker's use of the sociobiological materials to develop the correlations with a theoretical model of altruism within an economic system.[41]

III.1.3.   The literature on altruism is already immense, even though it is by no means yet sufficient to explain altruism fully — and this is only one of the wants and needs that are pertinent to the philosophers' arguments. Nevertheless, this scientific study of altruism, together with the theoretical conceptualities, enables us to begin to understand concretely and to follow out the implications of what the philosophers have pointed us towards — the character of the *is* experiences of needs and the nature of the *oughts* contained in them. These scientific studies enable us to assess empirically whether the philosophers I have relied upon are correct in their rejection of the categories of the naturalistic fallacy, the *is-ought* dichotomy, and in their questioning that reasoning cannot arrive at an evaluative conclusion if it has only descriptive premises from which to begin. Here in the scientific studies of altruism we have the basis for the philosophical psychology that Anscombe asks for, the careful comparison of needs that Midgley requires, the objective base of a "fundamental human need" that will illumine Hare's comment that pro-attitudes are what they are because they are relevant to such needs. Here we have the sort of scientific description that makes sense of Foot's provocative suggestion that analysis of justice is incomplete until it shows that and how and why justice is *needed* by human beings.[42]

III.1.4. One more example may illumine how the scientific study challenges and amplifies the philosophy. Consider this passage from Hare's essay on "Wrongness and Harm":

> It is not univerally the case that if we want something, it is in our interest to have it, nor that if something is in our interest, we want it. I do not think that anyone would maintain so crude a connexion as this between the notions.[43]

The sociobiological materials (let us say, on altruism) compel us to ask what Hare means by the term "want." Is it a *felt* need or lack? This is certainly one dimension. Or is it an *unfelt* need that manifests itself in our feelings and behaviour? As, for example, the genetic processes that underlie altruism — these are not *felt* as such, and yet they manifest themselves in both feelings and behaviour. Or is a want the end-product of reflection upon what has manifested itself in feelings and behaviour, with the judgment that reflection can add, pro or con? Furthermore, on what basis do we say that a want is *not* in our interest? If wants, such as altruism have their basis in the genes, or, as others argue, in culture, and both genes and culture are subjected over the millenia to selection processes, in what sense are these wants not in our interest? How could they not be in our interest? Has the selection process gone wrong? Or do we mean that although the underlying genetic (or cultural) processes are correct, even good, in their own right, we have falsified them by allowing them to eventuate in wrong feelings or behaviour. What is the source of this wrong, falsifying expression of undeniably valuable genetic (or cultural) processes? Or do we mean that valuable genetic (or cultural) dynamics have been embodied in behaviour that was once adaptive, but which now, due to changing environmental conditions, is maladaptive? In the case of wrong or maladaptive behaviour, what is it that is not in our interest? The genetic (or cultural) dynamic? Or the secondary expression of that dynamic in feeling and behaviour? What Hare stated as a simple cliché has become much more complex and possibly false when viewed in the light of contemporary science.

III.2.*Dyck's Gap-Induced Requiredness.*

III.2.1.   We have mentioned briefly Dyck's argument that the ought is given to experience in the experiences (the *is*) of gap-induced moral requiredness. The scientific enterprise as we have discussed it is illumined by Dyck's schema, even as that enterprise provides, within Dyck's terms, the *is* which he speaks of. The sociobiologists do engage in a gap-closing argument that goes something like this: If certain basic need *x* is not *attended to*, the human (or natural) system is threatened, i.e., it will not continue or at least will not continue well, or as it is designed to function. There is an inferred gap here: we *ought* to do *x*, or *y* or *z*, in order that this gap not continue to exist: *x* or *y* or *z* become values, oughts, obligations. For example, Pugh demonstrates that such items as the opportunity to dominate, the opportunity to contribute to the common enterprise, face-to-face relations of talking and listening, humour, fairness — that these items are fundamental human needs. His argument is an indirect form of: If these basic needs are not attended to, human beings will not continue to exist, or at least will not continue to exist well, or as they are designed to exist.

III.2.2.   Here we have a very clear case of moving from *is* to *ought*, from fact to value, from science to ethics. The fundamental issue is survival or the enrichment of surviving human life. If Pugh is correct, dominance, face-to-face relations, *et al.*, are basic needs, then without them human life will cease or become less than it could and should be. This gap induces us to respond by closing it, that is, by insuring that there will be opportunities to dominate (whether by becoming a superb pianist, a champion tennis player, or a sadistic bully), for intimate relations, and the like. The experience of the gap includes the experience of the *is* which constitutes the requirements of the human living system and also the sense of imperative that something must be done to close the gap by fulfilling the system's requirements. Scientific fact has provided the ought.

III.3.   *Searle's Institutionalization of Fact.*

III.3.1.   Searle's point is that facts are not simply "brute" (to refer to Anscombe's discussion of "brute facts")[44] but are also, on occasion, encased in the very experience of them within institutions or contexts of meaning that bring an oughtness with them. Searle, as we indicated, uses the institution of promising as his chief example.

III.3.2.   The sociobiological interpretations of life suggest that our very existence takes place within the institution of evolution, governed by the dynamics of natural selection. This context could be said to be a Searleian institution. One does not have to make a decision to "evolve" in order to live. One does not decide to set the genetic dynamics in motion in order to live. It is not legitimate to hold a person accountable for his or her genes' following the laws of natural selection on the grounds that the person accepted that accountability in the act of existing. Rather, the very occurrence of genes entails development according to the dynamics of evolution and natural selection. Therefore, survival is a value, in some sense, that is embodied in the evolutionary institution in which we all live. All of Pugh's values could be said, likewise, to be institutional facts.

III.4.   *Hare's Concept of Wrong.*

III.4.1.   In his essay on "Wrongness and Harm," Hare is building bridges between himself and his critics. His interesting argument goes like this: Harm is the act of preventing some interest being satisfied, in that such an act would prevent being fulfilled some prescription which another person had assented to. Such prevention of a prescription's fulfillment is a wrong and harmful act. Hare extends, in a provocative manner, the concept of prescription to animals and inanimate things by asserting that when objects are used by a conscious being, the prescriptions of that being may be attributed to the object. Further, if an animal engages in goal-directed behaviour, that may be said to imply a prescription. Thus, our actions towards animals, objects, as well as towards other persons may be termed harmful and wrong if they prevent prescriptions being fulfilled.

III.4.2.   Scientific investigation and theorizing describes Hare's prescriptions in the same manner that it illumines needs. In that moment, scientific fact becomes *ought*-laden, in accord with an argument that goes like this. The ecosystem (world, human species) has needs (goal-directed behaviour); to fulfill these needs is a prescription; to prevent such fulfillment is harmful and wrong; therefore, we ought to fulfill these needs.

III.5.   The conclusion to be drawn from this discussion is that since science can and does furnish massive description and interpretative theorizing with respect to the *is* which philosophy insists contains the basic *oughts* for human life, that science may become perhaps the most

72

persuasive means for understanding values available to us.

III.6. Our purpose here is to describe how it is that science does make a claim to be able to bridge the *is/ought* gap. However, it is necessary to step back briefly and comment critically on the scientific effort. Science (here sociobiology) does (or promises to) make a considerable advance in illumining an *ought* dimension in the *is*. Science gives us reliable information on basic needs — human needs and those of the ecosystem. Further, science provides some information on how a hierarchy of competing needs could be formed. Finally, science throws light on what strategies may be most or least suited for filling those needs. Science fails to bridge the gap between *is* and *ought*, however, in that it cannot tell us which strategy is best suited for a specific case in any given time. Nor can it finally determine which of a set of competing needs should receive most attention. Human responsibility to decide (Moore's "open question test") continues to be the final word.

IV

IV.1. I am now ready to deal directly with my central concern — the relationship between science and Christian theology. There are several reasons why I was constrained to wander through so much underbrush and attempt to clear it away. Perhaps the most important reason is that theology and theologians who attempt to deal constructively with science are continually being challenged as to why they take it seriously in a constructive manner, *i.e.*, as to why they permit it to influence their theological formulation.[45] Further, such theologians (among whom I count myself) are often charged with moving naively from scientific description and theory to theological affirmation, from *is* to *ought*.[46] It is no over-statement to say that the majority of theologians and religious philosophers who take account of science devote themselves to probing the *is-ought* problem under the assumption that Moore and Hume (as interpreted from a Mooreian perspective, which Hunter calls the BGI, the Brief Guide Interpretation)[47] are unassailably correct, that the naturalistic fallacy is to be avoided like the plague, that one cannot derive evaluative conclusions from descriptive premisses.[48] Far too many fine minds in theology and religious philosophy have devoted too much ink and paper to reiterating that *is* and *ought* shall never meet, that the cliché about descriptive premisses and evaluative conclusions is indeed unquestionably true.

The result is that, despite their ingenuity and admirable subtlety of mind, these theologians and philosophers never get around to substantive statements about science and theology, never permit the substance of scientific discovery to inform theological formulation. They are often victims of philosophical paralysis.

What I hope for the first three-fourths of this essay is that it has cast at least a shadow of doubt on the BGI of the possibilities for the conversation between science and Christian theology. I hope that it has raised the possibility that one can seriously propose that the substance of scientific discovery is not only relevant to values, but that it is also a resource for discovering values and *oughts* — that one can propose such a thesis and nevertheless truly be neither naive nor uninformed. This thesis stands as a candidate for reasonableness, insofar as science has met the criteria which have been set by the intellectual gatekeeper of the road over which science and theology must traverse in their attempts at rendezvous, the gatekeeper which is called philosophy.

IV.2.   If my argument is cogent, that scientific description and theory stand, under philosophical scrutiny, as a significant source for understanding value and *oughts* for us to day, the consequences for theology are significant indeed. In the earlier discussion, I set forth the view that religion begins its discussion in the intellectual marketplace with symbols which claim to unify *is* and *ought* in the most intimate bond. Now, if the scientific enterprise be an important source of description of what is and also of what ought to be, theology is forced to assume one of three possible stances in the marketplace. It may insist that the descriptions of what is and what ought to be that come embodied in religious symbol are the only true descriptions, and thus remain fully indifferent or hostile to science. Or theology may leave the scene of the marketplace altogether, allowing scientific description to be the most important and adequate presentation of what is and ought to be, thereby rendering religion secondary, or else quite obsolete. Or, finally, theology may insist that science and religion are both essential to the whole truth of what is and what ought to be.

IV.3.   The first position runs the risk of obscurantism. For theology to insist that religious symbols present their claim to set forth what is and what ought to be with no relationship to science is an option that seems unreal in intellectual circles. It is a stance that is seldom licensed by the best authorities. Nevertheless, it is a widespread stance, and it flourishes in many quarters. So much does it flourish that it is often caricatured by the cultured despisers of religion and used as a straw man for polemics against religion.

The second position runs the risk of theology's being the object of a reductionism by the forces of scientific materialism. Such reductionism does take place, because science can claim so persuasively to be the sufficient source of knowledge about what is and what ought to be. E. O. Wilson's latest book, *On Human Nature,* which won the Pulitzer Prize in 1979 in the United States, is remarkable for its daring and straight-forwardness in admitting that science is the source of mythology as well as of description. He calls this mythology the "evolutionary epic," and he challenges scientist and religionist and John Q. Citizen alike to recognize how questions of human destiny and human responsibility are dealt with in the scientific worldview-become-mythology. As this mythology of scientific materialism reaches into the human limbic system, it will replace the other two grand mythologies — traditional religion and Marxism. Alexander Morin has advanced the thesis that sociobiology's claim to be a mythology has contributed to the bitter criticism of the fledgling science. He states the issue thus:

> Sociobiology is based on the tenets of scientific materialism. These tenets are taken largely for granted in *Sociobiology* and made explicit in *On Human Nature.* They consist essentially of a belief in the existence of an objective reality, in which all events are determined by consistent forces that are themselves part of the reality and that are . . . . capable of description by the application of the methods of scientific inquiry. The world view that results from this belief system has no room in it for the immaterial, for ultimate purpose, or for any class of events that is exempt from its universality. There is little comfort for humanity in this doctrine.[49]

Morin's point is that although most scientists may believe something like what Wilson and his colleagues set forth, the scientific community becomes uncomfortable when "faced with any statement of faith, even one that purports to be based on scientific principles."[50] In any case, although it is as unpalatable to many scientists as the first stance is to theologians, scientific materialism is alive and well in this world, and it bids fair to clear religion, including the Christian religion, away from the marketplace of ideas.

The third position is the only one that is fully permissible for theology. Each of the first two stances is rooted in the claims of religious symbol and scientific description, respectively, to represent most adequately the unity of *is* and *ought*. The third stance is rooted in the same matrix, with the difference that theology finds in that rootage the courage to maintain its own claims in the marketplace, as well as the honesty to admit that precisely because religious symbol brings *is* and *ought* to light in their interrelatedness, it must respect authentic manifestations of what is and what ought to be wherever they arise.

IV.4.   The third stance, that of the necessary coexistence of science and religion as representations of *is* and *ought*, holds its own risks. Scientific description and theory is persuasive today, and that persuasiveness is grounded in the success with which science works to make our world understandable and also in the success with which science enables us to do things that we want to do. The chief risk for theology in coexisting with science in the marketplace is that the power of the scientific description irresistibly moves the discussion of *is* and *ought* into the arena of survival and non-survival. Dyck's analysis brings this risk to the fore. The most urgent gap experienced by humans — and therefore the most pressing gap-induced requiredness — is the gap created by the possibility of not surviving.

Theology, therefore, has no alternative today but to speak its truth about what is and what ought to be in terms relevant to survival — the survival of the species, of the world, of values, of human worth, of all the conditions upon which the human spirit is dependent. In our time, theology is not accustomed, by and large, to speak in survival concepts with a survival vocabulary. Theology must learn so to speak. But as it learns, it runs yet another risk — the risk that it will fail to recognize that the concepts and vocabulary of survival must be transvalued, given new meanings, when they enter the theological precincts. These meanings, which are new with respect to the scientific concepts of survival, are old as far as theology is concerned. They are the meanings that relate all of earthly existence to God and his will. These meanings will augment the scientific discussion of survival; indeed theology will often conflict with science at this point — particularly, for example, when science argues that survival refers only to genes and not organisms. If these meanings are not added, reduction to materialism will have taken place automatically. This would threaten the credibility and survival of theology. More importantly, it would, I believe, betray the hopes of mankind itself, which looks to theology to speak survival language with new and more satisfying meanings. Theology discovers that the risks it runs, as well as its

76

capabilities to deal with the risks, take their shape from the same source — from the adequacy of both science and religion to present the *is* and *ought* in the marketplace of ideas where men and women come looking for a word of truth.

REFERENCES AND NOTES

1. Ferkiss, V., *The Future of Technological Civilization* (New York, George Braziller, 1974), p. 90.
2. Spinoza, *Ethics*, Book IV, Prop. xxxviii, quoted in Frankena, W. " 'Ought' and 'Is' Once More", in *Perspectives on Morality, Essays by William K. Frankena*, ed. Goodpaster, K. E. (Notre Dame, Univ. of Notre Dame Press, 1976), p. 137.
3. Essays by these writers appear in *The Is-Ought Problem*, ed. Hudson, W. D. (London, Macmillan, 1969). Also: Foto, O., "Moral Arguments", in *Moral Philosophy*, ed. Feinberg, J. and West, H. (Encino, Dickenson Publ. Co., 1977), pp. 430–36; Midgley, M., *Beast and Man* (Ithaca, Cornell Univ. Press, 1978).
4. Hare, R. M. "Descriptivism", in Hudson, *Essays on the Moral Concepts* (Berkeley, Univ. of Calif. Press, 1972); *The Language of Morals* (Oxford, The Clarendon Press, 1952).
5. Frankena, p. 141.
6. Hare, "Descriptivism", p. 257.
7. Wilson, E. O., *Sociobiology, The New Synthesis* (Cambridge, Belknap, 1975).
8. *Ibid.*, p. 4.
9. See: *The Sociobiology Debate*, ed. Caplan, A. L. (New York, Harper and Row, 1978); Ruse, M., *Sociobiology: Sense or Nonsense* (Dordrecht, D. Reidel, 1979).
10. Wilson, *Sociobiology*, p. 562.
11. *Ibid.*, p. 563.
12. Wilson, *On Human Nature* (Cambridge, Harvard Univ. Press, 1978), pp. 5–6.
13. See note 3.
14. See note 4. Gewirth, A., *Reason and Morality* (Chicago, Univ. of Chicago Press, 1978).
15. Searle, in Hudson, p. 120.
16. Hare, "Descriptivism", p. 257.
17. Hare, *Essays*, pp. 105–9.
18. Frankena, p. 141.
19. Gewirth, p. 158.
20. *Loc. cit.*
21. Searle, in Hudson, pp.120–35.
22. Dyck, A. J., "Moral requiredness: Bridging the Gap Between 'Ought' and 'Is' — Part I", *The Journal of Religious Ethics*, 6/2 (Fall, 1978) 293–318. Also, *A Gestalt Analysis of the Moral Data and Certain of Its Implications for Ethical Theory*. Unpublished Ph.D. dissertation, Harvard University, 1965.
23. Dyck, *Gestalt Analysis*, pp. 70–73.
24. *Ibid.*, pp. 50–70.
25. Pepper, S. C., "Survival Value", *Zygon*, 4, 1 (March, 1969) 4–11. Also: "On a Descriptive Theory of Value: A Reply to Professor Margolis", *Zygon*, 4, 3 (Sept., 1969) 261–65; Leavenworth, M., "On Integrating Fact and Value", *Zygon*, 4, 1 (March, 1969) 33–43 and "On the Impotence of Unnatural Values", *Zygon*, 4, 3 (Sept., 1969) 281–5; Edel, A., *Ethical Judgment* (New York, Free Press, 1955) and "The Relation of Fact and Value: A Reassessment", in *Experience, Existence,*

and The Good, ed. Lieb, I.C., (Carbondale, Southern Illinois Univ. Press, 1961), pp. 215–229.

26. Edel, in Lieb, *Op. cit.* p. 221.
27. See, for example, discussions by Berger, P., *The Sacred Canopy* (Garden City, Doubleday and Co., 1967), chap. I.
28. Tillich, P., *Morality and Beyond* (New York, Harper and Row, 1963), chap. I, esp. pp. 19–20, *et passim*.
29. Leavenworth, "Impotence", p. 281.
30. Ricoeur, P., *The Symbolism of Evil* (New York, Harper and Row, 1967), pp. 347–57.
31. Smurl, J. F., *Religious Ethics: A Systems Approach* (Englewood Cliffs, Prentice-Hall, 1972), pp. 2–10. I am indebted to my colleague Franklin Sherman for this reference.
32. Hare, "Descriptivism", p. 256.
33. Anscombe, in Hudson, p. 179.
34. Foot, in Hudson, pp. 206–8.
35. Midgley, p. 182.
36. Midgley, pp. 182, 189.
37. Trivers, R. L., "The Evolution of Reciprocal Altruism", *Quart. Rev. Biol.*, 46 (1971) 35–57; Dawkins, R., *The Selfish Gene* (Oxford, Oxford Univ. Press, 1976).
38. Pugh, G. E., *The Biological Origin of Human Values* (New York, Basic Books, 1977).
39. Campbell, D. T., "On the Conflicts between Biolgical and Social Evolution and between Psychology and Moral Tradition", *American Psychologist*, 30 (1975) 1103–26. Burhoe, R. W., "The Source of Civilization in the Natural Selection of Coadapted Information in Genes and Culture", *Zygon*, 11, 3 (September, 1976) 263–303. It should be noted that the scientists differ on the question whether altruism is transmitted exclusively by genetic evolution or by psychosocial (cultural) evolution. It is not germane to the purposes of this essay to comment on this debate, although the discussion here does presuppose that Campbell, Burhoe, and others are correct in their insistence that genetic evolution is inadequate to convey altruistic behaviour beyond close kinship groups.
40. Katz, S., "The Anthropological Basis of Values", unpublished paper, 1979.
41. Becker, G., "Altruism, Egoism, and Genetic Fitness: Economics and Sociobiology", *Journal of Economic Literature*
42. Foot, in Hudson, pp. 211–13.
43. Hare, *Essays*, p. 97.
44. Anscombe, in Hudson, p. 178, and "Brute Facts", *Analysis*, 19 (1958)
45. For example, Holmer, P. L., "Evolution and Being Faithful", in *Changing Man: The Threat and the Promise*, ed. Haselden, K. and Hefner, P. (Garden City, Doubleday and Co., 1968), pp. 156–168.
46. See Gustafson, J., "Theology Confronts Technology and the Life Sciences", *Commonweal*, June 16, 1978. Gilkey, L., *Religion and the Scientific Future* (New York, Harper and Row, 1970), especially chap. I.
47. Gilkey, *op. cit.;* Barbour, I., *Myths, Models, and Paradigms* (London, SCM Press, 1974).
48. See works cited in footnotes 45, 46, 47.
49. Morin, A. J., "Revelation and Heresy in Sociobiology", *Science, Technology, Human Values*, 27 (Harvard University Program on Science, Technology, and Public Policy, Spring 1979) 24–35.
50. *Ibid.*, p. 27.

Part II

NATURE, MAN AND GOD

Chapter 4

DIVINE AND CONTINGENT ORDER

T. F. Torrance
University of Edinburgh, U.K.

I

Scientific and theological world-views
In our day we have reached a turning-point in the history of thought at which natural science and theological science are confronted each in its own way with the need to adopt a fundamental attitude to the universe as a whole.

Natural science has always tended to generate a world-view or cosmology, such as the Ptolemaic or Copernican orientation toward the cosmos, and has since Newton been concerned to develop a system of the world; but it has also tended to renounce anything like a scientific world-view on the ground that this would mean stepping across the frontier of exact science into metaphysics, and allying itself with unwarranted cosmological presuppositions and speculations. Hence in modern times natural science has claimed to be neutral or non-committal in respect of any specific cosmology. Today, however, the situation is radically changed. On the one hand, the relentless pressure of its own inquiries has carried science to the very limits of being where it can no longer avoid the question as to initial conditions or the basic relation between concept and reality; and, on the other hand, there has steadily emerged through these inquiries an underlying conceptual unity in objective scientific knowledge ranging from microphysical to astrophysical aspects of the universe. This change is marked by the fact that there has now arisen a science of cosmology, for the profounder our understanding of nature throughout the universe gets, the more we are forced to grapple with meta-scientific and cosmological questions and are committed to adopting a basic attitude to the universe as a whole, which cannot but affect every fundamental theory and every theory-laden experiment.

In modern times theology also has been widely concerned to abjure commitment to any specific cosmology. Some theologians, in acceptance of the Kantian and Laplacian rationalisation of Newton's system of the world into a self-containing and self-explaining deterministic framework, have gone to great lengths in seeking to detach understanding of the Bible and Christian theology from any world-view and indeed to cut off faith from any empirical correlates in physical space-time reality. Thereby, however, they have replaced a God-centred and objective outlook with a radically man-centred and subjective outlook. Other theologians who take seriously faith in God as Maker of heaven and earth, and therefore reject any conception of the universe as a self-contained and self-explanatory system, nevertheless claim that faith does not generate a distinctive view of the universe and cannot be tied up with any particular cosmology. Theology, they say, on its own proper ground can operate freely and non-committedly within various cosmologies. Justification for this is offered on the ground that the biblical revelation does not contain any ontology of heaven and earth and is therefore not concerned with cosmology. Because theology has to do with God and man, it operates only on the cosmological border where the universe of space and time is limited by the invisible transcendent reality of the divine. On the other hand, it is admitted that faith in God as Creator of the universe implies that a cosmos detached from its Creator loses its natural axis and that man detached from the cosmos is an abstraction. Hence even on this view theology cannot operate on its own proper ground in complete detachment from cosmology.

Is it actually the case, however, that there is no distinctively biblical or Christian view of the universe? Can theology, concerned as it is with interrelations between God and man-in-the-universe, be pursued properly without consideration of its empirical correlates in the continuities and structures of space and time? It seems clear to me that both these questions must be answered in the negative. Undoubtedly faith in God finds itself restricted, if not altogether suffocated, in some cosmologies rather than in others, which implies that it cannot disregard views of the universe within the society or culture in which faith arises and seeks to take root. Likewise, theology functions more freely in some cosmologies than in others, and the fact that it may find itself in conflict — as has often happened in the past — with conceptions governing a particular outlook upon the universe, reveals that theology operates with basic cosmological conceptions of its own which it cannot give up. It is indeed distinctive of the Judaeo-Christian outlook that God interacts with man within the physical reality and order of the cosmos to which man belongs, and does not merely relate himself to man in some 'external' or 'indirect' way which could only be given mythological expression. It is in and through the medium of space and time that God acts upon man and makes himself known to him, and man is called to responsive acts of obedience and knowledge. That is to say, the fact (so essential to both Judaism and Christianity) of God's self-revelation to man within the objectivities of this empirical world carries with it spatio-temporal coefficients which faith in the living God cannot give up without defection from its foundation. By the same token theology finds itself committed to a distinctive understanding of the created order of space and time which implies basic cosmological convictions of far-reaching significance.

It is a serious fault of much modern theology with its rather one-sided emphasis on history that, while it recognises that faith in God cannot be cut loose from temporal factors, it has nevertheless sought to cut off faith from its involvement with spatial factors. Thereby, however, theology of this sort makes faith in the God of history irrelevant for this world and renders even its own historical enterprise highly questionable, for time detached from space is empty and meaningless. This goes far to account for the current debâcle of what is called the historico-critical method in biblical interpretation, in its failure to grapple with the spatio-temporal reality of the historical Jesus, not to mention the incarnate presence and redemptive act of God in our world of space and time.

The orientation of classical Christian theology in the early centuries of our era was very different. The seriousness with which it took the incarnation of the Creator in space and time forced it to think out radically the whole idea of creation out of nothing, and the continuing relation of God to space and time which are the bearers of all rational order in the created universe. The basic convictions implicit in this Christian view of God and the universe quickly brought Christian theology into sharp conflict with the conceptions governing the cosmologies prevailing in the ancient world, so that the great theologians were forced not only to make the distinctively Christian view of the world explicit but to reconstruct the rational foundations of ancient cosmology. And what is more — admittedly this is a startling claim — classical Christian theology generated those basic conceptions upon which any scientific cosmology must rest if it is to be true to the actual nature of the universe.

On the other hand, it must be said that a theological view of the universe, in accordance with which the natural axis of the universe is to be found not within the universe itself as an independent cosmological system but in its relation to God its transcendent Creator, cannot be identified with any particular cosmology, even one that arises on the basis of distinctively Christian conceptions. From a theological perspective the physical universe is to be regarded as an open intelligible system which constitutes a consistent whole only in so far as it is completed beyond itself in God as its creative ground. Hence so far as theology is concerned the material content of any scientific account of the universe is treated as a partial, provisional and revisable cosmology which can never be completed or therefore explained merely in terms of its own internal constituent relations but which, on its empirico-theoretical level, can nevertheless be highly meaningful for theology when it is co-ordinated with a higher level of rational order in God as its sufficient reason. It is a significant fact that a rigorously scientific approach to the universe today, which carries its inquiries into the immanent intelligibilities of the universe to the very boundaries of empirical reality where natural science breaks off, approximates to just such a theological understanding of it. The common factor between those two very different views of the universe, making them open to each other and such an approximation possible, is to be found in the concept of *contingent order*.

II

Contingent order
Contingent order is not a concept that was produced, or indeed could have been produced, by natural science, ancient or modern, on its own. It is the direct product of the Christian understanding of the constitutive relation between God and the universe which he freely created out of nothing, yet not without reason, conferring upon what he has made and continues to sustain a created rationality of its own dependent on his uncreated transcendent rationality. It was the injection of that concept into science that so altered its very basis that the rise of modern empirico-theoretical science was possible. Ancient science realised that if there were no order in the universe but only chaos the universe would not be open to rational knowledge, but it identified order with what is logically and causally necessary as well as timeless. And ancient science was not without a certain notion of contingence, in the sense of chance or the accidental, but it was regarded as the antithesis of what is orderly or rational, and therefore as defective of reality and no more than transient appearance. Thus the idea of contingent order, so far as ancient science is concerned, would have been an impossible contradication in terms. The determining presuppositions of Greek science which lay behind that way of

thinking had to be uprooted and rejected before the notion of contingent rationality or the rationality of the contingent could even be entertained, let alone accepted. That is what happened through the radical Christian doctrine of God's creation and sustaining of the universe in form as well as matter out of nothing. It liberated nature conceived as the timeless embodiment of eternal forms from a necessary relation to God, which made it impossible to distinguish nature from God; and it destroyed the bifurcation of form and matter, affirming each as equally created out of nothing and equally real in their indissoluble unity with one another in the one pervasive rational order of the contingent universe under God.

Today natural science assumes both the contingence and the orderliness of the universe. The universe is contingent for it does not exist of necessity: it might not have been at all and might very well have been different from what it is. Yet in coming to be the universe is characterised by an open-structured order which partakes of its contingence. If the universe were not characterised by contingent order but by an immanent necessity, the laws of nature would be derived from it immediately and necessarily by logico-deductive operations without experimental questioning of nature, which would make empirical science quite pointless. Only in comparatively recent times, however, when scientific investigation has come up against the limits set by the initial conditions of nature, including the finiteness of space and time, and explanations are pushed back to the ultimate assumptions or beliefs about the nature of the universe which regulate all our working scientific conceptions, has contingence been forced into the open, compelling acknowledgment from us, even though it is not scientifically, far less logically, derivable or provable. Such is the position we have now reached, as the contingent nature of the universe challenges science to reckon with it no longer as a negligible hidden parameter in its theories but as an essential and integral factor in rigorous scientific understanding and interpretation of the natural order. This change has the effect of making us realise that all scientific truth is contingent and limited for it is correlated to contingent and limited realities, yet that does not detract from the intelligibility and the validity of scientific conceptions, for scientific conceptions do not have their truth in themselves but in the realities to which they refer and on which they are grounded. Because of the contingent and limited nature of those realities science must reckon with the fact that the orderly connections which it seeks to trace within the universe cannot be followed through scientifically to any final end, for they break off at the limits imposed by space and time, but that nevertheless through their contingent intelligibility they refer our thought meta-seicentifically beyond those empirical limits to an ultimate intelligible ground on which all orderly connections within the universe must finally depend if they are to remain intelligible and consistent. Thus contingence and order which our science presupposes throughout all its operations imply a fundamental outlook upon the nature of the universe which points back to the Christian doctrine of creation.

We note again that it is through the concept of contingent order that theological and scientific views of the universe are not only compatible but may be coordinated significantly with one another. Contingence, however, has a double aspect deriving from its theological roots which needs clarification. On the one hand, it means that the universe depends entirely upon the beneficent free will and act of the Creator for its being and form, and is not a necessary emanation of the divine, but, on the other hand, it also means that the universe is given an independent reality of its own completely differentiated from the self-sufficient eternal reality of God. Thus in virtue of its contingence the universe has an orientation at once toward God and away from him. Theology is more concerned with the former orientation of the universe, its dependence on God, and natural science understandably is more concerned with the latter orientation of the universe, its independence of God — yet neither can be held properly without the other. For theology the radicalisation of contingence implies that in creating the universe out of nothing God gave it a natural condition and status of its own such that if we are to respect the universe as it came from the hand of God and do justice to its creaturely nature we are obliged to direct attention to it for its own sake, as well as for God's sake. Thus there is theological warrant for the independent empirical investigation of the universe by natural science — indeed such an investigation is a duty toward God laid upon us by his work of creation. For natural science the radicalisation of contingence implies that the universe is endowed with an autonomous character both as a whole and throughout its immanent relations, with features and patterns and operational principles which belong to it as by intrinsic natural right, such that if natural science is to be rigorously faithful to the nature of the universe it must bracket off the universe from relation to God and develop autonomous modes of investigation appropriate to the independent reality of the universe which allow it to disclose its own inherent rational order. Hence reliance upon experimental questioning, together with the forswearing of rationalistic deductivism, is a duty imposed on natural science by the contingent nature of the universe and not an optional extra.

86

It is evident that theology cannot develop an adequate understanding of the relation of God to the universe which he has made without accepting the radical implications of contingence. If it does not accept them it is tempted to turn in upon itself and to treat theology as a closed rationalistic system of thought, in which 'God' is defined by reference only to what man can conceive. However, if theology does accept the radical implications of contingence, it provides ground for the rise of a methodological secularism in natural science which through an orientation in inquiry away from God runs the risk of over-reaching itself in a dogmatic secularism or atheism. The problem of natural science, on the other hand, is that in developing autonomous modes of scientific investigation it is tempted to treat the universe as a wholly self-supporting and self-explaining necessary system, and thus by closing in upon itself runs the risk of lapsing into an empiricist rationalism in which contingence is abjured and genuine empirical science is pushed aside. Both theological science and natural science require the double aspect of contingence, dependence on God and independence from him, in order properly to be what they ought to be. For theology concentration on dependence alone would exclude freedom unless dependence becomes the ground for a genuine independence; while for science concentration on independence alone would also exclude freedom, for it would degenerate into a pointless circularity consistent and complete in its own internal necessities, unless independence is limited by dependence on God. Clearly theology needs dialogue with natural science to keep it properly free and open toward God, and natural science needs dialogue with theology to keep it properly free and open toward the universe.

III

The rationality and freedom of creation
Let us explore the implications of contingent order a little further by reference to the cognate conceptions of contingent rationality and contingent freedom as they derive from the Christian understanding of creation. Just as the doctrine of God's creation of the universe out of nothing operates with a relation between the creative rationality of God and the created rationality of the universe, so it operates also with a relation between the creative freedom of God and the created freedom of the universe. The rationality which God has conferred upon the creation is not incongruous with his own uncreated rationality but is a limited, contingent reflection of it. Likewise the freedom

which God has imparted to the creation is not incompatible with his own transcendent freedom, but since the freedom of the universe is grounded in that divine freedom it is also limited by it and thereby established as contingent freedom. This combination of contingent rationality and contingent freedom, which excludes both arbitrariness and necessity, makes the universe an open dynamic system of contingent order in which nature is capable of a variety of possible interpretations consistent with each other, evident, for example, in several equally valid formulations of some physical law. Behind this inherent openness and variability in nature lies the correlation of the rationality and freedom of the universe to the unlimited rationality and freedom and therefore to the endless possibilities of the Creator, whereby nature is endowed with its power constantly to surprise us in the spontaneous emergence of increasingly complex forms of order in the expanding universe and thus in the manifestation of unexpected features and structures at different levels of reality which nevertheless always turn out to be consistent with features and structures at other levels. Such is the indefinite range and richness of contingent order which we are unable adequately to grasp, not because it is deficient in rationality but because the depth of its rationality exceeds our human capacity to apprehend it beyond limited levels. By its very nature, however, the contingent order of the universe grips our thought in such a way that it is harnessed to a reference beyond empirical reality, when very much more is indicated to us than we can express merely in terms of intramundane relations and possibilities. Nevertheless, if we insist on contriving for ourselves some sort of controlling formalisation of what is thus indicated, we find that the truth becomes turned into a lie. That is to say, the kind of intelligible order everywhere inherent in created reality contingently reflects an ultimate reality infinitely greater than we can conceive, which calls into radical question all the idolatrous surrogates of our human minds.

IV

Factors detracting from and promoting contingence.
There is, however, another story to be told. Throughout modern times it has generally been held proper for natural science to confine itself to intramundane connections and explanations, in methodological exclusion of all reference to extramundane relations. It would seem no less proper for natural science to recognise that this exclusion is only methodological and does not imply that there is no reality beyond

what is open to investigation through its own methods and instruments or is accessible to understanding and formalisation within the limits of its own conceptual framework — otherwise it would be guilty of the fallacy of identifying the real with what is conceivable to the natural-scientific reason alone. If this exclusion is acknowledged to be only a methodological convenience, but nevertheless remains practically in force, then it will clearly be difficult for natural science to have much to do with contingence in its double aspect as contingence away from God and contingence on God which we have found to be essential to it.

Undoubtedly modern science does accept the idea that the universe is contingent, for that is the regulative assumption behind its reliance upon experiment and its operation with the interlocking of experiment and theory. Nevertheless science has not been without certain problems in this respect. By focussing on the determination of observable regularities in nature and their formalisation as logico-causal continuities, to the exclusion of all extra-causal and extra-logical factors, science has steadily created an immensely powerful and successful conceptual machinery which has generated a momentum of its own and functions as though it were a law to itself. In this way rigorous, exact science tends to develop a prescriptive framework from which contingence appears rather like a surd which finally baffles scientific analysis, representation and explanation. Hence too frequently in on-going science contingence comes to be identified with what does not fit into exact scientific formalisation and therefore to be treated as a negligible irrelevance. Thus in spite of the fact that contingence is the *sine qua non* of empirical science there are evidently factors in modern scientific activity undermining its status and tempting science to resolve it away. On the other hand, there are factors in recent developments which reverse this trend, so that contingence once more comes into its own in a powerful way.

Factors detracting from the notion of contingent order all appear to be bound up with the view of the universe as a closed mechanistic system. For short we shall call this the 'Newtonian world-view' since Newton supplied the controlling concepts and equations, although strictly speaking it was only after Newton's time that it developed into the sophisticated deterministic outlook which dominated thought until the first quarter of the twentieth centry. Basic to this view of the world was its atomism, on the one hand, and its unchanging overall structure, on the other hand. All nature was regarded as comprised of separated corpuscles which even at a distance act instantaneously on one another through empty and uniform space, while retaining their substantial identity throughout all change. This enabled science to offer an explanation of all empirical phenomena in the universe strictly in terms of mechanical causes and with precise mathematical quantification; but it had the effect of imposing artificially upon an admittedly dynamic universe of bodies in motion a rigid homogeneous frame-work reckoned to be needed if science is to offer an account of nature irrespective of all observers. Such an objectivist view of the world from a point of absolute rest resulted in the conception of a closed necessary order in which contingence was inevitably suppressed or at least tolerated only under condition of a necessary relation to immutable physical law.

Clearly there was a basic contradiction in the Newtonian world view between its rigid unchanging conceptual framework, absolute time and space, and the dynamic nature of the universe which more and more came to light throughout the nineteenth century in physics and biology alike. Since on these assumptions 'reality' was restricted to what can be predicted and controlled through the instruments and calculations of physics and mechanics, the gap, inherent in the dualist basis of Newtonian science, between the conceptual apparatus employed by natural science and the on-going empirical universe, widened considerably until it came to be held that science is not after all a search for reality, as Newton thought, but a necessary pragmatic device for human existence in this world, making for convenient arrangements of conceptual symbols and fictions through which we may describe scientific activity, classify observational data, and derive economical generalisations, without exerting the claim that they have any ontological bearing upon empirical reality. That is to say, an unbalanced concentration upon theoretical formalisation and mathematical idealisation, to the detriment of the empirical ingredient in scientific knowledge, gave rise to a positivist and conventionalist outlook in which the formulation of physical law is cut off from the ontological basis on which natural science rests, and genuine contingence is resolved away. This recurring difficulty that science, especially after Kant, Laplace and Mach, evidently has with contingence would seem to indicate that modern science, like ancient science, by itself could not come up with the notion of contingence but that, essential though it is to natural science, it derives from elsewhere, i.e. as we have claimed, from Christian faith.

Factors promoting the idea of contingent order are evidently bound up with the view of the universe as a unitary open system. For short we shall call this the 'Einsteinian world-view' since it was with Einstein's early work in relativity and quantum theory that the decisive change to a new basic notion of order set in. Already deep in the nineteenth century, especially with Faraday and Maxwell, there was a growing realisation that to understand the nature of the universe a rather different concept of order was needed to replace that of a necessary and mechanical order. Investigation into the properties of electromagnetic induction revealed that the idea of instantaneous action at a distance is untenable, and called for a new idea of material substances as convergent points of force rather than as discrete corpuscles in empty time and space; while the discovery that all forces such as electricity, magnetism and light are interrelated called correspondingly for a new theory of the world as a complex field of forces within which all movement and change involve time. It was left to Clerk Maxwell to provide mathematical clarification and interpretation of these insights, to develop a unified theory of electricity, magnetism and light, and to come up with the laws of the field. However, Maxwell's acceptance of the notion of ether (which Faraday had rejected) created problems, for it meant that he had to retain a mechanical interpretation of the force field, and called in question Faraday's interpretation of matter and field. Out of this came Maxwell's famous partial differential equations for the electromagnetic field, which have been so outstandingly fertile for subsequent scientific discovery and advance. At the same time Maxwell attempted a different type of field interpretation, not dependent on Newtonian mechanism, which while operating with matter and field as separated realities nevertheless held that in some way they interpenetrate one another. Thus Faraday and Maxwell opened the way for a new understanding of nature in terms of field theory which could be set against the Newtonian outlook and which, in spite of Maxwell's acceptance of Newtonian dualism and mechanism, pointed to a non-mechanical view of the universe in which matter and field are unified.

The decisive step in this direction was taken by Einstein in his rejection of Newtonian dualism and mechanism. Following on clarification particularly by Hertz and Lorentz of difficult problems resulting from contradictions between Maxwellian and Newtonian mechanics, Einstein introduced a fundamental change into field theory, coordinating it with a startlingly new view of the universe and its unitary dynamic order, very different from the Newtonian worldview. He dethroned time and space from their absolute, unvarying, prescriptive role in the Newtonian system and brought them down to empirical reality, where he found them indissolubly integrated with its on-going processes. At the same time he set aside the idea of instantaneous action at a distance, but also set aside the existence of ether (still maintained by Lorentz) and all idea of the substantiality of the field (in Faraday's sense). There now emerged the concept of the continuous field of space-time which interacts with the constituent matter/energy of the universe, integrating everything within it in accordance with its unitary yet variable, objective rational order of non-causal connections. Thus instead of explaining the behaviour of the field and all events within it in terms of the motion of separated material substances characterised by unique unchanging patterns and defined by reference to the conditioning of an inertial system, and therefore in terms of quantifiable motion and strict mechanical causes, Einstein explained it in terms of the objective configuration of the indivisible field and the dynamic invariant relatedness inherent in it — that is to say, in terms of the principle of relativity. It was the radical break with Newtonian mechanics and the Newtonian world-view that made relativity so difficult to grasp, but it was in coherence with this new understanding of the universe and its intrinsic order that Einstein also sought to develop quantum theory, without a duality of particle and field, which, as he believed, calls for the determination of relativistic field-structures in a proper scientific description of empirical reality rather than a statistical account of quantum-experimental events and conditions. All this implied the unification of matter and field in a dynamic unbroken continuum (i.e. without the contiguous particle-connections of the Cartesian 'field'), which prompted Einstein to devote so much attention to developing a unified field theory and thereby determining the general laws of the whole indivisible field. Although Einstein himself was not able to achieve this specific aim, nevertheless he succeeded, particularly through general relativity, as the staggering unfolding of its implications and the verification of its predictions have since shown, in opening the way toward a unified view of the universe with a very different conception of order.

V

Cosmolgical implications of relativity
The revolution in cosmology which all this entails represents a complete inversion of the Newtonian picture. For Newton the empirical world of phenomena characterised by relative apparent time and space was overarched by an unchanging infinite framework of absolute mathematical time and space which, while detached from empiri-

cal reality in that it remains completely unaffected by it at any point, causally conditions it throughout so that it is imprisoned within a rigid geometrical structure of a Euclidean sort. Here we have in effect a vast cosmological synthesis of the immutable God and the created universe. Such a universe is both infinite in its coordination with God and closed in upon its immanent necessities, which finally leaves no room for contingence or freedom. For Einstein, however, all that is, as it were, turned upside down. The controlling concept of the space-time metrical field, defined by reference to the finite speed of light, implies the integration of finite space and time with physical reality, with the result that the universe may be described as 'finite and unbounded'. That is, so to say, instead of being closed from above down, the universe is to be regarded as open from below upward. The finite universe certainly has frontiers, but they are not frontiers at which it is turned back to be imprisoned in itself so much as frontiers where it is open indefinitely to what is beyond. Hence the finite universe cannot be what it actually is even as finite without being relativised by what transcends it. This may be expressed otherwise, in a more Einsteinian way. Instead of empirical reality being construed in terms of absolutely certain mathematical propositions clamped down upon it, which would inevitably introduce both rigidity and infinity into physics, mathematics is to be understood from its ground in objective, empirical stuctures of space-time, without distorting idealisation which would make it irrelevant to experience. Thus it is through open mathematical structures appropriate to its nature that the universe really discloses to us the secrets of its latent order, which is of an open, contingent kind, with variables and spontaneities which we are unable to constrain and confine within our abstractive, logicist and mechanist patterns of thought. Such an integration of the empirical and the mathematical in our interpretation of the universe allows its immanent rationalities to articulate and resonate in such a way that they point naturally and freely beyond their finite conditions and limits without being obstructed through artificial foreclosure. In this event natural laws, in terms of which science seeks to describe the orderly behaviour of reality, may be formulated under conditions of the contingence of the universe, and thus without being cut off from the contingent basis upon which natural science rests, which would be the case if they were converted into necessary timeless truths of reason. As such, of course, natural laws are essentially and always open to revision in the light of what the universe may yet reveal of itself to our inquiries, for if they are true they are implicated in a dimension of rationality ranging indefinitely beyond them, and therefore must refer to much more than can be expressed in explicit terms at any time.

It must now be pointed out that these two different world-views, the Newtonian and the Einsteinian, and the different kinds of order they entail, are not to be thought of as merely contradictory to one another. There are certainly contradictions between a closed mechanist and determinist conception of the universe and an open-structured and non-determinist conception of it, but the reconstruction of the Newtonian outlook which we have to carry out on the basis of the Einsteinian outlook deduces the Newtonian as a limiting case of the Einsteinian on a lower level of scientific interaction with nature, much as classical physics is to be regarded as a limiting case of relativistic physics. That is to say, the Newtonian model of the universe cannot after all be regarded as a complete, self-contained and self-explaining, system, for if it is consistent as a scientific model it can be justified only by being completed beyond itself through coordination to a model characterised by a profounder and more comprehensive system of rational order. Thus the Newtonian model requires relation to the Einsteinian model if it is to retain any validity on its own limited basis.

A primary ingredient in this new Einsteinian model, which helps to give it a radically different character, is *time*, not time as an external geometric parameter as in the Newtonian model, but time as inherent in the empirical processes of physical reality which demands that even inanimate matter must be considered as a dynamic and temporal state of affairs. However, with the introduction of time as an integral factor into our understanding and interpretation of the universe we are no longer able, like the later Newtonians, to exclude from the spectrum of scientific inquiry all questions as to whence and whither, thereby restricting natural science artificially to questions as to what and how. That is to say, questions about ultimate origins and ultimate ends must be entertained by scientific inquiry and, what is more, the question why there is a universe at all rather than nothing — if only because such questions help to open up to view the distinctive nature of the universe. They have the effect, of course, of considerably reinforcing the recovery of genuine contingence in our grasp of the rational order in nature. Here, then, we have an approach to the universe as a finite yet continuous and unified whole which is to be interpreted in terms of unbroken rational continuities rather than patterns of static causality — i.e., in terms of reasons rather than causes. All this is not to say that natural science through the properly autonomous modes of inquiry which it develops can itself answer questions about origins and ends, which in rigorous fidelity to the nature of its empirical and contingent subject-matter it must raise, but only that it should pursue its natural investigations in such a way as to recognise these further questions as rationally continuous and consistent with the questions which it normally raises. Of course, if natural science thought it could come up with answers to those questions, in actuality it would only shut the door they open for us.

In accordance with its own nature this new understanding of the universe, opened out for us through the Einsteinian model, demands to be considered as a limiting case of a still profounder and more comprehensive realm of rational order. This is not to imply that the relation between this and the Einsteinian system is precisely similar to that between the Einsteinian and the Newtonian, for the different conceptions of order involved would introduce real dissimilarities in the cross-level connections, but only that this Einsteinian type of order, particularly as it embraces contingence in such a profound way, requires relation to an order of rationality transcending it, if it is to retain rational integrity on its own natural level.

VI

Order/contingency as limiting case of divine order
The kind of relation envisaged here may perhaps be indicated by borrowing language from David Bohm as to the intersection of 'explicate' and 'implicate' orders,[1] for the kind of open contingent order disclosed in this new understanding of the universe is evidently implicated invisibly in a higher level order beyond space and time as its ground which cannot be articulated reductively in terms of the manifest explicate patterns of the lower level order of space and time. Of course, the kind of ultimate intelligible ground with which theology is concerned is infinitely beyond any invisible implicate order with which we may be concerned in physics.

We have now returned to the two-fold orientation of contingent order, which we described theologically as contingence away from God and contingence toward God: contingence away from God toward an independent state of affairs in the created universe, and contingence toward God as the creative ground and reason for the unitary rational order and relative autonomy of the universe. The deeply based intersection between these two approaches, and the two worldviews to which they give rise, does not involve anything like a cosmological synthesis of the Creator and the contingent order. Nor does it involve the development of a specific theological cosmology of the kind which could be held in a one to one correspondence with the coordinates of a natural scientific cosmology, or even in a partial differential relation to it. Full justice must be done to contingence on both sides of the intersecting relation: the free contingent activity of God in creating the universe out of nothing and ceaselessly sustaining it in being, and the free continget existence of the universe with a rational order of its own by divinely given creaturely right. How are we, then, to spell out what is involved or at least required of us in the two-fronted orientation of contingent order?

(1)   The fact that the universe, as we understand it in theology, is coordinated to the unlimited rationality and freedom of the Creator, implies that it has a freedom and flexibility in its order which makes it capable of a variety of consistent interpretations and cognate cosmological formalisations. Theology can make no specific contribution to the development of any such cosmology: that belongs to the purview and freedom of natural science. Because the universe is God's creation, theological science cannot but be deeply interested in the uncovering through natural scientific inquiry of the rational patterns which God has conferred upon it, if only in Christian concern for praise and worship of the Creator.

(2)   The fact that both theological science and natural science have a stake in the contingence of the universe and its order, implies that the intersection between their different world-views has to do with basic forms of rationality in the space-time universe in which each shares in its own distinctive way. This gives theology no ground for standing aloof from the cosmological discoveries made by natural science, but rather ground for seeking a fuller understanding of their rational basis in the space-time universe within which also theology must develop adequate accounts of its own convictions about incarnation and resurrection, for example, as well as creation, with proper respect for their empirical correlates in the spatio-temporal structures of empirical reality. Yet theology can do this only as at the same time it clarifies for science as well as for itself the transcendent relation of the Creator to what he has made and continues to uphold through his sustaining power and rationality.

(3)   Since the new scientific view of the universe is not hostile to the Christian faith, theology has no need to be on the defensive as it felt it had to be when confronted with the dualist and determinist conception of the universe as a closed continuum of cause and effect, which axiomatically ruled out of consideration any real notion of God's providential interaction with the world or therefore of prayer, let alone notions of incarnation and redemption. Rather is it now

possible for theology to engage in constructive dialogue with natural science, not only for its own good but for the good of science also. Dialogue can help theology purify its apparatus of concept and term from time-conditioned and pseudo-theological as well as pseudo-scientific lumber, freeing it to unfold knowledge of the living God on the proper ground of his self-revelation to mankind. Dialogue can also help natural science, in view of its recurring temptation to resolve contingence away, to remain faithful to the nature of created or contingent reality, upon the recognition of which its empirico-theoretical activity is based, and therefore to remain open to the realisation that the universe is what it is as a whole because of its implication in a transcendent rational order, in God.

REFERENCE

1.   For David Bohm's notion of implicate order, see *Foundations of Physics* 1, No. 4 (1971) 359–381; 3, No. 2 (1973) 139–168.

Chapter 5

DID GOD CREATE THIS UNIVERSE?

John Bowker
Department of Religious Studies, University of Lancaster, U.K.

I

The Intersection of Theology and Science
During the course of our discussions, Professor Sykes made the point
very strongly that as a theologian it was impossible for him to engage
with Science; he could only engage with scientists and with many
competing interpretations of the scientific enterprise, since that is
what is presented to him, rather than a unified 'Science'. The same
point could be — and was — made about Theology, that it is not a
single activity, and that there are several different 'theologies'.
Indeed, some of the more popular writing at the present time in this
area explores the connection between science and Eastern metaphysics which involve characterisations of theistic reality very different
from those in Christianity.[1]

So theologians and scientists undoubtedly have their own work to
do, and their own subject-matter to attend to. But at the same time,
the conclusion was equally strongly resisted in the discussion that they
are engaged in autonomous language games which arise from and have
reference to their own distinct subject-matters. The reason for that is
obvious, that at various points they are both commenting on the *same*
subject-matter, or on overlapping subject-matter, the human subject
and the cosmos in which that subject is set. Such concepts as creation,
providence, incarnation, *maya* and *lila*, involve propositions about
the same cosmos which scientists also investigate. They are not necessarily the sort of propositions which would come within the scope of
scientific inquiry, but on the other hand they carry with them an
implication that there are points or modes of interaction between God
and this universe. If these claims are to have any consequence where
we are concerned, it follows that there are necessary points of intersection between theology and science where the relation of God to
humanity or to the cosmos is involved.

The issue then becomes what sorts of interaction are believed to occur, and what kinds of argument are then used to comment on the intersection of theology and science. The purpose of this paper is to exemplify some of the arguments which occur in one of the areas in question, and to ask which, if any, of them seems to be fruitful, and what sort of conclusions we can draw. The example I have chosen is 'creation', because that potentially is a concept or doctrine which connects somewhere with the cosmos about whose nature and origin scientists also speculate and draw conclusions. It must, of course, be stressed that the doctrine of creation does very much more for theology than offer proposals about origins, just as, on the scientific side, proposals about the origin of the universe are highly speculative and at present inconclusive. Nevertheless, the concept of creation in Western theology does seem to imply some sort of connection between God and this particular universe which presents itself evidentially to us.

II

Order and design

The word 'teleology' has fallen into such disrepute that the mere mention of it has the same effect as the whispered words 'Black Douglas' used to have, according to Scott, on mischievous English children — the evocation of a panic-stricken terror. And yet one of the curiosities of recent writing, both in philosophy and natural science, is the rehabilitation, not indeed of teleology, but of teleonomy. Teleonomy is not a word which theolgians have dreamed up as a last-ditch way of rescuing providence. It is a word which has been evoked by the sheer pressure of data — by the sort of universe this appears to be, and by the evolutionary process being the sort of process that it is. And yet the use of this word is often fraught with the kind of coy ambiguity which we associate with the character of Estella, whose meaning never quite coincided with her manner. The ambiguity arises because even the restricted word 'teleonomy' seems to flirt dangerously with the possibility of programmes and of design, and that possibility has been equated with a finalism which belongs to the teleology which has been rejected.

This is a very pervasive confusion (and one which will be exemplified in more detail further on), but at the same time it is a very understandable confusion. It reflects a determination to exclude even the least trace of vitalism and/or of a masterplan of the final state of the universe imposed upon it by an original design and designer. All this is tied to a belief which many people still hold that, after Hume, all arguments to the existence of a designer from design in the universe have been nailed down so conclusively in a secure coffin that no risen body of new argument could ever hope to break the seal and walk again. And yet the seal *has* been broken, and the argument is undoubtedly alive and (some would add) well.

As an example, we may take the way in which Swinburne has reformulated the argument. Swinburne certainly accepts that some of the detailed points in Hume's case against Cleanthes are conclusive. But the form of teleological argument attributed to Cleanthes is not the only form that the argument can take. In particular, Swinburne insists, it is necessary to distinguish between the two kinds of regularity or order in the world,

> "the regularities of copresence or spatial order, and regularities of succession, or temporal order. Regularities of copresence are patterns of spatial order at some one instant of time. An example would be a town with all its roads at right angles to each other, or a section of books in a library arranged in alphabetical order of authors. Regularities of succession are simple patterns of behaviour of objects, such as their behaviour in accordance with the laws of nature — for example, Newton's law of gravitiation, which holds universally to a very high degree of approximation, that all bodies attract each other with forces proportional to the product of their masses and inversely proportional to the square of their distance apart."[2]

Obviously, the argument discussed in Hume is almost entirely an argument about regularities of copresence, not of succession; and Swinburne makes the point that *that* form of the argument is in principle *always* liable to erosion:

> "There is always the risk that scientists might show that most states of apparent disorder were states of latent order, that is, that if the world lasted long enough considerable order must emerge from whichever of many initial states it began."[3]

Swinburne therefore concluded:

> "The 18th century proponents of the argument from design did not suspect this danger and hence the devastating effect of Darwin's Theory of Evolution by Natural Selection on those who accepted their argument. For Darwin showed that the regularities of copresence of the

100

animal and plant kingdoms had evolved by natural processes from an apparently disordered state and would have evolved equally from many other apparently disordered states. Whether all regularities of copresence can be fully explained in this kind of way no one yet knows, but the danger remains for the proponent of an argument from design of this kind that they can be."[4]

"Of this kind": but this is not the only kind of argument from — or perhaps better, as MacPherson points out, to — design.

"It has frequently been suggested that the Argument should be called not the Argument *from* Design but the Argument *to* Design. The reasoning behind this . . . has to do with whether the argument assumes its own conclusion. In the sense of 'design' where we may be inclined to say that design implies a designer, to acknowledge the presence of design in the universe is virtually to have arrived at the conclusion that there is a divine designer. So what really needs to be established, it is claimed, is not that if the universe exhibits design it must have a designer, but that it does exhibit design in the first place. What is needed is an argument *from* order *to* design; that is, the universe is of the kind called design: if that is established the question of God can largely take care of itself."[5]

So Swinburne suggests:

"For these reasons, the proponent of the argument from design does much better to rely for his premiss more on regularities of succession. St. Thomas Aquinas, wiser than the men of the 18th century, did just this. He puts forward an argument from design as his 5th and last way to prove the existence of God, and gives his premiss as follows: 'The 5th way is based on the guidedness of nature. An orderedness of actions to an end is observed in all bodies obeying natural laws, even when they lack awareness. For their behaviour hardly ever varies, and will practically always turn out well; which shows that they truly tend to a goal, and do not merely hit it by accident.' "[6]

So Swinburne reformulates what he calls

"the most satisfactory premiss for the argument from design" as "the operation of regularities of succession other than those produced by men, that is, the operation of natural laws. Almost all things almost always obey simple natural laws and so behave in a strikingly regular way."[7]

So the question then becomes:

"Given the premiss, what is our justification for proceeding to the conclusion that a very powerful free non-embodied rational agent is responsible for their behaving in that way?"[8]

Swinburne's answer to that is formed in two parts, first, "by showing that there can be no other possible explanation for the operation of natural laws than the activity of a god"; and second, by seeing "to what extent the hypothesis is well confirmed on the basis of the evidence."[9] This sounds an ambitious programme, and part of it (the assessment of evidence for the strength of the analogy) is left to others to complete.[10] But the first part, the activity of personal agency, *is* open to analysis, and it depends on the distinction between scientific explanation and personal explanation — a distinction which is elaboraged in *The Coherence of Theism*.[11]

There, Swinburne resists the attempts of Davidson[12] and Goldman[13] to reduce personal explanation (whereby E is explained as the result of an action A done by an agent P (not by an event) in order to realise an intention) to scientific explanation (whereby an event E is explained by past events or states C and natural laws L). Davidson and Goldman had argued in effect that the brain states in P creating the intention are the initial conditions, C, which bring about the future event under the operation of natural law. Thus 'intentions' become like 'desires' or 'wants', which an agent has and which operate effects through him.

But in fact 'intentions' are *not* like 'desires' or 'wants' in that respect. As Swinburne puts it (relying here on R. Taylor, *Action and Purpose*, pp. 248f.):

"If P brings about E as a result of his intention J to bring about E, is this intention something which he may just find himself having or something which in some way he must choose to have? If the latter, then we are still left with personal bringing-about. If the former, it is possible that the intention might cause E without the agent having in any way intentionally (in the ordinary sense of this term) brought E about."[14]

That is the paradox which, Swinburne claims, prevents the reduction of personal explanation to scientific explanation being brought about. And to make the point clearer, Swinburne illustrates it:

"Let E be the agent's arm going up. Now if an intention is something which an agent may find himself having, then an intention is like a desire, and P may find himself having an intention to raise his arm (say in order to attract attention), but be too reluctant, hesistant, or shy to act on his intention. Nevertheless, the intention could suddenly cause E, to the agent's surprise without his intentionally having raised his arm. So bringing about an effect intentionally is not just a matter of an intention bringing about the effect (where an intention is a state which a man might find himself having), I conclude therefore that personal explanation is *sui generis*, and is not reducible to scientific explantion."

It hardly needs to be pointed out that Swinburne is not claiming that intentional action is unlawful, or that it is not enabled by naturally scientific conditions. In other words, he is not dissenting from Geothe's more elegant summary:

"Nach ewigen, ehrnen,
Grossen Gesetzen
Müssen wir alle
Unseres Daseyns
Kreise vollenden"

Swinburne is simply arguing that the circle is not a closed circle, and that within it personal action is consequential, but in a way that does not suspend the natural order:

"Now in order that a human agent's intentions may have the intended effects, often various states of affairs must hold and various laws must operate in the world . . . So, then, although scientific explanation often explains the occurrence and operation of the factors involved in personal explanation — it may explain our having the capacities we do or our having the intentions we do — nevertheless, personal explanation explains, whether or not it involves or is backed by scientific explanation. Clearly the theist, in claiming that there is an omnipresent spirit, God, who makes or brings about (or permits the bringing about of) all logically contingent things apart from himself, is using personal explanation."[15]

This distinction has a clear neurophysiological counterpart in the familiar arguments of Sperry, based on the observation of his patients in whom the cerebral commissure had been cut — remembering that we are exemplifying arguments, not claiming that a final word of truth has been spoken. Sperry's argument is that even if behavioural science were to establish that none of us had any real choice to be anywhere else, or that our presence was "already 'in the cards', so to speak, five, ten or fifteen years ago", it does not follow that "in the practice of behavioural sciences we must regard the brain as just the pawn of the physical and chemical forces that play in and around it."[16]

Sperry's point is that the configurational properties of complexity master the more elementary components that make them possible. Thus the inner atoms and electrons of a molecule are 'hauled and forced about' in chemical interactions by the over-all configurational properties of the molecule. And if that molecule is itself part of a single-celled organism, such as *Paramecium*, it too is obliged to follow what Sperry calls "a trail of events in time and space" which is largely determined by the over-all dynamics of *Paramecium caudatum*. Therefore Sperry concludes:

"When it comes to brains, remember that the simpler electric, atomic, molecular, and cellular forces and laws, though still present and operating, have been superseded by the configurational forces of higher-level mechanisms. At the top, in the human brain, these include the powers of perception, cognition, reason, judgement, and the like, the operational, causal effects and forces of which are equally or more potent in brain dynamics than are the outclassed inner chemical forces."[17]

The distinction here is that although neurophysiological research like that, to take an example, of Kornhuber (measuring the electrical potential generated in the cerebral cortex prior to the initiating of voluntary action)[18] will always be able in principle to discern the electrical or chemical activity of any brain behaviour (since otherwise the subject would presumably be dead), that *in itself* cannot comment on what Sperry called 'the configurational properties' of the behaviour in question. It certainly cannot rule out the observation that there are operational, causal effects and forces which are derived from personal agency, which may form the basis for an analogy to theistic agency in the production of a universe of this sort. However, if that seems to arrive at God a little too fast, the conclusion at the moment is that

"although the apparent freedom and rationality of the human will *may* prove an illusion", and although man "may have no more option what to do than a machine and be guided by an argument no more than is a piece of iron, . . . this has never been shown and, in the absence of good philosophical and scientific argument to show it, I assume, what is apparent, that when a man acts by free and rational choice, his agency is the operation of a different kind of causality from that of scientific laws"[19] — although it depends upon them for the effecting of its intentions.

So the critical point in Swinburne's argument is this:

"The free choice of a rational agent is the only way of accounting for natural phenomena *other than* [my italics] the way of normal scientific explanation, which is recognised as such by all men and has not been reduced to normal scientific explanation."[20]

Might that reduction take place, even though it has not yet been successfully achieved — supposing, for example, that we knew more, or even everything, about the brain states preceding and accompanying intentionality? The answer must be no, because the operations of those states of brain behaviour produce precisely that conflict of data, in respect of action, which requires a language to talk about it. Thus Swinburne concludes:

"Almost all regularities of succession are due to the normal operation of scientific laws. But to say this is simply to say that these regularities are instances of more general regularities. The operation of the most fundamental regularities clearly cannot be given a normal scientific explanation. If their operation is to receive an explanation and not merely to be left as a brute fact, that explanation must therefore be in terms of the rational choice of a free agent. What then are grounds for adopting this hypothesis, given that it is the only possible one?"[21]

The grounds are "that we can explain some few regularities of succession as produced by rational agents and that the other regularities cannot be explained except in this way." Swinburne then exemplifies these, and concludes: "Hence knowing that some regularities of succession have such a cause [of a rational agent acting freely], we postulate that they all have. An agent produces the celestial harmony like a man who sings a song."[22]

But obviously the agent of the laws which govern the appearance of a universe such as this is critically different from an agent who operates within it. Thus

"our argument proves to be an argument by analogy and to exemplify a pattern common in scientific inference . . . The proponent of the argument from design stresses the similarities between the regularities of succession produced by man and those which are laws of nature and so

105

between men and the agent which he postulates as responsible for the laws of nature. The opponent of the argument stresses the dissimilarities. The degree of support which the conclusion obtains from the evidence depends on how great the similarities are."[23]

Swinburne then reinforces his argument by observing:

"If the conclusion is true, if a very powerful non-embodied rational agent is responsible for the operation of the laws of nature, then normal scientific explanation would prove to be personal explanation. That is, explanation of some phenonmenon in terms of the operation of a natural law would ultimately be an explanation in terms of the operation of an agent. Hence (given an initial arrangement of matter) the principles of explanation of phenomena would have been reduced from two to one . . . So then in so far as regularities of succession produced by the operation of natural laws are similar to those produced by human agents, to postulate that a rational agent is responsible for them would indeed provide a simple unifying and coherent explanation of natural phenomena."[24]

With such an attractive economy as the invitation, "what is there", as Swinburne asks himself, "against taking this step?" Only that having achieved economy in one direction we have thereby become prodigal in another. As Swinburne answers his own question:

"Simply that celebrated principle of explanation — *entia non sunt multiplicanda praeter necessitatem* — do not add a god to your ontology unless you have to."[25]

But perhaps we *do* have to. Perhaps the inference of personal agency is necessary. Swinburne therefore concludes:

"The issue turns on whether the evidence constitutes enough of a *necessitas* to compel us to multiply entities. Whether it does depends on how strong is the analogy between the regularities of succession produced by human agents and those produced by the operation of natural laws. I do not propose to assess the strength of the analogy but only to claim that everything turns on it. I claim that the inference from natural laws to a god responsible for them is of a perfectly proper type for inference about matters of fact, and that the only issue is whether the evidence is stong enough to allow us to affirm that it is probable that the conclusion is true."[26]

Here, then, is an example of an argument which keeps alive the possiblity that this universe is derived from God as the unproduced producer of all that is. Its strength depends, as Swinburne emphasises, on the extent to which the actual evidence reinforces or demands the analogy — and in that respect, his position is similar to the point made by MacPherson (p. 101). Swinburne is concerned with the fact of natural law and order as a general condition of the universe, but clearly natural law can only be discerned and established by us in our observation of its operations and appearance. It is not that the argument would require us to find instances of personal intervention on the part of God, creating one event rather than another, but rather that the regularities of order as a whole are of a kind similar to those which we attribute to personal agency in our own experience. Thus in relation to any particular example, one would expect to find (if the argument is well-founded) *not* opaque problems which can be solved only by the invocation of a personal agent, but an eventual solution to such problems in conformity with the regularities which have evoked the analogy to personal agency in the first place. We can therefore say, paradoxical though it seems at first sight, that the more successful the regularities of succession are in eliminating the direct intervention of God in the transactions which constitute the universe, the stronger the analogy will become which suggests that he is the resource of it. But *is* this what we find in the progress of scientific argument about origins? To answer that we must begin by returning to the shift from teleology to teleonomy.

III

From Teleology to Teleonomy
Teleology has in general been abandoned as a word principally because of its Aristotelian associations, and above all because it implied a final end or state in the mind of a designer from the outset, toward which the process of the universe is constrained. However, some features of the evolutionary process seem to exhibit goal-directedness or channelling, somewhat of the kind found in programmed behaviour, and as a result some other word has been required, or one might say evoked, by the data — and that word is 'teleonomy'.

But what has then happened is that the ghost of teleology has been allowed to haunt and dominate the use of the word teleonomy: almost *any* hint of delimitation, programme or design (which are concepts which arise very naturally from teleonomic considerations) has been equated with teleological finalism, as though that is the only meaning of programme or design. The resulting confusion has been considerable and anti-theological, to say the least. To give just one example: although the shift from teleology to teleonomy is usually attributed to Pittendrigh,[27] Ernst Mayr wrote an influential summary of the point, in a paper in 1961 called 'Cause and Effect in Biology'[28]:

"It would seem useful to restrict the term teleonomic rigidly to systems operating on the basis of a programme, a code of information. Teleonomy in biology designates 'the apparent purposefulness of organisms and their characteristics', as Julian Huxley expressed it.

Such a clear-cut separation of teleonomy, which has an analysable physico-chemical basis, from teleology, which deals more broadly with the overall harmony of the organic world is most useful because these two entirely different phenomena have so often been confused with each other.

The development or behaviour of an individual is purposive, natural selection is definitely not. When MacLeod stated 'What is most challenging about Darwin, however, is his reintroduction of purpose into the natural world', he chose the wrong word. The word purpose is singularly inapplicable to evolutionary change, which is, after all, what Darwin was considering. If an organism is well adapted, if it shows superior fitness, this is not due to any purpose of its ancestors or of an outside agency, such as 'Nature' or 'God', who created a superior design or plan. Darwin 'has swept out such finalistic teleology by the front door', as Simpson has rightly said."

Mayr has here, in effect, equated 'design' and 'plan' with 'finalistic teleology'. Not surprisingly, therefore, when Mayr introduced the issue of *Scientific American* devoted to evolution, the basic ambiguity becomes very obvious: on the one hand, everything is a product of chance and necessity, but on the other, it is nevertheless possessed of order and direction; but such order cannot in principle be programmed because that would imply finalism:

"Man's world view today is dominated by the knowledge that the universe, the stars, the earth and all living things have evolved through a long history that was not foreordained or programmed, a history of continual, gradual change shaped by more or less directional natural processes consistent with the laws of physics. Cosmic evolution and biological evolution have that much in common . . . 'Evolution' implies change with continuity, usually with a directional component."[29]

The analogy from order to personal agency on the basis of this description would be as natural as Swinburne suggests, except for the fact that 'personal agency' and 'programme' have been equated by Mayr with a final end or state in mind of the agent or programmer; and on that basis the equivalent of personal agency in Swinburne's sense has been — not surprisingly — ruled out. But a programme does not necessarily have a final state or condition in view: it may simply create the boundary conditions which delimit — and therefore make available — particular operations, thereby economising on their possible diversity. Some programmes *are* finalistic: a programme for a concert delimits all the possible musics which might be played and has a clear final state in view; but a programme for a cricket match does not: it delimits the actions which are possible if a cricket match and not a football match is to be the outcome, but it does not have a final state or result in mind, although it allows a general predictability. Similarly, a programme for a universe, while it would certainly, by definition, delimit total randomness, would not need to have a final state in view as a consequence of the boundaries implicit in the programme. Such a programme could certainly contain chance and randomness, but within limits.

Whether this particular universe in which we participate *is* that sort of universe may certainly be questioned; what cannot be questioned is that goal-seeking behaviour in biological process requires *some* language to speak of it. We may, with Waddington, prefer to talk of chreods and trajectories, but we still end up with exactly the same content, but in novel language: a chreod is "a canalized trajectory which acts as an attractor for nearby trajectories"; or in other words, it is "the most general description of the kind of biological process which has been referred to as 'goal-directed'."[30] Waddington then commented — making exactly the right distinction between ordered regularities of succession and finalism:

> "The nature of such processes has always been recognized as one of the major problems of theoretical biology. The words to be used for describing them and discussing them are still matters for debate. The earlier expressions 'teleological' and 'finalistic' are usually thought to carry an implication that the end state of the chreod has been fixed by some external agency and that the end state is in some way operative in steering the trajectory towards itself. To avoid such implications I have spoken of such phenomena as 'quasi-finalistic', and the word 'teleonomic' (introduced I believe by Pittendrigh in *Behaviour and Evolution*, 1958) has been used as a substitute for teleological. On the whole,

however, I believe it is preferable to use words (such as chreod) which do not lay such stress on the final state but draw attention to the whole time-trajectory."[31]

But then the pressure toward personal agency, or toward what Polanyi called "an orderly innovating principle"[32] becomes very strong indeed. Polanyi's point is that one can only raise questions of chance and probability against a background of already discerned order — as he exemplified by his famous white pebbles on Abergele station: when we see an inscription laid out in white pebbles on the station lawn, saying, 'Welcome to Wales by British Railways',

"no one will fail to recognize this as an orderly pattern, deliberately contrived by a thoughtful station-master. And we could refute anyone who doubted this by computing as follows the odds against the arrangements of the pebbles having come about by mere chance. Suppose that the pebbles had originally all belonged to the garden and would, if left to chance, be found in any part of this area with equal probability; we could compare the large number of arrangements open to the pebbles, if distributed at random all over the garden, with the incomparably smaller number of arrangements in which they would spell out the inscription 'Welcome to Wales by British Railways'. The ratio of the latter small number over the former very large number would represent the fantastically small chance of the pebbles having arranged themselves in the form of the inscription merely by accident; and this would crushingly refute any supposition of this having been the case."[33]

However, Polanyi then makes the point that if we return to the station some years later and find "the previously eloquent pebbles" scattered in a random confusion, "might we not get into serious difficulty if we were now asked once more: what is the chance of the pebbles having arranged themselves in this particular manner by mere accident?" For clearly the same computation will yield exactly the same "fantastically small value for the probability of this particular arrangement. Yet obviously we are *not* prepared to say that this arrangement has not come about by chance."[34] Therefore Polanyi argues that discussions of chance and probability are relative to the discernment of order:

"Now why this sudden change in our methods of inference? Actually, there is no change: we have merely stumbled on a tacit assumption of our argument which we ought to make explicit now. We have assumed from the start that the arrangement of the pebbles which formed an intelligible set of words appropriate to the occasion represented a distinctive pattern. It was only in view of this orderliness that the question could be asked at all whether the orderliness was accidental or not. When the pebbles are scattered irregularly over the whole available area, they possess no pattern and therefore the question whether the orderly pattern is accidental or not cannot arise."[35]

So if we stay with the pebbles, but now of a slightly smaller size, we can say that the aggregate of gravel, before it is excavated, lies in the earth in a form determined by random processes, but that its incorporation into the concrete form of a motorway fly-over is not so decisively determined by random processes, although still dependent on them. In this case, personal agency imposes shape and order, within boundary limits of possibility, on the outcome.

To what extent can that be applied analogously to the shape and order apparent in the universe or in the evolutionary process? The answer is, not at all, if it implies a direct analogy to God as the one who, out of the randomness of the universe, constructs some of its actual occurrences — its, so to speak, motorway bridges. If *that* were the argument, then the more chance and randomness there is in the universe, the more opportunity there would be to claim that a personal agent is required to produce its lawful outcomes. To put it another way, the more improbable the universe and its evolution are, the more one requires the equivalent of an observer to collapse its indeterminacy into its singularity — its particular outcome. Such arguments have occurred theologically — and indeed in a way Islamic occasionalism is an early version of them.

But the argument we are examining is almost the exact reverse of this. It is predicting that if God is the unproduced producer of all that is, the fundamental indeterminacy of the universe will not obscure the regularity of the evolutionary process, and that we can consequently expect to find probability rather than zero-probability in such occurrences as the origin of life. But is this in fact what we find? To answer this, we need to look at the progress of the arguments that have actually been used.

IV

The Origin of Life and the Anthropic Pinciple
The term 'zero-probability' was used deliberately in the preceding

paragraph to supply an obvious point of departure, Monod's *Chance and Necessity*. For Monod, the origin of a self-replicating organism posed "not so much a 'problem' as a veritable enigma". [36] The problem lies in the fact that the genetic code has to come into being in the first instance when it can serve no use or purpose unless or until it is translated. As Monod put it:

> "The code is meaningless unless translated. The modern cell's translating machinery consists of at least 50 macromolecular components *which are themselves coded in DNA: the code cannot be translated except by products of translation.* It is the modern expression of *omne vivum ex ovo*. When and how did this circle become closed? It is exceedingly difficult to imagine."[37]

But since, according to Monod, everything is occasioned by chance and necessity, it can only be by wholly improbable chance that the right macromolecules combined in a way that was ultimately to prove fruitful but had no virtue or logic in itself. "Our number', as he put it, "came up in the Monte Carlo game."[38] And in less colloquial form:

> "The enigma remains, masking the answer to a question of profound interest. Life appeared on earth: what, *before the event*, were the chances that this would occur? The present structure of the biosphere certainly does not exclude the possibility that the decisive event occurred *only once*. Which would mean that its *a priori* probability was virtually zero."[39]

How have the arguments developed since then? A quick way of pursuing this is to take, as an example, Calow's *Biological Machines: A Cybernetic Approach to Life*,[40] not least because he concludes explicitly:

> "I am a reductionist because I hate gaps and because I can see nothing in biology which looks as though it will not yield to the laws of physics. I am a mechanist because I believe that driven properly machine analogies will help to bulldoze facts into the gaps which appear to remain between beings and things. Hence my mechanism is reductionism and there is no ghost in my biological machine."[41]

Calow certainly recognises the problem:

> "Did the biocybernetic organism that we now see originate out of a

passive open system, a primordial chicken, or instead, did it arise out of some original programme, a primordial egg?"[42]

Two somewhat different routes have been proposed toward a solution — sometimes summarised as metabolism *vs.* reproduction, or protein *vs.* nucleic acid:

> "One traces the phenotype to genotype pathway right through the first primitive organism into the 'chemical soup' and then into the world of physics. This is a somewhat speculative argument but its appeal rests on the continuity it perceives between physical, chemical and biological worlds. The other begins with a single 'chicken'; a protein with enzymatic powers, and uses this to build and then replicate a single template."[43]

The first of these is a kind of Whiteheadian programme, as Calow acknowledges, but with Whitehead's 'mentalism', or to be more precise, his 'subjective aim' implicit in all 'occasions of experience', very firmly excised. In its place Calow proposes, on the basis of the work of S. Black,[44] the quality of shape,

> "a property of objects which varies independently from their substance. For example, while the energy and mass of a potter's clay may remain constant its shape can take on an almost infinite variety of patterns."[45]

Because shape does play an important part in many communication systems, and certainly in cellular communication, it is undoubtedly a very fundamental property in matter. We know that "proteins 'transmit' information to metabolism on the basis of their ability to select between differently shaped metabolites, and the transcription, translation and replication of DNA proceeds on the basis of the physico-chemical surface laid bare when the complementary strands part." Consequently Calow concludes:

> "At the heart of these processes is a fit-fill mechanism, something like a molecular jigsaw, in which molecules are recognised and ordered on the basis of whether or not they fit into templates (complementary shapes) in the 'transmitter' molecules. This depends on the 'transmitter' molecules being able to form shapes which fit only certain other molecular species."[46]

113

Calow therefore proposes

> "a series of fit-fill-fit systems, each based on slightly different shapes, the continuation of each depending on the ability of a shape to attach, retain and shape matter from the surrounding environment. Furthermore, if one of the shapes were a little better at doing this than the others it would tend to have a slightly better chance of transmitting itself. In other words we find in these simple fit-fill-fit systems the potential for prebiotic selection based on communication efficiency. Also, since molecular shape can be altered by molecular bombardment (thermal noise) we also have the potential for molecular mutation; changes in shape which might by chance increase the communication efficiency of the system."[47]

This, then, is the first way in which organic life might have originated: "From a primordial polymer, possibly an inorganic crystal . . ., the simple fit-fill-fit mechanism evolved into an ever more efficient communication channel, ultimately transmitting information to a nucleotide template."[48]

The second possiblity is based on the work of Sumper and others, who have shown that

> "a replicase enzyme, derived from a bacterial virus, can generate RNA molecules from nucleotide precursors *in vitro* and then copy them. Hence given an environment in which there were spontaneously formed nucleotides and a spontaneously formed protein which had replicase power it would be possible to conceive of the genesis of a primitive, self-replicating system."[49]

Obviously, the problem remains of the odds against the right combination at the right time in the right place. But still: how effectively do these possibilities account for the origin of life?

In some respects, extremely well. The process of information is now well established, and Calow summarises it:

> "The message passing along the communication channels established by these self-replicating systems (from one template to another) was, and still is, basically very dull and very simple — being just 'transmit me'. Sooner of later it became associated with other subsidiary instructions which specified more effective ways of bringing about the basic command under particular conditions. This occurred through the evolution of a second major communication system fixed 'laterally' to

114

the main channel and concerned with the flow of information from genotype to phenotype. It is in this context that we tend to talk more about the code having meaning and the nucleotide sequences giving instructions. Typical of semantics there is no obvious reason why one base triplet should specify for one amino acid rather than another. It seems as if the genetic code is established by convention rather than by the laws of physics. There is no mystery as to how this works, however, for the dichotomy resides in a tangible system of allosteric molecules, like tRNAs, which are capable of plugging in at one end to the template shape formed by the nucleotides and at the other end to a specific amino acid molecule."

All this, as Calow observes, is straightforward and can be coherently envisaged on the basis of a fit-fill-fit system. But still, quite rightly, he returns to the fundamental difficulty:

"The difficulty comes in envisaging how the system of definitions was established in the first place. Consider what is needed: a self-replicating template, a collection of amino acids, and then a system of allosteric molecules which by chance was able to make some sense (giving meaning to) of the information carried in the template shape. That is, by chance the 'defining molecules' had to plug into amino acids and then into the nucleotide template, so bringing the amino acids into such a relationship that they could combine to form a polypeptide. Finally, this polypeptide had to catalyse the self-replication of the template. Added to all this is the difficulty of introducing a transcription stage and then of postulating the chance occurrence of spontaneously formed enzymes capable of catalysing these transcription-translation processes. What is more, all the necessary machinery had to originate at the same time and in the same place."

Calow concludes that although the chance still seems low, the only alternative is "the involvement of special forces", so the conclusion of Monod must be correct: "If such a system did arise by chance it could only have happened once and the universal nature of the genetic code and the mechanism of protein synthesis is strong evidence for a singular origin. This, of course, is back to the weak argument of Monod, but so far it is the only one we have."[50]

But in fact it is not, and the next stage in the history of the argument (not chronologically but logically, if the universe is regular) must be to reduce the improbability by showing that despite these initial appearances to the contrary, the emergence of life in this sort of universe is

115

highly likely rather than unlikely. That particular response takes many different forms. One line is to demonstrate that the fit-fill-fit mechanism is a natural and unsurprising consequence of the properties of the component parts. Thus Lacey and Weber have argued that the origin of the genetic code lies in the direct correlation between the properties of amino acids and their anticodonic nucleotides (for example, their hydrophobicity and hydrophilicity).[51] Another approach accepts the improbablity of life emerging on this planet in isolation and suggests that there must have been a decisive contribution from surrounding space. Examples of this response are Crick and Orgel's theory of panspermia, or Hoyle and Wickramsinghe's appeal to the contribution of comets or planetesimals:

> "The essential biochemical requirements of life exist in very large quantities within the dense interstellar clouds of gas, the so-called molecular clouds. This material became deposited within the solar system, first in comet-type bodies, and then in the collisions of such bodies, with the Earth. We might speak of the Earth as having become 'infected' with life-forming materials."[52]

A third and more comprehensive example is the head-on response of Prigogine and Eigen, who argue that far from the evolution of life being improbable, it must be regarded as inevitable if it is based on derivable physical principles, even though the route to the actual historical occurrence of life is unpredictable. Prigogine's point of departure was "to consider the problems [of living organisms being characterised by complex organisation, maintained by constant interactions with the external environment] from the point of view of the thermodynamics of irreversible phenomena."[53] His theorem (put forward in *An Introduction to the Thermodynamics of Irreversible Processes*[54]), which concerned the minimal rate of development of entropy in the course of stationary irreversible processes, specified a simultaneous maximising conversion of potential energy into working processes, with the effect that an open system (one which interacts by way of exchange with its environment) has the potential of self-conservation as a result of its working processes. Put a little more directly, if there are a number of open systems, the one which will acquire the greatest input of available energy will be the one in which the efficiency or intensity of the working processes is greatest in the conditions of the surrounding environment. The consequence of that would be that the intensity of the working processes of an open system, far from reducing the chances of survival (by demanding a greater input of energy), enhance the probability of survival.

The paradigm example of new structures and patterns being generated and maintained from initially homogeneous conditions is the
convectional instability which generates regular patterns beyond a
particular threshold from an initially uniform temperature gradient –
of which the classic illustration is the so-called Bénard instability, in
which a horizontal fluid layer is heated from below and cooled
uniformly on the upper surface: at a critical value of the temperature
gradient, an internal convection movement is developed which is
established spontaneously and which is organised in a highly regular
pattern of hexagonal cells. As Prigogine puts it, "It is only because the
external constant (temperature gradient) drives the system far from
equilibrium that the system may give rise to ordered, highly co-
operative structures."[55]

The consequence of the attainment of a dissipative structure of this
kind is a genuinely novel state of matter induced by the flow of free
energy under non-equilibrium conditions. As Prigogine observes: "In
this new state we have a new physical chemistry on a *supermolecular
level* while the laws referring to the molecular level remain unchanged
and given by the quantum mechanical or classical equations of
motion."[57] Applied to the problem of the origin of life, the consequence is of enormous importance, since the amplification of fluctua-
tions *is itself regular:* thus if a new structure arises beyond instability,
and this effect is possible within the boundary conditions of the
system in question, then it will occur, not with a near zero-
probability, but with a probability of one — provided that there is
some mechanism and input of energy to create the fluctuation in the
first place; otherwise there will be no compensation for the return to
equilibrium (the production of entropy).

Applying this and his theory of a self-instructive catalytic hypercycle as the simplest model for an ensemble of nucleic acids and proteins
organizing itself into a stable self-reproducing and further evolving
unit, Eigen concluded:

"Nucleic acids provide the inherent prerequisite of self-organization.
However, they require a catalytically active coupling factor of high
recognition power in order to build up a high structural capacity.
'Information' becomes its meaning only by functional correlation. Any
fluctuation in the presence of potential coupling factors leading to a
unique translation and its reinforcement via the formation of a catalytic
hypercycle offers an enormous selective advantage and causes a breakdown of the former steady state of uncorrelated self-reproduction. As a

117

consequence of such an instability the nucleation of this functional correlation (we may call the origin of life) turns out to be an inevitable event – if favourable conditions of free energy flow are maintained over a sufficiently long period of time. The primary event is not unique. Universality of the code will result in any case as a consequence of non-linear competition."[57]

However, although "evolution appears to be an inevitable event, given the presence of certain matter with specified autocatalytic properties and under the maintenance of the finite (free) energy flow necessary to compensate for the steady production of entropy",[58] the fact remains that this 'probability of one' cannot explain how the exact route of historical evolution came about, because of the stochastic nature of the underlying processes – nor can it predict the future deterministically, for the same reason. Thus the strong recognition of necessity in the evolution of life has not eliminated the elements of chance – indeed, it rests upon them, by being the sort of necessity that it is. But it follows also that chance and necessity have become very different indeed from their conceptualisation by Monod.

We have now moved in a short space from near zero probability to inevitability in the origin of life. Although the former might seem to offer the clearest opportunity to invoke the agency of God (as one who is necessary to bring about the near-impossible), that is simply another instance of the 'God-of-the gaps' argument. It is the latter – the very fact of regularity which compels the argument to search (successfully) for inevitability – which supplies the most powerful illustration of the coherence of the appeal to personal agency.

The same point can be illustrated in many different ways. A particularly obvious example is the so-called anthropic principle – often misunderstood as returning man to nature, whereas in fact it is the exact reverse, a returning of nature to man. The anthropic principle is derived from what appears to be the extravagant and prodigal size of the universe. But in fact for life to appear, elements such as oxygen, carbon, phosphorous and nitrogen, which are much heavier than hydrogen, require several billion years heating up in the interior of a star. But general relativity requires that a universe providing several billion years of time must be several billion light years in extent. Thus from the point of view of the possibility of life, the universe, far from being extravagantly large, could not be other than it is if life is to emerge.[59]

There is, then, a kind of boundaried coherence in the very narrow

118

pathways of possibility along which the universe moves. As Bernard Lovell put it, in his Presidential address to the British Association in 1975:

"It is an astonishing reflection that if the proton-proton interaction were only a few per cent stronger then all the hydrogen in the primeval condensate would have turned into helium in the early stages of expansion. No galaxies, no stars, no life would have emerged. It would be a universe for ever unknowable by living creatures. The existence of a remarkable and intimate relationship between man, the fundamental constants of nature and the initial moments of space and time, seems to be an inescapable condition of our presence here tonight."

It is a similar pressure of argument which led Wheeler and Patton to ask, 'Is Physics Legislated by Cosmogony?' – the title of the paper they contributed to the Oxford symposium on quantum gravity.[60] Their problem was the paradox arising from gravitational collapse in combination with the Big Bang: supposing we set a commuting machine to

"calculate onward instant by instant towards the critical moment, and let it make use of Einstein's standard 1915 geometrodynamics. Then a point comes where it cannot go on. Smoke, figuratively speaking, rises from the machine. Physics stops. Yet physics has always meant that which goes on its eternal way despite all the surface changes in appearances. Physics stops; but physics goes on: here is the paradox"[61]

Not surprisingly they search for a deeper underlying structure:

"Whatever the deeper structure is that lies beneath particles and geometry, call it 'pregeometry' for ease of reference, it must be decisive for what goes on in the extreme phases of big bang and collapse. But is it really imaginable that this deeper structure of physics should govern how the universe came into being? Is it not more reasonable to believe the converse, that the requirement that the universe should come into being governs the structure of physics?. . .Towards the finding of this 'pregeometry'. . .no guiding principle would seem more powerful than the requirement that it should provide the universe with a way to come into being. It is difficult to believe that we can uncover this pre-geometry except as we come to understand at the same time the necessity of the quantum principle, with its 'observer-participator', in the construction of the world. Not 'machinery', but a guiding principle, is what we seek."[62]

119

V

Science and Theology

These examples of arguments about the origin of the universe and of life are intended to illustrate the obvious, namely, the indispensable pre-supposition of regularities of succession which guarantee (to use a deliberately strong word) the successful solution of even the most opaque problems – in principle: it does not follow that all problems can therefore necessarily be solved by us! The extreme alternative would be Margenau's model of a world not ruled by laws but governed by an irrational demon who decides every Sunday what is going to happen during the following week. Somewhere in between the two is the constant temptation to theology to identify *particular* instances of God's activity out of the many occurrences in the Universe. The most that particular instances will do is to illustrate and reinforce the coherence of supposing that the universe, or the regularities which govern it, are a consequence of personal agency; and that the possibility of particular interactions between God and his creation is not ruled out as incoherent. They cannot do more than that, because even if we came to those conclusions as the ones most clearly demanded by the evidence (the occurrence of a universe of this sort), the universe will not suddenly beome a different place. Whether God is or is not, the universe will still present itself evidentially in exactly the same way (except insofar as the observer's participation in this universe collapses probabilities into singular outcomes, which presumably makes relevant the motivations of particular observers to engage in particular experiments).

But the general point remains, and is a consequence of a part of one of Gilbert Ryle's familiar dilemmas, the dilemma of how one can tell a false coin from a genuine coin if all coins are false. If all examples are examples of the same thing, what do they exemplify? If all coins are counterfeit, of what are they counterfeits? If the whole universe is in the condition of either having been created by God, or not having been created by God, it is not possible to discern the difference in either case in any particular universe. "Ice could not be thick if ice could not be thin."[63]

So the universe does not become a different place even if its regularities of succession seem to suggest the analogy to personal agency, or if, in the economy and narrow balance of its pathways, it exhibits the characteristics of programmed design, if . . . then so-and-so. It is because the universe *is as it is* that it seems to demand this account of itself. Consequently, what can be looked for in the relation between science and theology, as people in each activity attend to and reflect on the data which present themselves to consciousness, is independence insofar as the data are entirely different, and the exploration of consonance and dissonance where the data intersect. It is certainly possible for an extension of scientific understanding to contradict particular propositons which occur in religious discourse (say, that the cosmos took literally six days to come from chaos to its present appearance); but religions and theologies are not extinguished by such corrections: the corrections are accepted insofar as they are relevant, often immediately, sometimes belatedly, and they act as constraint over subsequent utterance. But they cannot defeat the whole theological and religious exercise, because that is dependent on a far wider range of experience and data. And at the same time, on the positive side, the extension of scientific understanding may highlight and reinforce the coherence of some theological propositions, where, as in the case of the origin of the cosmos and its continuity, the theological and scientific concerns overlap or intersect.

But does this approach leave us with, at most, a kind of remote and ineffectual deism? The answer is no, because what reinforces the correctness of the analogy to personal agency and the inference of God is that we seem to be able to relate to the resource of the programme and thus of the universe by a direct , but not unmediated, communication. Even in the brief hints in this paper the fundamental importance of communication as a mode of energy transaction in the constitution of this universe has surely been inescapable. Maybe then it is not surprising that we who are constituted in our nature as personal agents seem to be able to enter into a network of correspondent communication with the one who is believed to be the agent of the universe. That mode of communication or of transacted energy is known as worship and prayer.

It is in this way that we become established, to use Péguy's phrase, as outposts of God's activity on the frontiers of life; and it is in this way also that God *is* of effect in the universe, as a resource, constraining us at least, into outcomes which would not otherwise obtain. We at least are collapsed by God into singularities of love – or should be, if we are attending faithfully to him and to our neighbour.

The continuity between science and theology is that what we observe in all cases in this universe, including ourselves, is the transaction and transformation of energy. Much of our analysis, therefore, focusses on the question of constraint:[64] what is it that constrains an event (short-lived or long-lived, from a molecule or less to a mountain or more) into the particular outcome which presents itself evidentially and makes demands on our comprehension? What cannot be ruled out at present (i.e., on the basis of our present understanding of the universe and of ourselves) – and in my guess is unlikely ever to be ruled out – is the possibility that among the constraints, which control energy transacted through the human system into its outcomes, are those which are derived informationally from a resource external to the human subject, which has traditionally been characterised theistically – as God. To put it in a different and more speculative language, in the programmes which set boundary markers on the unfolding of a universe such as this, the possibility cannot be ruled out that God can participate in the human programme, particularly where it is looked for in faith.

It is here that incarnational Christology is potentially prosaic and factual in relation to science. It is not the least incoherent (which is not to say that it is therefore true) to realise that among the constraints which controlled Jesus into the particular outcome which evoked both Church and creed is the constant (and therefore wholly embodied) input derived from God: the humanity in this case is not destroyed, nor is the aseity of God compromised or diminished. If the retrieval and the constraint are constant, this is not other than the Word made flesh.[65]

It follows that virtually all our judgements are highly corrigible and are often corrected; yet they frequently manifest a provisional and somewhat surprising reliability, which is derived partly from our extensive intersubjectivity and partly from the fact that the constraints of data are not wholly created in the mind, although they are not indeed 'raw', and can only be handled in networks of interpretation. Here again the continuity between science and theology is obvious, once it is recognised that the data in each case are not identical, although at points they intersect. The final and absolute connection between science and theology lies not in a territorial mapping of domains, but in the unification of judgement in human lives which are prepared to accept the constraints in each activity where they are appropriate to a proposed utterance, and are prepared also to participate in those modes of attention and discipline (learning and experiment, prayer and sacrament) which lead beyond themselves toward a condition which is legitimately described as truth.

122

JOHN BOWKER

REFERENCES AND NOTES

1. For example, Zukav, G., *The Dancing Wu Li Masters* (New York, 1979); Capra, F., *The Tao of Physics* (London, 1976).
2. 'The Argument from Design', *Philosophy*, XLIII (1968) p. 200.
3. *Op. cit.*, p. 201.
4. *Ibid.*, p. 202.
5. MacPherson, T., *The Argument from Design* (London, 1972), p. 9
6. Swinburne, *op. cit.*, p. 202.
7. *Ibid.*, p. 202
8. *Ibid.*, p. 202f.
9. *Ibid.*, p. 203.
10. *Ibid.*, p. 206, 211.
11. *The Coherence of Theism* (Oxford, 1977), pp. 131-41.
12. 'Actions, Reasons and Causes', *Journal of Philosophy*, LX (1963) 685-700.
13. *A Theory of Human Action* (N. Jersey, 1970).
14. Swinburne, *op. cit.*, pp. 136f.
15. *Ibid.*, pp. 137f.
16. 'Problems Outstanding in the Evolution of Brain Function', in *The Encyclopaedia of Ignorance, I, Life Sciences and Earth Sciences*, ed. Duncan, R. and Weston-Smith, M (Oxford, 1977), p. 432.
17. *Ibid.*, p. 432.
18. 'Cerebral Cortex, Cerebellum and Basal Ganglia: an Introduction to their Motor Functions', in *The Neurosciences: Third Study Program*, ed. Schmitt, F. O. and Worden, F. G. (Cambridge, Mass., 1974), pp. 267–80.
19. Swinburne, 'The Argument . . . ', p. 204.
20. *Op. cit.*, p. 204.
21. *Ibid.*, p. 204.
22. *Ibid.*, p. 204.
23. *Ibid.*, p. 205.
24. *Ibid.*, p. 206.
25. *Ibid.*, p. 206.
26. *Ibid.*, p. 206.
27. 'Adaptation, Natural Selection and Behaviour', in *Behaviour and Evolution*, ed. Roe, A. and Simpson, G. G. (Yale, 1964), pp. 390–416: "The biologist's long-standing confusion would be more fully removed if all end-directed systems were described by some other term, like 'teleonomic', in order to emphasize that the recognition and description of end-directedness does not carry a commitment to Aristotelian teleology as an efficient causal principle" (p. 394).
28. The paper was originally published in *Science*. It was reprinted, as a precirculated paper for the I.U.B.S. Symposium in *Towards a Theoretical Biology, 1*, ed. Waddington, C. H. (Edinburgh, 1968), pp. 42–54. Waddington replied that Mayr's sharp distinction between the behaviour or development of an individual (which can be purposive) and natural selection (which cannot) cannot be sustained. In Waddingtons view, "quasi-finalistic types of explanation are called for in the theory of evolution as well as in that of development". (*op. cit.*, p. 55).
29. 'Evolution', in *Sci. Am..*, CCXXXIX, 3 (1978) p. 39.
30. 'The Basic Ideas of Biology' in *op. cit.*, ed. Waddington, pp.13f.
31. *Op cit.*, pp. 14f.
32. "The [evolutionary] process must have been directed by an *orderly innovating principle*, the action of which could only have been *released* by the random effects

123

of molecular agitations and photons coming from the outside, and the operation of which could only have been *sustained* by a favourable environment." *Personal Knowledge: Towards a Post-Critical Philosophy* (London, 1958), p. 386.

33. *Op. cit.*, p.33.
34. *Ibid.*, p. 34.
35. *Ibid.*, p. 34.
36. *Chance and Necessity* (London, 1972), p. 135.
37. *Op cit.*, p. 135.
38. *Ibid.*, p. 136.
39. *Ibid.*, p. 136.
40. London, 1976.
41. *Op. cit.*, p.121.
42. *Ibid.*, pp. 115f.
43. *Ibid.*, p. 117. It is not, of course, necessary to decide between these as exclusive alternatives. We may prefer , with R. E. Dickerson, to conclude, "Today nucleic acids cannot replicate without enzymes, and enzymes cannot be made without nucleic acids. To the question, 'Which came first, enzymes or nucleic acids?' the answer must be, 'They developed in parallel'." ('Chemical Evolution and the Origin of Life', in *Sci. Am.*, CCXXXIX, 3 (1978) p. 65). However, Dickerson is still left at the stage in the history of the argument where the envisaging of the process, whereby the 'machinery' for replication evolved, is still remote:
"Many attempts have been made to find a natural fit between protein sequences and nucleic acid sequences that could have existed before the appearance of the present-day elaborate machinery involving transfer–RNA molecules, ribosomes and charging enzymes. None of these attempts has been fully convincing. In all present-day life a charging enzyme attaches a specific amino acid to a transfer–RNA molecule that has at its other end an anticodon for that amino acid. [Compare the approach to the origin of life in n.51 below.] . . . The specificity of matching amino acids to codons lies neither in the codon nor in the transfer RNA but in the charging enzyme. How did the matching arise before charging enzymes existed? This looks like another chicken-and-egg paradox, since the charging enzymes themselves are synthesized by the translation machinery they help to operate. The answer to the original chicken-and-egg paradox was that neither the chicken nor the egg came first; they evolved together from lower forms of life. The same must be true of the genetic machinery; the entire apparatus evolved in concert from simpler systems now driven out of existence by competition. Although we can examine fossil remains of chicken ancestors, we have no fossil enzymes to study. We can only imagine what probably existed, and our imagination so far has not been very helpful."
44. *The Nature of Living Things* (London, 1972).
45. Calow, *op. cit.*, p. 117f.
46. *Ibid.*, p. 118
47. *Ibid.*, p. 118f.
48. *Ibid.*, p. 119.
49. *Ibid.*, p. 119
50. *Ibid.*, p. 120.
51. Lacey, J. C. and Weber, A. L., 'The Origin of the Genetic Code: an Amino Acid-Anticodon Relationship', in *Protein Structure and Evolution*, ed. Fox, J. L., Deyl, Z. and Blažej, A., Intl. Union of Biochemistry Symposium, 74, (N. York, 1976)), pp. 213–22:
"The data considered thus far, although incomplete, suggest that the code

JOHN BOWKER

originated and evolved through some special relationship between amino acids and their anticodon nucleotides . . . The basic model is that each of the four mono-nucleotides would be responsible for recognising and activating a class of amino acids; ATP for hydrophobic amino acids, UTP for hydrophilic and GTP and CTP for those of intermediate hydrophobicity . . . Perhaps the crux of what we are saying is that early in the evolution of the code, recognition and activation of the amino acids must have taken place simultaneously through the agency of a domain having the proper hydrophobicity to be attractive to the amino acid and its anticodon nucleotide. Such a domain would be the precursor of the active site of the aminoacyl–tRNA – synthetases. We thus envision the evolution of the genetic code as an evolution of appropriate active sites" (pp. 219, 221).

52. *Lifecloud: The Origin of Life in the Universe* (London,1978), p. 157.
53. 'Problèmes d'Evolution dans la Thermodynamique des Phenomènes irréversibles', in *The Origin of Life on the Earth*, ed. Oparin, A. I., *et al.* (London, 1959), p. 418.
54. New York, 1955.
55. Prigogine, I. and Nicolis, G., 'Biological Order, Structure and Instabilities', *Quart. Rev. of Biophysics*, 4 (1971) pp. 111f.
56. *Ibid.*, p. 143.
57. Eigen, M., 'Molecular Self-organization and the Early Stages of Evolution', *Quart. Rev. of Biophysics*, 4 (1971) pp. 197f.
58. *Ibid.*, p. 202.
59. The anthropic principle, which claims that for human life to emerge the universe could not be other than it is, is then extended further by drawing attention to the post-quantum transformation of the observer-observed distinction into the observer as participant in the universe, so that at the quantum level the observer is required in order to collapse probabilities into singular outcomes. J. A. Wheeler, therefore, asks whether "the very mechanism for the universe to come into being is meaningless or unworkable or both unless the universe is guaranteed to produce life, consciousness and observership somewhere and for some little time in its history to be": "Chance mutation, yes; Darwinian evolution, yes; yes, the general is free to move his troops by throwing dice if he chooses; *but he is shot if he loses the battle* [my italics]. Deprived of all meaning, stripped of any possibility to exist, is any would-be universe where Darwinian evolution brings forth no community of evidence-sharing participants, according to the view of 'self-reference cosmogony' under examination here.' (Wheeler, J. A. and Patton, C. M., 'Is Physics Legislated by Cosmogony?' in *Quantum Gravity: an Oxford Symposium*, ed. Isham, C. J. *et al.* (Oxford, 1975), p.567.) However, the anthropic principle is not undisputed, to say the least, and there are others who do discern profligacy in the universe. Thus P. C. W. Davies concluded his recent book, *The Forces of Nature* (Cambridge, 1979), with "the remarkable thought" that the world would apparently be much the same place with only the two lightest quarks (u, d) and the two light leptons (e, v_e), since they seem to make up all of ordinary matter: "How extended is this overprovision How many quarks and leptons will there turn out to be? Perhaps there is no limit . . . One reason for the superabundance of species might be that nature produces everything it *can* rather than everything it *needs*"(p. 229). But if that *is* the reason, it would reinforce rather than contradict the argument to boundaries and design.
60. For details, see note 59 above.
61. *Op. cit.*, p. 541

125

62. *Op cit.*, pp. 558, 575.
63. *Dilemmas* (Cambridge, 1954), p. 95.
64. It should perhaps be emphasised that the word 'constraint' in the cybernetic sense is a positive, not a negative, concept: see my *The Sense of God: Sociological, Anthropological and Psychological Approaches to the Origin of the Sense of God* (Oxford, 1973), for a discussion of this point, and for a quotation from Ashby's summary of it. In a more general sense, a constraint is an alternative or additional description of a dynamic process which ignores the fact that the laws of motion are already a total constraint over the detailed behaviour of any system – *i.e.*, the identification of constraint is a conscious abstraction of detail for the solution or analysis of particular problems or data.
65. The application of this perspective of information-process to theology and Christology can be found in my two related books. *The Sense of God . . .* and *The Religious Imagination and the Sense of God* (Oxford, 1978).

Chapter 6

PROFANE AND SACRAMENTAL VIEWS OF NATURE

Sigurd Daecke
Rheinisch — Westfälische Technische Hochschule
Aachen, W. Germany

"FIE, IT IS NATURAL!", said the princess in the tale of the Danish poet Hans Christian Andersen, when the prince presented her with a natural rose and she preferred the artificial toys of the supposed swineherd. "Fie, it is natural!", said also continental theology, when it regarded *nature* and the *environment* and with disgust turned to the artificial world of *man* and *society* — God, man and society are the concerns of the belief in creation, but nature is not. This is the way in which the three (quantitatively) prevailing theological positions of recent times in Germany — the kerygmatic, the existential and "political" theology — have understood the doctrine of creation. Thus nature and the environment, which could quite simply be called "creation", were never the main objects of belief in creation, as it was understood by most German theologians. At best, nature was mentioned indirectly by way of speaking about God, human existence and society.

I

God and nature in German theology of recent times
In *kerygmatic* theology, belief in creation is, rather, belief in the creator, belief in the word of God, especially in Jesus Christ. For "the reality of the creation is known in the person of Jesus Christ" (Karl Barth[1]). Nature here is "theatrum gloriae Dei" (Calvin), nature is only the stage on which "salvation history" (*Heilsgeschichte*) is performed, but which has nothing to do with this history itself. Nature here is profane creation and different from the Creator, whose word is the single object of faith. Adolf Schlatter, probably the last German theologian who acknowledged the "book of nature" beside the "book of the Bible", once said that such a theologian is speaking of nature as if he did not *see* it, but only heard of it through the words of Holy

Scripture. Of course it is necessary to hear and to read what the word of God is telling us about creation, as it was in the programme of Karl Barth in his preface to his doctrine of creation in volume III, 1 of the *Kirchliche Dogmatik*. It is necessary, but not enough.

If kerygmatic theology reduced the object of the doctrine of creation to the word of God, *existential* theology reduced it to human existence. *Entweltlichung* was the task of faith, according to Rudolf Bultmann. Belief in creation here consists in man confessing himself as a creature. Luther had already begun his explanation of the first article of the *Credo* in his "Small Catechism": "I believe that God has created *me* ..." And Schleiermacher's concept of belief in creation is the "feeling of absolute dependence" of human existence (*schlechthiniges Abhängigkeitsgefühl*). From Luther and Schleiermacher to Bultmann and Gogarten, "creation" has been reduced to the anthropological and personal dimension. Friedrich Gogarten definitively divided the object of faith which is exclusively God, from the object of reason, which is competent for the study of profane nature. So theology abandoned nature to the sciences, and no more conflict was possible between faith and science. *"Political"* theology, or the so-called theology of society, also considers nature as profane, as secularised. Belief in creation here becomes hope for the liberation of mankind, hope for a better world, and thus faith is only interested in societal matters, not in nature.

All these three theological positions — the kerygmatic, the existential and the political — understand nature as secularised, as profane. Therefore theology is not concerned with nature, but only reason is, and that means science. A positivistic science and the so-called *Offenbarungspositivismus* in theology agree on this dualistic division of reality. Reality here is divided like the house of Faraday, who locked his prayer-room when he went to his laboratory, and who locked the door of the laboratory, when he returned to his prayer-room. This attitude was called "schizophrenia" by Pierre Teilhard de Chardin: a split reality and a split consciousness of man.

Of course there were, and are not, only these three theological positions in Germany. Besides Barth and Bultmann, there was Paul Tillich with his unitary view of God and the world, but he did not stress the notion of nature in his system. Today, the theology of Wolfhart Pannenberg is an important and impressive antithesis to all those positions which divide God, human existence or society from nature and which limit belief in creation to God, man and society. Pannenberg's unifying view of the *one* reality, which tries to reconcile God and nature, is one of the most important theological positions of

128

our time. He is even better known abroad than the present kerygmatic, existential and "political" theologians (as measured perhaps by
the number of dissertations on Pannenberg's theology, not only in
English but in many other languages). In spite of that the other
positions prevail quantitatively in German universities. Other
attempts to unify the concepts of God and of nature are made by
scientists and philosophers, but rarely by theologians. Most of them
still continue to advocate the profane view of nature.

Nevertheless this concept of secularisation was called into question
in Germany when ecological consciousness was growing and when the
desacralisation of nature by the Old Testament — especially the
division of Creator and creation, of God and nature — were held
responsible for the exploitation and destruction of nature and so
responsible for the environmental crisis. But the Cartesian division of
subject and object was incriminated even more than that particular
division between a holy God and profane nature. Even O. H. Steck in
his excellent book on the Old Testament understanding of "world and
environment"[2] has now again confirmed that the Old Testament
stresses the transcendence of God in contrast to a desacralised nature
and a profane world. Moreover man, in the Old Testament view,
stands above nature as the *imago Dei*, the representative of God. On
the basis of this view, nature could be understood instrumentally as an
object of human use, or even abuse.

II

God and nature in ecumenical papers of the last five years
The Old Testament scholar Klaus Koch is German too. Therefore one
could anticipate that his view would be: "In Genesis 1 the whole
programme of modern natural science and technique lies 'in nuce'
before us".[3] On the other hand — and this is quite new — Koch
stresses the connection not only between man and earth — *adam* and
adama — but also between God and earth — *Jahweh* and *adama*.
More than that, Koch dares to derive from Old Testament texts a
concept of the correlation between God and nature which, as he says
in his paper for the ecumenical consultation on "Humanity, nature
and God" in Zurich 1977,[4,5] is somewhat surprising. For the general
opinion is, writes Koch, that an unbridgeable gap between God and
nature is the general tenor of the Old Testament. Now he describes, in
spite of these usual presuppositions, the relation between God and
nature according to the Old Testament as "God *is* nature", or more

precisely: "God including nature".

This is indeed surprising. For the first formula usually means pantheism, the second panentheism — doctrines which are thought to be rejected as well by the Old Testament as by the Christian Church. To support his thesis, that this view of "nature in God" or "God including nature" is really the message of the Old Testament, Koch refers to Hosea 2, *v.* 21, 22: "I will give answer, says the Lord, I will give answer for the heavens, and they will answer for the earth, and the earth will answer for the corn, the new wine, and the oil; and they will answer for Jezreel" (N.E.B.). Here the prophet is thinking of a coherent chain in which God is the initiator, but an initiator who acts in interdependence with earth, man and nation. God is the beginning and the end of that chain, of that natural process, which sustains the functions of elementary life.[5]

Klaus Koch is the first German exegete of the Old Testament I know who has dared to contradict the dogma of the big gap between the transcendent God and nature, between the holy Creator and the profane creation. He is the first to find evidence of the unity of God and nature in the Bible — perhaps except for the original, pre-Paulinian version of the hymn in Col. 1 *v.* 15 ff., where Christ and the cosmos are conceived as the unity of head and body. But in spite of Koch's paper, and also of those by Birch, Gregorios and Hartshorne — all of them emphasising a unitary, holistic view of God and nature — the report of the Zürich consultation states: "God is not equated with nature; the Old Testament is no pantheist". The belief, that God is One and Supreme, and therefore de-supernaturalises the world, rids it of superhuman personal power, whether divine or demonic, adds the Zürich report (p. 29, 31).[4] Perhaps the report is here balancing and harmonising the contrary views of the participants of the consultation, the dualistic and the holistic points of view.[6]

Nevertheless the papers and reports of the ecumenical consultations in Mexico[7] 1975 and Zürich[4] 1977, like those of the 1979 World Council of Churches Conference on "Faith, Science and the Future" in Cambridge, Mass., tried to correct the misunderstanding of a doctrine of creation which forgets nature (cf. I, above) through an epistemological concentration on the knowledge of God, an anthropological concentration on human existence and a political concentration on the improvement of society. All these models of the concept of creation are an insufficient basis for the dialogue between theology and science and for the solution of ecological problems. For if theology does not care about nature and if theology abandons nature to the sciences, there is no common level, no common basis for a dialogue: they have no common object. And theology must abandon nature to science, if it does not succeed in finding a real relation between God and nature, in overcoming the dualism of God as the object of theology and nature as the object of science.

For if nature is understood as profane, as secular, then it has only an instrumental value for us and can be objectified, used and even abused and exploited. It then has no intrinsic value to itself, no inner significance, which can induce man to protect and to save it. Yet the ecumenical consultations in Mexico reported: "In our use of plants and animals we need to discover a balance between the instrumental value to us and their own intrinsic value to themselves and to God .. The time is ripe to speak about the world and its inner significance and nature".[7] But in that Report we do not find more than these proposals, suggestions and demands. "How can the intrinsic value of nature be established?", "How can it be understood?" — to these questions there is no answer in the report.

The Zürich Report of 1977 begins with a similar question: "How is the conflict between the instrumental value of nature and its intrinsic value to be resolved?"[8] It is already a gain — compared with the usual German discussion — that this question is actually asked. But the report is also the first to concede that there are several different views of nature in the Bible and that one of them is the vision of an integral relation between humanity, nature and God. This conceptual unity has been disrupted by wrong interpretations, since the 17th century, that detached humanity as well as God from nature. Now we need — that Report says — to rediscover the intrinsic value not only of non-human creatures, but also of the inanimate creation. For it is not the Christian tradition to value nature merely as an instrument. But the ascription of an intrinsic value to nature is dependent on a unitary view of God, humanity and nature, which itself has to be rediscovered.

The reports of the ecumenical consultations only postulate and demand this new unifying theological vision of nature, humanity and God, this "harmonious unity". The problem how to arrive at this unitary vision of God, man and the cosmos, how to overcome the separation of God and nature, the dualism of immanence and transcendence, of the natural and the supernatural, of matter and mind, of subject and object, how to relate creator and creation — that problem is realised and described, but nowhere resolved in the reports of the consultations and conferences, not even at the world conference in Cambridge, Mass., in 1979. The Zürich report does indeed affirm: "God is no longer seen as a reality 'outside of' or apart from the reality of humanity and nature. Humanity and nature can exist only in God ... God, humanity and nature are thus seen not as three separate realities, but as one reality".[9] This is an exact definition of a panentheistic concept. If we compare it with the individual papers, it is the voice of the Metropolitan Paulos Gregorios. Today panentheism can be presented as the solution of the problem of the relation between God and nature — in spite of the theological verdicts. But for overcoming the dualistic view of reality, we need better-founded arguments. We need at least arguments instead of proclamations, especially if subsequently it is affirmed: "This is not to blur any of the distinctions ... The tensions remain, between God's transcendence and his involvement in the creation". But this is not the answer — this exactly is the open question: Do there really still exist tensions and distinctions?

Klaus Koch has indeed found surprising exegetical grounds for a panentheistic view of the God-nature relation in the Old Testament. But it is only one very small passage in Hosea on which he founds his thesis. With this support he merely shows that this unitary view, this concept of the oneness of God and nature is permitted by the Old Testament and not forbidden, as it was asserted by nearly all exegetes up to now. With the word of Hosea, Koch shows only that a dualistic view of the transcendent God and the profane, secular nature is not the only one which has been allowed by the Bible. This is really a great release for all those who hitherto thought that a holistic, unitary concept of God, humanity and nature — if we absolutely want to get it — must be asserted *without* assistance by the Bible, especially against the Old Testament. The Danish theologian Ole Jensen for example suggests that the concept of the sacredness of creation, which he thinks to be the only view possible considering the environmental crisis, must be developed without assistance from the Bible by a *Tendenz-Hermeneutik* opposite to the usual one.[10] This now seems to be no longer necessary, and a unifying, holistic concept of God and nature, a view of nature as sacred, may now be developed with a better conscience. But, as it is a single position among opposite ones, it seems to be insufficient just to refer to Hosea 2 *v.* 21 f. The unity of God and nature must be established systematically. Dogmatic reasons are necessary for the concept of sacred nature. For the question remains: Who or what is sanctifying nature? Why can nature be considered as sacred?

The last passage of the Zürich report does in fact give "elements of a new vision of the relation of humanity, nature and God".[11] But the relation between *humanity* and nature is here also substantiated only in terms of the personal, ethical category of "responsibility", and in a very short assertion at that. Furthermore, the report on "Humanity, Nature and God" of Section II of the 1979 W.C.C. Conference at Cambridge, Mass., similarly restricted itself to using the terms "relation", "relationship" and "connection" — not "unity" or "oneness" of God, humanity and nature, as Birch and the process-theologians do. This "relation" or "connection" is here also founded on the idea of responsibility, on the biblical concepts of the *imago Dei* and the *dominium terrae*, which means simply a personal, ethical conception of the relation of man to God and nature. This is only a social-ethical foundation for an ecological theology and does not need a genuine "theology of nature" with a concept of the relation between God and nature. The concept of "dominion", which the W.C.C. Conference report refers to, means that man is responsible for nature because he is God's representative — his steward or his caretaker and manager (T. S. Derr[12]).

But to base environmental ethics only on the idea of man's responsibility to God, because of his status as God's steward, is insufficient: first, because the reason for preserving nature from destruction is not founded on nature itself, on its relation to God and its sacredness; and secondly, because man's responsibility is primarily demanded for fellow-men and not for nature, there is the possibility of conflict between the responsibility for man and the responsibility for nature. In spite of the participation of several process-theologians in these various consultations, and in spite of their papers, the reports say nothing about divine immanence in natural processes, nothing about deification of the evolutionary process; they do not claim that nature is an object of reverence, regarded as sacred, or even that matter is divine — as we read it in the publications, for example, of Barbour, Birch, Bonifaci, Cobb, Rust and Schilling on the relation between God and nature, or between theology and science. The process-theological ideas, for example of Charles Birch, who has read papers at the consultations and conferences in Mexico and Nairobi, in Zürich and in Cambridge, Mass., scarcely influenced the official reports. Perhaps the transcendence of God, his distinction from nature and the concept of a personal God seem to be insufficiently emphasised when Birch, as in his 1979 W.C.C. paper, stresses a unitary approach to the problem against the disjunctive view of God, humanity and nature, referring to Gregory of Nyssa's concept of nature *in* God. A possible reason for the lack of emphasis on the process-theological view in the official reports is that it lacks a specifically biblical, or at least theological, foundation. In his 1979 paper, Birch merely refers to Whitehead's concept of God, except for quoting some verses from the book of Job. But the Whiteheadian view is not the only one able to form the basis for a unitary view of God and nature. So we come to

III

God and nature in contemporary theology
In his essay "The 'Elements of the Universe' in Biblical and Scientific Perspective"[13] Walter Wink has shown a remarkable route to a unifying concept of God and nature. His approach avoids both the error of separating nature from God and that of identifying them; he considers nature as profane as well as divine. For he brings into the discussion the New Testament idea of the "*stoicheia* of the world" (Gal. 4v. 4, 9; Col. 2v. 8, 20) which he understands as irreducible and basic entities, fundamental principles of nature, invariances and unchanging laws of the cosmos, which are powerful and irresistible, which transcend us and which modern scholars think of as "spirits", he says.[14] While, for example, G. A. Riggan sees a theophany in the stability of DNA or R. W. Burhoe interprets God as the meaning of natural selection, Wink sees these manifestations as *stoicheia* and says: Indeed DNA *is* God — but only at the level of genetics; and indeed God *is* manifest as natural selection — but only at the level of biology. God is not reducible to DNA or natural selection: God is rather that power that penetrates all being at every level and is related to every level, for God's reality is never exhausted in what is made manifest at any given level. What is called "God" at the level of biology in fact is a *stoicheion*. Indeed the *stoicheia* are numinous and powerful, they participate in the divine and are to be revered and honoured — but not themselves worshipped. If they are elevated to a higher level they will become demonic, and to do this is idolatry, Wink says, referring to Tillich.[15]

This is one possible solution of the problem. Nature here is neither profane nor divine; on the one hand, God is manifest in nature; on the other hand, he is not manifest there as the Christian God appropriate to the spiritual level, but only as *stoicheion*. Nature therefore is related organically to God — but it is not equated with God. But it seems to me, that the better — because still more biblical and christological — way is the *sacramental* view as proposed in the ecumenical dialogue by the Metropolitan Paulos Gregorios (Paul Verghese) in several papers since the consultation at Bucharest 1974 and in his book *The Human Presence*[16] — but even earlier in Anglican theology by A. R. Peacocke[17] and other authors in the book edited by

H. Montefiore,[17] (as well as their 19th-century Anglican and earlier predecessors), and nearly 60 years ago also by the French scientist and theologian Pierre Teilhard de Chardin.

Teilhard's motive for his vision of the continuity of the universe and God, the unity of nature and God, for his attempt to overcome the dualism of reality, the dichotomy of faith and thought, the opposition of theology and science, was the problem of his own existence as scientist and theologian at once. He suffered from his "divided life between two worlds", which caused a "schizophrenia", as he once said, in somebody who was at once theologian and scientist. Therefore he tried to unify God and nature, to integrate in a consistent whole the two sources of his understanding of God. He tried to overcome the opposition between the model of God which he derived from his contemplation of the natural world and the view of God which he received from revelation. To support this unification of God and nature, he developed, after about 1930, his *evolutionary* concept of God: God as the immanent motor of evolution and at the same time as the transcendent attractive pull of the natural, creative processes — a concept very similar to that of the North American process-theology some decades later.

But during the first ten years of his work, especially in 1918 and 1923, he conceived the unity of God and universe in *sacramental* terms and noted the vision of the universe which changed into the eucharistic host. In the desert of China he celebrated in 1923 the "Mass over the World": "Receive, O Lord, this total host, which is offered to you by the creation moved by your attractive pull at the new sunrise ... All matter now is incarnated, God, by your incarnation".[18] This sacramental vision stresses the presence of God, or more exactly, of Christ in matter and in the cosmos; and it expresses the understanding of nature as an offering, as a sacrifice, not as a possession of man. The destiny of nature is not to be dominated and utilised, but to be offered to God. Matter for him is not material for man, not a resource to be exploited, but a unity with God: not secular, but sacred, sanctified by the incarnation of God in Christ. For God has not only become man in Christ, but also matter.

Quite similarly P. Gregorios writes: "Here a totally fresh attitude is necessary, one which is different for our objectifying-analysing technique. We shall call it the reverent-receptive attitude".[19] The scientific-technological attitude on the one hand and the reverent-receptive attitude on the other hand Father Gregorios also calls "mastery and mystery": "It is not science and theology that need to be reconciled. It is rather these two attitudes — the mastery and mystery

— which have to be held in tension ... We may give nature, as our extended body, into the hands of the loving God in the great mystery of the eucharistic self-offering ... This eucharistic union-mysticism, in which we are one with the whole creation in our responsive self-offering to God, is the mystery that fulfills human existence ... The mastery of nature must be held within the mystery of worship".[20] The sacramental view of nature, which leads us to accept nature from God and to offer it again to God instead of objectifying and analysing it (which induces us to have reverence for nature instead of abusing and destroying it) is, according to Gregorios, a necessary complement to the scientific attitude, not an alternative to it. Gregorios does not pretend to replace the modern concept of reality, the scientific and technical attitude to nature, by reverence and devotion to a sacred or even divine nature — for then science and technology would become impossible.

In his paper at the 1979 W.C.C. Conference in Cambridge, Mass., with the title "Science and Faith — complementary or contradictory?" Gregorios again emphasised that "faith needs science, must come to terms with it, and work for new perceptions in both faith and science, through respectful collaboration and healthy self-criticism": thus science and faith are not contradictory, but complementary. Science which is related to faith in this way can overcome the Cartesian dualism of subject and object. Of course, science is compelled to objectify nature. But the reverent-receptive attitude of a faith regarding nature as a sacrament, sanctified by the incarnation of God in Christ, does not allow science to abuse and to destroy such sacred nature — sacred not in itself, therefore not divine, but accepted by God in his incarnation.

More particularly referred to God's acting in Jesus Christ than the concept of the Gregorios — which in the Orthodox manner is more liturgical than systematical — is A. R. Peacocke's "sacramental view of nature",[17] which is dominant also in the report of a Working Group of the Doctrine Commission of the Church of England, with the title "Man and Nature".[21] In a way similar to Gregorios' speaking of complementarity between science and faith, Peacocke writes that they "converge in a view of the cosmos which can therefore be properly called 'sacramental' ". And according to the report by the Working Group "the Christian sacramental understanding of the natural universe is congruent with the contemporary scientific perspective on the evolution of the cosmos ... ".[22] Thus Peacocke stresses still more than Gregorios the fact — which is so necessary for the dialogue between scientists and theologians — that it is the same nature which is analysed by the scientists and which has been sanctified by the manifestation of God within the creation, by his incarnation in Jesus Christ. And still more evidently than in the texts of Gregorios, Peacocke here emphasises that a unitary view of God and nature is founded on belief in God as a Trinity. The summary of his sacramental view of nature is: "The world is created and sustained in being by the will of God ... The Son, the Logos, is the all-sufficient principle and form of this created order", and its "continuing creative power ... is the Holy Spirit himself".[23]

Such ideas are to be found in ecumenical discussion only in a small passage of the 1975 Mexico City report,[7] which nowhere later seems to have been used, on "the Logos-centred presence of God in and with nature": "This specifically Christian Logos-based doctrine of creation, which affirms the inseparable, active, transcendent-immanent involvement of God in creation, has always to be understood as hope for both humanity and nature".[24] But we find the sacramental view of nature not only in Anglican and Orthodox theology. The Swedish Lutheran Jonas Jonson also writes[25] that the sacraments are "the expression of the unity of creation, man and redemption". Baptism and Holy Communion are the symbols of this unity of God and creation, man and nature, which is founded by the incarnation, interpreted as the identification of God with the biological, healthy world. By this "sacramental view of creation" Jonson stresses the "intrinsic value of all which has been created", the "sacredness" of nature: The flower, the whale, the river and the air, which we breathe, are sacred, are the answer of God. The "social" and "political" consequences of this sacramental "unity of God, man and nature" is "the classwar of the unborn, threatened by poisoning ... together with the classwar of the waters, the sea-eagles and the woods against a profit-orientated exploitation". For the sacramental view of nature as sanctified by the Incarnation prohibits the exploitation of nature as well as the exploitation of man.

Pierre Teilhard de Chardin changed from his sacramental view of nature to the evolutionary concept of the unity of God and nature about 1930, after having written the *Le Milieu Divin*. But he did not link these two concepts of the relation between God and nature, the mystical one and the evolutionary one. Is there any contradiction between them? In any case Teilhard did not try to reconcile his later scientific approach with his former sacramental approach to a unified view of God and nature. This led to two misunderstandings: first, that the sacramental view is not useful for dialogue between theology and science, because it is supposed not to be scientific, but mystical; and secondly, that the evolutionary view of God and nature and of their relation is not theological, but philosophical, because it is supposed to be incompatible with the personality and transcendence of God, and because it has neither a Christological nor a pneumatological foundation. This reproach is at least partly right with respect to Teilhard's own concept, and thus his attempt to unify the views of God and of nature does not satisfy entirely.

It is still less a solution of this problem simply to equate God with nature, or with the selective processes as for example R. W. Burhoe does, when he says, that "the scientist's 'nature' and the supreme God or ultimate reality ... translate to essentially the same thing".[26] As Philip Hefner has shown this is neither a scientific nor a theological concept, but rather a metaphysical one.[27] In contrast to these approaches, P. Hefner,[27] H. Montefiore[29] and A. R. Peacocke[17,28] seem to have succeeded in combining the evolutionary and the sacramental approach in a unifying concept of God and nature. They show that it is possible to understand the natural processes sacramentally: that means to refer them to incarnation, redemption, sanctification and to the Holy Spirit. Thus A. R. Peacocke writes: "The understanding of Jesus as God Incarnate also acquires a new relevance when he is seen as the consummation of a process of cosmic evolution which occurred as an expression of God's creative will ... For God-becoming-man, the Incarnation ..., can now be seen as the consummation of that evolutionary process in which the rise of man succeeded the general biological sequence". Because "the Incarnation has been expounded" thus by Peacocke " as the culmination and chief exemplification of the creative, dynamic activity of God in the cosmic development of the 'world-stuff' ",[28] God and nature have been related not only theologically, but precisely Christologically. H. Montefiore does the same by using the idea of redemption: "Man ... acts not only as co-creator with God in nature but also as co-redeemer in the sense that he assists the purposes of God in the natural world".[29] And both of them, Montefiore and Peacocke, connect God and nature by the concept of the Holy Spirit as operating in matter,[30] as "the power and presence of God as he fulfills the potentialities of the world-stuff ('matter') at each level and stage of the cosmic process through the laws it obeys".[31] "This concept of spirit as an aspect of matter is surprisingly similar to the Christian doctrine of sacraments ... Christians claim that the whole process of evolution is the outworking of the Holy Spirit, that is, the outworking of the creative being of God in his world".[32] Also Philip Hefner understands "the presence of the Spirit ... as a transformation which approaches the fulfilment of the intrinsic potentialities of a living being".[33]

Thus the unity of God and nature is founded not only on Christology and soteriology, but also on pneumatology. And thus the desacralisation of nature has been overcome, which "has tended to divorce the spiritual from the material, leaving the world God-forsaken and therefore beyond the scope of redemption" (Montefiore[34]). But the separation of God from nature has been overcome by the idea, that "God has so honoured matter with his own presence and ... matter is capable of Incarnation, then it must be worthy of great respect",[35] for matter is then no more profane, but sanctified, having now intrinsic value (Montefiore) in a "sacramental universe" (Peacocke[36]). If we look for a biblical foundation of this sacramental view of nature, in addition to the New Testament message of Incarnation, we can refer to the hymn in Col. 1 v. 15 ff., which originally — before the Pauline ecclesiological redaction — expressed the unity between Christ the head and his body, the universe, the cosmos, which has been created and reconciled by him. As the head with the body, so Christ is organically connected with nature. Also in this hymn the natural world is the body of Christ, in accord with a sacramental view of nature.

"Natural theology" seems to be no more possible today. We cannot claim to have knowledge of God in nature. But it is another thing to know that God is related to nature and the sacramental view of nature is a good model for this tight relation between God and nature.[37]

REFERENCES AND NOTES

1. Barth, K., *Kirchliche Dogmatik III, 1*, "Die Lehre von der Schöpfung" (Zollikon-Zürich, 1945), p. 29.

2. Steck, O. H., *Welt und Umwelt* (Stuttgart, 1978), pp. 78 ff., 120, 139.

3. Koch, K., "The Old Testament View of Nature", in *Anticipation* No. 25 (Geneva, 1979), p. 49.

4. Report of the Zürich Consultation "Humanity, Nature and God", in *Anticipation* No. 25 (Geneva, 1979).

5. Koch, *ibid.*, p. 47.

6. On the one hand: God "is One and Supreme, and therefore transcendent", but on the other hand: God is not "the remote and transcendent", he "is no longer seen as a reality 'outside of' or apart from the reality of humanity and nature. Humanity and nature can exist only in God. They cannot be outside God for God has no outside": here we hear the voice of Birch, Hartshorne and especially Paulos Gregorios. And "God is intimately and enduringly involved with nature" (*op.cit.*, ref. 4, pp. 31, 27, 29). But *cf.* the statement "Christian Hope and the natural Sciences" from the Commission on Faith and Order 1978 in Bangalore: "The Christian doctrine of creation meant that nature itself was not sacred and might be approached as object, not subject" (*op.cit.*, ref. 4, p. 75).

7. "Science and Faith", Report of a Consultation in Mexico City on *The Christian Faith and the Changing Face of Science and Technology* (1975), in *Anticipation* No. 22 (Geneva, 1976) 21.

8. *Op. cit.*, ref. 4, p. 22.
9. *Ibid.*, p. 27.
10. Jensen, O., *Theologie zwischen Illusion und Restriktion* (München, 1975), pp. 273 ff.
11. *Op. cit.*, ref. 4, p. 37.
12. Derr, T. S., *Ecology and Human Liberation*. (Geneva, 1973), pp. 48, 72.
13. Wink, W., "The 'Elements of the Universe' in Biblical and Scientific Perspective", in *Zygon* 13 (1978) 225-248
14. *Ibid.*, pp. 235-237.
15. *Ibid.*, pp. 240-243.
16. Gregorios, P., *The Human Presence — An Orthodox view of nature* (Geneva, 1978), especially Chapter VII, "Mastery and Mystery", pp. 82-89.
17. Peacocke, A. R., "A Sacramental View of Nature", in *Man and Nature*, ed. Montefiore, H. (London, 1975), pp. 132-142. (This is a version of Chapter 7 of his earlier *Science and the Christian Experiment* (Oxford University Press, London, 1971) and of "Matter in the Theological and Scientific perspectives — a sacramental view" in *Thinking about the Eucharist*, ed. I. T. Ramsey (SCM Press, London, 1972) pp. 14-37.)
18. Pierre Teilhard de Chardin, "La messe sur le monde", in *Hymne de l'univers* (Paris, 1961), pp. 19, 23. Cf. *ibid.*, p. 25: "En ce moment ou votre Vie vient de passer ... dans le Sacrament du Monde ..."; p. 27: "Vous êtes incarné dans le Monde ..." and already (1918): "Je m'agenouille, Seigneur, devant l'univers devenue secrétement ... votre Corps adorable et votre Sang divin ... Le Monde est plein de vous!" ("Le Prêtre", in *L'Ecrits du temps de la guerre* (Paris, 1965) p. 290).
19. Gregorios, P., *op. cit.*, p. 86.
20. *Ibid.*, pp. 88 f.
21. *Man and Nature. op. cit.*, ref. 17, pp. 3-83.
22. Peacocke, A. R., *op. cit.*, ref. 17, p. 142; The Report, *op. cit.*, ref. 17, p. 60.
23. *Ibid.*, p. 140.
24. *Op. cit.*, ref. 7, pp. 20 f.
25. Jonson, J., "Global och nationell jämvikt som utmaning till kyrkan", *Teologernas svek*, in *Vår Lösen*, 1 (1977).
26. Burhoe, R. W., "What Does Determine Human Destiny? — Science Applied to Interpret Religion", in *Zygon* 12 (1977) 381.
27. Hefner, P., "To What Extent Can Science Replace Metaphysics?", in *Zygon* 12 (1977) 88-104, especially pp. 93-103.
28. Peacocke, A. R., "The Nature and Purpose of Man in Science and Christian Theology" in *Zygon* 8 (1973) 389, 391.
29. Montefiore, H., "Man and Nature: A Theological Assessment" in *Zygon* 12 (1977) 206.
30. *Ibid.*, p. 209.
31. Peacocke, A. R., *op. cit.*, ref. 28, p. 390.
32. Montefiore, H., *op. cit.*, p. 209.
33. Hefner, P., "The Self-Definition of Life and Human Purpose: Reflections upon the Divine Spirit and the Human Spirit", in *Zygon* 8 (1973) 399.
34. Montefiore, H., *op. cit.*, p. 205.
35. *Ibid.*, p. 209.
36. Peacocke, A. R., *op. cit.*, ref. 28, p. 392.
37. I thank Dr. A. R. Peacocke for his excellent grammatical revision and correction of my manuscript.

Chapter 7

THE RETURN OF MAN IN QUANTUM PHYSICS

Richard Schlegel
Department of Physics, Michigan State University, U.S.A.

I

Physics and Theology

The development of physical science is generally seen as having played a significant role in the transition from medieval Christian faith to the high component of non-believing in Western culture today. In an obvious way, the factual descriptions of astronomy destroyed the very groundwork of popular Christian thought; for, it became evident that there was no Heaven in the sky where God could dwell or man enjoy an eternal life. On a deeper level, the successes of a universal mechanics in prediction and control tended to diminish traditional explanatory roles of a divine being. And, during the nineteenth century the application of scientific historiography to Biblical writings still further eroded the credibility, and consistency, of centuries-old Christian doctrines.[1]

And yet, we know that such an account, suggesting a Comtean advance of positive science over superstitious dogma, is too simple – a kind of unwarranted scientific fundamentalism. I believe that we should all be grateful to science for its incomparable truth-obtaining capacities. Science, however, tends to give us knowledge on its own terms, tellling us not what we necessarily most want to know, but, rather, what science has learned at a particular time. Further, science too is a belief system. Its particular facts about nature do not change over the centuries, but its first principles do, and it is they that largely form our natural philosophy.

I could now go on and say that, since certainly our ideas about the natural world must to some degree influence our religious beliefs, there clearly is an influence of physics on theology. In part I shall be saying this and, indeed, the central concern of my paper will be with what I take to be a theological significance of twentieth-century developments in physics. But again, it is a mistake, I believe, to see religious ideas as altogether derivative–as following rather than leading–in their relationships to science. For, suppose we briefly consider the underlying ideas of the classical, Newtonian science that preceded the much altered and now dominant physics of today. Whence came those conceptions of the earlier physics: of a science with laws that absolutely governed the motion of every iota of matter, and on the basis of which Laplace[2] presumed that he could by calculation predict the future state of the universe at any time whatsoever? These are, I suggest, but a new statement of God's properties of omnipotence and omniscience, although ascribed not to him but to what today we call the science of physics.

In an oft-quoted discussion[3] A. N. Whitehead has asserted that the scholastic logic prepared the Western mind for scientific thought; that the mediaeval insistence on the rationality of God led eventually to a search for general principles in natural science. I believe that White-head's proposal can be given surprisingly strong support. It is not my desire in this paper to do so in any detail, but we can cite two parallels in addition to those of power and knowledge just noted. In classical physics, the locus and source of control over nature is in natural law; this is not a physical entity or force in the usual sense, but an intellectually discerned set of principles, often obtained and express-ed only with the assistance of mathematical reasoning. But likewise we are told of God in Thomistic theology: " 'God is incorporeal.' Therefore He can be seen 'only through the intelligence.' "[4] Also, to give the second parallel, in the physics that succeeded medieval thought, and held sway until our own century, it is a prime charac-teristic that the knowing scientist can be separated from the nature he describes. This means that physics, by the grace of its independence, may tell of a world that is in no way altered by the scientist's act of knowing. Similarly, the God of medieval thought is completely removed from any influence by man; as with the natural world of classical physics, he is intrinsically defined without relation to man. Thus, in the words of St. Thomas Aquinas[5]: "Now, a relation of God to creatures, is not a reality in God, but in the creature . . . Since therefore God is outside the whole order of creation, and all creatures are ordered to Him, and not conversely, it is manifest that creatures are really related to God Himself; whereas in God there is no real relation to creatures, but a relation only in idea, inasmuch as creatures are referred to Him".[6]

It is I would judge, not at all unreasonable that the natural philosophers of the fifteenth, sixteenth, and seventeenth centuries should carry over into their science the long established root ideas to which they had been accustomed with respect to the ultimate properties of the universe. Eventually, those ideas, *in their religious expression*, were of course much criticised by the science that developed from them; the child did come, so to speak, often to disavow the parent. In consequence, Christian theology from the sixteenth to the nineteenth centuries was much changed by science, as we have noted. But nonetheless we can conclude that scholastic theological ideas had a merit, in their own right, and that they were an important factor in forming the classical, Newtonian physics. It is not too much to say that theology pioneered the basic ideas of that physics, which although now much modified, did seem so right that it quite captured men's minds for two hundred years or so.

Today we are again in a situation where physics has given us an altered natural philosophy and, I suggest, the novel outlook is important for theology. But also, again, physics in its new philosophy has in part come where theologians have already been. Although perhaps not to as great a degree as in the development from scholastic thought to Newtonian physics, I shall be able to give evidence showing again a key role for general philosophical outlook in forming the new physics.

II

The Change to Quantum Physics

I shall go at once to the central new physical concept. In the older physics, and as we find in everyday experience on the human scale of magnitude, an object has one and only one set of physical properties for an observer. It is, we say, in a single physical state. But we have learned in quantum physics that this is no longer true when we consider micro-scale particles – roughly, of the size of atoms or smaller. A proton, say, may be distributed over a range of spatial positions; or, for one and the same observer it may be moving with several or many different velocities, with respect both to direction and to speed. We say that the particle, then, is not in a single state but is in a superposition of different dynamical states. Not every property of a particle can be multi-valued in the manner just illustrated. Electrical charge, for example, is fixed, and is always the same. But a particle can simultaneously be in different states of non-linear as well as straight-line motion, and, if it has an intrinsic spin, the effective axis of that spin may be distributed over more than one direction.

I am well aware of how incredible my assertions may seem to be. We are accustomed to the motion, say, of a motor car, but still we can fix a location for the car, at least approximately, at any one instant of time;

or, even more convincingly, we can do so for our own selves as we walk down a path. And, as for either the car or our own body having two different quantities and discretions of motion, at one and the same time: that seems quite directly inconsistent. We must remind ourselves, however, that we have no *a priori* warrant that the space-time properties of matter on the micro-level of quantum physics are the same as we have found at larger spatial magnitudes. The same empirical evidence and theoretical development which have led physicists to accept the physical existence of different dynamical states for a particle have also entailed restrictions on what can be observed for a particle. With those limitations we find that we cannot come to inconsistency or contradiction.

I shall return to this point. But first a few words are in order about why physicists accept the existence of particles in multiple physical states. In brief, the answer to that question is that inferences from observation have forced them to do so. Particles in fact do behave in ways that can only be reasonably interpreted by assuming that they are in a superposition of different physical states. The dilemma of wave *vs.* particle behaviour for both matter and radiation is an illustration, but there are also many other phenomena that show superposition effects.[7] However, to consider the wave-particle dualism, because it is relatively well-known, we recall that in a typical experiment electrons, for example, pass through two closely spaced parallel slits in a metal foil. The observed intensity pattern of the electrons on a film, after they have gone through the slits, directly shows what physicists call an interference pattern; this results from interaction between electron in state 1, "passed through slit 1", and the same electron in state 2, "passed through slit 2". The experiment can be performed with, in effect, only one electron at a time in the apparatus; hence, we know that *each* electron had to be in a superposition of the two states as it traversed the slits.

With the existence of particles in more than one physical state, as defined, we clearly have a groundwork of nature that is utterly at odds with that envisaged in pre-quantum physics. To quote one of the founding fathers of quantum theory, P. A. M. Dirac: "The nature of the relationships which the superposition principle requires to exist between the states of any system is of a kind that cannot be explained in terms of familiar physical concepts. One cannot in the classical sense picture a system being partly in each of two states . . . . There is an entirely new idea involved, to which one must get accustomed and in terms of which one must proceed to build an exact mathematical theory, without having any detailed classical picture."[8]

It is natural to ask, what determines the extent of multiplicity of states. Why can an electron occupy more than one position state, whereas you and I are manifestly localized in a single state? The answer to this question rests with the magnitude of Planck's constant, usually referred to as 'h'. This number is basic in quantum theory, as is the speed of light in relativity theory. If h were zero, we would not find particles in more than one state. But, even though quite small by standards of everyday life, h is not zero. And, it is the way of nature that particles must distribute themselves over a range of states such that for appropriate pairs of physical variables the product of two ranges is approximately h; in any event, no less than h. Thus, to cite the most celebrated example, the extension of a particle over different velocity states in some one direction, multiplied by the extension over position states in that same direction, must at least be equal to h. For an electron, say, this required multiplicity of states gives a behaviour, as noted, that is very different indeed from that of, say, a one kilogram mass. The required different states do exist, we believe, for the latter mass too; but they are so nearly identical, because of the smallness of h, we are not possibly able to distinguish one state from another. Also, because the kilogram mass is not a single particle but a lattice-work of many billion particles, we cannot coherently place it in a state in which the product of velocity and position ranges is so much greater than h that we detect a superposition of observably different states.

It is because the required different states are for conjugate pairs of physical quantities, as position and velocity , or time and energy, that we do not come to inconsistency. Nature shows herself in quantum physics to be by our judgements wonderfully ingenious in avoiding the traps that classical concepts lead us to formulate for the multi-state particle. Thus, we might say, if the interference behaviour of an electron requires that it go through both of two slits, let us observe it at the location of one of the slits; then we shall have directly shown the contradiction in asserting that it is in a superposition of two states, one for passing through each slit. In fact, we readily can arrange a detector at the slits, and it will show us the electron to pass through one and only one of them. But, the relation to h that we have mentioned for the product of position and velocity ranges will then require a large range of different velocity states for the particle, since in making the measurement of the electron at a given slit we have decreased the range of locations to a slit width. And, because it is in the different velocity states, the electron would no longer show the interference pattern which leads us to say that it passed through both slits. Many other physical situations could be cited in which physicists have looked for inconsistency; to date, they have always failed to find it, even in hypothetical "in principle" experiments.

Please let me now summarise what I have said about quantum physics. I have discussed material particles, but roughly similar statements apply to radiation. A particle does not subsist as an entity with a set of intrinsically defined dynamical properties. Rather, it is distributed over a superposition of different properties, and, in response to its environment the extent or range of superposed magnitudes for a given physical variable will change. Thus, a particle may be quite sharply localized by having it pass through a small opening. But that restriction will bring an increase in the range of superimposed velocity states of the particle; for, there is a natural minimum value for the combined ranges of certain conjugate pairs of variables, location and velocity being one of those pairs. This minimum value is given by Planck's constant h, and hence it sets the scale on which we find matter showing its superposition-of-state properties.

We are now ready for the key point. In our *direct observation* of a matter or radiation particle we do find it to be in but one state. An electron, for example, interacts with a detector screen to form a black spot at substantially a point region. Or, a proton, even though known to be in a superposition of velocity states, will in a direct measurement be found to manifest only one of those velocities. Our large-scale world is one in which physical systems have the single-state variables of classical physics. So, we have the obvious question: How does the micro-level particle make the transition from a superposition of different physical states to the single state in which it is observed? Or, to put the problem a bit differently, what determines which state of a particle is the one that becomes its physically observed state?

It is here that the oft-discussed element of chance enters into the quantum theory. As far as we know, there is no strictly determining factor in the selection of the observed state. For a given physical system, a probability function can be calculated for the expectation of finding the different values of a physical variable: the electron that has passed through a small opening toward a detecting film is more likely to strike the film at a point along its original line of motion than at a point a millimeter removed. But not all the mathematicians and computers in the world will enable one to do more than calculate a likelihood measure for its striking at a given point. *Only* by observing where it strikes can one ever know the location of that point on the screen.

The discovery of an essential indeterminacy in nature is a radical innovation of quantum physics, even though, we must remember, a substantial degreee of determinism still remains for the large-scale phenomena that present the observations on which classical physics was based. In a physical system that consists of many particles, as for the kilogram mass, the quantum-scale superposition effects tend to cancel out. Yet, it remains true that the non-determined individual atomic particle can have large scale effects, for much of biological process occurs at the microparticle level. Or, to take a more purely physical example, an apparatus can easily be contrived by which the motion of a large object–an electric locomotive, say–does or does not occur, depending on the chance event of whether an electron does or does not strike a given area of a detector surface.

We accept then, that there is a probablistic element in the passage from a superposition of physical states to some one single *observed* state. We still have the question, why does the passage occur? In reply, there are two things to be said. First, the single state appears in an observation and that involves a transfer of energy or momentum from the object system to the observer. Second, the transferred energy or momentum is a definite, natural amount associated with the object system in some one physical state; and, it is only such a definite *quantum* that can be transferred from object to observer. Hence, that restriction, to the transfer of a whole quantum, has the consequence that some one of the states of the superposition be selected as one that interacts with the observer's apparatus. Thus, the electron in giving up energy to a detector does so in a quantum at some one location, not in partial quanta from several locations. If nature were cntinuous in all its quantities, as presumed in the older physics, there would be no need for such a limitation on interaction possibilities. But it is not; and, in the words of Niels Bohr[9], " . . . the indivisibility of the quantum is itself, from the classical point of view, an irrational element which inevitably requires us to forego a causal mode of description . . . "

It is, then, in the interaction between object and observer that the individual micro-system, initially in a superposition of states, comes into a single (or approximately single) state, for the particular physical variable that is observed. Necessarily the object is then in a required superposition of states for the conjugate physical variable; and, with the observation there may, depending on the physical circumstances, be a development of a new superposition of states in the observed variable. All this will be in accordance with the required "at least as large as h" that we have discussed in quantum physics for the product of ranges of superpositions.

I have discussed the transition from a superposition to a single state for the interaction that is involved in an observation of a particle. But suppose the interaction that might have been observed actually occurs in the absence of the observer; suppose, for example, that an electron makes a spot at a given point on a detecting screen, but the spot is not observed until later, or, perhaps never at all. Has the reduction of state, from a superposition to a single location state, occurred even if not observed? The formal structure of quantum theory, and the dependence on observation for knowledge of the values taken by the physical variables of a particle, conspire to make it surprisingly difficult to answer this question within the theory. In recent decades some exotic answers have been proposed by physicists.[10] However, I shall not here consider the problem, but rather, will assume a traditional physical realism. This implies, I will take it, that interactions which result in bringing a system into a single state with respect to some physical variable are occurring throughout the universe, and not only in the relatively small domain of human-observation interaction.

III

Man and Natural Science

The natural world disclosed by quantum theory has a flexibility that was altogether lacking in the machine-like universe of classical physics. Particles like tiny billiard balls, self-determined in their physical properties and behaving in strictly causal patterns, have simply failed as hypothetical constructs; they do not allow the development of models that have nature's richness of process and structure. And, with the establishment of the new quantum physics there is, obviously, a notable change for the role of the observing scientist. Observation is of course a necessary element for all of the natural sciences. Further, even in classical physics the acts of observation may disturb the nature that is being described, as when the insertion of a thermometer slightly changes the temperature of the liquid that is being studied. Due regard may generally be taken, however, of that kind of disturbance. But quantum physics has shown us *natural properties that are defined only in the act of observation*. We ask, say, what is the direction of motion of an electron? It has emerged from a small opening, in a superposition of motional states, each with a different direction. Only through an interaction, such as is associated with an observation of the electron, will it take up a definite single velocity state.

148

We see that the scientist has become, in the words frequently used by Niels Bohr, an actor as well as a spectator in the drama of existence. Nature does not abide in a definite form, available for man to describe if he chooses. Nature takes its shape only with the occurrence of the interaction that is necessary if there is to be a description. Physics has here established a subjectivism that is, I believe, an epistemological innovation. It is not asserted that the physical system gains existence by virtue of the observer's awareness, as in Bishop Berkeley's *esse* is *percipii*; nor, is there an implication that man's own nature gives the content of experience, as for Locke's secondary qualities, or more completely as with Kant's transcendental aesthetic and categories of the understanding. Physicists do generally accept that the object system exists independently of the knower, before and after an observation; but, to repeat, the specific physical properties of a described object are generally determined–in their natural occurrence–only when they enter into the interaction that gives rise to the description of measurement.

It perhaps needs to be emphasized again that the explicit interaction-dependence obtains for individual particles, on the level where h is a factor of significant magnitude. The position of the Moon in the sky is not a consequence of our making a measurement. Nonetheless, a nature which is intrinsically dependent on the interacting scientist for important dynamical properties has given us a new partnership between man and nature. When the appearance of an electron as a localised particle in a spatial region depends on whether or not a particle detector is placed in that region, we do indeed have for the scientist a role of partially creating as well as observing the particle.

It may be objected that man is involved in but a tiny fraction of all the events of nature, and hence his influence cannot be so very great. In reply, one can point out that the altered role is in any event of paramount importance for man. He becomes a part of the ongoing processes of nature, exerting some effect upon them. In contrast, in the view of the older physics he was something of an anomaly: in a mysterious way able to describe and conceptualize nature but not essentially a part of the great inanimate machine. Further, the entity that we call an individual person interacts with a total nature that includes all the parts of his own body. We see that the possibility for more than one outcome of an interaction, because of the selection of one physical state from a superposition, gives rise to a capacity for flexibility and novelty in the behaviour of a human being. There is that possibility too, of course, in other biological organisms, and even

149

in some complex artefacts, but it seems to have been developed to a uniquely high degree in our species.

Inevitably, the question of the role of quantum-theory uncertainty in human free will now come close upon us. It should be readily granted that the establishment of a statistical, chance element in nature does not in itself in any significant way give an explanatory ground for freedom of choice, for, as has often been remarked, effectual choice requires causal reliability. But it is also true that the presence of chance in natural processes clearly does break the iron grip of determinism that was envisaged in pre-quantum physics. There is no basis now for regarding freedom of the will as illusory, with a denial of the sense of making a free choice that each of us has, at least in some circumstances.

I believe that we properly may see as relevant the interaction-reduction of a superposition to one of several different states. As already noted, we here have a plasticity, a capability for the novel and unpredictable, in the natural micro-processes. It therefore can appear reasonable that living organisms should be flexible in response to their inner and outer experiences; that they should, in a word, be able both to adapt and to innovate. At present we do not at all know how the distinctive quantum properties of matter are effective in psychic-physical relationships. But, given the basic characteristic of individual micro-particles, that specific properties are completely determined only in the interactions of physical process, we have at least a framework for understanding the responsiveness of sentient beings to alterations in experience.

On the scale of ordinary human dimensions we in fact see an approximately predictable pattern of biological behaviour. Thus, people seek food when they are hungry; they generally in their behaviour acknowledge physical hazards, such as falling from a cliff, or being burned by fire; youngsters come to an age when they have explicit sexual interests; and so on. But also, especially in traits that are distinctively human, behaviour clearly can be much less predictable. Thus, in the development of a person there seems to be a role for unpredictable inner factors. Here the concept of man in part creating the nature he studies lends an intelligibility quite lacking if the natural world is regarded as a domain independent of a man in its properties. For, using again the simile of a partnership between man and nature, we see the biological organism as forming itself in consequence of a conjunction: natural factors of inheritance and circumstance joined with contributions from the persisting and remembering individual biological entity. Man has been returned into physics, after an absence of several hundred years, because we have learned that in its detailed properties the natural world which he describes does not exist independently of his description. It follows, therefore, that we may now legitimately see man as naturally contributing to the creation of his own being, including his personality and his capacities.

IV

Theological Implications

In my opening comments, I elaborated upon Whitehead's proposal, that classical physics was made possible, in the form it took, by the late mediaeval theology. If that suggestion is correct, an identification of God with components of the cosmos, external to man, is not surprising. Certainly, such has often been the Christian way of conceiving of the divine reality: God not as within us but as an external force, extra-mundane except in the grace of sending his Son to us. This view may have been reinforced by developments in physical science. Thus, in the seventeenth century, Henry More, the Cambridge Platonist, proposed physical space as being the manifest indication that we have of God, and for Nicholas de Malebranche "space practically became God Himself".[11]

It is fair to say, I believe, that in the past hundred years there has been a shift in Western theology toward a conception that places God much more in man's direct experience than before. Also, in some current theology God is regarded as subject to alteration by man, and even dependent upon him. I shall quote a few statements that are indicative of this doctrinal change. William James, in lectures given at Manchester College, Oxford, in 1907, asserted that " . . . because God is not the absolute, but is himself a part when the system is conceived pluralistically, his functions can be taken as not wholly dissimilar to those of the other smaller parts–as similar to our functions consequently."[12] The theological views of A. N. Whitehead have been widely influential, and particularly, I judge, in their emphasis on the role of God as participant in ongoing processes everywhere in the universe. In his *Process and Reality* Whitehead writes, " . . . the doctrine of an aboriginal, eminently real, transcendent creator, at whose fiat the world came into being, and whose imposed will it obeys, is the fallacy which has infused tragedy into the histories of Christianity and of Mahometanism."[13] For, Whitehead asserts, God is "not *before* all creation, but *with* all creation."[14] He may be regarded as " . . . the principle of concretion–the principle whereby there is initiated a definite outcome from a situation otherwise riddled with ambiguity."[15] To a physicist the last statement seems almost to be referring to formation of a definite single state from a superposition, and I want later to comment on it. But I now give one more statement by a theologian, this time from Martin Buber. He writes in his *I and Thou* (which was published in 1922): "You know always in your heart that you need God more than anything ; but do you not know too that God needs you–in the fulness of his eternity needs you? How would man be, how would you be, if God did not need him [man], did not need you? . . . Creation happens to us, burns itself into us, recasts us in burning . . . We take part in creation, meet the Creator, reach out to Him, helpers and companions."[16]

It is not difficult to see–nor, I think, is it at all far-fetched to do so–that there is a parallel between the twentieth-century developments in physics and in theology. Quantum theory has taught us that on the atomic level, where indeed much of biological process does occur, including that of our own bodies, the description of nature involves the partial determination of its properties. Likewise, it is now acceptable for God to be seen not as separate and immutable, but in his nature involved in the natural world of change; and at least in the view of some, not without dependency upon man. The evidences of God, in contemporary theology, tend to be found in individual personal experience, rather than from the properties of the external natural world, as proposed, for example, by William Paley in the eighteenth century.

In accord, then, with a major theme of current theology, we can consider God to show his being in the significant, non-routine experiences of living. Particularly, we might for example see inspiration, resolve, insight, love, courage as divine aspects of experience. Our notable human properties, and perhaps especially those traits that we regard as ethically good, would then be somewhat in the domain of God, as traditionally they are in religious beliefs. Incidents of intense feelings, which frequently bear strongly on our attitudes, or on our entire life, could reasonably be accepted as unusually intimate experiences of God. And, indeed, if the divine being is defined for man by qualities such as those I have suggested there scarcely can be an atheist, since all tolerably normal people would have direct knowledge of the divine aspects of inner experience.[17]

If we accept that quantum physics requires that man does have a role in forming his or her own natural self, we may, further, consider that components of God, present in the natural world, are identical with formative factors in human behaviour. It is indubitable that quite as much as established patterns of biochemical change, for example, are present in human beings, so also are elements of desire, of evaluation, and of purpose. It is such elements that determine free choice of behaviour, and we have proposed that they are to be considered as part of the divine being. God is, then, in the material world, interwoven with other of its parts, such as inanimate atoms, and quite as existent and irremovable as they. Or, to express the association somewhat differently, we say that a person matures as an entity of the existing world, with an interplay between factors described by the regularities of natural science and those that contribute individual personhood and achievement. The latter are associated with God; and, in instances of unhappiness and human failure, perhaps to a degree with an inadequacy of divine component. The contribution of quantum theory to this theological suggestion is that it gives a physically valid scheme whereby we can envisage a person's natural being as formed in part as a response to his or her own decisions and activities. Because man plays a role in the formation of self, and because divine elements are present in him, he too participates in the becoming and being of God.

I would not think that it is theologically justified to limit the factors in nature that are regarded as divine to the members of our human species. For the other animals too, there are moments of intense emotion, factors of motivation and discipline, perhaps intrinsically good and bad behaviour. Recall our proposed identification of divine aspects of nature with distinctively personal behaviour or experience in human beings. It would be in keeping with that association to see notable conscious experience and behaviour everywhere in nature as manifestations of aspects of God.

However, considering the theological tradition, I believe that God as the proposed divine aspects of experience is hardly an altogether adequate concept. For, more is wanted from divinity than what is subjectively experienced in important and critical moments of life. Some reliance on God for understanding the whole universe is an essential element. It is noteworthy that another key theologian of our day, Paul Tillich, suggests that God is encountered primarily in human-problem situations, but does also give for him the basic defining property, the ground of all being. It has been my intent, however, to take note of the movement in theology toward a subjectively defined, man-dependent concept of God, and to suggest a summary definition of divine factors of experience, appropriate to that concept. It is not my purpose, and, indeed, is not at all within my competence, to propose a synthesis, or completion, whereby the God defined by subjective experience is validly extended to one who is warrantor for the cosmos. It perhaps is relevant, though, to point out that in physical theory we have virtually no linkage between overall, large-scale features of the universe and the properties that have been discerned by quantum physics. Possibly there is a comparable gap in theology, between guidance and emotion, given in individual personal experience, and God as ultimate cosmic being.

V

The Keystone of Quantum Physics

Can we say that theology had a non-trivial role in guiding physics to its new natural philosophy, required by the quantum theory, somewhat as scholastic philosophy was important in setting the foundation concepts of the classical Newtonian physics? Strictly, I think the answer must be "No". But if theology be broadened to philosophy, then I believe we can reply affirmatively: that metaphysical speculation did significantly contribute to the philosophy of quantum theory.

We might first consider the quoted passage from Whitehead, to the effect that God acts continuously to bring definiteness out of ambiguity. It is plausible to see Whitehead's statement as vividly in accord with novel results that appeared in physics at about the time he wrote it. At the least, a remarkable perception of deep currents of change in the philosophy of nature is indicated. But, the historical facts do not support a conjecture of influence by Whitehead on the developments in quantum physics contemporary with him. His own technical contributions to physical theory were in the general theory of relativity, some years earlier, and there is no record of interactions between him and the founders of quantum theory. In the mid- and later 1920's, when the climactic papers on quantum theory were being published, he was at Harvard, at the wrong Cambridge for hearing of the new developments at dinner conversations. He was immersed in philosophy at this time and, although he well knew the earlier quantum theory, there is no indication that he followed the revolutionary new literature. His conclusion, that there is a need for resolutions into single states in physical process–a need which he saw as supplied by God–is all the more remarkable for coming, it appears, from his general metaphysical considerations.

To understand how historically the radical new role of man came into twentieth-century physics we can better look directly to the physicists who formed it. I take the authority of Max Born[18] for the

154

statement that four men are pre-eminent among them: Einstein, Bohr, Heisenberg, and Dirac. (I would add, that others too, including Born himself, made invaluable essential contributions.) Of the four, it was Niels Bohr who both led the root change in natural philosophy, and who to a significant degree was philosophically trained and concerned. Einstein, somewhat like his master-physicist counterpart Isaac Newton, was philosophically conservative. Heisenberg in his writings shows a continuing awareness of Greek thought, but, although he might be said to have contributed the central insight in the way of technical physics, his was not the philosophical pioneering. Professor Dirac, as indicated in the quotation given earlier, clearly saw epistemological implications in the new theoretical developments, but at least in his writings, has not been concerned with stating a coherent new natural philosophy.

We return to Bohr. His role in forming the ideas of quantum physics is well stated by J. Robert Oppenheimer:[19] "Our understanding of . . . what we call the quantum theory of atomic systems, had its origins at the turn of the century and its great synthesis and resolutions in the nineteen-twenties. It was a heroic time. It was not the doing of any one man; it involved the collaboration of scores of scientists from many different lands, though from first to last the deeply creative and subtle and critical spirit of Niels Bohr guided, restrained, deepened, and finally transmuted the enterprise."

The key alteration needed to give quantum physics a coherent theory was the acceptance of a substantial role for the observer in the determination of natural entities, on the micro-level. Bohr led the world of physicists to this new basic tenet by virtue of his own persistent struggle with the problem of the relation between knowing subject and known object. From boyhood days he had a strong interest in philosophy, and as a university student at Copenhagen he was much influenced by Harald Høffding. In particular, the situation in which subject and object are apparently identical intrigued him, as when a person is concerned with his own thoughts. Here, a parallel to the situation that came to be manifest in quantum physics could especially benefit from Bohr's philosophical sophistication; I refer to physical measurements in which the observed object is also the carrier of the information, as may well be, say, for an electron or a photon.

In particular Bohr was impressed by the writings of Søren Kierkegaard, who had strongly influenced Høffding. It is not now appropriate to enter into an account of the influence of those two philosophers upon him. And I shall only mention the novel by Paul Møller, *Adventures of a Danish Student*, in which the problems of thinking about one's own thinking are semi-humourously treated. It is legendary that Bohr pressed this book upon physicists who worked with him at his Institute in Copenhagen. William James' *Principles of Psychology* also influenced his physical thinking, Bohr acknowledged, especially for its concern with the coupling of subject and object. Without his background of philosophical reading and thought, Bohr would surely not have made the carefully formulated statement, as he did, that the situation in quantum mechanics "bears a deep-going analogy to the general difficulty in the formation of human ideas, inherent in the distinction between subject and object."[20] For a careful study of the philosophical influences on Bohr I refer you to the book, *The Conceptual Foundations of Quantum Mechanics*, by Max Jammer. In his detailed discussion Jammer is concerned with, to use his words, ideas that for Bohr "contributed to the creation of a philosophical climate which facilitated the surrender of classical conceptions."[21]

I would like to suggest that taking a broader perspective we may see the involvement of epistemological idealism in nineteenth-century thought as a preparation for the discovering of an intrinsic role for man in the microphysical processes he describes. The idealistic epistemology begins, of course, with the philosophy of Immanuel Kant. With him we have a proposal, in a detailed, technical manner, for a contribution of the knowing person or scientist to the properties of the natural world. As I have stated, the mode of subjective determination was for Kant far different from that eventually established by physicists, but nonetheless his critical philosophy discloses a novel possibility for the source of even the primary properties of nature. By the early twentieth century that possibility had been extensively explored, and had become a vital part of Western philosophic thought. But physics remained strikingly apart from any subjectivist epistemology until the work of Bohr. His mind philosophically prepared, he saw that experimental and theoretical features of quantum physics implied that observation itself contributes to what until then had been regarded as purely objective properties of matter.

VI

Concluding Remarks
A juxtaposition of first ideas of physics and theology has given support to a point of view expressed, for example, by Philip Hefner: "that all human perceiving and thinking–whether scientific, artistic,

philosophical or theological–are of a piece, cut from the same cloth."[22]
It is obvious that theology has learned from physics, but I think my
presentation argues too that physicists need philosopher-theologians
for the long-run validity of their science. Physics is highly partial,
constrained to a set of aspects which although universal are also but a
fragment of nature; hence, it requires fresh insights from those who
attend to a wider set of experiences.

Certainly, mankind needs more for its guidance than physics, or
broadly speaking, more than the natural sciences, for which physics is
the foundation. It is that fact, I take it, which leads to our now
discussing twentieth-century theology and science, rather than,
perhaps, having only a history of theology to discuss, with no contributions having been made, as some expected, after the time of the
philosophes. We need more than physics because, again to quote
Professor Hefner, religion is concerned with how human beings are to
live optimally in the world;[23] and, it is evident enough that science is
not adequately telling us how that may be done.

We can expect that both science and theology will be maximally
effective when they can harmoniously re-enforce each other. It is now
acceptable for us to regard the making of a human being as within the
scope of natural processes, even with respect to factors of personality
and character. And, we can then come into accord with traditions of
God's immanence by making an identification, as is often done in
theology, between divine influence and human decision or achiev-
ment. Religion, then, has a focus on a particular aspect of the natural
world, but, likewise, nature is elevated by virtue of being seen as
possessing the possibilities for the best elements of human life. One
specific practical application of this point of view can be in opposing
spoliation and pollution of the natural world. The consequences of
man's exploiting nature, as if it were a domain apart from his own
being, do in any event nowadays give obvious reason for such an
opposition. The move toward living in harmony with nature gains
strength, however, from our understanding how much we are
altogether a part of it, even to sharing in its creation.

I have already stated that there does not appear today to be a
consonance between theology and physical cosmology, comparable to
the parallel development of subjectivist emphasis in religious thinking
and in micro-physics. Arthur Peacocke, for one, has shown that
Christian concepts do readily accommodate results in contemporary
astrophysical cosmology.[24] But, it does not seem to me that there is in
theology any kind of new theme that can be set along with what is
currently a golden age of discovery with respect to the physical

cosmos.

Returning to the similar importance for the human conscious response that we do find in physics and theology, I would like in conclusion to make a comment on the problem of the personhood of God. In a recent book[25] Richard Swinburne has found that among the properties usually ascribed to God in the Judeo-Christian-Islamic tradition the one of questionable coherence is that of being a person: of having the individuality, and continuity of identity, that we ordinarily associate with a person. Now, we have seen that the individual micro-particle gains its manifest value with respect to a physical variable only in an interaction; that is, physical definition of its personhood, so to speak, arises only in the course of physical process. Carrying this same motif from the level of inanimate nature, we envisage that human beings—constituted by the inanimate atoms—are also determined in thought and behaviour by processes of interaction and growth. At all levels of complexity, nature defines individual entities by induced passage to concrete actuality from potentiality (or, superposition, in quantum theory). One solution to the problem of God's individual *persona* is that he is manifested to varying degrees in the concrete, defined entities continually arising in nature. Some of these, as when they are human persons, have both relatively long continuity and relatively high individuality. We would say, then, that the divine aspects of nature are especially notable in human beings, with their manifestations of personality as contrasted with, say, individual atoms.

A conception of God as making his presence in nature's concrete events and organized families of events has the defect, we note again, that it does not give a coherent cosmic dimension for the divine being. Further, with that conception the personhood of God becomes multifaceted indeed, arising as it does in many persons, as that term is customarily understood. However, in any case we should hardly expect that the ordinary notion of person will be suitable for the being of God. A definition of God, even though involving a strong alteration of the usual concept of person, would gain merit if it were formed in accordance with basic concepts of natural philosophy. For, surely we do want the propositions of theology to have a foundation in human experience, including that which is encoded in natural science.

We have seen that there is historical precedent for theology actually giving guidance to science, probably because theology both makes conjecture that goes beyond the domain of science and is a human response to experience not normally considered in science at a given state of its development. This fact, I think, should give encourage-

RICHARD SCHLEGEL

ment to theology; in an age when science is so highly regarded, any activity that contributes to it is in the royal favour. But, conversely, I think the scientist, noting the inadequacies of science as a total philosophy and as a source of practical wisdom, should be eager to assist the theologian in what is a more difficult but also more critically important endeavour. I would like to think that the theological emphasis today on human experience, and the ineradicable role that physics finds for man, are unifying factors for a fruitful collaboration–between, let us say, a nature-respectful theology and a somewhat humbled we-do-not-know-it-all science.

REFERENCES AND NOTES

1. See, *e.g.*, Johnson, P., *A History of Christianity* (New York, Atheneum, 1977), pp. 374–80
2. Laplace, P. S. de, *A Philosophical Essay on Probabilities* (1796), trans. Truscott, F. W. and Emory, F. L. (New York, Dover Publications, 1951), p. 4.
3. Whitehead, A. N., *Science and the Modern World* (New York, Macmillan, 1931), pp. 17–18.
4. Taylor, H. O., *The Mediaeval Mind* (London, Macmillan, 1938), vol. II, p. 478.
5. *Summa Theologica*, Sec. 95, Reply Obj. I, quoted in Hartshorne, C. and Reese, W. L. *Philosophers Speak of God* (Univ. of Chicago Press, 1953), p. 120
6. In a summary statement, Hartshorne and Reese write: In the orthodox view, "God is altogether immutable, absolute, wholly independent, and incapable of receiving any good from his creatures". (Ref. 5, p. 351).
7. See, *e.g.*, "Evidences of Superposition", Chap. II in Schlegel, R. *Superposition and Interaction* (Univ. of Chicago Press, 1980).
8. Dirac, P. A. M., *The Principles of Quantum Mechanics*, 3rd ed. (Oxford Univ. Press, 1947), p. 12.
9. Bohr, N., *Atomic Theory and the Description of Nature* (New York, Cambridge University Press, 1934), p. 10.
10. I give a survey and discussion in Ref. 7, Chaps. VII and VIII.
11. Burtt, E. A., *The Metaphysical Foundations of Modern Science* (London, Routledge and Kegan Paul, 1932), p. 140. My assertion about More is also from Burtt's book, p. 137 *et seq.*
12. James, W., *A Pluralistic Universe*, Lecture VIII (Conclusions).
13. Whitehead, A. N., *Process and Reality* (New York, Macmillan, 1929), p. 519
14. Ref. 13, p. 521
15. Ref. 13, p. 523.
16. Buber, M., *I and Thou*, quoted in Hartshorne and Reese, Ref. 5, pp. 304–305.
17. I have discussed the point of view of this paragraph in a paper, "Quantum Physics and the Divine Postulate", *Zygon*, *14*, (1979) 163.
18. Born, M., *My Life: Recollections of a Nobel Laureate* (New York, Scribner's, 1978), p. 234.
19. Oppenheimer, J. R., *Science and the Common Understanding* (New York, Simon and Schuster, 1954), p. 37.
20. Bohr, N., Ref. 9, p. 91.
21. Jammer, M., *The Conceptual Foundations of Quantum Mechanics* (New York, McGraw-Hill, 1966), p. 173. Also, see the discussion by Gerald Holton in his

Thematic Origins of Scientific Thought (Harvard Univ. Press, 1973), pp.133-142; and, Leon Rosenfeld's essay in *Niels Bohr*, ed. Rozental, S. (New York, Wiley, 1967), p.121.

22. Hefner, P., "Christian Assumptions about the Cosmos", in *Cosmology, History and Theology*, ed. Yourgrau, W. and Breck, A. D. (New York and London, Plenum, 1977), p. 349
23. Ref. 22, p. 350.
24. Peacocke, A., "Cosmos and Creation", in *Cosmology, History, and Theology* Ref. 22.
25. Swinburne, R., *The Coherence of Theism* (Oxford, Oxford Univ. Press, 1977).

Part III

EPISTEMOLOGICAL ISSUES

Chapter 8

WHAT DOES IT MEAN TO SAY THE TRUTH?

Rubem A. Alves
Universidade Estadual de Campinas, Brazil

"On a cursory view of the present work it may seem that its results are merely *negative*, warning us that we must never venture with speculative reason beyond the limits of experience. Such is, in fact, its primary use. But such teaching at once acquires a *positive* value when we recognise that the principles with which speculative reason ventures out beyond its proper limits do not in effect *extend* the employment of reason, but, as we find on closer scrutiny, inevitably *narrow* it. The principles properly belong — not to reason but — to sensibility, and when thus employed they threaten to make the bounds of sensibility coextensive with the real, and so to suplant reason in its pure (practical) employment." *I. Kant.*

I

The ideal of truth
The great ideal which has inspired philosophy and science is the ideal of truth. Even the sceptics never denied it. They simply believed that it cannot be reached. The centrality of the epistemological debate in our tradition, regardless of our presuppositions and conclusions, is a sure indication of the fact that the ideal of truth is the great regulative horizon for our endeavours. Philosophy and science are not after "edification", as Hegel pointed out. They are after reality, no matter how un-edifying it might appear.

Only a few deviants had the courage to question the ideal of truth.[1] But since they were deviants, their visions remained outside the main stream of our tradition and they were often branded with the stygma or "irrationalism".

I wish to take the side of the deviants. It is my conviction that a totalitarian employment of the concept of truth, as defined by the rules of science, has made it impossible for us to understand *action* and the *expressive* discourses which it creates. Science and action are two different games, and the rules of the former must not be applied to the latter. My hypothesis is that, within the limits of scientific language, the meaning of truth is determined by a *contemplative posture*. Contemplation intends towards the *given*; it looks for entities and structures which are actual, already present before the subject. Expressive discourses like religion, ideologies, utopias, poetry, and dreams, on the contrary, emerge out of the context of action. In action, however, as opposed to contemplation, the subject intends towards the *possible*. Given objects and structures are not the end of its search. These elements are here taken as mere *raw materials* to be used in the construction of realities not yet in existence. The ideal of scientific truth, therefore, is not and cannot be the tribunal which judges action and the expressive discourses which it creates. In this context, scientific truth is *instrumental*. Take a plastic artist as an example. He must have objective knowledge of the materials with which he works. This knowledge, however, is impotent to determine the shape which the work of art is to take. Just as we cannot use the truth about raw materials as an ideal for art, we cannot use the concept of truth, as defined by scientific discourse, as a criterion for our judgement of expressive discourses.

Let us explore this hypothesis.

II

The "silent agreements" behind the concept of truth.
What do we mean when we say "truth"? We know that meanings are not inherent in words. Meaning depends on a number of "silent agreements" which lie hidden behind articulated discourse.[2] Truth is one word among others. Its meaning, therefore, depends also on the "silent agreements" of the discourse within which it appears. What are these "silent agreements" which remain unspoken but which, out of the darkness of their silence, control our meaning-giving activity?

Our quest takes us back to the origins of Greek philosophy. Even at its first founding and groping moments we already find in it a basic problem which will determine its development: nature, as it is given immediately to our sense-perception, has the mark of fluidity and transitoriness. Nothing is repeated. It flows endlessly like a river. But amid fluidity and transitoriness, we find not chaos and disorder, as would be expected, but rather order and law. Under the visible face of phenomena, the thinking mind was able to detect the invisible operation of a *logos* which has to be postulated as that "x" which explains our sense-perceptions. When the philosopher raised the ontological question "what is?" he was, indeed, asking about this "x". On the one hand, he was formulating the programme of his work: this "x" must be found. On the other hand, he was stating an ideal for the philosophical discourse: philosophy is not called to describe the fleeting, visible face of things. Philosophy must speak about reality. It must articulate, through its discourse, the invisible foundation of things.

"What is?" The ontological question affirms silently that reality is objectively given. It is "out there", to be discovered. Philosophers are not called to *create* anything but simply to *contemplate*. A human subject can do nothing to transform, abolish or recreate the *logos*. But he can understand it. Greek tragedy is the artistic expression of this silent agreement. It describes man in revolt against reality (fate) and, nevertheless, doomed beforehand to be defeated. Tragic is the confrontation between the man who fights against "what is", the opposition between the psychological and the ontological, the conflict between the particular and the universal. The tragic hero struggles in vain; the philosopher contemplates and understands calmly. It is in this context that the meaning of truth emerges, as the conformity between the spoken word, the discourse, and the ontological, the hidden structure of laws which exhibit eternal necessity.

Greek philosophy was unable to develop its programme down to its ultimate consequences. The philosophers knew that sense-perceptions are shadows of reality but not reality itself. But they lacked a method to translate their insight into discourse. If, to use Kant's suggestive analogy, the philosopher must not behave as "a pupil who listens to everything that the teacher chooses to say, but as an appointed judge, who compels the witness to answer questions which he has himself formulated",[3] we could say that the Greek philosophers knew that the witness was withholding informations, but they did not know which methods to use in order to force it to reveal the truth.

Modern science transformed this insight into realization. It learned, with Galileo, that true answers were not given because questions were not correctly asked. Nature speaks the language of mathematics. Mathematics became the "open Sesame" which unlocked the doors to the hidden chambers of reality where eternal laws abide. Laws are to modern science what the ontological was to the ancient Greeks. What are laws if not the permanent behind the fleeting?

For science to speak the truth about reality, therefore, it must depart from the common, unreflected language which refers to phenomena in their given immediacy. Indeed, "scientific truth is always a paradox, if judged by everyday experience, which catches only the delusive appearance of all things".[4] There is a gap between appearance and reality. "All science would be superfluous if the appearance, the form, and the nature of things were totally identical."[5] I believe that all scientists will agree with these two statements. They were made by Karl Marx. I quoted him on purpose. His world seems to be far removed from the world of natural sciences and even from other types of social sciences. Indeed, many believe that marxism is no science at all. Marx is a heretic. And if inquisitors and the heretic, in spite of all disagreements, agree on this matter, we may have an idea of how deeply ingrained this ideal of knowledge is. Their silent agreements are the same. Their common credo states that (a) there is a gap between the visible and the invisible; (b) the purpose of science is the contemplation of the invisible which alone deserves the name of reality; and (c) scientific discourse, as a consequence, is not concerned with the visible but with reality. Scientific truth, therefore, is not satisfied with statements of the type "snow is white" or "an A-bomb was dropped in Hiroshima". This is not the kind of truth science is after. Science wants to construct statements which give, to intellectual intuition, the picture of that system of laws which is at the foundation of perception. This system alone deserves the name of reality. Everything else is contingent and fleeting.

I know that some will object that my description of science, as dominated by a contemplative attitude, does not do justice to the practice of science. Contemplation might have been central to Greek philosophers, but modern scientists are committed to experimentation. Without experimentation, no science. And what is experimentation if not a form of action?

But, let me ask: is experimentation the end-product of science? If I am not mistaken, both inductivists and deductivists agree that the function of experimentation is either to produce or to test statements about reality, statements which say what the world is like. These statements only, and not experimentation, are the goal of science. Indeed, experimentation is possible only in the context of theories and hypothesis. The function of scientific statements is to provide an *in-sight*, a vision, no matter how precarious and provisional it might be, of the hidden structure of reality. Experimentation thus, is subordinated to contemplation.

III

The battle against imagination

As you know, the meaning of a word is determined by the way it is used. [6] How has the regulative ideal of truth been used? Does it appear only in the context of the epistemological discourse? Has its use had any other implications which go beyond the limits of the epistemological debate?

Suppose that scientists had recognised science as one game among other possible games. For one to play a game at least two things must be known:

(a) The *purpose* of the game.

(b) The *rules* which have to be obeyed, if the purpose is to be achieved.

The purpose of the scientific game is *truth*: a discourse which reflects the given laws of reality.

Its rules are made up of all methodological procedures which control the construction of the true discourse.

When one speaks about rules, however, one implies silently a number of possible procedures which are forbidden. One cannot move any piece of chess as if it were checkers; one is not supposed to touch the ball with one's hand, if one is playing soccer. In the game of science, likewise, there is a number of cards which cannot be used. A scientist is fobidden from using in the game of science any words or concepts which emerged out of the context of action. These words and concepts, to the degree that they are *expressive* of the subject's creative intention, are charged with emotional elements. They are *subjective*. But science wants to be objective: it is committed to the object only. For one to play the game of truth one must be value-free. A scientist is not called to speak but rather to allow reality to speak through his discourse. His role is that of an *interpreter*, and not that of someone who utters an original statement. The scientist, as an *empirical subject*, must be absent from his discourse. Scientific discourse is universal and this universality, this freedom from the particularity of the subject, this commitment to laws, is what makes possible the process of inter-subjective testing of statements. The silent agreement behind the inter-subjective testing of statments and the demand for objectivity is, therefore, that the subject must be absent from the discourse, since the discourse must be totally taken up by the object.

For the game of science to be played, therefore, a radical *assepsy* of the discourse is required. Everything which bears the mark of the empirical subject must be eliminated. Emotions, desires and values must be gotten rid of, just like a surgeon aseptically cleans his field, before operating. Much of the discussions about epistemology, indeed, deal with the problem of the pathology of discourse: it becomes incapable of telling the truth when it is infected by subjectivity.

Thus, Bacon proposed his theory of idols. Idols are the illusions of subjectivity which make impossible the knowledge of the object.

Thus, all secondary qualities were eliminated from scientific discourse. Odours, sounds, tactile impressions, colours — they are all subjective translations of data and, as such, express how the subject react to objects. For this very reason, they vary from individual to individual, from occasion to occasion and lack the elements of universality and necessity which belong to laws.

Thus, psychoanalysis classified our common discourse in the archives of neurosis, as being determined by desire and love, in opposition to scientific discourse, which is the only one to reflect truth, since it has submitted itself to the reality principle.

Thus, in marxism, ideology is clearly distinguished from science. Ideology is a discourse which expresses our social disorder, and as such is devoid of any epistemological significance.

Thus, in philosophy of science, the context of discovery of theories has been equally dismissed as being void of cognitive significance, since it contains nothing but the accidental psychological and social conditions within which a discovery was made. It points to the subject and not to the object, and can therefore, be totally forgotten with no harm being done to knowledge itself.

Is the scientific ideal of truth a mere statement of the programme of the game of science, a game among others? When one assumes that truth is to be found only in a discourse which reflects the object as a mirror, does not one silently agree also that all other forms of discourse are false? If science had understood itself as one game among others, it could simply say of other forms of discourse that they belong to other kinds of games. And it is likely that some sophisticated philosophers of science will say that this is, indeed, the case. But we must ask if this has been the actual *use* of the ideal of truth. It seems, on the contrary, that science has been fighting a battle against all other forms of discourse, not as discourses which belong to other games, but as either false on meaningless. If this is the case, we are drawn to the conclusion that the ideal of truth has not been used only within the epistemological debate about the rules of the game of science. On the contrary, the ideal of truth has been part of a totalitarian therapeutic and political programme for all discourses.

"When we run over our libraries, persuaded of these principles, what havoc must we make? If we take in our hands any volume — of divinity or school metaphysics, for instance — let us ask, 'Does it contain any abstract reasoning concerning quantity or number? No. Does it contain any experimental reasoning concerning matters of fact and experience? No. Commit it then to the flames, for it can contain nothing but sophistry and illusion.'"[7]

A clear division is made between two types of discourse. One of them is constructed according to the rules of science. It contains knowledge. All other kinds of discourses are "sophistry and illusion". Society is thus divided between two groups; those who know (they receive the name of experts today) and those who do not. It is not necessary to explore the political implication of this social distribution of knowledge, present in the regulative ideal of truth.

Karl Popper has similar feelings about the way words like "nonsensical" and "meaningless" have been used. "If by the words "nonsensical' or 'meaningless' we wish to express no more, by definition, than 'not belonging to empirical science', then the characterization of metaphysics [as other sorts of non-scientific discourses] as meaningless non-sense would be trivial; for metaphysics has usually been defined as non-empirical. But, of course, the positivists believe that they can say much more about metaphysics than that some of its statements are non-empirical. The words 'meaningless' as 'nonsensical' convey, and are meant to convey, a derogatory evaluation; and there is no doubt that what the positivists really want to achieve is not so much a successful demarcation, as the final overthrow and the annihilation of metaphysics."[8]

Popper's point, if I am not mistaken, is that beyond the immediate purpose of clarifying the rules of the scientific game, one finds here the totalitarian assumption that all other games must be abolished, since they do not make sense. Science has not understood itself as one game among others but rather as the only legitimate employment of language. In science there is truth or, in a more modest version of the same ideal, the criteria for the detection of error. Otherwise, there is only sophistry and illusion, non-sense and meaninglessness. Non-scientific discourses, therefore, do not deserve to survive. I question, therefore, the often praised openness of scientific discourse. This is indeed true, when small bits of knowledge are at stake. But it is not true, however, when it speaks about itself. The moves of the game may be questioned. Just as one questions the wisdom of a certain move in chess. But the game itself, is never questioned.

169

It is curious to notice that the therapeutic and political programme we just mentioned even became a respectable philosophy of history. As you know, the main stream of XIXth century philosophy looked at history as an *educational* process through which mankind was being cured of its madness. Primitive, childish, expressive thought, was being left behind. Darkness and irrationality were being exorcized by the light of science. The idea that science is a game among others, one possible way, among others, of coming to terms with reality, never passed in the heads of the advocates of this philosophy of history. The expansion of science implied the shrinking of the expressive discourses. This is the reason why, according to their view, religion was doomed to extinction.

IV

Truth and action

The meaning of concepts can be clarified by means of a simple heuristic device: take the concept and explore ideally its consequences to its utmost limits. By this means it is possible to bring to light hidden implications which would have remained in a kind of dormant state, if left unexplored. Let us play with the concept of truth.

Let us imagine this ideal being fully realized. Let us imagine that consciousness has been cured of its madness and is no longer disturbed by images and symbols expressive of desires. Let us imagine a transparent consciousness which sees nothing but the given reality.

If the ideal of truth is realized historically, we are entitled to believe that, from this moment on, behaviour will no longer be irrational. It will be expressive of truth. Indeed, there is no other option, since reality fills all the spaces of consciousness. Phantasies and illusions are gone. What shape would behaviour take if it is informed by truth, nothing but the truth?

Rebellion against reality, the essence of neurosis and the twin brother of imagination, according to Freud, will be over. Devoid of any symbols which open the doors to the imaginary world, we would be totally adjusted to the given. As Prescott Lecky remarks, under these circumstances "the normal person, presumably, would find fault with nothing and accept everything".[9]

Ours would be a situation similar to that of a chess player. The options open to action would be those of shifting the pieces of reality around, according to the dominant rules of the game. "We would no longer have either a future in the historical sense or temporality as we

170

know it", says Henry Lefebvre. "We would enter into a kind of eternal present, which is likely to be very monotonous and boring." The new future would be the future of "machines, of combinations, arrangements and permutations of the given elements". "The only novelties would be the introduction of new techniques ... unless the deviants [those who are not yet dominated by reality and truth] who, by the way, would be harassed with wild cruelty [they would be defined as either sick people or subversive], intervene in order to disrupt the system".[10]

Karl Mannheim is a scientist who got very disturbed by this prospect. He was convinced that freedom as well as all turning-points where qualitative changes occured in our historical development, are unthinkable without the element of utopian imagination. The utopian discourse is far removed from scientific discourse, since it is expressive of sufferings, desires, aspirations and longings. Its symbols, indeed, do not describe that which is empirically given, as social reality. The utopian mentality intends towards a social order which does not exist in any place. Nevertheless, according to Mannheim, this utopian element is of basic importance, if qualitative changes are to be brought about in history. It is with deep concern, therefore, that he sees that the utopian mentality is living its last moments.

> "It is possible, therefore, that in the future, in a world where nothing new happens, when each moment will be the repetition of the past, a new condition will emerge in which thought will be totally purged from ideological and utopian elements. The total elimination of all reality-transcending elements will issue into an 'objectivism' which, in the last instance, implies the decomposition of human will. The disappearance of utopias bring with itself a state of stagnation, in which man himself will become a thing. We would be, then, before the greatest imaginable paradox: man, after reaching the highest degree of rational control of existence, no longer has any ideal and, as a consequence, becomes a simple plaything of impulses. ... With the relinquishment of utopias man will lose the will to shape history and, with it, the ability to understand it."[11]

The triumph of truth will be sterile. Cured from the madness of imagination and subjectivity, the man who speaks only the truth, will become totally integrated in the system of the given, be it nature, be it society.

Had science adopted Kant's modesty, evident in the short paragraph at the beginning of this paper, our prospect would be different.

Kant's point is that scientific knowledge is strictly limited by the very rules of the game of science. Science is not contemplation of reality face to face. It has no metaphysical competence. If one extends unduly the application of science, in a totalitarian fashion, so as to cover the whole of reality, action will suffer. This is, precisely, my point. Truth, as a valid regulative ideal of the game of science, cannot be the tribunal which judges action and the discourses which belong to it. If the ideal of truth is used as an overall therapeutic and political programme, action, as we know it, will vanish. Action moves according to different rules than those of contemplation. Scientific cognition aims at seeing and stating the hidden laws of the given. Action aims at creating different structures, not yet in existence. The rules of a game are not valid for another. And since our problem has to do with the relationships between science and religion, I will advance the crucial question: *"Where does the religious discourse belong? To the game of science or to the game of action?"*

V

The truth of action

My hypothesis is that the religious discourse belongs to the context of action. We cannot understand its meaning if we interpret it with the help of the rules which test the truth of scientific knowledge.

What are the silent agreements behind action?

My answer to this question is, to a great degree, influenced by Uexküll, Goldstein, Merleau-Ponty, Cassirer and Nietzsche.[12] Since the limits of this paper do not allow me to go into details, I ask you to keep their thought in mind, as I attempt to summarize the main points of my position.

I would like to quote a short paragraph taken from Cassirer's *An Essay on Man*, in which he presents a summary of Uexküll's perspective for the interpretation of animal behaviour:

> "It would be a very naive sort of dogmatism to assume that there exists an absolute reality of things which is the same for all living beings. Reality is not a unique and homogenous thing; it is immensely diversified, having as many different schemes and patterns as there are different organisms. Every organism is, so to speak, a monadic being. It has a world of its own because it has an experience of its own. In a world of a fly we find only 'fly-things'; in the world of a sea urchin we find only 'sea-urchin-things'."[13]

If Uexküll is right, it becomes obvious that the problem of objective truth is totally foreign to an animal. Behaviour is determined by vital demands and, as a consequence, its cognitive explorations can never be neutral. An organism can know reality only as it has a vital meaning for itself.

Is this true of animals only? "We need to recognize", says Dewey, "that the ordinary consciousness of the ordinary man left to himself is a creature of desires rather than of intellectual study, inquiry or speculation. Man ceases to be primarily actuated by hopes and fears, loves and hates, only when he is subjected to a discipline which is foreign to human nature, which is, from the stand point of natural man, artificial." "If we are willing to take the word dreams with a certain liberality", he adds, "it is hardly too much to say that man, save in his occasional times of actual work and struggle, lives in a world of dreams that is organized about desires whose success and frustration form its stuff."[14]

Kant's categorial structures are here displaced by the living structure. This living structure, the organism itself, is the hypothesis with the help of which the environment is organized and known. We do not find here anything which resembles contemplation. Organisms are after functional relationships. Behaviour, thus, finds its truth when it succeeds in establishing functional relationships with its environment. This functional circle (Uexküll: Funktionskreis) is the only reality that an animal can know.

Much before Uexküll, Feuerbach had a similar insight. In the epistemological discussions which are found in ¶1 of chapter I of *The Essence of Christianity* he develops a similar understanding of knowledge. We never know objects in themselves, but always objects as they are related to ourselves. There are as many realities as there are vital centres which organize the mass of raw materials at hand. "The life of an ephemera," he says, "is extraordinarily short in comparison with that of longer-lived creatures; but nevertheless, for the ephemera, this short life is as long as a life of years to others. The leaf on which the caterpillar lives is for it a world, and infinite space." "If plants had eyes, taste, and judgement, each plant would declare its own flower the most beautiful; for its comprehension, its taste, would reach no farther than its natural power of production."[15] Every organism is its own Absolute. Thus, when we look at the immense variety of living forms, we may conclude that *reality is an orchestra which can play many different melodies*. In each and every organism, reality takes on a specific form: behaviour actualizes one of its many possibilities which remained dormant and hidden under the cold eyes of contemplation.

Are we proposing a retreat back into subjectivism? Back to inwardness? Back to emotions? The cartesian dualism forces us into dilemmas which are far removed from reality. The very survival of organisms for millenia — and its likely that they will survive man and his science — should make us aware of the fact that they are in close contact with reality. Otherwise, how could they have survived? The fact that action is not based in objective, value-free knowledge, does not mean that it is divorced from knowledge, being thus irrational, but rather that it is based on a different kind of knowledge, a knowledge which probes reality not in terms of its mathematical and formal properties, but in terms of its vital significance and promise. Indeed, it is the repression of life and its demands, implicit in science's option for formalism and objectivism, which is, to a great degree, responsible for our problems. Indeed, within the strict rules of the scientific game, there is never room for the question: is this bit of knowledge conducive to life? Science does not ask vital questions. It is after formal and abstract relations. Instead of dismissing knowledge, as it is concretely given in the experience of life·and action, as tainted with particularity and emotions, science should rather learn from the wisdom of life itself, in order to regenerate itself.

We cannot understand human behaviour according to the patterns of animal behaviour without further ado. There is a gap between man and animals. But the analogy might prove fruitful. Maybe the difference between man and animals is to be found in the fact that whereas each animal species is prisoner of its own melody, man is able to compose new ones. This, indeed, is Merleau-Ponty's suggestion: "what defines man is not the capacity to create a second nature — economic, social or cultural — beyond biological nature; it is rather the capacity of going beyond created structures in order to create others".[16] Behaviour, therefore, is never quiet acquiescence in the given. It is an active shaping and reshaping of the raw materials at hand, in order to create a new reality, a human reality. Reality, in its immediate givenness, is a formless mass of materials which have not yet become a home. Truth, therefore, is never the pure description of this mass. It lacks the marks of humanity. Nature must humanized. The humanization of nature, however, is not a fact like stones and stars. Neither is it the system of laws which explain stones and stars. The humanization of nature is a *task* which becomes reality only through the mediation of action. This is the reason why, from the perspective of behaviour, truth is not a given which antecedes it, but rather the result which follows it. In this context truth takes on a clear ethical meaning. Truth is not to be found in contemplation of the given but in one's commitment to the possible. Truth is something to which one commits one's own life. I quote Camus:

> "I have never seen anyone die for the ontological argument. Galileo, who held a scientific truth of great importance, abjured it with the greatest ease as soon as it endangered his life. In a certain sense, he did right. That truth was not worth the stake. Whether the earth or the sun revolves around the other is a matter of profound indifference. To tell the truth, it is a futile question. On the other hand, I see many people die because they judge that life is not worth living. I see others paradoxically getting killed for ideas or illusions that give them a reason for living."[17]

The capacity of going beyond created structures in order to create new ones implies also the capacity to *negate* the given. But negation is an indication that *body* and *environment* are in conflict. It should be noticed that the human body is not the organism, in its immediacy. Man has enveloped its organism with symbols and values. This is the reason why it can be said that whereas an animal *is* its organism, man *has* his organism.[18] Man is the only animal which can negate its organism, for the sake of values. He is free to commit suicide. We, thus, speak about the human *body* and not about the human organism.

It is in the conflict between body and environment that *desire* exists. Desire is the immediate awareness, on the part of the body, that something is lacking in its environment. Desire is a symptom of absense. One does not long for the now: one longs for bygone or future periods of time. One does not long for the present beloved person; one longs for those who are away. If consciousness were totally objective, longing would be impossible, as it would be impossible to plan the recovery of the lost presence. Expressive symbols, which grow out of desire, are confessions of an absence, negations of the real as it is immediately given, and statements of purpose for action: the absent must become present. Devoid of these symbols, no purposeful and intelligent action could ever happen. We would be condemned to a sort of random activity, in which behavioural reactions follow a trial and error pattern, with no direction, in the hope that somehow, someday, one will hit the jackpot.

Intelligent and purposeful action, thus requires symbols which represent the absent, the possible, the desirable. But these were exactly the symbols which were the target of science's aseptic and therapeutic programme! Truth and objectivity demanded their elimi-

175

nation. Does this mean that action is doomed to be irrational and opposed to science? Not at all. Action is opposed to science to the extent that science expands its rules in a totalitarian fashion. When this happens, science becomes metaphysics and establishes the rules for all meaningful discourses.

From the perspective of action *science is the exploration of raw materials*. Its purpose is the knowledge and control of entities at hand. When one extracts a metaphysics from science one silently declares that reality exhausts itself on the level of raw materials. Action cannot believe this. Its basic hypothesis is that there are many possible worlds which have not yet become actual. When we define truth according to the rules of the game of science and apply it to all possible discourses we silently agree that action and creativity do not belong to reality. From the standpoint of action science has no metaphysical competence. It does not exhaust the meaning of the world because, given its rules, the world is meaningless.[19] But scientific reason has a place because it is one of the intstruments of creativity. As Nietzsche put it poetically:

> "The body is a great reason ... An instrument of your body is also your little reason, my brother, which you call 'spirit' — a little instrument — and a toy of your great reason."[20]

In the context of action science and scientific truth must be understood as hierarchically subordinated to and instrumental of the purposes of action.

We have come to a point where we must correct something which was said before. I affirmed that science is determined by a contemplative posture: value-freedom, truth for its own sake. Indeed, this is what science has said of itself. But this is nothing but a piece of self-deception. As Werner Stark remarks, "value-free thinking may be an ideal, but it is certainly nowhere a reality."[21] Even our science grows out of a certain system of action. Why has science grown and expanded the way it did? Sheer accident? Have we become more committed to knowledge? Is science being subsidized by governments and corporations because they love truth? Or is it because it is functional? Is not science the cognitive organ of certain specific demands for action? As Max Scheler has pointed out, our science is totally incomprehensible if it is not understood as an organ of a new and specific kind of will to power, will to manipulate, will to control.[22] The scientist, from within the ivory tower of his theories and experiments says to himself: "Truth! This is what I am after! This is what I am discovering!" What he ignores is that his is a very specific kind of truth, a truth which is functional to a very specific and concrete system of action — one system of action among many other possible ones.

> Things become clear by means of images.
> An organist sits at an organ he has never seen before.

He looks, examines, probes, tests. He knows that his performance will depend on the range of possibilities which are objectively given. He proceeds like a scientist. He also asks: "What is?". But then he stops and starts playing. The "thus it is" becomes now an instrument of the "thus I will it to be". The object is transformed into an instrument of will. A new reality emerges. The world becomes different. There was nothing, absolutely nothing, in the object at hand, the organ, which would allow one to deduce the form of the melody. A symphony cannot be deduced from an orchestra. The orchestra is the condition of the possibility of the symphony. But a symphony *is* not the orchestra.

> What is reality?
> The organ?
> The music?

When science attempts to give an account of reality by reducing it to its basic elements, it proceeds as if the reality of the symphony were the instruments of the orchestra. Action is accidental. It might have been otherwise. Just like the music: a dream of the human mind, fleeting. It does not pass the test of the ontological question.

The artist, on the other hand, will say: "Reality? It is the music. The organ is nothing but a "little instrument and a toy" of my creative activity. Creation is my final truth."

VI

The locus of the religious discourse
Where are we to locate the religious discourse? Where does it belong? What is its purpose and function? Contemplation and objective cognition? Or is it an expression of desire and a programme for action?

Suppose that we accept the scientific ideal of truth as valid for all forms of discourse. What are the alternatives left for our understanding of religion?

Alternative one: we could classify religion as a pathology of knowledge and isolate it in the asylum of meaningless statements. In this case religion has nothing to say.

Alternative two: we could try to find a place for God in the gaps of the universe constructed by scientific discourse.

"There was a "Big-Bang"! The Universe had a beginning! We may still speak about "Creation" without contradicting science. We have found the First Cause, the Unmoved Mover again."

"Heisenberg's universe has an element of indeterminism right at its deepest foundation. May be this indeterminism is the secret door through which divine freedom sneaks into the world."

"Can the marvellous element of purpose and adaptation present in life be explained by pure chance? Can we understand it if we stick to a mechanical view of reality? Does not this kind of explanation require too much faith, more faith than the simple postulation of purpose and intelligence as presiding over the evolutionary process?"

I must confess that these issues fascinate me. But, no matter how hard we try, they remain scientific questions. They have nothing to do with religious experience. To quote Paul Tillich, to be religious is to be "ultimately concerned" about the meaning of life. Now, there is nothing in this "X" which was present at the Big-Bang, which sneaks into the world through the gates of indeterminacy, which presides over evolution, which corresponds to one's ultimate concern. As Feuerbach indicated, "religion is the solemn unveiling of a *man's* hidden treasures, the revelation of *his* intimate thoughts, the open confession of *his* love secrets".[23] In what way is this "X" related to this religious experience? It remains as another scientific hypothesis. And, as Kierkegaard indicated, there is nothing given in objective knowledge which can be the object of one's infinite passion.

We are left with empty hands. Religion is either reduced to nonsense or assimilated into science. But the God of science is not the God of religious experience; it might be the result of a logical necessity, but it is not a symbol which expresses man's love secrets.

The other possibility which remains open is to locate religious discourse in the context of action. In this case the symbol God expresses our sense of an absence. God is a symbol which is a protest against reality as it is. In Paul's words, it is uttered by a creation which groans in travail, in the hope of a transforming event, redemption. In this case God appears as the highest project of action, as the horizon towards which we move.

You could object that this God could be nothing more than an illusion. You might be right. Indeed, in religion, as it is given empirically, we find not one God, but myriads of gods, gods who cannot be brought into harmony, except by the process of philosophical abstraction which robs them from any vital meaning. Gods are vital hypotheses. They are symptoms of an immense variety of life projects. And one cannot ask of them: "Which one is true?" Just as you cannot ask: "Which is the true organism, the butterfly or the elephant?" The religious discourse is part of our body. And the question which one can ask of the body is this: "Which, of the immense variety of its possible forms, is most conducive to survival and happiness?"

Kant's Copernican revolution was a shift from the object to the subject. His subject, however, was universal and formal, free from emotions and desires and even unconcerned about happiness. This subject, however, does not exist anywhere. It is a product of a process of abstraction whereby our cognitive functions are cut off from any relationships with life.

I am proposing that we start from man as body, as ultimately concerned about life and happiness. Religion, in this anthropological context, is man's bet, his act of faith as to the possibilities which can be actualized through action, out of the mass of raw materials at hand. One can no longer ask of the religious discourse: "Is it true?" Would you ask this question of your own body? For action to take place, a belief in the possibility of the not yet born is necessary. The problem of religion, therefore, is not posed by action, since creative action pressuposes it. As Nietzsche put it beautifully:

> "This, indeed, is bitterness for my bowels, that I can endure you neither naked nor clothed, you men of today. All that is uncanny in the future and all that has ever made fugitive birds shudder is surely more comfortable than your 'reality'. For thus you speak: 'Real we are entirely, and without belief or superstition. (. . .) Your are sterile: that is what you lack faith. *But whoever had to create also had his prophetic dreams and astral signs, and faith in faith.*"[24]

We are destined to religion. We may opt for one God or another. But we do not have the option to live without gods. Very often our gods get old and die. But they die because new gods are being born. It does not matter if they no longer wear the sacred robes of former times. Indeed, today, to a great degree, our gods have become secularized. They present themselves under new masks which make them

179

more plausible to the modern world-view. No matter how modern and secularized they have become, however, we find always in them the expression of the "cor inquietum", the restless heart which longs for a world capable of being loved. As Durkheim once affirmed, "there is something eternal in religion which is destined to survive all the particular symbols in which religious thought has successively enveloped itself."[25] But this religion, far from being a hypothesis as to the scientific foundation of the universe, is rather man's bet as to the possibility of transforming the mass of raw materials at hand in a world expressive of love and desire. This is the only truth to which man is after, the truth which is at the service of happiness. As the philosophers of former times used to suggest God is the horizon of the quest for the "summum bonum", implicit in man's action.

REFERENCES AND NOTES

1. Among the deviants we find Soren Kierkegaard. See: his *Concluding Unscientific Postscript* (Princeton, Princeton University Press, 1968), chapter II: "The Subjective Truth, Inwardness; Truth is Subjectivity". Also: Friedrich Nietzsche, *Thus Spoke Zarathustra*, in *The Portable Nietzsche* (New York, The Viking Press, 1965), pp. 233-235, "On Immaculate Perception"; Albert Camus, *The Myth of Sisyphus* (New York, Random House, 1955), pp. 3-4, where he states that the meaning of life and not truth is the basic philosophical problem.
2. Wittgenstein, L., *Tractatus Logico-Philosophicus*, § 4.002.
3. Kant, E., *Critique of Pure Reason* (New York, The Modern Library, 1958), p. 14.
4. Marx, K., *Value, Price and Profit* (1865), p. 37. Cf. Selsam, H. and Martel, H., *Reader in Marxist Philosophy* (New York, International Publishers, 1963), p. 138.
5. Marx, K., *Capital*, vol III (1894), p. 951.
6. Wittgenstein, L., *Philosophical Investigations* (New York, The Macmillan Co., 1968), p. 20, §: "the meaning of a word is its use in the language".
7. Hume, D., *An Inquiry Concerning Human Understanding* (New York, The Liberal Arts Press, 1957), p. 173.
8. Popper, K., *The Logic of Scientific Discovery* (New York, Harper & Row, 1968), pp. 35-36.
9. Lecky, P., *Self-Consistency: A Theory of Personality* (Garden City, Doubleday & Co., 1969), p. 123.
10. Lefebvre, H., "Reflexões sobre o Estruturalismo e a História", in *O Método Estruturalista* (Rio de Janeiro, Zahar, 1967), p. 89.
11. Mannheim, K., *Ideologia e Utopia* Rio de Janeiro, Editora Globo, 1954), p. 244.
12. Uexküll, J. von, *Theoretische Biologie* (2nd ed. Berlin, 1938) and *Umwelt und Innenwelt der Tiere* (1909, 2nd ed. Berlin, 1921); Goldstein, K., *The Organism* (Boston, Beacon Press, 1963); Merleau-Ponty, M., *The Structure of Behaviour* (Boston, Beacon Press, 1968); Cassirer, E., *An Essay of Man* (Toronto, New York, London, Bantam Books, 1979).
13. Cassirer *op. cit.*, p. 25.
14. John Dewey, *Reconstruction in Philosophy* (Boston, The Beacon Press, 1962), pp. 5-6, 7.

15. Ludwig Feuerbach, *The Essence of Christianity* (New York, Harper & Row, 1957), p.8.
16. Merleau-Ponty, *op. cit.*, p. 175.
17. Albert Camus, *op. cit.*, pp. 3-4.
18. Peter Berger & Thomas Luckmann, *The Social Construction of Reality* (Garden City, NY, Doubleday & Co., 1967), p. 50.
19. Max Weber, " 'Objectivity' in Social Science and Social Policy", in Maurice Natanson (ed.), *Philosophy of the Social Sciences: a Reader* (New York, Random House, 1963), p. 363: "The fate of an epoch which has eaten of the tree of knowledge is that it must know that we cannot learn the *meaning* of the world from the results of its analysis, be it ever so perfect; it must rather be in a position to create this meaning itself."
20. Walter Kaufmann, *The Portable Nietzsche* (New York, The Viking Press, 1965), p. 146.
21. Werner Stark, *The Sociology of Knowledge* (London, Routledge & Kegan Paul, 1967), p. 71.
22. Werner Stark, *The Sociology of Knowledge* (London, Routledge & Kegan Paul, 1967), pp. 115-116: "It was not 'pure reason', not 'the spirit in itself' which at the inception of the modern age sketched out the tremendous programme of a comprehensive mechanistic explanation of nature and man, long before its implementation in physics, chemistry, biology, psychology, sociology, etc., but the new will to power over nature ..."
23. L. Feuerbach, *op. cit.*, 13.
24. Walter Kaufmann, *op. cit.*, p. 232.
25. Emile Durkheim, *The Elementary Forms of the Religious Life* (New York, The Free Press, 1969), p. 474.

Chapter 9

THE EVIDENTIAL VALUE OF RELIGIOUS EXPERIENCE[1]

Richard Swinburne
Department of Philosophy, University of Keele, U.K.

I

I believe that arguments for the existence of God are best regarded as inductive arguments. The various phenomena which they cite – the existence of the Universe, its conformity to order etc., support or confirm the existence of God, but they do not make it certain. However, taken together, the various arguments form a strong case for the existence of God.[2] I seek in this paper to investigate one such argument, the argument from religious experience. Or rather, somewhat more generally, I seek to investigate the evidential value of religious experience in showing that there is a God or any other supernatural reality. Many and varied experiences have been called "religious experiences", but for the purpose of my investigation I shall understand by a religious experience one which seems to the subject to be an awareness or perception of God, or some other supernatural reality, and in saying this I use the word "seems" in what Chisholm calls the epistemic use.

Chisholm's distinction between the epistemic and comparative use of such verbs as "seems", "looks", "appears", etc. is of importance for me, and so I had best set it out at the beginning[3] To use such words in their epistemic use is to describe what the subject is inclined to believe on the basis of his sensory experience. If I say "the ship appears to be moving" I am saying that I am inclined to believe that the ship is moving, and that it is my present sensory experience which inclines me to hold this belief. If I am using "looks" in this way when I say "the penny looks circular", I am saying that I am inclined to believe that it is circular, and that my inclination to hold this belief arises from my visual experience. By contrast to use "looks" etc. in the comparative use is to compare the way an object looks with the way other objects normally look. In this use "the penny looks elliptical" Means "the penny looks the way elliptical things normally look".

The speaker is not saying and does not imply that he believes or is inclined to believe that the penny is elliptical; he may know very well that it is not. Again, in the comparative use "from here it looks red" means "from here, it looks the way red things normally look". When I describe an experience in terms of the way things seem (epistemically) to the subject, I shall say that I describe it epistemically.

So then on my definition what makes an experience a religious experience is the way it seems (epistemically) to the subject. What is it for the subject to be right, in fact to perceive God (believing that he is so doing)? It seems to me, for reasons which others have given at length, that the casual theory of perception is correct – that S perceives x (believing that he is so doing[4]) if and only if the experience of it seeming to S that x is present was caused by x[5]. So S has an experience of God if and only if it seeming to him that God is present is in fact caused by God.

One often perceives one thing in perceiving something else. In seeing a man dressed in such and such a way I may see John Smith. In seeing the print of such and such a shape in the sand I may see the footprint of a bear. In seeing an especially bright star in the sky I may see Venus near to the Earth. In these cases my very same visual or other sensations (described comparatively) which bring about my perceiving the first thing also bring about my perceiving the second thing. In perceiving the second thing one does not see anything extra in the sense of a new item which had escaped one's notice before; rather one perceives the first thing as the second thing. In these cases one man may perceive both things, and another man perceive only the first thing and yet both have the same visual sensations. This relation which holds between perceptions may also hold between experiences described epistemically. In seeming (epistemically) to see the man dressed in such and such a way I may seem to see John Smith. In such cases the same sensations (described comparatively) which bring about the first experience also bring about the second. Or two men may both have the same visual or other sensations (e.g. a bright spot in the middle of their visual fields) and through having those sensations one may have a certain experience described epistemically (e.g. seeming to see a lighthouse in the distance) and the other may not. Or of course the same visual or other sensations may give rise to totally different experiences (described epistemically) in different men.

With these points in mind, it will be useful to classify the different kinds of religious experience. In due course I shall make similar points about all of them, but it is worth while at this stage pointing out the diversity of experiences which fall under our definition. First, we have experiences which seem (epistemically) to the subject to be experiences of God or something else supernatural, but where he seems to perceive the supernatural object in perceiving a perfectly ordinary non-religious object. Thus a man may look at the night sky, and suddenly "see it as" God's handiwork. Secondly there are the experiences which men have in perceiving a very unusual public object.Take the appearance of the risen Jesus to the disciples as described in Luke 24, *v* 36–49. A man looking and talking like Jesus who had been crucified three days earlier suddenly turned up among them and eat some fish (looking and talking the way that Jesus used to look and talk.)Yet in perceiving this public event, the disciples had the religious experience of taking the man to be the risen Jesus Christ. Their religious experience was that he looked like Jesus in the epistemic sense, and so they believed him to be. A sceptic might have had the same visual sensations (described comparatively) and yet not had the religious experience.

The other three classes of religious experiences are ones which do not involve taking public phenomena religiously. In the third place we have cases where the subject has a religious experience in having certain sensations private to himself, sensations of a kind describable by the normal vocabulary used for describing the sensations which result from the use of our five senses. In his dream described in Matthew 1.20f. Joseph dreamed that he saw an angel who said to him certain things. Here there were no public phenomena, but Joseph had certain private sensations which he might have been able to describe by means of normal sensory vocabulary–e.g. he had the visual sensations like the sensation which he would have had if he had been looking at a man dressed in white, and the auditory sensations which he would have had if someone had been saying such and such to him. (He might have been able to tell us the actual words which the man in the dream seemed to be saying to him.) What made the dream a religious experience was that in having the sensations , and after he had woken up, it seemed to Joseph that an angel was talking to him, i.e. he took the man-in-the-dream to be a real angel and not a mere angel-in-a-dream, and the words-in-the-dream to be words uttered by the angel.

Fourthly we have the case where the subject has a religious experience in having certain sensations private to himself, yet these are not of a kind describable by normal vocabulary. The subject has some sensation analogous to sensations of normal kinds, e.g. visual or auditory sensations, but only analogous –such that if his experience was of a public phenomenon we might say that it was the experience of a sixth sense. Presumably mystics and others who find it difficult if not impossible to describe their religious experiences, and yet feel that there is something to be described if only they had the words to do the describing, are having experiences of this kind. Fifthly and finally we have religious experiences which the subject does not have by having sensations. It seems to the subject, perhaps very strongly, that he is aware of God or of a timeless reality or some such thing, and yet not because he is having certain sensations; it just so seems to him, but not through his having sensations. Just as it may seem to me strongly that my hand behind my back is facing upward rather than downward, yet not because of any sensations. Many mystics who claim to experience God via "nothingness" or "darkness" may be making the point that their experience of God is not mediated via any sensations. More ordinary cases however also fall into this category. A man may be convinced that God is telling him to do so-and-so, and yet there may be no auditory or other sensations occurring.

There is no doubt at all that very many men down the centuries have had religious experiences of one or more of the above kinds. Indeed that statement rather underplays the situation. For many people life is one vast religious experience. Many people view all the events of their life not merely under their ordinary description but as God's handiwork. For many people, that is, very many of the public phenomena of life are viewed religiously and so constitute religious experiences of the first type. What seems to one man as simply a wet day is seen by another as God's reminder to us of his bounty in constantly providing us with food by means of his watering plants. What seems to one man as merely a severe illness is seen by another as God's punishment for the sins of his youth. That God is at work is no inference for these men but what seems (epistemically) to be happening. As well as such experiences of the first kind, very many men, both those who are much of the time religious believers and those who are not, have had many religious experiences of the other kinds. The question must now be faced as to the evidential value of all this. Is the fact that all these experiences have occurred evidence for the existence of God (or some other supernatural reality)?

II

In discussing religious experience philosophers have sometimes made the claim that an experience is evidence for nothing beyond itself, and that therefore religious experience has no evidential value. That

185

remark reflects a philosophical attitude that those philosophers would not adopt when discussing experiences of any other kind. Quite obviously having the experience of (apparently) seeing a table is good evidence for supposing that there is a table there. Having the experience of (apparently) hearing my lecture is good evidence for supposing that I am lecturing. So generally, contrary to the original philosophical claim, I suggest that it is a principle of rationality that (in the absence of special considerations, if it seems (epistemically) to a subject that an object x is present, then probably x is present. What one seems to perceive is probably there. How things seem to be is good grounds for a belief about how things are. From this it would follow that, in the absence of special considerations, all religious experiences ought to be taken by their subjects as genuine, and hence as substantial grounds for belief in the existence of their apparent object–God, or Ultimate Reality, or Poseidon.[6] This principle, which I shall call the Principle of Credulity, and the conclusion from it seems to me correct. It seems to me, and I hope to my listeners, intuitively right in most ordinary cases such as those to which I have just been referring, to take the way things seem to be as the way they are. I shall now argue that attempts to restrict the principle in ways which would rule out its application to religious experience are quite unjustified. I shall consider two such attempts to argue that while it appearing to me that I am perceiving tables, chairs, houses, etc. is good grounds for supposing that I am, it appearing to me that I am perceiving God's handiwork or angels or Ultimate Reality is not good grounds for supposing that I am.

The first argument is that our supposing that the way things seem is the way they are is not an ultimate principle of rationality, but itself requires inductive justification (i.e. justification in terms of past experience) and that that inductive justification is available in the ordinary cases but not in the religious cases. More particularly, a philosopher may claim that the fact that it appears that something is x is good grounds for supposing that it is x only if we have evidence that when in the past it has appeared that things are x, they have proved so to be; or at any rate the supposition that they are x has proved a successful assumption to work from. Hence, the philosopher might argue, it is all right to take what looks like a table as a table, because our past experience has shown that such appearances are not misleading; but he might go on to question whether we had the kind of inductive evidence which was necessary to justify taking religious experiences seriously.

A major difficulty with the view of the first argument is that its suggested principle clearly needs modification to deal with cases where the subject has no past experience of x's but does have experience of properties in terms of which 'x' is defined. Thus a centaur is defined as a being with the head, trunk and arms of a man, and the body and legs of a horse. A subject has seen men and horses but not centaurs before. It then appears to him that a centaur is present. Is that good reason to suppose that it is? Surely yes. So the principle behind the first argument had better be modified to read: the fact that it appears that x is present is good grounds for supposing x is present only if we have evidence that when in the past it has appeared that x or any property by which x is defined is present they have proved so to be, or at any rate the assumptions that they were present proved successful assumptions to work from. But then the argument is quite inadequate to rule out taking religious experiences seriously. For "God", like "centaur", is defined in terms of properties of which most of us have had experience. He is defined (in a wide sense of the term) as a "person"[7] without a "body" who is unlimited in his "power", "knowledge", and "freedom", and in terms of other similar properties, of all of which we have had mundane experience. A man might well, through visual, auditory, tactual, etc experience of recognizing persons of various degrees of power, knowledge and freedom be able to recognize when he was in the presence of a person of unlimited power, knowledge, and freedom. Indeed it is plausible to suppose that a man might be able to recognize extreme degrees of these qualities, even if he could not so easily recognize lesser degrees straight off without inductive justification.[8] So once the inevitable modification is made to the first argument, whatever its merits, it has no force against the claims of religious experience.

The second attempt to restrict the application of the principle of credulity, allows that the principle holds in ordinary cases (without needing inductive justification) but denies that (in the absence of inductive justification) it holds in less usual cases. One writer who has thus restricted the principle is Chisholm. He claims that whenever we take something to have a certain characteristic (or relation) we have adequate evidence for the claim that it does have this characteristic (or relation); but that whenever we take something to have some non-sensible characteristic (or relation), that is not in itself adequate evidence to suppose that it does. And what are these "sensible characteristics and relations? Chisholm writes:

> The characteristics include being blue, red, green, or yellow; being hard, soft, rough, smooth, heavy, light, hot, or cold; and that of

sounding, or making-a-noise. The relations include; being the same, or different with respect to any of the characteristics in question; being more like one object than another with respect to any of the characteristics, or with respect to hue, saturation, and brightness, or with respect to loudness, pitch, and timbre. The class of characteristics and relations also includes the "common sensibles" – that is, "movement, rest, number, figure, magnitude" – as well as what is intended by such terms as "above", "below", "right", "left", "near", "far", "next", "before". "after", "simultaneous", and "to last", or "to endure". In short, the characteristics and relations in question are coextensive with what Aristotelians have traditionally referred to as the "proper objects of sense" and the "common sensibles" and what Reid described as the objects of "original" perception.[9]

So, according to Chisholm, if something seems (epistemically) to you to be brown or square or solid, that is good grounds in itself for believing that it is. But if something seems to you to be a table, or a Victorian table, or a ship, or a Russian ship, that is in itself not good grounds for believing that it is. You need further justification for these beliefs. Thus you would be justified in believing that something was a Victorian table if it seemed to have a certain shape, colour, and mass, and you had past experience of the testimony of witnesses that things like that were made in Victorian times. (The "testimony of witnesses" might need to be spelled out in terms of noises uttered by objects.)

Let us say that if it seeming that an object is *x* is grounds for supposing that is without need for further justification then you have an *experience* of *x*. But if this does not hold, then it seeming that an object is *x* is an *interpretation* of your experience which stands in need of further justification. If you have an experience of *x* and in fact *x* causes your experience, then you *really perceive x*; if you conclude that *x* is present without experiencing *x*, you merely *infer x*. Attempts to draw such lines as Chisholm draws between experience and interpretation, real perception and mere inference are of course as old as the empiricist tradition in philosophy.

That there is such a line to be drawn is a common and seldom argued assumption in many discussions of religious experience. Once the line is drawn, the consequences are evident. For the line always leaves the typical objects of religious experience as matters of interpretation rather than as true objects of experience. It follows that even if it seems to you strongly that you are talking to God or gazing at Ultimate Reality, this fact is no reason in itself for supposing that you are. You are having an experience which is properly to be described in a much more mundane way –e.g. as the experience of hearing certain noises – which you *interpret* as the voice of God but which you have no good reason for so doing unless further evidence is produced.

However, no such line as the one which Chisholm attempts to draw, can be drawn between experience and interpretation. For clearly we are justified in holding many perceptual beliefs about objects having non-sensible characteristics which cannot be backed up in terms of beliefs about objects having "sensible" characteristics. Few would doubt that I am justified in believing that a certain woman is my wife. Yet if asked what it is about the woman I take to be my wife which makes me believe that she is my wife, I would be utterly unable to give a satisfactory answer. I could only give a very vague description of the Chisholmian "sensible" characteristics by which I recognize her, a description which would fit tens of thousands of other women whom I would not for one moment mistake for my wife. That one can recognize does not entail that one can describe, or that knows what the features are by which one recognizes. I may be justified in claiming that you are tired or angry, just by looking at your face, and yet be unable to say what it is about your face which makes you look tired or angry. Again, I can recognize my wife's voice over the telephone although I certainly cannot say what it is about the noises which come through the telephone receiver which are especially characteristic of her voice. For senses such as smell and taste most of us have no vocabulary for describing sensible characteristics. Asked about the liquid we are drinking, "What is it about it that makes it taste like tea?", we would be stuck for an answer. But that fact casts no doubt on our justification for believing that we are drinking a cup of tea. The fact that it tastes like tea is good reason in itself for supposing that it is – whether or not we can say in more primitve terms what it is about it which makes it taste like tea.

Men differ in the kinds of objects and properties which they learn to pick out. Sometimes they can describe the "sensible characteristics" of those objects and sometimes they cannot; and even if they can, the recognition of objects of some kind and their more sophisticated properties may be a more natural process that the description of their sensible characteristics. There is no reason of principle why we should not grow so adept at spotting Russian ships, or Victorian tables, or blue-dwarf stars or elliptical galaxies that we can recognize them straight off, without being able to say what it is in way of Chisholmian sensible characteristics about what we see which makes us identify them as we do.

So this second argument against the original principle of credulity fails, and the principle stands. If it seems (epistemically) to S that x is present, that is good reason for S to believe that it is so, in the absence of special considerations – whatever x may be. And it is some reason too for someone else too whom S reports his experience to hold the same belief. For the fact that someone tells you that he thinks that he has perceived so-and-so is always some reason for you to believe that he has (in the absence of special considerations either for supposing that he is attempting to deceive you, or for supposing that he is himself mistaken. Considerations relevant to the latter are considered below. Considerations relevant to the former are the normal considerations which tend to show that a witness is or is not honest.) From all this of course it follows that if it seems to me that I have a glimpse of Nirvana, or a vision of God, that is good grounds for me to suppose that I do. And, more generally, the occurrence of religious experiences is prima facie reason for all to believe in that of which the experience was purportedly an experience.

III

However, all perceptual claims are defeasible. It is time to list the special considerations which operate in particular cases and give to a man or to others grounds for holding that although his experience was that it seemed to him that x was present (and so he is inclined to claim that x was present), really x was not present. Having listed these, we can then see whether they will normally be able to show that religious experiences are not to be taken at their face value.

There are basically four kinds of special consideration which defeat perceptual claims. The first two show that the apparent perception was of a kind with others which proved in the past not to be genuine perceptions. First one may show that the apparent perception was made under conditions or by a subject found in the past to be unreliable. Thus one may show that S's perceptual claims are generally false, or that perceptual claims are generally false when made under the influence of LSD, which is good inductive grounds for believing that a particular new perceptual claim made by S or made under the influence of LSD is false. Secondly one may show that the perceptual claim was to have perceived an object of a certain kind in circumstances where similar perceptual claims have proved false. Thus if S claims to have read ordinary-size print at a distance of a hundred yards, we can test him on a number of other ocassions and see if he reports correctly what is written at that distance; and if he does not we have good inductive evidence that the original claim was false.

The third and fourth considerations are ones concerned with the particular perceptual claim which do not involve inductive inference from the failure of similar claims. Since to perceive x is to have one's experience caused by x, one can challenge a perceptual claim to have perceived x either by showing that very probably x was not there or by showing that x very probably did not cause the experience. The third consideration then which defeats a claim to have perceived x involves showing that very probably x was not there.

I stress the word 'very'. We often think that we perceive what is a priori improbable, and are right on the basis of our apparent perception to judge that we do. It may seem to me, when I go to London, that I see Jones walking along the other side of Charing Cross Road. I may believe a priori that it is more probable than not that he is in Dover where he lives; and that even if he is in London, the odds are against his being in Charing Cross Road at that particular moment. But my experience suffices to outweigh this background evidence. We would indeed be imprisoned within the circle of our existing beliefs, if experience did not normally have this force. However background evidence may make it *very* improbable that x is present – e.g. because it makes it very improbable that x exists at all, or very probable that he is somewhere else. If it is very probable on background evidence that John is dead, then it is very very improbable that he is walking along the other side of Charing Cross Road at this moment; and my experience does not by itself suffice to push the latter into the category of the probable.

There are various ways in which it can be shown that very probably x was not present. One may show that x does not exist, or was in some other particular place at the time, or show that very probably x was not at the place in question more directly, in particular by showing that other observers who were rightly positioned with the right sense-organs and concepts did not perceive x. If I claim to have seen John in the corridor, my claim may be defeated by showing that although there were many others in the corridor with eyes functioning correctly, who were looking out for John and knew what he looked like and so would have been expected to see him if he had been there, they did not have similar apparent perceptions. Such a demonstration will only be conclusive if it can be proved that the other observers were attentive (i. e. would have perceived John, had he been there) and there will always be some doubt about how attentive observers are. But clearly the more observers rightly positioned with the right sense-organs and concepts who fail to observe x, the less likely it is that x was there. But if some other such observers have an apparent perception of x, that makes it very likely that x was there.

Fourthly, the claim to have perceived x may be challenged on the grounds that whether or not x was there, x was very probably not the cause of the experience of it seeming to me that x was there. One obvious way in which this can be done (without casting any doubt on other of my perceptual claims) is by showing that (very probably) something else caused my experience. We challenge the claim by producing a casual explanation of why it seemed to me that x was there, which does not involve x at any stage. If you show me the actor who was dressed up to look like John and who walked down the corridor, I realize that the experience of it seeming to me that I had seen John was probably caused by the actor, and so that I have no grounds for believing that John was in the corridor.

How far are these challenges available to defeat the claims of those who claim to have experienced God? The first challenge may defeat a few such claims, but is hardly generally available. Most religious experiences are had by men who normally make reliable perceptual claims, and have not recently taken drugs. The second challenge would consist in showing that normally religious perceptual claims were unreliable. If there was a good proof of the non-existence of God or anything similar, then of course that could be done. But the point here is that the onus of proof is on the atheist; if he cannot make his case the claim of religious experience stands. It might be thought that there was a general proof of the unreliability of the claims of religious experience in the fact that so many of them conflict with each other. "Religious experiences are enormously varied, ostensibly authenticating innumerable beliefs many of which are in contradiction with one another . . . The varieties of religious experience include not only those which their subjects are inclined to interpret as visions of the Blessed Virgin or senses of the guiding presence of Jesus Christ, but also others more outlandish presenting themselves as manifestations of Quetzalcoatl or Osiris, or Dionysus or Shiva".[10] Now of course devotees of different religions describe their religious experiences in the religious vocabulary with which they are familiar. In itself this does not mean that their different descriptions are in conflict – God may be known under different names to different cultures (as both Old and New Testaments acknowledge – see Exodus 6.2f. and Acts 17.23). Likewise a Greek's claim to have talked to Poseidon is not necessarily in conflict with a Jew's claim to have to talked to the angel who watches over the sea; it is so only if to admit the existence of Poseidon is to commit one to a whole theology, and there is no need to suppose that generally it is.

Admittedly, sometimes the giving of one description to the object of religious experience does carry commitment to a doctrine regarded as false by devotees of another religion. Claiming to have experienced the heavenly Christ commits one to a belief in a Incarnation which an orthodox Jew would not admit. But in these cases if the opponent of the doctrine can produce good grounds for regarding it as false, that is reason for the subject of the experience withdrawing his original claim. Among those grounds may be that the others have had conflicting experiences and that their experiences are more numerous and better authenticated; but there may be grounds of other kinds as well. The subject of the religious experience need not in such a case withdraw his original claim totally; he need only describe it in a less committed way – e.g. claim to have been aware of some supernatural being, not necessarily Dionysus (as originally claimed). The fact that sometimes (and by no means as frequently as Flew suggests) descriptions of the object of a religious experience are in conflict with descriptions of the object of another religious experience, only means that we have a source of challenge to a particular detailed claim, not a source of scepticism about all the claims of religious experience. Babylonian astronomers reported the movements of holes in the firmament; Greek astronomers reported the movements of physical bodies in the heavens. The conflict between their descriptions of what the specs of light in the sky really were meant that the perceptual claims of each group constituted arguments against the perceptual claims of the other group and further arguments were needed to adjudicate between them. Eventually the Babylonian astronomers had to admit that they had somewhat misdescribed what they saw. But this process need hardly lead to general scepticism about astronomical observation; nor need the similar process in religion. Nevertheless, it must be admitted that if there were a substantial number of religious experiences which entailed the non-existence of God, that would cast significant doubt on the credibility of claims to have perceived him. These might be, for example, religious experiences apparently of an omniponent Devil.

The third challenge to a claim of religious experience would consist in a demonstration that, very probably, God was not present to be perceived, and so the subject could not have perceived him. But if there is a God, he is everywhere. He is only not present if he does not exist. So to use this challenge, you have to prove that it is very improbable that there is a God, and, as stated above, the onus is on the atheist. It will not do to argue that some people do not have religious

193

experiences. For maybe they are spiritually blind. Only if you could first show that all persons with certain equipment and concepts would perceive God, if God were there to be perceived, would the failure of such a person to perceive God count against his existence. In any case plenty of people do have similar religious experiences corroborating each other.

The fourth challenge would consist in showing that the religious experience had a cause other than God. Now it is not enough to show that a man's upbringing or his taking drugs were necessary for him to have the experience. For the role of his upbringing or the taking of drugs might be to allow him to "see" what was there (to enable his spiritual "sight" to work) rather than to make him "see" what was not there. You have to show that its object is not *in any way* a casual factor in making the subject have his religious experience. But this is a particularly awkward challenge to apply when we are dealing with a purported experience of God (as opposed to, say, Mary or Poseidon). For there are two possible ways in which God might have caused my experiences – by intervening in the operation of natural laws, or by bringing about the operation of the laws as a result of which I have the experience. Now if the latter method of causation is suggested, the mere demonstration that I had the experience as a result of natural processes, has in itself no force against the suggestion that God was its cause[11] – for what is then at stake is whether God caused the natural processes. You do not show that I do not now see the table, by showing that its appearing to me that there is a table has a perfectly ordinary cause in goings-on in my optic nerve – what is at stake is whether the table caused those goings-on. A demonstration that God was not responsible for the natural processes which caused me to have the religious experience can only be attained by demonstrating that there is no God – for if he exists as defined, clearly he is responsible for the operation of natural laws. By contrast, lesser supernatural beings are not supposed to be responsible for the operation of natural laws, and so it is easier to show that they do not play any casual role in generating some experience.

The upshot of all this is, with respect to religious experiences purportedly of God, that unless there is a demonstration that very probably God does not exist, those who have religious experiences purportedly of God ought to believe them genuine. For others who do not have the experiences themselves, the great weight of testimony to the occurrence of a large number of experiences purportedly of God must give considerable probability to his existence – again, unless on other grounds it is very improbable that there is a God. (The special considerations are, I think, a little more easily deployed against claims to have experienced lesser supernatural beings.[12])

This conclusion followed from my principle of credulity that apparent perceptions ought to be taken at their face value in the absence of positive reason for challenge. There is no primitive description of what is perceived in terms of which all other claims to have perceived things needs justification. We are born with some conceptual scheme, no one part of which is more basic or more central than any other one. In terms of this we operate and describe what we perceive. The language game is played. If someone denies one of our claims on good grounds (formulated within the terms of our conceptual scheme), then we can withdraw it and re-describe the experience. And by this process whole conceptual schemes may be radically transformed – but, as in Neurath's analogy, like a ship at sea, only one plank at a time. Initial scepticism about perceptual claims – regarding them as guilty until proved innocent – will give you no knowledge at all. Initial credulity is the only attitude a rational man can take; there is no half-way house. However, claims which can subsequently be shown unreasonable can be weeded out. But the onus remains on the challenger. Unless we take perceptual claims seriously, whatever they are about, we shall find ourselves in an epistemological Queer Street. Religious perceptual claims deserve to be taken as seriously as perceptual claims of any other kind.

REFERENCES AND NOTES

1. This paper is a shortened version of Chapter 13 of my book *The Existence of God*, (Oxford, 1979), and is published here by kind permission of the publishers of the book, The Oxford University Press.
2. I argue this in my book *The Existence of God*.
3. Chisholm, R. M., *Perception* (New York, Ithaca, 1977), Ch. 4. Chisholm attempted to distinguish a third ("non-comparative") use of such verbs, but there is some doubt about whether there is such a use, and I am concerned only with the epistemic and comparative uses.
4. There is a use of "perceive" and other verbs of perception (e. g., "see", "hear") in which a subject may be said to perceive something which he does not believe that he is perceiving – e.g., I may be said to have perceived John without realizing that it was John whom I was perceiving. I am not concerned with perception of this kind, but only with perception of things which the subject believes that he is perceiving. I use "perceive" as the general verb for becoming aware by any of the five normal modalities of sense, and any other modalities of sense there may be.
5. The best presentation of the theory known to me is that by P. F. Strawson in his "Causation in Perception" (in his *Freedom and Resentment*, London, 1974).

However, having given the conditions stated above, he argues that they are still insufficient, although necessary, for perception. He claims (pp.79f.) that there are further restrictions for different senses, e.g., that "one can only see what is within one's arc of vision" or however loud the report of the cannon, if it is far enough away it will be out of earshot". But such restrictions seem only to be correct if we suppose that the meaning of such expressions as "within one's arc of vision" is defined by them. If there is an independent criterion of, e.g., "arc of vision" – say a geometrical one – then the stated restriction seems in no way obviously a necessary truth. There is nothing incoherent in supposing that some men can see round corners. I suggest therefore that my analysis gives sufficient as well as necessary conditions for perception. H. P. Grice in "The Causal Theory of Perception", (*Proceedings of the Aristotelian Society. Supplementary Volume* 1961, republished in *The Philosophy of Perception*, ed. Warnock, G. J., London, 1967, pp. 85–112, see pp. 102–106) argues in effect that if *S* is to perceive *x*, it is necessary that *x* cause *S*'s sense impression, but that this is not sufficient to guarantee perception. Grice's arguments against sufficiency however will not work if we understand by "sense impression" it's seeming to *S* that *x* is present, and if we take him as providing an analysis not of "*S* perceives *x*" but of "*S* perceives *x* (believing that he is so doing)".

6. C. D. Broad argues in this way for the *prima facie* justification of claims of religious experience in "Arguments for the Existence of God" in his *Religion, Philosophy and Psychical Research* (London, 1953). Many philosophers have made the obvious point that no experience entails the existence of its purported object but most seem to ignore the question whether it is *prima facie* evidence for it.

7. I write this without wishing to deny that in a special sense of "person" God is "three persons in one substance". For discussion of the meaning of terms by which "God" is defined, see my *The Coherence of Theism* (Oxford, 1977).

8. In this connection note that one does not need past experience of *x* in the same modality of sense in order to recognize *x* again. I may not have seen *x* before, only felt it; but my past feeling may enable me to recognize *x* when first I see it. Or I may not have tasted *x* before, only smelled it; but my past smelling may enable me to recognize *x* when first I taste it.

9. *op. cit.*, p.183.

10. Flew, A., *God and Philosophy* (London, 1966), pp. 126ff

11. This simple point is well made in William J. Wainwright "Natural Explanations and Religious Experience", *Ratio*, 15 (1973), pp. 98–101.

12. In their case, there is very little in the way of arguments other than arguments of apparent experiences of them, to demonstrate their existence. There is no cosmological argument to prove the existence of Poseidon! This may lead us to conclude that it is *very* improbable a priori that they exist, so improbable that the evidence of experience is insufficient to overcome the improbability. This paper cannot of course discuss just how probable or improbable it is on other grounds that there is a God. For argument on that see my book *The Existence of God*.

Chapter 10

THE VARIETIES OF SCIENTIFIC EXPERIENCE

J. R. Ravetz
Department of Philosophy, University of Leeds, U.K.

I

Introduction

People here will doubtless recognise the little twist in the title; I am adapting that of William James' classic study on religious experience. You will recall that he was trying to show that the disciplined approach of psychology could provide means for demonstrating both the variety and also the reality of those experiences we call 'religious'. We are not often reminded of the context of those lectures, in particular the studies of the eminent clinical psychologist Henry Maudsley on *Natural Causes and Supernatural Seemings* (1886). There we find, among other gems, the observation that

> 'The supernatural powers which were thought to possess and constrain the mind are in that case plainly no more than its natural nervous substrata engaged in disordinate, abnormal or, so to speak, *un*natural functions'. (p. 314)

One might say that William James was beginning the long job of re-establishing the respectability of religious experience in our educated common-sense, reversing a decline that had accelerated markedly around the sixteenth and seventeenth centuries. Although we are still far from comprehending such phenomena properly, certainly by this point in the twentieth century the existence of 'Altered States of Consciousness' is established for all except those who prefer not to look through this new telescope.

So I believe that the time is now ripe to extend the survey, and to consider that other pole of the classic dichotomy, namely 'Science'. Right away, I must distinguish between particular facts and theories about the external world, and the general view of reality with which they are commonly associated. Philosophers of science know well that

197

their task of establishing the credentials of the *materials* of science is far from trivial. But in a sense they are only rationalizing what is already obvious, for at least the stronger of these elements of science have an objectivity that for practical purposes needs no explanation or defence.

It is quite otherwise with the general view of reality and of its study, what we might call the *image* of science. This is very much more than a collection of the above-mentioned technical materials, or even a simple induction from their common characteristics. For the image of science performs many more functions than that of a synthesis of technical materials. It is unavoidably invoked in the many social and ideological struggles which scientists, and spokesmen for science, have engaged in over the centuries.

It is most important to realize that this image of science is not subject to the same rigorous tests against controlled experience that a matured technical science enjoys. But (and here is one of the crucial paradoxes of our dominant scientific world-view) those who project images of science do genuinely and sincerely believe that their personal speculations are objective hard facts. For otherwise, they themselves would, by their very own 'scientific' criteria, be talking nonsense. So, I conclude, a great deal of self-deception is necessarily practised in discussion at the level of imagery of science. The resulting confusion can be seen, for instance, Popper's writings when he talks about the philosophy of science rather than merely pronouncing on science. (See his criticism of Kuhn in *Criticism and the Growth of Knowledge*). This contradiction also affects the work in those sciences where the technical content has not yet become so strong as to dominate the ideological influences. As an example, we see that Henry Maudsley could and indeed needed to believe that he was doing no more nor less than Sir Isaac Newton in his determination of the laws of gravitation, when submitting human personalities and experience to his peculiar type of analysis. The same could be said, in a related field, of Sir Cyril Burt.

I would like to offer to you an idea which I consider to be as subversive as any, concerning the ideology of "scientism". This is conveyed by the term "immature science". For once we admit that there are fields which award themselves all the external regalia of science, and which assiduously mimic some version of "scientific method", but where there is still as yet nothing solid emerging, then we make a very different demarcation from those of the positivists. As an example I once argued that "nuclear strategy" is no better than astrology; I would now not give it even so much credit. Yet the fate of the whole world has depended in part on the judgements of "experts" in this institutionalized psychopathy. Less monstrous examples can be found in the various sorts of expertise by which our societies maintain social and ideological control, now that we are unable to force people to attend church every Sunday. Some of these would-be sciences are afflicted with cognitive problems that make theology seem like a fortress in comparison (take urban planning, for example); but given the fashions of this de-sacral age they are necessarily given credence. The sociologists of knowledge have recently begun to turn their attention to fields which may have some positive content but which are nonetheless denied legitimacy. Might I suggest that they next survey some fields which enjoy fame and favour in spite of being excluded, by a nearly logical necessity, from substantiating their claims?

The above are only among the more obviously grotesque examples of the harm that can be done by the sort of image of science that has been dominant in our culture since the seventeenth century. I believe that if we are to understand our present human predicament, which is technical and social as well as religious, we will have to employ history, dissecting and laying bare the various presuppositions that define our educated common sense; and for this a study of the images of science is essential.

But my task today is necessarily more modest: to make an analytical criticism of one aspect of the image of science. All I need is that you should rest comfortably with the awareness that images of science are not nearly so strictly determined as technical science itself. Also, it helps to remember that the history of science has both a scholarly and an ideological component; and so the picture that we get of the science of a past epoch is very strongly influenced by our present dominant image of science. What historians write about, say, seventeenth century science may tell us more about the twentieth-century image of science than about its origins in technique and ideology in the seventeenth.

II

The seventeenth-century origins

Let us turn, then, to that fateful century, wherein we will find many roots of our present understanding and images. There is an old, hagiographical history of that century, with an inspiring legend to tell. This has the general shape of a darkness, of Medieval origins, penetrated by bold spirits who simply dared to use common sense: putting experiment before speculation and reason before fantasy. Copernicus defied the orthodoxy of centuries and showed that the earth moves; Galileo turned from Artistotle's books to the actual experiment, to see how falling bodies accelerate. And so on — case after case of victory against metaphysics, dogma and superstition; first in physical science in the early modern period and then extended to other areas (as chronicled by Draper and White) in the course of general Enlightenment.

Historians of science have for some decades been exposing the defects of that tale. You are more likely than most to be aware of the 'revisionist' thesis, that modern science somehow *depends* on Christianity. And historians have shown how strong was the theoretical, *a priori* and speculative component in Galileo's work. The 'Copernican revolution' reveals unexpected paradoxes and anomalies. Thus we now ask at what point in time did the Copernican hypothesis seem scientifically justifiable, not merely for assent, but even as a reasonable hypotheses for the investment of resources in research? We may emerge with the paradox that the pioneers of the new astronomy and mechanics were far from having the better scientific case, until embarrassingly late in the seventeenth century.

Such peculiar results of the history of technical science must have an effect on the image of science. For, ever since the time of Galileo, Descartes and Bacon, the dominant image has involved their claim that there exists a correct Method that leads to Truth.

Indeed, we cannot make sense of the career of Galileo (to say nothing of Descartes or Bacon), until we cease to consider him as primarily a *scientist*, and see him as (by his own insistence) first a *philosopher* and then as 'mathematician' to his Ducal patron. The 'scientific revolution' itself becomes comprehensible if we see it as a campaign for a reform of ideas *about* science, introduced quite suddenly, injected into a continuous process of technical progress *within* science.

Those who have studied revolutions in other spheres have come to cope with some features that may easily mislead the unwary scholar; first, that they contain disparate and frequently contradictory elements, and second that these varieties are systematically suppressed in the offical history that needs to be written during and after the event. The simplification of the record of the scientific achievements of the heroic period is now beyond controversy among historians. But there is still a lively debate on natural philosophy itself, on what we may call the varieties of scientific experience. For, I believe, that

200

'scientific revolution' was primarily and essentially about metaphysics; and the various technical studies were largely conceived and received as corroborating statements of a challenging world-view. This consisted essentially of two Great Denials: the restriction of ordinary faculties as sympathy and intelligence to humans and to a remote Deity; and the relegation of the extra-ordinary faculties to the realms of the nonexistent or insignificant.

This metaphysical position was not newly invented in the seventeenth century; it was well known to have been advanced by the 'atomist' philosophers of classical antiquity. But there were novel elements in the circumstances of its announcement then. One was its close relation to a particular idea of natural science, based on disciplined direct experience of Nature and devoted to the achievement of control over Nature. This is well known. What is more difficult to comprehend (and I now begin to think more important), this reductionist philosophy was espoused not by atheists but by theists. Regardless of their private convictions, they generally (unlike their predecessors in atomism), did *not* see it as a vehicle for ideological attacks on established religions authority, but rather as a means of validating justifiable religious belief. This should tell us something about the special character of the problems of religious apologetics in that turbulent time.

Once announced, this 'new philosophy' required only a few generations to become obvious and nearly unquestionable. Capable of modification to fit the great variety of circumstances imposed by the changing contexts of intellectual work, this philosophy still serves, virtually unchallenged to provide the official demarcation between the genuine and the spurious in research about the behaviour of human and non-human worlds. Our current list of pseudo-sciences is precisely that defined by the Great Denials; while even patently absurd grandiose schematic programmes for reductionist human sciences (as Wilson's *Sociobiology*) are automatically entitled to a respectful hearing.

The great historical myth of this philosophy is that it was the necessary and sufficient cause of the great scientific progress of the seventeenth century. This was a central point in its propaganda, for itself at the time and in histories ever since. Yet the results of historical enquiry, some old and some new, contradict this claim. First we have the record of three great scientists, who made immortal discoveries, *outside* the programme of 'the scientific revolution'. These were Gilbert on the magnet, Kepler in astronomy, and Harvey on the circulation of blood. In each case the scientist operated within, and was motivated by, considerations that were soon to be rejected as 'occult'. Gilbert hoped to show that the 'world soul', the *anima mundi*, was located in the element Earth, whose purest realization was the lodestone. Kepler believed in astrology and in an intelligent, harmonious structure of the cosmos. Indeed, his 'harmony of the spheres' was his strongest argument for the Copernican system in his popular *Epitome* of 1619 and on. Finally, Harvey, we now know, did *not* discover the circulation on the analogy of a pump; rather he could thread his way through a mass of confused and contradictory data by the use of the Aristotelian methods and alchemical analogies which consituted the elements of the truly spiritual science in which he believed.

Thus the scientific side of the seventeenth-century 'revolution' was largely inaugurated by men who were, on these basic metaphysical issues, counter-reveolutionaries. When we come to the end of the 'revolution', in such figures as Boyle and Newton, a similar picture emerges. Newton very early saw the insufficiency of natural explanations of a purely atomistic nature: an immaterial Force and an intelligent Design were built into his scheme from the beginning. Further, he took very seriously indeed that ancient learning which claimed some Divine or supernatural authority, hence his extensive work on alchemy, chronology and prophecy. Of course, we find that Newton's sensibility, determining the goals of his studies, was that of a 'disenchanted' age. But his *problems* were shaped as much by the inherited materials as by current technical considerations. I think that the recent debate over the 'influence' of alchemy and magic on the new philosophy can be resolved when we cease to insist on simple extreme alternatives: Newton, for example, can be seen as attempting to *assimilate* the old materials to a new style.

I cannot take time now to go further forward in the history of science, and to show how significant 'positive' achievements were made by people who, in their own time and now, would be considered metaphysical deviants. Let it suffice that there were some; and a philosophy of science that leaves such events as 'irrational' thereby exposes its own inadequacy. I hope that the material I have sketched so far establishes the point that varieties of method and of metaphysics are not rigidly and uniquely paired. The sources of experience for the work that even *we* call science are far greater than hitherto admitted in the dominant philosophy.

III

The sources of knowledge
I have so far refrained from an attempt to specify what sources of knowledge, or particular 'varieties of scientific experience' are acceptable under the orthodoxy that has prevailed for some centuries now. For every author has put the matter slightly differently and it would be tedious to provide you with full details. We may content ourselves with Galileo's slogan 'sense experience and necessary demonstrations'. This is echoed in Hume's famous proclamation on the issue where he distinguished between the good 'abstract reasoning concerning quantity or number, or experimental reasoning concurring matter of fact and existence', on the one hand and the bad 'sophistry and illusion' on the other. We might well ask, what else is there to be accepted, as a source of knowledge about the external world?

I shall try to exhibit some other candidates — starting with the most plausible. Aristotle considered such a question in the *Nicomachean Ethics* Book VI; my question here is slightly different from his, and so my list is derived by stimulus rather than modelled on his.

From the philosophy of science of Thomas Kuhn we can derive that very ancient source of knowledge, tradition. For his puzzle-solving researcher accepts as unproblematic almost all the elements of his task, the 'paradigm'. One might say that the tradition embodied in a scientific paradigm cannot be an affair of the uncritical and enforced acceptance normally associated with that term; but then one should read Kuhn and see that his 'paradigm' is just such a conservative. 'tradition'. And to the extent that his picture is faithful to ordinary scientific work, we have a legitimate role for 'tradition' as a source of knowledge.

Another influential contemporary provides a new version of another element. This is Polanyi, with his 'tacit knowledge' that I shall label 'involvement'. For his essential point is that the knowledge of 'knowing that p is the case' is inseparable from the other sort of knowing, 'knowing how ... to establish p' — either by original discovery or learning. And 'knowing how' is partly a matter of kinaesthetic feeling, partly a matter of personal commitment. In this, Polanyi shows a path away from the disembodied intelligence of the Cartesian tradition. He provides a foundation for the intellectual respectability of 'craft' knowledge (which I have exploited in my own studies). And he brings back the whole person into the act of knowing; hence I call that 'involvement'. This sort of knowing has had its advocates, whenever either craft knowledge or the personal element

203

was stressed; for the former there is the 'chemical philosophy' of the seventeenth century; and for the latter, the 'romantic' tradition of the nineteenth.

One can look at 'involvement' analytically, observing that there is no standard sequence of explicit steps whereby the knower passes from ignorance to knowledge. The *act* of knowing is then named as 'intuition' — an instantaneous, undefinable process. This was recently brought back into philosophy, for a popular audience at least, by Robert Pirsig. His 'Quality' is the 'pre-intellectual awareness' of the world, which becomes indentified with the Tao, or participation in the universal flow. Not only mystically inclined philosophers will recognise this 'intuition'. The classic study in the psychology of invention in the mathematical field, by Hadamard, cited the cases where the 'flash of insight' brought materials from the subconscious mind to the field of awareness. I am inclined, therefore, to make intuition central to all the forms of knowing.

There remain two further sources of knowledge, one fairly straight-forward and the other deeply controversial. For the first, I discuss 'wisdom', that body of personal experience that has been so digested and synthesized that it cannot be fully demonstrated, but yet which is the mark of the master-craftsman as distinct from the beginner or ordinary practitioner. This is certainly an important category for an analysis of knowledge in general and I would defend it for science too, considering the whole body of knowledge required by a matured or leading researcher and not merely the explicit materials of students' exercises.

My final candidate for the present discussion is decidely controversial; indeed it was at the focal point for debates that may have been crucial for the adoption of our present dominant philosophy of nature. I shall call it 'illumination', using this as the type-case for the various manifestations of knowledge from an experience which, as regards the material world, is purely 'inner'. Such experiences may vary enormously in their content, cognitive and affective, and their verisimilitude, ranging from an undifferentiated 'cosmic consciousness' of pure bliss, to prosaic messages of advice from an immaterial intelligence, or to violent or bizarre manifestations of 'possession'. Nowadays all such knowledge is kept on the fringe, not very far from where Henry Maudsley assigned it; though the legacy of the 'consciousness revolution' of the sixties is far from exhausted, and the Churches view the new 'charismatic' movement with a nervous welcome.

It is hard for us to imagine how such knowledge could have any relevance to science; and in that difficulty lies a clue to the peculiarity and uniqueness of the post-Renaissance European world-view.

The full story of the progressive exclusion of such experience has not been told; a fascinating example is given by Owen Hannaway in his study *The Chemists and the Word*. There we learn that Paracelsus was, in twentieth-century terms, a theosophist. By contrast, the textbook-writer Libavius, a Ramist by persuasion, lived in a world as disenchanted as that of Galileo. In the middle were such figures as Oswald Croll and van Helmont, appreciative of a living cosmos but unable to commit themselves so totally to Paracelsus' astral sources of knowledge.

My feeling is that the intensity of such inner experience as Paracelsus had and used was, as a social phenomenon, ebbing all through the sixteenth century. By the seventeenth, 'enthusiasm' had become a term as pejorative as 'Bolshevik' or 'terrorist', and for the same reasons. For enthusiastical religion, sometimes related to populist science, had become the foundation of those lower-class rebellions that punctuated the whole Reformation period, and which brought horror to the established orders of society.

This source of knowledge actually became an issue in 'curriculum development' at Oxford University, when John Webster advocated Paracelsian chemistry and Fludd's mystical mathematics in a sort of 'Cultural Revolution' reform at Oxford in 1654. Further, he did so in the name of Bacon's experimental method. The scathing comment by Seth Ward was not entirely accurate, for Bacon's relations with 'enchanted' science were far from simple. But as a pronouncement for the future, it held good:

> There are not two waies in the whole World more opposite, than those of the L. *Verulam* and D. *Fludd*, the one founded upon experiment, the other upon mystical Ideal reasons...

The suggestion has been made, by Piyo Rattansi, that the move to the 'atomistic' philosophy by a number of English thinkers (including Robert Boyle) just at that time, was due in part to their political revulsion from 'enthusiasm' in religion. At the moment this is only very plausible, though very significant if true. But it may also be that by this point in the development of the European consciousness, only deviant or irresponsible elements would allow such experiences to be anything other than a strictly personal, private matter.

As a result of all this, I can present my proposed categories in a diagram, in mandala shape.

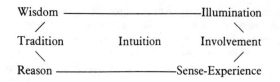

Wisdom ————————————Illumination

Tradition   Intuition   Involvement

Reason ————————————Sense-Experience

I have put 'intuition' at the centre, for it seems to be presupposed in all the others.

Let us see how the philosophers of the seventeenth century fit on this scheme. All put sense-experience and reason as primary; though Bacon, sharing with Newton the common idea of a *prisca sapientia* believed in a tradition extending at least to the Pre-Socratics. He and Descartes definitely believed in wisdom as a desirable source of knowledge; in his earlier years Bacon had hoped to distil wisdom from the aphorisms of the wise. The appeals to 'involvement' by both Bacon and Galileo were rather abstract and literary; neither really believed in the innate virtue of soiled hands. 'Intuition' is needed by Descartes to guarantee the validity of the mind's passage along 'those long chains of reasoning', and it is invoked by Galileo as the way that God knows. Finally, 'illumination' had some influence in the early careers of both Bacon and Descartes; though I believe that there we find the basic demarcation between our 'science' and all the other sorts. Should we consider Boyle, Newton and their successors, the pattern becomes even more complex. The sharp divisions proclaimed by the early prophets and reinstated by positivistic philosophers and historians, are lost in a tangle of beliefs and commitments.

IV

Conclusion

The moral of this story is *not* that the realms of 'science' and of 'religion' are indistinguishable. Rather, the boundaries between them, drawn over the various discrete sources of knowledge, are conditioned by the cultural environment. This analysis does not necessarily eliminate conflict as a part of the relation. But at least it may help us to escape from a sterile opposition of a pair of caricatured models of these two vast areas of knowledge and endeavour. We should be able thereby to do better history of the past, and perhaps even to cope better with the present and future.

206

Part IV

SOCIOLOGICAL CRITIQUE

Chapter 11

THEORY, THEOLOGY AND IDEOLOGY

Nicholas Lash
Faculty of Divinity, University of Cambridge, U.K.

I

Ideology and the problem of religious truthfulness
Truthfulness is integral not only to morality but to sanity. Few of us would survive for long if we seriously supposed our deepest convictions to be false or illusory. Our marriages would founder, our political and professional projects would atrophy; the darkness would silence our whistling. And yet, honest conviction is not easily won and is only sustained in counterpoint with an awareness of its fragility.

That was, if you like, a distant paraphrase of Karl Mannheim's characterization of 'the elemental perplexity of our time'.[1] That perplexity (and now my paraphrase moves closer to his text) can be epitomized in the question: 'How is it possible for man to continue to think and live, to believe, hope and pray, when problems of ideology are being radically raised and thought through in all their implications?'.[2] At the practical level, this is a question about likely or appropriate forms of survival (if any) of religious belief and practice. At the theoretical level, it is a question inviting theological reflection on the ideological status and function of religious practice and theological discourse. In attempting to respond to that invitation it is tempting to begin by offering a definition of 'ideology'. For a number of reasons, however, some of which will become clear in the course of this paper, I prefer to take a more indirect route.

II

Response to the problems
Many social scientists, influenced by any one of a number of strands in the Marxist tradition, would reply to my modified form of Mannheim's question by suggesting that religious belief and practice will

209

either wither away in the measure that social and economic conditions are effectively transformed or, failing such transformation, will survive as ideological expressions of an ultimately doomed social order. In the first case, theology would disappear with the erosion of its practical basis; in the second case, it would only survive either as the 'symbolic organisation' of a tale that continued, however falteringly, to be told, or as a form of dramatic and literary criticism.

The characterization of religious and theological discourse as 'ideological' is not, of course, confined to the Marxist tradition. It is also found in the work of those sociologists, from Mannheim to Parsons, whose method is classificatory rather than critical, and whose uses of the concept of 'ideology' correspondingly lack many of the pejorative overtones that it usually carried in Marx's writings.[3] Nevertheless, across a wide spectrum of sociological approaches, the characterization of religious and theological discourse as ideological frequently proceeds on a twofold assumption: firstly, that religious believers are not doing what, in the practice of their religion, they suppose themselves to be doing; secondly, that in the measure that they came to perceive this fact they would, at the very least, abandon all suggestion that religious believing implies or entails cognitive claims that cannot be redescribed, without remainder, in non-theological terms. This assumption, whatever the social conditions that generate and foster it, and whether its academic pedigree is traced, in individual cases, to Marx or to Durkheim, goes well byond such methodological atheism or agnosticism as is stipulated by the heuristic structure of sociological explanation.

Sociologists, even sociologists of religion, rarely exhibit any close and intellectually serious familiarity with the major traditions of Christian theological enquiry and argument. The sketch I have offered of approaches to the sociology of religion perhaps indicates why this is so: quite simply, they have no need to. They 'know' that 'the criticism of religion has been essentially completed',[4] or at least that the cognitive status of such alternative accounts as theologians continue to offer has been definitively discredited. Most sociologists, including many who are themselves religious believers, would, I suspect, agree that theological discourse is not in the business of making knowledge-claims that need to be considered on their own terms.

And what of the theologians themselves? There are, as I see it, at least three widespread forms of theological response to Mannheim's question. The first consists in responding to the question in a manner sufficiently selective as to escape its full force. Thus, for example,

210

Karl Rahner says that the concept of ideology has been used 'in so many different and contradictory ways that nothing is left to us but simply to give a brief definition ... of what *we* mean here by ideology'.[5] The definition that he offers, while by no means arbitrary, nevertheless too easily allows him to demonstrate that 'Christianity is not an ideology',[6] even though it is always in danger of interpreting itself as such. Professore Torrance, adopting a similarly selective approach, charges those theologians, such as Schleiermacher and Troeltsch, who reflect upon 'the phenomena of faith rather than [on] that in which we have faith',[7] with thereby converting theological into ideological statements.[8] What is missing from his treatment is any serious engagement with that complex tradition which would characterize *all* theological discourse as 'ideological', whatever 'objective reference and material content'[9] was claimed for such discourse by its exponents.

The second, and by far the most widespread, form of theological response to the question of ideology consists in simply ignoring it. Most theologians pay no more attention to sociologists than sociologists do to theologians. There is, in this mutual inattention, an epistemological paradox. The sociologist, I have already suggested, confidently ignores the theologian because he 'knows' that the theologian is not in the business of making knowledge-claims that need to be considered on their own terms. The theologian, for his part, confidently ignores the sociologist because he 'knows' that the object, springs and centre of theological enquiry are, in the last instance, resistant to the reductionism which is a constitutive feature of many sociological explanations of religion. This state of affairs is paradoxical because, central to the debates that keep both traditions of enquiry on the move are fundamental and fundamentally unresolved issues concerning the character and possibility of both 'knowledge' and explanation'.

There is a third form of theological response to the problem of ideology. It is exemplified by the work of the Spanish Marxist theologian, Alfredo Fierro, who resolutely and uncritically embraces an Althusserian form of the distinction between 'knowledge' and 'ideology'. According to Fierro: 'Only a positivist conception of theology can entertain the idea that theology contains some sort of knowledge';[10] no more than nonbelievers do 'Christians know anything about ... God, but they believe and hope nevertheless ... Hoping and believing are not knowing; they are a nonknowing illustrated by parables and images'.[11]

Fierro is one of a number of theologians (the others that I have in mind being Latin Americans) who have found, in Althusser's distinction between 'knowledge', or 'science', and 'ideology', an order of service according to which the marriage between Christianity and Marxism may be celebrated in tranquility.[12] This is intensely paradoxical in view of the use to which Althusser himself has put the distinction in order to 'save the appearances' of Stalinism.[13]

Considerations of space prevent me from exploring in detail my profound dissatisfaction with Fierro's characterization of 'believing' as a 'nonknowing illustrated by parable and images'. What would it be like, in the concrete, for 'believing' to take this form? What *kind* of 'illustration' of his nescience does Father Fierro expect from what ·'parables and images' as he stands before the firing squad? That question seems to me not improper, since any account of Christian believing, however formal or theoretical, must surely at least plausibly indicate something of the form which that believing might take when its 'material conditions' are contracted to the point of agony. The absence, in Fierro's study, of any discussion of questions of prayer and spirituality (the concrete forms of faith) is, I believe, significant.

To put it another way. My dissatisfaction with Fierro's definition of 'believing' arises primarily neither from his insistence that believing is a 'nonknowing', nor from his claim that it is in narrative and image, in picture and story, that faith finds expression (although these are issues of far greater complexity than he indicates), but in the uninformative casualness of his recourse to the metaphor of 'illustration' in order to describe the relationship between nescience and cognition, silence and language, in the dialectic of belief.

In Fierro, as in Althusser, abstract categories and distinctions freewheel at zero gravity, unconstrained by the discipline, derived from continual attention to the concrete and particular, which we are entitled to expect of a mode of reflection which declares itself to be 'historical-materialist'.[14] My mention of Fierro's Althusserian idealism, however, may at least have served to remind us that, even if problems of ideology may not be confined within the boundaries of the epistemological, epistemological issues nevertheless remain central to its exploration inasmuch as, throughout its history, the concept of ideology has been defined in at least partial contradistinction to concepts of knowledge. To describe religious practice, or theological discourse, as 'ideological', is always to characterize them, if not as 'simply false', or 'purely illusory', at least as lacking certain essential features of whatever is held to constitute 'true knowledge'.

The bewildering variety of contemporary uses of the concept of ideology arises partly from ambiguities and imprecisions in Marx's use of the notion and partly from the complexity of its subsequent history. It also partly arises, I suggest, from the fact that 'ideology' is one of those 'basic concepts' which, in Raymond Williams's phrase, have come to be 'seen to be not concepts but problems'.[15] However, I want to risk attempting just sufficient clarification as will enable me to isolate one or two of those aspects of the problem which should especially engage the attention of students of theological method. I propose to argue that there is, firstly, a *practical* dimension to the problem on which it is incumbent upon theologians continually to attend but which it outstrips their competence, as theologians, to 'solve', and that there is, secondly, a *theoretical* dimension concerning the status of theological discourse and the selection of appropriate theological 'cognitive strategies'.

III

Marx on ideology

Omitting consideration of what we might perhaps call the 'prehistory' of the term,[16] let me plunge in at the deep end and offer some reflections on Marx's use of the concept of ideology. Marx's critics frequently belabour him for what they regard as the radically inconsistent, even contradictory, character of his treatment of the relationship between social existence and consciousness in general, and of 'ideology' in particular.[17] But these criticisms, when not stemming from mere hostility, frequently misconceive the sense in which we might expect to find in his writings the elements, consistently laid out, of a 'theory of ideology'. Not only is this expectation precluded by the explosive restlessness of an original thinker most of whose relevant writings are heavily polemical in character, but we need to bear in mind that, ' in *The German Ideology* as in the Paris Manuscripts, Marx refuses to concern himself with epistemological questions'.[18] Such questions, at least as classically conceived, are, in the sense of the second thesis on Feuerbach, 'purely scholastic'.[19] It is one thing to argue, as I should wish to do, that Marxism has paid a heavy price for this refusal, as is indicated by the solipsistic manner in which Althusserians tediously reiterate the claim that, as the expositors of Marxist 'science', they and they alone possess the key to true knowledge, but of course they cannot discuss the matter in any terms other than their own, because to do so would be to lapse into 'ideological' discourse.[20] It is quite another thing, however, to criticize Marx for inconsistency

213

in respect of a theoretical programme which he never sought to undertake. If Marx's treatment of 'ideology' is obscure, as in many respects it undoubtedly is, that obscurity arises less from theoretical confusion than from an unfortunate choice, and a frequently slipshod use, of metaphor.[21] And few of his metaphors have caused more trouble than that of 'base' and 'superstructure', to which we shall return.

Seliger refers to Marx's 'exclusively pejorative, truth-excluding use of "ideology" '.[22] Both epithets are misleading. Neither of them are applicable, for example, to Marx's use of the term in the famous passage in the 1859 Preface to *A Contribution to the Critique of Political Economy*. In that passage, the use is, in Mannheim's sense, 'non-evaluative', and the insistence that 'It is not the consciousness of men that determines their existence, but their social existence that determines their consciousness',[23] while suffering from rhetorical overkill, says nothing about the truth of falsity of the products of consciousness, the 'ideological forms in which men become conscious of [social] conflict and fight it out'.[24]

In its most general sense, the concept of ideology refers to 'the general process of the production of meanings and ideas'.[25] If, in Marx's writings, the concept is usually employed more or less pejoratively, this is due to a series of further specifications to which he submitted it in the course of mounting his critique of the 'scientific', absolutist, ahistorical pretensions of bourgeois political economy.[26]

The first such specification arises from his insistence — the achievement of which marked the break with Feuerbach — that 'ideas are social products, which cannot be understood by the philosopher who stands outside history'.[27] The thought of those who suppose otherwise — be they philosophers, theologians, economists or politicians — is 'ideological'. And the concept has thus already acquired a sense according to which 'ideology' is a cognitively distorted and impoverished grasp of reality.

A second specification arises from Marx's preoccupation within the class-structure of society. Not only do 'the social circumstances in which the activity of individuals occurs condition their perception of the world in which they live',[28] but the particular social circumstances of nineteenth-century European societies, according to Marx, are those of societies locked in class conflict. 'Fundamental to Marx's "materialism" ' are 'the links which are drawn between *class structure* and ideology'.[29] The class struggle is not only largely invisible, but its invisibility is the result of the effective dissemination, as the accepted language and 'Weltanschauung' of a society, of the ideas and beliefs of whatever group wields economic power in that society. If Marx's polemical fire is directed most heavily at 'bourgeois' or 'capitalist' ideology, this is not because capitalist patterns of language and thought are, for some obscure reason, 'more ideological' than those of other forms of social and economic organisation, but because, in nineteenth-century Europe, the structure of economic power and dominance was, in fact, capitalist. Hence, his epigrammatic slogan that 'the ideas of the ruling class are in every epoch the ruling ideas'[30] demands different application in different historical circumstances. Thus E. P. Thompson, criticizing Kolakowski, has said: 'Political organisms select from the available stock of ideas those which best suit their interests ... they shape ideas into ideology ... What has happened in the Soviet Union is that Marxism as rationality or idea has been transformed into ideology'.[31]

Intellectually second-rate idealist sociologies, Marxist and other, solidify and reify Marx's analytic categories, transforming them into substantive descriptions. As such, they become historically and empirically unreferred generalisations, veering between the tautological and the patently false. Seliger is perfectly correct in saying that 'Marx did not use "ideology" according to a uniform definition, and the term itself did not occupy a central position in his work'.[32] But the moral that I would draw from this is that 'ideology', in Marx's writings, is not so much a theoretical concept as a variable pointer to a cluster of related problems his discussion of which is heavily impregnated with metaphorical usage of uneven quality. And, as E. P. Thompson has said: 'At least I know that the thinker who mistakes metaphor for fact is in for trouble'.[33] Meanwhile, he continues, 'in serious intellectual circles the argument about basis/superstructure goes *on and on and on* ... A whole continent of discourse is being developed ... which rests, not upon the solid globe of historical evidence, but on the precarious point of a strained metaphor'.[34]

If we bear such warnings in mind, I suggest that those features of Marx's treatment of ideology which I have so far sketched are not lacking in historical suggestiveness and social-scientific significance. When we take the next step, however, and ask, from an epistemological point of view (if Marx will forgive me), with what ideological discourse is appropriately to be *contrasted*, we move into deeper water.

'Where speculation ends — in real life — there', says Marx, in *The German Ideology*, 'real, positive science begins: the representation ... of the practical process of development of men. Empty talk about consciousness ceases, and real knowledge has to take its place. When reality is depicted, philosophy as an independent branch of knowledge loses its medium of existence'.[35] In the context, the general thrust of these remarks is clear enough. 'Speculation', 'empty talk about consciousness' is, to use an ancient distinction, at best 'opinion' and not 'knowledge'. Forgetful of its forgetfulness of the social, historical, 'practical' process of which it is an aspect, it 'mystifies', thereby distorting or 'falsifying' the consciousness of its practitioners. In its broad outlines, this realist criticism of freewheeling speculation, of what Sir Harold Wilson and E. P. Thompson regrettably persist in describing as 'theology',[36] is warmly to be welcomed, not least because the contents of such speculation tend to become absolutized both in the sense than an unwarranted universality is attributed to culturally and historically particular insights, and in the sense that they tend to become hypostatised. As Terry Eagleton has remarked of contemporary antihumanist Marxist atheism, such atheism 'signifies a rejection of that process whereby, out of the pluralistic play of our signs, a single one (God, the gold standard, paternal authority) is abstracted and enthroned as a standard by which all the others must be ranked.'[37]

Unfortunately, the metaphorical and conceptual framework within which Marx mounts his criticism is doubly flawed. In the first place, from the fact that 'ideology', as described, is defective as knowledge, it does not follow that 'real knowledge' may be identified, as Marx does, with 'real science'. This confusion persists to our own day. Thus, when Althusser insists that 'a "pure" science only exists on condition that it continually frees itself from the ideology which occupies it, haunts it, or lies in wait for it',[38] he appears to be reminding us not only of the irreducible tension between 'scientific' discourse and other modes of knowledge, but also of the heightening of that tension which results from the recognition that the ordinary language of social relationships and the language of literature, for example, are permanently exposed to ideological distortion. But does not the manner in which he expresses his concern for scientific 'purity' also carry the unwarranted reductionist implication that *only* 'scientific' discourse constitutes a mode of *knowledge*? Some such depreciation of the cognitive status of non-scientific discourse is certainly suggested by his announcement that 'ideology as a system of representations, is distinguished from science in that in it the practico-social function is more important than the theoretical function (*function as knowledge*)'.[39]

The 'purity' of discourse and the rectitude of practice are, of course, two sides of the same coin. Once question the assumption that Marxist 'science' has all other modes of discourse as its 'objects', and thus cannot possibly debate with them as if they were 'epistemological equals',[40] and the springs of revolutionary action have been fatally weakened. The reductionist identification of 'real knowledge' with Marxist 'science' allows the depreciative classification of all *other* modes of knowledge as mere 'opinion' or 'belief'. However, 'the Marxist does not have a relationship of belief with his science, but rather his science allows and formulates knowledge of its object'.[41] And why cannot the Marxist add: 'this, at least, is what I believe'? Because 'If Marxism admits "belief" as an epistemological category it will turn into its opposite, not a revolutionary praxis but an ideology of protest'.[42] Before breaking into a grin, the Christian, with his own unresolved legacy of the tension between the destructive singlemin- dedness apparently indispensable for effective action and the ineffec- tive 'generosity' of the 'liberal's' perpetual seminar, should consider whether he is in any position to scoff.

The tendency to depreciate the cognitive status of informal and literary modes of discourse is not, of course, confined to the Marxist tradition. Thus, for example, Talcott Parsons, who characterizes 'religious beliefs' as 'the non-empirical homologue of ideological beliefs',[43] defines 'ideology' as 'a system of ideas which is oriented to the evaluative integration of the collectivity', and adds: 'In so far as the cognitive interest has clear primacy the belief system is scientific or philosophical'.[44] No justification is offered for this historically and epistemologically jejune stipulative generalisation.

The second flaw in Marx's presentation stems from the manner of his characterisation of ideology as thought separated from the 'practi- cal process of development of men'. That separation, that dualism, is, for Marx, the hallmark of idealism. But his criticism of it can some- times be read (and, subsequently, has frequently been read) not as a passionate defence of the indissoluble *unity* of the single historical process of human thought and action, life and consciousness, but as endorsing a mere reversal of that dualism. On this reversal, which is at the root of 'reductionist' readings of Marxist materialism, ' "con- sciousness" and "its" products can be *nothing but* "reflections" of what has already occurred in the material social process'.[45] On this account, 'ideological' discourse is not only 'not scientific', but is merely 'epiphenomenal'.

I do not for one moment believe that this was Marx's own position. I believe that Michael Foster captured the central thrust of Marx's thought on these matters when he said that 'Historical materialism does not ... mean that ideas are devoid of all force, but that they are devoid of all original force'.[46] Nevertheless, it must be admitted that, by his choice of metaphors — above all, the metaphor of 'base' and 'superstructure', and (for example) the notorious *'camera obscura'* image in *The German Ideology* — Marx lays himself open to dualist, and hence reductionist, interpretations.[47]

IV

'Science' and 'Ideology'

If we allow that 'ideological' discourse may usefully be contrasted with 'science', nevertheless the restrictive identification of 'science' with 'real knowledge' must certainly be disallowed and for at least two reasons. Firstly, any such identification arbitrarily excludes from the range of modes of knowledge first-order, prereflexive modes of cognition. To follow Althusser in restricting 'knowledge' to *theoretical* apprehension is to deny that most people know the vast majority of the things that they not unreasonably suppose themselves to know. But the housewife *does* 'know' the price of butter and (to give a very different illustration of the irreducible variety of modes of knowledge) most of us may legitimately claim to 'know', albeit imperfectly, our friends.

That last illustration demands expansion, because it points the way towards my second reason for disallowing the reduction of 'knowledge' to 'science'. 'There is', says Mannheim, 'a type of knowledge ... whose first assumption is the fact that we come to know our associates only in living and acting with them'.[48] This consideration leads him eventually to the conclusion that 'political-historical thinking produces a kind of knowledge of its own which is not pure theory, but which nevertheless embodies real insight'.[49] Thus the possibility is opened up for familiar distinctions, of some importance for considerations of theological method, between 'theoretico-scientific' and 'hermeneutic' modes of knowledge. And the practitioners of both types of enquiry should, I suggest, learn from Marx's critique of ideology to seek always to be attentive to the *limits* imposed on their discourse and imagination by their historical and social location. 'In affirming that ideologies and social consciousness were not autonomous but, instead, were grounded in "social being" ', says Gouldner, 'Marx affirms that there are *limits* on reason and rational discourse'.[50]

Two further considerations, before moving on. Firstly, if there is *no* sense in which we may claim to 'know' our friends, or to 'know' ourselves, then, *a fortiori*, there is no sense in which we may be said to 'know' the mystery of God. And if our self-knowledge, and our knowledge of other persons, is 'conditioned' or 'determined' by the historical and social circumstances in which we exist — the stock of imaginative, conceptual and evaluative resources that are, *in practice*, available to us is indeed limited — then our knowledge of God is similarly determined. In this sense Christian belief, as the thematisation or categorial expression of faith's dark knowledge of God is, like other social expressions of personal knowledge, 'ideological'. It is ideological in the further sense that, in religious matters as in secular, we tend to be forgetful of the limits to which our knowledge is subject: 'Ideology', says Gouldner, 'dulls the tragic vision's alertness to limits'.[51] But to concede that religious belief is, in both these senses, 'ideological' is by no means indiscriminately to admit its 'false' or 'illusory' character. Whether or not human experience is experience of God, and hence 'experiential knowledge' of God (whatever the conceptual and symbolic forms, theistic or other, in which such experiential knowledge is categorially 'objectified'), is not a question which can even come up for consideration in terms of the discussion so far.[52]

The second consideration that I would raise at this point concerns the possibility of 'science' in Marx's, let alone in Althusser's sense. 'To be conditioned', says Seliger, 'is to be barred from comprehensive objective knowledge'.[53] Curiously, Seliger seems to suppose that Marx is to be criticized for endorsing this elementary truism. But in what sense, and in respect of what objects, do we usually suppose 'comprehensive objective knowledge' to be available? Gouldner highlights one important aspect of the distinction between science and ideology with his description of the 'analytic essence of ideology' as consisting in the fact that it is 'speech that does not recognize or make problematic its own grounds',[54] and by construing 'rationality' as 'the capacity to make problematic what has hitherto been treated as given'.[55] But he also comments, perceptively, that 'to make all things problematic at the *same* time is conducive not to rationality, but nihilism'.[56] And, with the shade of T. S. Kuhn peering over my shoulder, I am bound to ask: of what scientific practice that has ever occurred could it be said that it succeeded, or could hope to succeed, in making *all* of its grounds simultaneously and radically problematic?

In other words, is there not a sense in which the Marxist concept of 'science' is, in its contradistinction from 'ideology', to be construed as a *regulative ideal* rather than as the description of present practice?[57] Press this suggestion in one direction, and it would render the very notion of science practically vacuous. But, reminded by Althusser that 'the *theoretical* effects of ideology ... are always a threat or a hindrance to scientific knowledge',[58] it can perhaps also be read as indicating that scientific theory and practice have always attentively to struggle for the establishment and retention of their own 'scientificity'. And, from this point of view, it is perhaps the case that, amongst the concern characteristic of Christian theological enquiry, some at least are such that their pursuit is governed by a similar ideal.

V

Marx's critique of religion

Having so far said nothing about Marx's explicit critique of religion in general, and Christianity in particular, as ideological, I now propose briefly to remedy this. Marx is notoriously inconsistent in supposing that religion, alone amongst the forms of ideological discourse, cannot furnish genuine knowledge. On his account, whereas in a social order in which our alienation had been healed there would still be that which corresponded to law, polity, art and philosophy, there would not be that which corresponded to religion. Without being able to argue the case here, I believe that the clue to this anomaly is to be sought in the frequent analogies which Marx draws between political and religious forms of alienation. In some ideal future order, there might be that which corresponded to political practice and discourse, but the *state* would have 'withered away'. And the image of God is so unquestioningly identified, by Marx, with the image of an 'alien power', that questions concerning the forms of religion in a 'healed', nonalienated society simply do not and cannot arise.

Marx's criticism of religious practice — let us say, of religious ideology — as frequently contributive to and expressive of oppression, infantilism and social division, constitutes a far more devastating indictment of much past and present Christian practice and discourse, organisation, doctrine, hymnody and preaching, than most Christians — be they laypeople, theologians or church leaders — seem willing or able to recognize. But, from a *theoretical* point of view, the form and content of that criticsm are both uninformed and uninteresting. Centuries of strenuous, and by no means wholly unsuccessful, effort have been devoted to demonstrating that the God of Christian belief, a God of whom it is affirmed that the autonomy of his creation grows in direct, not in inverse, proportion to its dependence on him,[59] cannot *logically* be thought of as the alien presence (or absence) over against man which is posited by both Feuerbach and Marx.[60] Christian theology, like Jewish theology before it, has always contained its own protocols against idolatry. The dialectic between negation and affirmation, between the positing of 'images' of God, and the criticism of those images in the constructive silence of the apophatic, is a recurrent and central aspect of the history of Christianity to which Marx never at any point adverts.

A more interesting question might be: 'Why is it that Marxism needs to persist in the misrepresentation of Christianity?'.[61] Brian Wicker, who raises this question, suggests that the answer may be sought not far from 'scientific' Marxism's discomfiture when confronted with the question of ethics.[62] It is at least interesting to notice that the Althusserian participant in the debate to which Wicker was contributing, while quite prepared to expatiate on the tautological character of the proposition 'God made the world',[63] and the ideological character of the proposition 'I believe in God',[64] offered nothing by way of argument or evidence in support of his contention that the proposition ' "God exists" is always false',[65] and 'shuffled', as Newman would say, when challenged on the question of ethics.

VI

Social 'determination'

Before concluding, I must briefly return to the question of the 'conditioning' or 'determination' of language and thought by the social and economic contexts in which our language is produced. I have already noted the inadequacy of Marx's static, mechanical metaphor of 'base' and 'superstructure'. As E. P. Thompson remarks, 'the dialectic of social change cannot be fixed in any metaphor that excludes human attributes'.[66] But, when we have selected metaphors for the relationship between historical process and its ideological (and 'scientific') 'production' that do not contain an inbuilt tendency to reductionism, fundamental questions remain concerning our understanding of such concepts as 'conditioning' and 'determination'.

'No problem in Marxist cultural theory is more difficult', says Raymond Williams, 'than that of "determination" '.[67] Teasing out the complexity of the relevant group of German and English words, he distinguishes between being 'determined' in the sense of being powerless in respect of iron laws or powerful external agencies (a sense frequently evoked in the Marxist tradition, especially in some of its more 'scientific' forms) and being 'determined' or 'determinate' in the sense of being set within certain objective limits. Marx, he reminds us, repeatedly used the concept in this sense: 'New social relations, and the new kinds of activity that are possible through them, may be imagined but cannot be achieved unless the determing limits of a particular mode of production are surpassed in practice, by actual social change'.[68] He adds, however, that if we are to avoid a quietism quite alien to Marx's thought, we need to remember that 'determination is never only the setting of limits; it is also the exertion of pressures'.[69]

Are there not, in this cluster of meanings, reminders for a theological tradition which, in disciplining its own tendency to speculative self-indulgence, has not only insisted that the God of Christian belief is a God who, if I may so put it, disbarred idolatry by the self-destruction of his own image, but of whom we believe that, in his practical recognition of the tightest of limits, in Gethsemane and on Calvary, and not in any ideological 'forgetfulness' of them, he *thereby* exerted definitive pressure, 'determined' the course and outcome of human history?

VII

Conclusion
Let me now try to pull together the threads of this somewhat rambling discussion. Both the practice of faith and theological reflection are aspects of 'the general process of the production of meanings and ideas'.[70] As such, they are 'ideological' in a non-pejorative sense which should, nevertheless, remind biblical scholars and historians of doctrine that they too often neglect to study the social production of those beliefs and practices whose origins and development they seek to interpret.

The 'problem' of ideology arises, not from the fact that our ideas are social products, but from our 'forgetfulness' of this fact. We tend to be forgetful both of the objective limits set to our grasp of reality and of the extent to which the way in which we think and perceive and argue reflects underlying patterns of social division and dominance. The struggle for the accurate 'depiction' of reality, to use Marx's metaphor, thus becomes an aspect of the struggle for social change. In this sense, critical theory is an aspect of social praxis. But the quest for critical theory can, in turn, generate a 'forgetfulness' of objective limits. This, I suggest, is what happens when critical theory, or 'science' in Marx's sense, is contrasted with nonscientific modes of discourse in a manner which implies that only theoretical discourse can deliver 'real knowledge'. Thus, for example, if it is true that 'ideology dulls the tragic vision's alertness to limits',[71] it is also true that stimulating that alertness is as much the poet's duty as it is the critical theorist's. To suppose that only in theoretical discourse is truth told, reality 'depicted', is to succumb, once again, to that idealistic rationalism from which historical materialism was supposed to have delivered us.

The relevance of these remarks may become clearer when we remember that those primary modes of discourse which are constitutive elements of Christian religious practice are narrative, self-involving, autobiographical.[72] The Christian believer is a story-teller, and the story that he tells is of a process in which he acknowledges himself to be a participant. And if it is true that the tale that he tells is, like any autobiography, threatened with illusion and distortion, it is also true that only in the telling of the tale does the process achieve conscious expression. The telling of the tale is certainly not a sufficient condition of Christian truthfulness, but it is a necessary condition. The task of theology, as critical reflection on religious practice, is to elucidate the truth-conditions of the tale and thus critically to assess the truthfulness of its telling.

Implied in the distinction between 'religious practice' and 'theological reflection' is the claim that the responsibility for the critique of ideology devolves not only upon the social scientist (as 'critical theorist') but also upon the theologian. A few comments on this claim (which will seem highly implausible to many sociologists) are therefore in order.

In the first place, if, following Gouldner, we take 'rationality' to be 'the capacity to make problematic what had hitherto been treated as given',[73] then there will be 'objective limits', in practice, to the extent and the manner in which either the theologian or the social scientist can hope to realise this capacity. In the second place, I see no reason to suppose that, in principle, the theologian's rationality is any more circumscribed or inhibited than that of the social scientist.

In the third place, the claim that responsibility for the critique of religious ideology devolves partly upon the theologian raises the question of the possibility of 'scientific' theology. Perhaps, in view of the fact that, in current English usage, the concept of 'science' is considerably more restricted than either the French 'science' or the German 'wissenschaft', it would be better to ask about the possibility of theological discourse constituting a mode of 'rational knowledge'.[74] As I see it, this possibility could only legitimately be excluded if it could be shown that religious faith (the practice on which theology critically reflects) was in no sense 'experiential knowledge' of its object — even if it can never be demonstrated (and in *that* sense 'known') to be such knowledge.

These excessively condensed observations are, I hasten to add, offered as an 'agenda', as an indication of questions that arise from a consideration of the 'ideological' status of religious practice and theological reflection, not as conclusions to an argument.[75] I began by raising the question of 'truthfulness'. The 'truthfulness' of Christianity, as of Marxism, is primarily a practical matter: it is to be 'shown' in the transformation both of individuals and of social relationships. (Most people know this, rightly recognizing that saints are more important that theologians.) And because Christian religious practice (like all other beliefs and social practices) is, in the concrete, not only 'determinate' in form and content, but subject to distortion and 'false consciousness', therefore, as with other 'ideological forms', it needs to be set in continual tension with aspects of critical reflection: historical, literary-critical and philosophical.

I have referred to the question of the 'truthfulness' of Christianity rather than to the question of its 'truth', because no discussion of the latter topic is today entitled to sidestep the issues brought into focus in Marx's *Theses on Feuerbach*. As Ernst Bloch once said, commenting on those theses: 'Correctness is not yet truth'.[76] Nevertheless, correctness does indeed matter. The characteristic assertions of Christian belief are only 'correct' if cerain truth-conditions are fulfilled. The elucidation of those truth-conditions is, I have suggested, one of the responsibilities of the Christian theologian. And yet he can never afford to forget that 'the secret of the manner of their fulfilment lies with God'.[77]

REFERENCES AND NOTES

1. Mannheim, K., *Ideology and Utopia* (London, 1936), p. 38.
2. 'How is it possible for man to continue to think and live in a time when the problems of ideology and utopia are being radically raised and thought through in all their implications?' (Mannheim, *loc. cit.*). I have enough trouble with concepts of 'ideology' in this paper, without attending to Mannheim's idiosyncratic, and not always consistent, distinction between 'ideology' and 'utopia'.
3. Theologians tempted to see 'formal' sociological analysis as less challenging than Marxist criticism may be walking straight into a trap set by their own deep-rooted tendency towards idealism. In saying this, I have in mind Adorno's criticism of Mannheim: 'The sociology of knowledge expounded by Karl Mannheim ... calls everything into question and criticizes nothing'; 'In its neutrality the generalizing order of Mannheim's conceptual world is kindly disposed to the real world; it

employs the terminology of social criticism while removing its sting' (Adorno, T. W., "The Sociology of Knowledge and its Consciousness', *Prisms* (London, 1967), pp. 37, 38). According to Adorno, then, Mannheim, in issuing his reminders that no world-view, including Marxism, is immune from ideological distortion, is himself the unwitting 'idéologue' (in Marx's sense) of prevailing patterns of social dominance. In general, on the Frankfurt School's reaction to Mannheim, cf. Jay, M., *The Dialectical Imagination* (London, 1973), pp. 63,64.

4. Marx, K., 'A Contribution to the Critique of Hegel's Philosophy of Right. Introduction', *Early Writings* (London, Pelican Marx Library, 1975), p. 243.

5. Rahner, K., 'Ideology and Christianity', *Theological Investigations, VI* (London, 1969). p. 43.

6. *Ibid.*, p. 50.

7. Torrance, T. F., *Theological Science* (London, 1969), p. 28.

8. Cf. *ibid.*, p. 188

9. *Loc. cit.*

10. Fierro, A., *The Militant Gospel* (London, 1977), p. 239; cf. p. 290.

11. *Ibid.*, p. 412; cf. pp. 317-355.

12. 'The distinction between scientific analysis and ideology has enabled many Christians to look more favourably on Marxism', Hebblethwaite, P., *The Christian-Marxist Dialogue and Beyond* (London, 1977), p. 51. Cf. Gutierrez, G., *A Theology of Liberation* (London, 1974), p. 97, discussing 'the current vogue of interpreting Marxism in Latin-America according to Althusser'.

13. Which raises the interesting question of the sense in which *such* a use of the distinction is itself 'ideological': cf. Gouldner, A. W., *The Dialectic of Ideology and Technology* (London, 1967), pp. 286-287. 'How are we to understand Althusserian structuralism, not in its self-evaluation as "science", but *as ideology?*', Thompson, E. P., 'The Poverty of Theory', *The Poverty of Theory and Other Essays* (London, 1978), p. 197.

14. Thompson's sustained, detailed and devastating polemic against Althusser's idealism ('The Poverty of Theory') is all the more interesting in that it is the product of an historian standing, albeit at times uncomfortably, in the Marxist tradition.

15. Williams, R., *Marxism and Literature* (Oxford, 1977), p. 11. Cf. Wicker, B., 'Marxist Science and Christian Theology', *New Blackfriars* (1977), pp. 85-100, on category mistakes arising from the conviction 'that somehow the term "ideology", being an abstract singular, must — ultimately, in the last instance — denote a single idea, or concept' (p. 89).

16. For sketches of which, cf. *e.g.*, Mannheim, K., *Ideology and Utopia*, pp. 63-66; Seliger, M., *The Marxist Conception of Ideology* (Cambridge, 1977), pp. 13-19.

17. Cf. *e.g.*, Plamenatz, J., *Karl Marx's Philosophy of Man* (Oxford, 1975), pp. 86, 211; Seliger, *op. cit.*, pp. 22, 27.

18. Kolakowski, L., *Main Currents of Marxism, I, The Founders* (Oxford, 1978), p. 175.

19. Marx, *Early Writings*, p. 422.

20. Christian newly awakened from centuries of mutual intolerance should stir uneasily at all this talk of Marxism being now engaged in 'the purging of eclecticism from itself and the preclusion of united fronts with other discourses at the level of theory' (Barker, F., 'The Morality of Knowledge and the Disappearance of God', *New Blackfriars* (1976.) p. 403.

21. Cf. Raymond Williams' discussion of the 1859 Preface to *A Contribution to the Critique of Political Economy*, in *Marxism and Literature*, pp. 75-77.

22. Seliger, *op. cit.*, p. 76.

23. Marx, *Early Writings*, p. 425.

24. *Ibid.*, p. 426. Mannheim, commenting on this passage, seems to me justified in saying that 'the fact that our thinking is determined by our social position is not necessarily a source of error' (*Ideology and Utopia*, p. 111).

25. Williams, *Marxism and Literature*, p. 55; cf. pp. 70-71.

26. 'The entire notion of ideology, then, *as Marx used it*, was most crucially *a critique of the scientific pretensions of the new social science*' (Gouldner, *The Dialectic of Ideology*, p. 8).

27. Giddens, A., *Capitalism and Modern Social Theory* (Cambridge, 1971), p. 209.

28. Giddens, *op. cit.*, p. 42.

29. *Ibid.*, p. 209.

30. Marx, K., and Engels, F., *The German Ideology*, tr. Arthur, C. J. (London, 1974), p. 64.

31. Thompson, 'An Open Letter to Leszek Kolakowski', *Poverty of Theory and Other Essays*, pp. 177-178.

32. Seliger, *The Marxist Conception of Ideology*, p. 26.

33. Thompson, *op. cit.*, p. 119.

34. *Ibid.*, p. 120. Notice the ironic use of geographical metaphors derived from Althusser.

35. Marx, *The German Ideology*, p. 48.

36. For Thompson, theology, together with 'astrology, some parts of bourgeois sociology and of orthodox Stalinist Marxism', is not a 'mature intellectual discipline', but 'a merely-ideological formation' ('The Poverty of Theory', p. 204). Identified with the proposal of 'an ultimate system of truth' (p. 375), it is firmly contrasted with both 'knowledge' (p. 225) and 'reason' (p. 381).

37. Eagleton, T., ' "Decentring" God', *New Blackfriars* (1976), p. 149. Thus Jean-Joseph Goux speaks of 'le caractère profondément *théologique* du système monétaire' (*Economie et Symbolique* (Paris, 1973), p. 63, my stress). Of course, an ancient Christian theological tradition has always insisted that '*that* God really does not exist who operates and functions as an indiviual existent alongside of other existents' (Rahner, K., *Foundation of Christian Faith* (London, 1978), p. 63). But such reminders of what can *not* be said of God (as Aquinas would put it) hardly turn aside the atheist's criticism of uses to which, in *fact*, the concept of God is widely put in the practice of Christianity.

38. Althusser, L., *For Marx* (London, 1977), p. 170.

39. *Ibid.*, p. 231 (my stress). 'Although Althusser seeks to escape the polarity of ideology as "false", and science as "valid", his standpoint in fact rests upon a peculiarly ungrounded version of such a differentiation' (Giddens, A., *Central Problems in Social Theory* [London, 1979], p. 181).

40. Cf. Barker, F., 'The Morality of Knowledge . . .', p. 404.

41. Barker, *art. cit.*, p. 405.

42. Barker, *art. cit.*, p. 410. It is not difficult to see why Lucien Goldmann's declaration that 'the phrase *Credo ut intelligam* provides a common basis for Augustinian, Pascalian and Marxist epistemology' (*The Hidden God*, tr. Thody, P., (London, 1964), p. 94) should make him unpopular in certain circles.

43. Parsons, T., *The Social System* (London, 1951), p. 367.

44. *Ibid.*, p. 349.

45. Williams, *Marxism and Literature*, p. 61.

46. Foster, M. B., 'Historical Materialism', *Christian Faith and Communist Faith*, ed. MacKinnon, D. M. (London, 1953) p. 88.

47. Cf. Giddens, *Capitalism*, pp. 208-209; Plamenatz, *op. cit.*, pp. 211ff; Seliger, *op. cit.*, pp. 32-33; Williams, *op. cit.*, p. 58.
48. Mannheim, *Ideology and Utopia*, pp. 150-151.
49. *Ibid.*, p. 165.
50. Gouldner, *The Dialectic of Ideology*, p. 14.
51. *Ibid.*, p. 75.
52. Cf. Rahner, K., 'Experience of God Today', *Theological Investigations, XI* (London, 1974), pp. 149-165.
53. Seliger, *The Marxist Conception of Ideology*, p. 21.
54. Gouldner, *The Dialectic of Ideology*, p. 45.
55. *Ibid.*, p. 49; cf. pp. 214-215.
56. *Ibid.*, p. 144
57. 'Scientific' Marxists would presumably resist this suggestion. Yet, in the course of doing just that, one of them asserts that, 'because Marxism is a scientific practice, a *praxis*, it is only in the process of changing the world that it can constitute itself as a science' (Barker, 'The Morality of Knowledge ...', p. 407). In which case, it may be some time before this science is 'constituted'.
58. Althusser, *For Marx*, p. 12.
59. Cf. Rahner, K., 'Thoughts on the Possibility of Belief Today', *Theological Investigations, V* (London, 1966), p. 12.
60. Cf. Wicker, 'Marxist Science and Christian Theology', p. 95.
61. Wicker, *art. cit.*, p. 97.
62. Ethical systems that view morality, ideologically, as 'some "autonomous region" of human choice and will, arising independently of the historical process' (Thompson, 'The Poverty of Theory', p. 363) invite Marxist criticism, but do not excuse Marxist silence: 'The project of Socialism is guaranteed *by nothing* ... but can find its own guarantees only by *reason* and through an open *choice of values*. And it is here that the silence of Marx, and of most Marxisms, is so loud as to be deafening' (*loc. cit.*).
63. Barker, F., 'Science and Ideology', *New Blackfriars* (1977), p. 477.
64. *Ibid.*, p. 476.
65. *Loc cit.* Marxism may 'say firmly that there is no God' (Barker, 'The Morality of Knowledge ...', p. 405), but firmness of assertion is no substitute for argument.
66. Thompson, 'The Peculiarities of the English', *The Poverty of Theory*, p. 79; cf. pp. 119ff, 275-276.
67. Williams, *Marxism and Literature*, p. 83.
68. *Ibid.*, p. 86.
69. *Ibid.*, p. 87.
70. *Ibid.*, p. 55.
71. Gouldner, *The Dialectic of Ideology*, p. 51.
72. This feature of the discourse of faith does not necessarily appear in its grammatical form: the distinction between 'religion' and 'theology' is more fundamentally a distinction between *uses* of language than between sets of propositions (consider, for example, the range of possible uses of the proposition 'God is just', which could either be an expression of personal trust, or a thesis in a theoretical theodicy).
73. Gouldner, *op. cit.*, p. 49.
74. Cf. Wartofsky, M. W., *Feuerbach* (Cambridge, 1977), p. 448.
75. Elsewhere, I have tried to pursue the discussion along the lines indicated: cf. Lash, N. L. A., 'Ideology, Metaphor and Analogy', in *The Philosophical Frontiers of Christian Theology*, ed. Hebblethwaite, B. and Sutherland, S., to be published

by the Cambridge University Press.

76. Bloch, E., 'Changing the World, Marx's *These on Feuerbach*', *On Karl Marx* (New York, 1971), p. 81.
77. MacKinnon, D. M., *Explorations in Theology* 5 (London, 1979), p. 165.

Chapter 12

COMPARING DIFFERENT MAPS OF THE SAME GROUND

David Martin
Department of Sociology, London School of Economics and Political Science, U.K.

THE PRIMARY foci of concern so far in the interchange between sociology and theology have been determinism and relativity. However neither determinism nor relativity are new problems, and it is not even clear that they are sharpened or seriously altered by sociological analysis. Of course whoever engages in sociological work will be conscious of the pressure exercised by the problem of more or less strict casuality in human affairs, and will be exposed to a persistent practical relativisation of his perspective. He will regard norms and ideas as systematically related to a context of time and place, culture and social exigency. He will see how truths which men suppose to be eternal mutate according to the several necessities of modes and styles of social life. But that is, perhaps, just his psychological problem. At the level of philosophy it is difficult to see how his personal difficulty gives rise to a new question for ontology. He simply lives with an acute and troubling version of old questions.

So in what follows I will try to desert the ancient stamping ground of determinism and relativity, and at least attempt to begin elsewhere. I shall select certain statements from the body of Christian belief and see whether my reflections on them yield anything problematic for theology. I will put on a naive stare, looking at statements and seeing whether the sociological categories embedded in my mental equipment start to generate oddities, difficulties, problems. It may well be that as I do so the old issues of determinism and relativity will creep back, asserting their usual primacy.

The statements at which I intend to stare are not theological propositions but ordinary working religious sentences. They are respectively from an epistle, a gospel and a psalm. First, 'If any man be in Christ he is a new creature'. Second, 'That they may all be one'. And third, 'Behold thou hast made my days as a span long and mine age as nothing in respect of thee; and verily every man living is altogether vanity . . . And now, Lord, what is my hope? Truly my hope is even in thee'. I select these working sentences because they are likely to tie in with religious institutions. The first touches on a crucial transition, or shift of religious condition, and therefore will be a leit-motif both in liturgical enactments and personal biography. I will in due course discuss it with particular reference to Baptism. The second touches on the bond of solidarity constantly invoked in social and religious language alike. It also has ramifications in the idea of unity as such: the unity of God, of the Trinity, of God and Man, of Christ and the Church, of Christians one with another. The third is an eloquent response to the limits of the human condition, more especially contingency and death. Death and life are the primary counters of religious experience, and provide the ground from which grows a huge tree of symbolism.

If we turn now to the first statement it is first of all necessary to define what it means, or more realistically to hint at what it contains and implies. At one level it is little more than a bare tautology, saying that a man who is in Christ is not as he was previously. At another level it contains in a little space almost the whole of Christian theology. You are not likely to make much sense of such a sentence unless you already know the rest of the doctrines in which it is lodged. However, these doctrines are also themselves dense statements of the same kind, and comprise an arc of intimately related signs and symbols. So all that can be done is to select some points on that arc of cognate signs.

According to Christian faith Christ is the head of the new creation and the first born of many. These are not born by the processes of natural generation but spiritually regenerated, and thereby inducted into a new order of brotherhood, summed in Christ. This new order cancels mere legality and opens up a process of regeneration within the universe itself. Not only is the law of sin reversed within the self but the powers which dominate the universe have received a signal of defeat. So when a man is 'in Christ' he is reborn into a new order where 'the former things are passed away'. To be joined to Christ is to undergo a birth, death and resurrection of the spirit. The old Adam is supplanted by the new Adam, and this means that all our losses are now to be reversed, including the most severe loss of all, which is death. Christ by dying cancels death, and any one who is 'in Christ' dies with him, sharing in the redemptive triumph of love over frustration and negativity. Of course, this is not to say that all who call themselves Christians grow up into the full stature of the new man. Rather, the benefits of new manhood are open to all men by grace. The tincture of newness is implanted in whoever is open to it.

All this is, of course, fundamental theology and the reader may easily wonder where sociological reflection will begin to take over from theological exposition. But I am, after all, staring naively at a tiny sentence, and I have already underlined how the tiniest of sentences contains a taut spring of implication. The smallest atom of religious discourse is a creative and explosive ball. Moreover, I could have begun from any of these tiny micro-statements and traversed the whole arc of meaning. Every point on the arc is integral to the complete cycle of related centres. These centres also subsume each other and thereby provide an analogy of their own meaning. By their own inherent nature they mutually subsume and incorporate, and also point to subsumption and incorporation as fundamental to spiritual relationships. They speak of the logic of relations and exemplify them. And sociology is of course concerned with the logic of relations.

How then does this logic of subsumption and incorporation work out? To be 'in Christ' is to be taken in spiritually and incorporated: 'I yet not I but Christ in me'. There is an I in him, and he is in me. Likewise that I is joined to 'all them that are Christs'. 'He' and 'I' are conjoined with 'they'. This refers to the act of incorporation which constitutes the Church. Christians absorb his body into themselves that their 'sinful bodies may be made clean by his body'. Thus incorporation is also transference: the essential unity covers an essential difference. A transference is also a transition. What was once polluted and alien becomes clean and acceptable. It therefore repeats the sacrifice whereby it has been redeemed. The Christian presents himself sacrificially, receiving the benefits of loving sacrifice, offering them up and symbolically repeating them in his approach to the divine. So we find that within this thought-world relationships constantly repeat themselves in analogical mirrors. To partake of the benefits of sacrificial love, offered a priori and without condition, you place the sacrifice before God and you remake the sacrifice in yourself as an offering to God. Whereas previously you were 'unworthy to make any sacrifice' you now find that sacrifice is your 'bounden duty and service'. This brings us back to the relatonship between transference and transition. You enjoy a change of status, from alien to citizen, from child of wrath to son of God. The term 'rite de passage' as used by anthropologists can be applied to the enactments of baptism and the Eucharist quite literally. Those who entertain faith enter upon a passage or journey, and are caught up in a kind of movement. The movement takes them from unworthiness to worthiness, old man to new man, death to life. The journey or passage is a sequence existentially appropriated and symbolically objectified.

Sociology deals in sequence and transition, as well as in subsumption and incorporation. Journeys and joinings are the basic repertoire of the discipline. So also is the difference between in and out: what sociologists call the maintenance of boundaries. Those who join for the journey are different from those who do not. They belong to a different city. The logic of in and out, moving and remaining behind, will generate all kinds of distinctions and boundary markers. Out and in, before and after, will be defined and demarcated by sin and salvation, world and church, new man and old man, glory and shame, pilgrim and sojourner, City of God and City of Man, the Kingdom of heaven and the principalities and powers. The sociologist will see the boundaries of belonging sharply framed in these mighty opposites. Each mighty opposite will express transfers and transits, exclusions and incorporations.

Nothing in the world of thought or of enactment will escape the opposition. If we turn, for example, to baptism, we see how a man shifts from the prior condition of wrath to the subsequent condition of acceptance, conveyed in all the symbolism of crossing. The transition is conveyed by the crossing of water and the sign of the cross made in water. Here the properties of a natural element are deployed to convey multiple meanings. Water is an element through which you cross, in which you are immersed and by which you become clean. Here we see implicit and explicit one of the great religious sentences: 'in whom, by whom, and through whom'. The little prepositions 'in', 'by' and 'through' characterise the basic structure of spiritual relations. They contain incorporation and transit and mediation. In baptism they link with a triple transition: from enslavement to liberty, from death to life, and from journey to arrival. The water is simultaneously the Red Sea, the Jordan and the river of death. All involve crossing and transition. Thus sacred history becomes linked to individual history and the isolated individual is set within a vast field of holy images and significant transits. He simultaneously enters the social movement and the movement of history.

All this is ground which the sociologist shares with the theologian. For the sociologist the analysis of symbols and sentences is an essential prolegomenon to understanding how religion works, and for the theologian it is the substance of his discipline. However, the sociologist takes leave of the theologian immediately he considers how religion is woven into the social fabric, i.e. how it relates and adjusts to different types of social formation. So I will take the sentence 'if any man be in Christ he is a new creature' as it relates to Baptism and then outline a sociological procedure. This procedure may or may not yield a 'correct' result. I mean that my sociological analysis may not be entirely convincing. But what matters is the approach itself and whether it throws up some characteristic difficulty for the theologian.

When one considers Baptism, i.e. the ritual incorporation into the new manhood, one of the major theological issues turns on whether the rite of initiation should be administered to children. The sociologist takes note of this issue and asks the following question: under what social circumstances are Christians likely to perceive this difficulty and to opt for adult baptism? This question cannot be settled by taking all instances of adult baptism and correlating them with a characteristic social environment. Rather one has to construct a piece of plausible social logic and then to see how far the logic is exemplified and contradicted in historical instances. This is a complex and disputable point of methodology into which I cannot go at the present juncture.

Baptism signifies and objectifies the entry into 'newness'. It is not however coextensive with the process of redemption in the individual soul. Rather the rite works as a demarcation point objectifying the point of entry into the company of the redeemed and signifying who belongs. Now, insofar as Christianity becomes coextensive with a natural community, that is to say with organic and primordial solidarities, the sacrament of baptism will *function* as entry into that natural community. The 'new creature' remade in the image of Christ will also become, in practice, the 'new creature' who has just arrived in the community. Baptism, as Kierkegaard observed, will be enacted as a Christian version of circumcision. This is not to say the specifically Christian meaning will be obliterated, but it will undergo a partial mutation under the fuctional pressure exercised by the natural community. It will be remade in the image of the organic and primordial relations which obtain in close-knit, solidary societies where religion is woven into the whole social fabric.

However, Christianity is by nature also an aspect of the fundamental process of differentiation, setting spiritual brotherhood against blood ties, and heavenly citizenship against secular belonging. The mighty opposites within which it is framed include this crucial differentiation, and thrust strongly against mere ordinary, *automatic* membership in a sacralised, natural group. Yet that thrust in part is neutralised by primordial solidarities. The original meaning, if that can be identified, is left stranded in the symbolism, unable to escape the grip of the organic pull. The Church talks as if baptism were a kind of pre-emptive strike for redemption, trying to give a persuasive gloss to a paradox thrust upon it by the social relations in which it is embedded.

No doubt you already observe the multiple problems which attend on the analysis so far. Quite apart from the (perhaps) foolhardy identification of an 'original' meaning I have attributed a theological paradox to a social contradiction. I have suggested that a symbolism of distinctive belonging, rooted in a premature differentiation, is practically subverted by the undertow of an organic social process, and thereby throws up an insoluble problem, How, I could go further and argue that when that natural pull is slackened, and the individual given space and room vis-a-vis social solidarity then the original symbolic thrust can reassert itself. More than that, it can strengthen the whole individualistic tendency, objectifying a new sense of *chosen* faith, even though the emphasis is on God's elective choice of the individual. The symbolism of the new creature which is embedded in baptism can now make straightforward sense*.

Now, we come to the question as to whether the link posited between infant baptism and organic, solidarity relationships and between adult baptism and a more voluntaristic type of society, bears at all on the *status* of the doctrines. Does the fact that a contradiction at the level of theologic parallels a condition at the level of sociologic affect the issue as such? And, in spite of assurances to the contrary, are we sliding back towards the old question of relativity?

Let me place this dilemma within a concrete situation. A member of the Church of England on the verge of the 1980's may observe that as the Church slips anchor with the natural community and moves towards the open sea of voluntary association it begins to reconsider the doctrine and practice of baptism. Such a person would observe that the shift towards denominational status is accompanied by a demand for greater explicit commitment. As belonging ceases to be automatic and becomes open to erosion from various alternatives the criteria governing access to baptism are tightened up. This can be seen as a partial shift to the Baptist position insofar as commitment receives a new emphasis. However, infant baptism remains *in situ* for various reasons, including inertia. The sins of the parents are now visited on the child, since the decision whether or not to baptise turns on their degree of attachment to the Church.

Supposing this sociological analysis were correct, could it have any

---

*   I will not go into such questions as to why a voluntaristic Church like Methodism retains infant baptism, and why the Baptist Church does not revert to infant baptism wherever it re-enters the solidary pull of the community, as in the Southern States of the U.S. There are mechanisms of conservation which can be cited to explain such awkward instances. However the instances do indicate why we cannot mechanically correlate types of baptism with types of community.

bearing on how baptism ought to be understood? In asking the question let us recollect that we are considering various ways in which the transition to the 'new man' may be objectified by way of a demarcated entry into the 'household of faith'. We have observed a loose empirical link between organic solidary bonds and infant baptism, and this link can be rephrased as a degree of 'fit'. When the organic community dissolves then automatic belonging by birthright ceases to be 'fitting'.

Here lies the crux, because the empirical 'fit' which we observe from the sociological perspective is translated by some into a sense of what is 'fitting' i.e. appropriate. In the new social situation the transition to the 'new man' is seen as released from the old solidarities, as no longer embedded in the bond of ineluctable belonging. So the *proper* approach stresses choice.

However, the shift from empirical fit to theological propriety crosses the line between 'is' and 'ought'. It designates an appropriate normative response on the basis of an observed social connection. But this only pushes the normative issue towards the question: Why should anybody adjust to the new situation? Adjustment is not a moral imperative. Indeed, adjustment is often seen as moral capitulation.

At this point the arguments become very complicated, because it is perfectly possible to enquire how far the essence of the transition to the 'new man' may be conveyed by infant baptism in one social situation and by another form of baptism in a different social situation. Controversy is couched in terms of necessary core and expendable variable periphery, and this distinction of core and periphery itself tends to flourish and appeal in the modern situation. Equally characteristic of the modern situation is an argument based on the notion of a Babylonish captivity experienced by the Church either by reason of links to the structure of power, or in this case, by embeddedness in solidary, organic bonds. However, now the captivity is over the distortions which it induced may be thrown off, the truth of original Christianity recovered.

These arguments cannot be pursued further in this paper, since the object has been to stare at the root concept of the 'new man' and then see how this is ritually objectified according to the type of social order. The basic conclusion may, however, be underlined, which is that a 'fit' observed at the empirical level cannot be translated into what is theologically fitting.

We can now consider the second sentence; 'that they all be one'. This too is a statement of incorporation, in which the vertical unity of Father and Son is linked to the horizontal unity of all the sons and

235

daughters of God. It is not necessary to go into the exegesis expounded for the first sentence. Rather, we may turn to the deployment of this statement in the theological justification of ecumenism. The phrase 'that they may all be one' is set to work in an ecumenical context.

Before considering phrase and context we have to note two historical facts. One is that some scholars assure us that Jesus never envisaged a church. Moreover many commentaries do not attribute the phrase to Jesus. The other is that sentences of this kind are not only part of the logic of a theological position but are deployed in a legitimating role. Not only is the phrase a normative injunction to unity but it is also deployed authoritatively. Just as 'thou art Peter etc., is deployed to legitimate the Pope of Rome so 'that they may all be one' is deployed to bolster the W.C. C. and ecumenism. So we must distinguish carefully between unification as an element in a religious logic and the use of a phrase as an authoritative pronouncement. The latter is of course subject to a philosophical criticism.

The idea of unity is extremely general in its scope and what follows concerns only its application to the cause of ecumenical aspiration. One such application might run as follows: The Holy Spirit cannot be released because of the sin we are in by reason of our unhappy divisions. This might mean that our unhappy divisions are sign and proof of the frustration of the Spirit, in which case it is merely circular. The theologian is pointing to a particular condition characterising it as spiritually defective.

However, he may have something else in mind. He may be saying that disunity is a bar to any renewal of Pentecost. As he observes the 'deadness' of the contemporary church he may attribute the advent of *rigor mortis* to division and lack of full ecumenical fellowship. Such a statement appears to contain a hint of explanation as well as mere characterisation. He is not only saying that disunity signifies spiritual frustration but attributing the frustration to the disunity.

Of course, this may still be another circular statement which has simply travelled by a larger roundabout. The theologian challenged by an instance where the spirit apparently moves in a situation of disunity might say that the Spirit cannot be *fully* expressed until disunity is removed. Or he may say that a spiritual movement tolerant of disunity or, worse still, giving rise to schism, is *ipso facto* not moved by the true spirit of God. If he does protect his assertion in these ways there is nothing to be done with him. The glancing empirical reference is in fact vacuous.

If on the other hand the statement is not protected in these ways we may then adduce our contrary instances. For example we can point to

Methodism and ask whether or not this movement was 'of the Holy Spirit', and if the answer is positive we can point to the multiple schisms to which it gave rise. Indeed, we can give lots of similar instances, such as the rise of Franciscan spirit, which resulted both in heresy and rejuvenation. Of course, we do not put it past a theologian to say God the Holy Spirit was having to work at that time in a distorted situation and that therefore His activity was also subjected to a complementary distortion i.e. heresy, enthusiasm, spiritual excesses. But we have at least shown that in those instances where the Spirit has plainly been at work, at least by the standards of our straw theologian, there also is to be found lively schism and disunity. Spiritual rejuvenation and breakage of fellowship historically often go together. It follows that if our theologian's statement has empirical content then it is inaccurate. The Spirit *can* work in divisive situations. More than that it even appears to be positively associated with them.

Another move still remains whereby our theologian can wriggle sideways by developing the distinction between the distorted past and the potential in the present. He may concede that in the past the movement of the Spirit has been associated with lively schism, beginning with the division between Christianity and Judaism and the controversy between the followers of Apollos and the followers of Paul. However, in the modern situation, loosely defined, the 'Spirit' is calling us to unity, and He cannot be manifest until unity is in train. Again, this may mean no more than a benediction bestowed on attempts at unity. But it may also be a quasi-empirical statement about the special situation of the modern churches. If so, it lies within some overall view of historical periodisation which probably has a metaphysical loading. I mean that a theologian talking about the special characteristics of this present age may be using categories from a philosophy of history. The seeming statement about spiritual movements at the 'present time' is not really an empirical judgement about factors increasingly operative since, say, 1760 or 1860 or even, God save us, since 1960, but a theological apprehension of the current scene, an inspired 'sense' of the new age to which a specific kind of action is uniquely appropriate i.e. unification.

This 'apprehension' is itself validated by reference to the Spirit and is not susceptible to proof or disproof, verification or falsification. One may, however, observe the criteria by which the new age is marked off and staked out, and these may be a mixture of empirical observation and prophetic judgement. Thus the theologian may say 'We see today that such and such is the case . . . ' And then he may

237

interpret this as a 'sign'. The event and its train of consequences is treated as a gestalt which holds together as a comprehensive 'sign'. Once the sign is identified, the theologian argues that we are thereby warned to pursue a particular kind of action i.e. to be 'led' into unity.

This vocabulary of 'sign', 'age', 'inspiration' and 'leading' is of course specifically theological and is practised by sophisticated theologicans as well as by enthusiastic sectaries. Modernists and ecumenists make free with 'signs' as much as any sectarian, even if their language is less luridly biblical and blatantly eschatological. A liberation theologian discerning the signs of the times in Marxism or student revolt is not less in this particular mode than a sectary surmising he is in the time of the latter rain.

However, the interpretation of signs and the proclamation of ages is not open to empirical test. The Kingdom is at hand. The lame walk and the blind see. Repent and believe the Gospel. These are notes of urgency, divinations and demands, insights and commands. One cannot confute them. It makes no sense to say that as a matter of sober calculation the number of one-time lame now observed to walk has risen above the critical point. No. We are being enjoined to wake from the dead, and the signs which belong to that awakening are anticipatory instances of what resurrection and restoration mean and embody. This proclamation is a demand which simultaneously tells you the nature of the restoration now present or potentially available to you.

Here, of course, we are at the heart of the Gospel itself, and when the ecumenist identifies the Spirit with the cause of unification then we can only appeal to criteria internal to the proclamation itself. We may, for example, ask what in God's name the raising of the dead has to do with the faith and order committee of the World Council of Churches and other organisational entities. We may ask whether, in the original documents, the Spirit is not defined as inherently divisive, so that one shall be taken and one shall be left.

All such arguments, internal to theology, are curiously flexible in their application. We appeal to a general spiritual 'sign' and draw whatever application suits us – or seems good to the spirit within us. It is, of course part of the work of a sociologist to observe these flexible applications as they are utilised in religious suasion, whether by Popes or earnest followers of Seventh Day Adventism or Mr. Moon. The flexibility allows room for manoevre, and any attempt at hardening up such statements interferes with their social efficacy.

For example, that famous justification of tolerance by Gamaliel is often quoted against inquisitorial action. It affirms that 'if this thing be not of God it will come to nought'. However, when the statement is reversed it seems to imply that whatever makes a successful stir in the world is to be regarded as blessed of God. Actually, there are theologians who implicitly hold such a view, but its implications are very unpleasing, even if amended to mean that whatever stays successful over a long period is 'of God'. However, though this statement is used flexibly, it may perhaps be less flexible than most theological forms of suasion, since it is at least formally reversible. Most theological justifications have a much more open texture, the most open of all being the invocation of the Spirit. (Even Series 3½ has been justified by the direct operation of the Spirit in the Revision Committee, and that moreover by a diocesan Bishop.)

But to return more directly to our theme: We have looked at glancing empirical statements locked in theological injunctions. Not all empirical statements are so indirect or so bound in to the broader philosophical context. For example, a theologian may say; 'Lack of unity is the principal obstacle to the work of God in England today.' Now this is almost a direct empirical claim. It depends of course on how 'work of God' is defined, but assuming that this refers to a definable extant condition then it is open to falsification. A sociologist may then proceed to show what factors are actually involved, by the normal processes of social scientific reasoning. He may show, for example, that where, as in Scandinavia, the Church has no serious problem of disunity, spiritual life is singularly dormant. He may suggest that it is to such united death that the ecumenical movement seductively invites us.

But it is clear in this instance that the theologian has stepped outside his *opus proprium* He has made a refutable, falsifiable statement. He is thereby a scientist *malgré lui*. The difference between theological and sociological statements remains, in principle, as unbridgeable as ever.

So let me take a third religious statement which is not at all about multiple incorporations or about unification. It is from the Psalm 39 used in the Burial Service: 'Behold, thou hast made my days as a span long and mine age as nothing in respect of thee. And now Lord what is my hope? Truly my hope is even in thee'. There is very little to be said about such a statement except to notice two characteristics. It conveys the sense of an unavoidable limit; the empirical fact of death. It acknowledges ineluctable frustration and the contingent character of human being. However, it transcends that frustration with 'hope in God'. So within the final social rite of transition, whereby a man is placed with his ancestors, there is reference to another transition. The shift from life to death, socially acknowledged in the burial service, is theologically acknowledged and then placed in the context of another shift, from death to life. There is, if you like, a crossing in two directions; life-death, death-life. The religious statement contains both, acknowledging the universality of death and anticipating the triumph of life. It is simultaneously the language of limits and of transcendence. Nothing a sociologist can say about the social transitions involved in burial can have any bearing either on the undisputed limit represented by death or on the act of faith which denies its finality.

However, our examples may allow us to make some concluding observations about religious language. We noticed how it has to do with incorporation and unification, and how such social acts were rooted in a dense forest of symbols, each entwined with every other. These symbols were 'signs' of transition. They were imperatives which symbolically described relationships. They were also a language of alteration, giving these relationships an altered aspect. The 'elements' in the symbolic language were transubstantiated. Certain relations and certain hopes were organised in a unified symbolic field by the power of signs and images. But nothing a sociologist might tell us about the social reality of the various transitions where they come into play, whether baptism, or eucharist or death, could conceivably bear on the realities to which signs claim to refer.

Chapter 13

SENSES OF THE NATURAL WORLD AND SENSES OF GOD: ANOTHER LOOK AT THE HISTORICAL RELATION OF SCIENCE AND RELIGION.

Martin Rudwick

Unit for the History and Social Aspects of Science, Vrije Universiteit, Amsterdam, The Netherlands

Summary

THE 'CONFLICT' model of the historical relation of science and religion is still dominant both in the public mind and as a myth in the service of a 'triumphalist' view of natural science. The most important critique of scientific triumphalism now comes, not from 'radical science' but from an increasing coherent 'strong programme' in the sociology of natural-scientific knowledge (e.g. Barnes, Bloor, Shapin). This calls for causal explanations of changes in what is claimed as scientific knowledge, in terms that are impartial and symmetrical with respect to modern judgments of the validity of the claimed knowledge. It also programmatically looks out for the effects of social circumstances, experiences and interests on the constructed content of scientific knowledge. Despite criticism from some philosophers, the strong programme is proving increasingly successful in handling problems in the history of science. Its generally Durkheimian treatment of religious issues poses an important challenge to traditional historical accounts of 'science and religion'. It needs to be enriched, however, by extending its constructivist view of scientific knowledge from the collective to the individual level, and by taking more seriously the constraining and differentiating effects of the externality of the natural world itself, on the construction of claimed 'knowledge'. But the strong programme should also be ready, by its own canons, to treat claimed religious 'knowledge' symmetrically with claimed scientific 'knowledge'. It should therfore not exclude *a priori* the possible differentiating effects of whatever is claimed as externality characterised in theistic terms, on the construction of human senses of the natural world. A more adequate interpretation of specific episodes and broader trends in the historical relation of science and religion would thus become possible, if the strong programme's emphasis on the social construction of scientific knowledge were combined with Bowker's theory of religion as information process.

I

Introduction

The traditional stereotype of historical conflict between natural-scientific knowledge and religious belief has long ago been abandoned — or so we are often assured. But those who say so are wrong. The old stereotype is alive and well and living in television studios — and therefore also in millions of living rooms. Honest Galileo is still threatened with torture by a malevolent Inquisition; Darwin and his 'bulldog' Huxley still triumph by sheer virtue over a fundamentalist Fitzroy and a devious Wilberforce.[1]

The persistence of such powerful images indicate at once the rather obvious point that conceptions of the historical relations between science and religion are a socially distributed form of knowledge, just like any other collective belief. What is *passé* to enlightened theologians and historians of science may be very much a live concern to others. But this is not just a matter of popular stereotypes showing cultural lag in relation to scholarly knowledge. For the alleged knowledge of what the conflict involved is socially distributed even within the intellectual sector of society. For example, the trial of Galileo was travestied most recently, not by some trendy television producer but by a self-proclaimed polymathic scientist, who chose to ignore the historical research that had been digested for his benefit. And this was not a matter of unavoidable over-simplification for the sake of television, for the same theme runs through all Jacob Bronowski's published work. He was bound to show Galileo before the Inquisition as a simple confrontation of good and evil, because a more truly historical presentation would have compromised the confident scientistic vision of the 'Ascent of Man'.[2]

What is striking about this kind of scientific triumphalism is that it remains so persuasive, not only among self-defined top scientists but also among the general public. We should not over-estimate the impact of recent critiques of the whole enterprise of natural science. Yet those critiques have undeniably been important; and one of their effects has been to make most of the traditional discussions of the relation between science and religion simply obsolete. Traditional studies of religious belief in relation to science were almost always grounded ultimately in the acceptance of natural-scientific knowledge as paradigmatic, at least within a broad area of rational thought. But that paradigmatic character of science has now been thrown into doubt in three distinct ways; or rather, it is rejected by three broadly distinct social groups.

242

Firstly there are the self-styled 'radical' scientists, for whom the enterprise of science now stands unmasked as ideological through and through, as a tool in the hands of those with a political interest in maintaining an exploitative *status quo*. Secondly there are those for whom science has lost its paradigmatic character because of the perceived strength of the claims of rival systems of knowledge, the pseudo-sciences or — to their adherents — 'alternative sciences' that are generally borrowed *ex oriente*. Thirdly — and far more significant than the others — there are those for whom science now takes its proper place as just one of many culturally constructed enterprises, as a 'relativistic science' that requires analysis and evaluation on a par with other human activities. (Distinct from these three numerically small groups of critics there is of course the much larger zone of public fear about the social and political consequences of the technological uses of scientific knowledge; but for this much larger group the knowledge itself is still objective and instrumentally certain — indeed all too certain — and only its desirability is questioned).

II

Some negative criticisms

In this paper I want to explore the implications of the third and most significant of those critiques of scientific knowledge, namely that deriving from the tradition of the sociology of knowledge, in the hope that it may point towards a fresh approach to the historical study of the relation of science and religion. But first I must make some rather negative criticisms of the traditional treatment of this theme.

One such criticism must be directed at the very way the problem has often been posed, namely as a relation — whether of conflict or reconciliation — between two entities termed Science and Religion. It may be protested that the use of such global terms is unavoidable or at least desirable for the sake of brevity (I have after all used them myself in the title of this paper); but the distorting effects of this usage should not be under-estimated. For it can seduce us into thinking that there really are two monolithic entities which need to be related to each other, when instead we ought to be attending to the enormous variety of the activities that are covered by the terms Science and Religion. Even the term Science is highly problematic, as I myself have been forced to realise since I moved from a culture where it has been narrowed down to 'natural knowledge' to one where it still means *'Wissenschaft'*. Furthermore, even among the natural sciences themselves there is so much variety of cognitive and social forms, in relation to such alternative goals as understanding, prediction and control, that we ought to ignore the monopolistic claims of some physicists and attend also to what other natural scientists say and do. For the other term, Religion, there has been too much attention to the supposedly contrasted roles of Protestantism and Catholicism in the development of the relationship, and too little attention to the variations of attitude and practice in relation to science, that have existed at different times and places within both those traditions (and indeed within others too).

A second criticism must be directed at two contrasted ways in which the historical relationship has generally been handled, either in terms of abstract concepts or with an exclusively individualistic emphasis. The first or abstract approach reduces both scientifc and religious behaviours to a formal comparison of propositional statements; it strips away as irrelevant all the passions and purposes that have sustained those behaviours, leaving only a skeleton of formalised conceptual structures. The second or individualistic approach, by contrast, sometimes gives all too much attention to the particulars of individual personality that informed a specific confrontation of representatives of Science and Religion, such as that between Huxley and Wilberforce. The limitation of this second approach is not over-intellectualism, but rather the failure to take adequate account of the social dimension of any such episode.

In place of either the abstract or the individualistic approach, I suggest that what is needed is a study of scientific and religious behaviours, treated as processual activities which have not only a conceptual but also an emotional dimension, and not only an individual but also a social dimension. Of course this is easier said than done, but at least we should try.(This emphasis will also explain why I have deliberately used the term Religion in the title of this paper in place of the more intellectualist term Theology).

In one important area the approach I have just argued for is already being adopted, at least to some extent, and is already yielding some results. Among professional historians of science there is a growing awareness of the vital role that religious beliefs have played in the past in the construction of scientific world-views on both individual and collective levels. (And under 'religious beliefs' must of course be included in some cases strongly anti-religious beliefs). What is still more important is that these beliefs are no longer regarded as embarrassing for the reputation of a great scientist, nor are they dismissed as irrelevant to the 'real' work of science in past periods. Furthermore they are no longer treated only as 'external' factors that in particular circumstances may have retarded or advanced the intrinsic 'internal' development of valid scientific conclusions. A growing number of historians of science now routinely treat religious beliefs as a possibly constitutive factor in the formulation and acceptance not only of generalised world-views but also of quite specific scientific theories and even of alleged observational 'facts'. Religious beliefs, in other words, are taken seriously in the task of understanding not only the context but also the content of the scientific work of past periods. There is a growing readiness on the part of historians of science to enter empathetically into those beliefs, however alien or even bizarre they may seem to a late-twentieth-century mind, in order to gain a deeper understanding of the scientific work that was produced within the framework of those beliefs.

This empathy has limits, however, which suggest that behind the appearance of scholarly tolerance, religious beliefs are not really taken a seriously as it seems. For historians of science are paying more attention to the role not only of religious beliefs but also of beliefs in for example astrology, natural magic and alchemy. It is no coincidence, I think, that they are doing so at a time when the monopolistic claims of modern science are under attack by proponents of similar beliefs in their modern form of 'alternative sciences'. This is significant, because by implication or at least by association, religious beliefs seem to be given much the same ontological status in the historian's mind as magic and astrology. This inference is supported by the observation that the strength of the historian's empathy for religious beliefs often seems to be directly proportional to the space of time that separates him from them, fading away as one approaches the present day.

I suggest therefore, that even scholarly historical studies of science have escaped only superficially from the powerful triumphalism of modern science, at least as far as religious beliefs are concerned. Modern science in relation to social policy and political ideology has been forced in recent years on to the defensive. But modern science in relation to religious belief remains unshakeably triumphalist in its rhetorical tone.

This might be attributed to the social and cognitive marginality of religious belief in a modern science-based culture like our own. But this assertion, that our culture is indeed one in which religious belief is marginal, is itself no neutral claim. It is a claim made by those groups in our society — including a highly vocal sector of the scientific élite — which possess the cultural power to press that view on to the rest of us. In others words, at every level of sophistication, including that of professional history of science, current conceptions of the historical relation between natural-scientific knowledge and religious belief are heavily influenced by the cultural hegemony of specific groups for whom religious belief is indeed marginal or vestigial. Once this hegemony is recognised for what it is, the way is open for a more actively critical stance towards the triumphalist interpretation of the historical development of scientific behaviours in relation to religious behaviours.[3]

III

Scientific knowledge as a cultural product
I have suggested that the most significant contemporary critique of scientific knowledge is not that of the proponents of 'radical science' or 'alternative science', nor even that of the opponents of nuclear power stations and the like. Far more unsettling in the long run for traditional views of science is the critique, or rather re-interpretation, of scientific knowledge as a relativistic cultural product. The emergence of this new view of science, and in particular the erosion of the privileged epistemological position of natural-scientific know-ledge, is still often identified with Thomas Kuhn's notions of paradigm-guided 'normal science' and anomaly-induced 'revolutio-nary science'.[4] Looking back, however, over the twenty years (no less!) that Kuhn's work has been publicly available, it seems clear that despite all the fuss it once caused among philosophers of science, certain aspects of Kuhn's work were absorbed quietly and naturally by historians of science. Indeed some historians even claimed that in so far as these notions were valid, they had long been part of good historical practice. This was less than fair to Kuhn's originality in formulating explicitly much that had previously remained implicit. But it is certainly true that much good recent historical work on science has made effective and explicit use of categories such as 'scientific tradition', which take for granted the importance of social as well as conceptual continuity in scientific activity, as a necessary context of any innovative originality that may arise.

Kuhn's work can now be seen, however, as just one contributory factor to a much more far-reaching erosion of the old certainties about science, and to the rise of an increasingly coherent view of science as a cultural product. It is convenient to refer to this new view as the 'strong programme' in the history and sociology of natural-scientific knowledge. That is the term used by one of its leading spokesmen, David Bloor; but I do not mean to imply that all research in this direction has been derivative from, or even influenced by, that of Bloor and his Edinburgh colleagues, nor is there any monolithic unaminity among those writers themselves or between them and others. Nevertheless there is enough consistency to make a general description of the strong programme both possible and useful.[5]

The strong programme is 'strong' in relation to weaker forms of the sociology of science which are limited to an analysis of the social circumstances that may retard or accelerate the development of scientific knowledge.[6] In this weaker programme the actual content of science is regarded, if only implicitly, as an intrinsic process derived primarily from the interaction of external nature with human rationality. By contrast, the strong programme deliberately explores the possibility that the social circumstances and social goals of scientists may affect the actual content of the claimed knowledge which results from their activity. The strong programme thus lies clearly in the mainstream of traditional sociology of knowledge, yet it programmatically rejects Mannheim's assumption that the *Naturwissenschaften* could not be subjected to the supposedly relativising effects of such an analysis.[7]

The strong programme aims at offering explanations of the development of natural-scientific knowledge in terms that are causal, impartial, symmetrical and reflexive. This means in particular that scientific ideas that are currently judged 'correct' are to be treated impartially alongside those that modern scientists would reject as 'erroneous' or 'unscientific', and that both categories pose exactly symmetrical problems of explanation. If a particular notion is judged correct by modern scientists, we cannot explain its acceptance at a certain time in the past simply by pointing to its 'truth': we must still ask, how and why was it accepted by particular scientists in a certain cultural situation at a specific period? And we must ask exactly the same question about any notion that is currently judged erroneous. Acceptance and rejection are always and irreducibly social acts by specific social groups in specific cultural circumstances.

The kinds of causal explanation that are given within the strong programme need not be exclusively or even primarily social in character; but social influences on the content of scientific knowledge are programmatically not excluded from consideration. That double negative is necessary, in order to contrast the strong programme with what has been in practice the ruling orthodoxy about science. That orthodoxy has excluded the possibility of social influences, either dogmatically and completely, as foreign to the nature of 'real' or 'hard' natural science, or at least methodologically, by shifting the burden of proof on to the other side. In contrast, the strong programme urges that each case should be considered on its own merits: at certain times and places, particular kinds of science *may* be such insulated sub-cultures that their content is not influenced perceptibly by any but the most general characteristics of the wider society. But we should not assume *a priori* that this is the norm, and we should approach the study of any particular episode open to the possibility of finding some much more specific social influences.

In fact, however, most writers following the strong programme reject the notion of historical 'influence', with all its dubious connotations of contagion and its suggestion of quasi-automatic cultural transmission. Instead, they utilise more and more the notion of use, often calling on the later Wittgenstein to act as the programme's patron philosopher. The question then is: how has a particular piece of scientific knowledge — or more accurately, claimed knowledge — been used, by whom, and to serve what interests? Again, it is not assumed that all interests must be social, only that social interests may be operative alongside, for example, technical-instrumental interests, and that that possibility must not be excluded *a priori*. Scientific knowledge is regarded above all as a cultural resource which is constructed, evaluated and used, always by particular social groups in the service of their specific interests.

This view need not in fact reduce scientific knowledge to 'nothing but' a product of social circumstances; but it is understandable that some of its critics fear its apparent relativism. This is not least because it makes increasing use of explicit analogies from social anthropology, and claims that there is no intrinsic contrast between modern scientific knowledge and the claimed knowledge of so-called primitive cultures. But if in this respect it is somewhat neo-Frazerian in orientation, it is also strongly Durkheimian in its exploration of possible parallels or even isomorphisms between the content of scientific knowledge and the social circumstances, social experience or social interests of those who accept that knowledge as valid. If Wittengenstein is the patron philosopher, than Durkheim is surely the patron social scientist of the strong programme. But the more general point is that the anthropological perspective is seen as breaking through what is otherwise an inpenetrable barrier to a realistic view of science, namely the 'sacralization' of modern scientific knowledge. It provides resources for studying science realistically as a social institution and as a cultural product, without assuming *a priori* any intrinsic uniqueness that would preclude or limit the scope of such a study.[8]

There have been plenty of strong defensive reactions to the emergence of this view of science, particularly from philosophers who feel that the rationality of natural-scientific knowledge is threatened. Many of their points may well be valid; but the splenetic tone of some of their criticism, like that of Lakatos's attacks on Kuhn a decade ago, leads one to suspect that a sacred cow has been attacked.[9] I am not competent to evaluate these philosophical attacks, and I will not attempt to do so. But many features of the strong programme are now being incorporated successfully into what seems to me to be some of the best and most original research in the history of science; and I believe that this empirical challenge is what will count in the end.[10]

The passive voice that I have used in this bare and somewhat crude summary of the strong programme for the study of science is not intended to conceal my own sympathy with it, or indeed my own attempts to use it to re-evaluate the area of science with which I am most familiar.[11] It is true that all the historical case-studies that have been carried out broadly along the lines of the strong programme can be, and indeed have been, criticised on particular points by other specialist historians. Nevertheless I think it is clear that any future interpretations of these and other episodes in the history of science will have to face the challenge posed by the strong programme.

Relating these 'strong-programme' interpretations to more conventional 'internalist' accounts of the same episodes will be one major challenge; but here I only want to point out that they pose a challenge of equal importance to more conventional accounts of the historical relation between science and religion. Few of these case-studies relate explicitly to religious concerns in a narrow sense.[12] But any future account, for example, of the long-standing historical alliance between science and religion in European culture will have to face the challenge of the more Durkheimian view of religion that is implicit in many of these studies. To put it more precisely, it has long been recognised that from the late seventeenth century to the mid-nineteenth, there was a widespread sense of compatibility or mutual reinforcement between one of the dominant views of scientific research, as delving into the wonders of creation, and a specific Christian tradition that placed great emphasis on the providential character of the created world. But the strong programme obliges us to ask causal questions about the explanation of the origin and maintenance of this particular view of science and religion. Who put it forward, who used it, and what (and whose) interests did it serve?

Likewise the breakdown of this alliance during the nineteenth century, with the rise of scientific naturalism — of which the Darwinian debates can now be seen as just one facet[13] — will also need to be studied with the same perspective in mind. This example should serve to show how the strong programme is — or should be, by its own canons — as corrosive of complacently anti-religious interpretations as it is of complacently pro-religious ones. For it is now clear that the broad movement of scientific naturalism, and within it the propagation of theories of materialistic transformism (or evolution) in biology, was just as much a resource used to serve specific social interests as was the providentialist veiw that it opposed. Naturalism was above all the weapon of the newly rising group of 'professionalised' scientists, struggling to wrest cultural power — influence over education, for example — from an older élite that in most European countries was closely identified with the institutional Church.[14] The strong programme applies here symmetrically, by its own canons, even though this may· be little to the liking of some of its supporters: it must demythologize the old positivist view of the victorious struggle of science against religion just as much as the older view of science as the natural ally of religion.

IV

Limitations of the strong programme
The strong programme has two serious limitations, however, at least in my opinion. The first concerns the way the strong programme handles the individual level of scientific activity. Its proponents are rightly concerned to give a social dimension to the very texture of scientific knowledge. But in reaction to the traditional view of science, the personal dimension is then devalued until it is almost out of sight.

The reason for this anti-individualist tendency seems to be that an emphasis on the individual scientist and his thought-process is equated with a concern to insulate the scientist from his social environment. In other words, the individual level of analysis is seen as an alternative to the social; it is seen as a way for the historian to preserve the 'sacred' or 'totemic' purity of the 'real' work of the scientist, particularly the great scientist, undefiled by contamination from so-called 'non-scientific' influences from his environment. It is undeniable that historical research on individual scientists has sometimes had this effect, as Shapin and Barnes rightly point out in a recent critique of research on Darwin and Darwinism.[15] But it does not follow that this is an intrinsic characteristic of all studies of individual scientists.[16]

250

The strong programme embodies a conception of scientific knowledge as an active social construction. Scientific knowledge is regarded, in my view rightly, as something actively constructed by specific social groups in particular historical circumstances; it is not merely discovered or uncovered in Nature. But there is no reason why the same constructivism should not be adopted also on the individual level, as it is for example quite explicitly in Howard Gruber's phenomenological 'evolving systems approach' to scientific creativity. Gruber speaks of the cognitive 'network of enterprises' that a creative scientist pursues in the service of a 'web of abiding goals'.[17] Evocative phrases like these call attention to the reality of personal purposes in scientific work; but they do not in any way exclude the possibility, indeed the probability, that these purposes are constrained within and partly shaped by the multitude of social realities that surround the individual.

Scientific knowledge, like other cultural resources, is clearly often used to further a variety of group interests, including specifically social interests. But that is no reason to deny that it may also be used by individuals to further their own personal purposes, as a resource for the construction of their own life-ways. The attribution of personal purposes to historical actors is indeed fraught with problems of evidence and interpretation, but that is no good reason for denying altogether the accessibility of such purposes. Like the behaviourists' denial of the reality of the consciousness of the subject, such a high-minded refusal to contaminate one's methodological purity ends only in dehumanising the subject-matter, which is, after all, our forebears and ourselves.

The second limitation in the strong programme is even more serious. It is expressed most succinctly by Barry Barnes, in the preface to his main book on the sociology of scientific knowledge: "Occasionally, existing work leaves the feeling that reality has *nothing* to do with what is socially constructed or negotiated to count as natural knowledge".[18] Yet much of the distinguished work in this field by Barnes and his colleagues does leave me at least with precisely this feeling; or rather, to be somewhat fairer, the way in which 'reality' becomes an input into the cognitive situation, and the way in which that input is related to all sorts of social input, remain obscure. By adhering to the maxims of impartiality and symmetry — admirable though they are as methodology — the possible differentiating effects of externality on the social construction of scientific knowledge tend in practice to be relegated to the background. Yet the ontological question is crucial, and ought to be kept central in the discussion.

251

Scientific knowledge may indeed be a social construction through and through, and therefore a cultural product, but it does also claim to have a more-than-random relation to the externality of the natural world. It has become a commonplace of current thinking about science that the natural world greatly under-determines the form that theories about it can take; but that insight should not lead us inadvertently into the position of implying that the natural world does not determine our theories at all. It is clear that, without doing violence to our experience, our conceptions of the natural world can be organised in many different, even apparently incompatible ways, according to the kinds of technical-instrumental or other interests that they are intended to serve. But this does not eliminate the framework of constraints that the externality of the natural world imposes on the possible variety of our constructions; nor does it preclude the learning processes by which we come to modify our constructions as a result of our cumulative experience of those constraints. To put it more simply, to see scientific knowledge as a social construction does not rule out the possibility of cumulative scientific progress. This is because it does not eliminate the possible differentiating effects of the input from externality on that social construction. It does not absolve us from asking whether the survival and continuing plausibility of some characterisations of the natural world, and the decline or extinction of others, may not be due in part to their relative match or mis-match with the externality that they claim to describe and interpret.

This is emphatically not a plea for a return to the old asymmetry that the strong programme has rightly criticised: one kind of explanation for the history of correct scientific ideas and another kind for the history of erroneous ones. On the contrary, what I have suggested would be an extension of the strong programme's insistence on symmetry in explanation. But it would imply a deliberate decision to enrich the repertoire of the inputs that must be considered. It would mean treating the inputs from the externality of the natural world, alongside and on a par with the manifold inputs from the social world, as possible factors in the history of *all* scientific ideas. Human senses of the natural world would then be treated as fully human, as the products of active cultural construction through and through; yet at the same time the input from the externality of the natural world itself would be treated programmatically as an equally significant source of constraints on the character of that construction, and more particularly as a possible source of differentiating effects during the ongoing process of cognitive construction.

252

V

Scientific knowledge and religious knowledge
I suggested earlier that historical research within the strong programme in its current form already poses an important challenge to
more traditional accounts of the historical relation between scientific
knowledge and religious beliefs. This challenge would be streng-
thened, however, but also paradoxically reflected back in criticism of
much of this recent research, if the strong programme were to be
enriched in the ways I have just proposed.

The strong programme, by its own canons, requires us in any case
to speak not of 'religious beliefs' but of 'religious knowledge', impartially with 'scientific knowledge', as soon as certain claims about the
effects of God or gods become collectively shared by a social group, as
of course they are in any actual religious tradition. For this does not
imply our own acceptance of the validity of what is claimed as either
religious or scientific 'knowledge'; it only implies that that 'knowledge' is accepted as a valid guide to action by the group concerned.
But if we now re-assert the feasibility of studying the individual
construction of scientists' personal routes through life, using the same
ordinary historical methods that are used to study the social construction of scientific knowledge, then the same labels of 'religious knowledge' and 'scientific knowledge' must also be applied impartially to
whatever resources the individual uses in the construction of a personal life-way.

For example, Gruber's study of Darwin's manuscripts leads him to
claim that Darwin's research was powered and guided by 'images of
wide scope' that were too private to be shared.[19] These 'images' must
be regarded as part of Darwin's scientific 'knowledge' just as much as
the overt models and metaphors that he derived from them, which
later became part of the collective 'knowledge' of his scientific community. But we must also treat in the same way those aspects of
Darwin's thinking that can properly be termed religious (they were
religious concerns, even though their content eventually had an anti-
religious or rather agnostic effect). Darwin himself noted with some
sadness the gradual fading of his early religious beliefs. But we could
re-state this by saying that the resources of religious 'knowledge'
which his upbringing had mediated to him gradually lost their plausibility and therefore their power and use in the construction of his
personal life. Of course this was both influenced by, and later helped
to accelerate, a much wider collective decline of plausibility of those
resources; but the continuous interaction between the individual and

his society does not negate the reality or the historical accessibility of the individual level.

The symmetry and impartiality advocated in the strong programme must be extended, however, not only from the collective to the individual level; it must also apply on both levels in relation to all kinds of claimed input from external reality, whether the actors themselves label these inputs naturalistically or theistically or both at once. If the maxims of symmetry and impartiality have any operational content at all, then advocates of the strong programme are in duty bound to treat the claimed inputs that lead to religious knowledge in exactly the same way as those that lead to scientific knowledge.

The anti-discriminatory prescription seems unavoidable; but it may well be unpalatable to some proponents of the strong programme who, in the name of a 'naturalistic' approach, claim to follow a robust 'no-nonsense' materialism in relation to all aspects of scientific knowledge and its construction. A scientific naturalist who also upholds the strong programme for the analysis of science might well protest that the cases are entirely different: that scientific knowledge does at least claim to be about the observable natural world around us, whereas religious claims concern only a world of unobservable supernatural entities. But of course that glosses over the crucial point that the strong programme itself has rightly emphasised: namely that even in the case of science, what counts as knowledge is a social construction with a highly mediated relation to whatever is directly experienced of the natural world. And this is no different from what is claimed as religious knowledge, which is likewise manifestly a social construction, a cultural product, with a highly mediated relation to those claimed effects in experience which are labelled — whether appropriately or not — as the effects of God. What is important in both cases is the nature and operation of the claimed input from externality in the construction of meaning and the pursuit of concrete goals, both for the individual person and for the social group.

By neglecting the question of the possible differentiating effects of externality upon the social construction of knowledge, the proponents of the strong programme are in danger of landing even natural science in the same situation in which Freud placed religion, namely as *nothing but* a projection of meaning by human beings on to a faceless universe. But as John Bowker pointed out in his Wilde Lectures a few years ago, even Freud admitted that another kind of externality *could* have the differentiating effect in experience that he denied categorically in the case of religion. In any deep human relationship, such as marriage, one person's initial 'knowledge' of the other may well be highly projective; yet this may be gradually constrained in the course of the relationship into an outcome that is manifestly affected by the differentiating effect of the independent reality of the other person. In other words, what is initially claimed as 'knowledge' may indeed be largely wishful thinking, but it can gradually — though never totally — be corrected.[20]

This example can of course be used equally as an analogy for either scientific or religious knowledge. Indeed by formulating the problem in terms of information process and learning behaviour the supposed contrast between scientific and religious behaviours almost fades away. In my discussion of scientific knowledge up to this point I have in fact deliberately used language borrowed from Bowker's general theory of religion as information process, in order to bring out this similarity. This tends to support the argument that the historical relation between what we now label respectively as 'religious' and 'scientific' has been that of a gradual differentiation and divergence, rather than the replacement of one by the other, as the older positivistic tradition maintained.

In Bowker's formulation, religions have come to be differentiated through their continuing attention to proposed routes through the more intransigent limitations of human lives, such as the inpenetrability of death and the irreversibility of time. Such routes operate as guides to action in the construction of both individual and collective life-ways. The religious traditions in which they are embodied are necessarily conservative in character, because they are bound to try to conserve for the future those resources that have been found effective in the past in mediating the plausibility of the proposed routes and their undergirding sense of God. But traditions are not immobile: they may be modified by defensive reaction to the undermining of plausibility from without; but they may also be renewed from within by those who claim that the existing resources do not do justice to their own sense of God. If a tradition is not so renewed, it may become extinct.[21]

This kind of formulation should no longer seem strange as a description that could be applied with little modification to the intrinsically conservative but frequently renewed traditions that make up science. Here too it is a matter of proposed routes through various human limitations, operating as guides to action on both individual and collective levels. And here too the survival or extinction of traditions is a question of the maintenance and renewal, or the undermining and collapse, of the plausibility of the proposed routes. But scientific traditions have come to be labelled 'scientific' as a result of their successful focussing on human limitations that have turned out to be less intransigent than they once seemed. These include not only limitations that have been surmounted eventually by technologies, such as the human inability to fly, but also those that pose problems for the construction of human meaning, such as the fact that the human perspective on the whole natural world is limited to the viewpoint from the Earth at one moment in cosmic history, with the limited equipment of the human sense-organs. Indeed, one could write the whole history of science in terms of projects for the trans-cendence of such limitations.

I want to suggest, therefore, that the classic crisis-points in the historical relation of science and religion can be re-interpreted as crises in the plausibility of proposed routes through various human limitations, particularly when the intransigence of these routes in terms of claimed senses of the natural world and of God was in doubt.

For example, a fully historical understanding of the confrontation between Galileo and the Roman church must take account of the underlying power-struggles between Jesuits and Dominicans, and between Tuscans and other tribal groups within the Curia; it must also be aware of the dilemma of international politics in which the Pope was caught.[22] Beyond that kind of historical context, however, it must also explore the possibility that both sides in the dispute were using what they claimed to be good science as a resource in an underlying struggle for cultural power — a struggle between the older élite of the professoriate in alliance with certain elements of the religious orders, and the newer and more pragmatically oriented élite to which Galileo belonged. But even research along those lines, which could well be brought within the strong programme, would fail to do justice to Galileo's clear sense that Copernicus's heliostatic theory successfully penetrated the human limitation of an earthly viewpoint, while the Church authorities equally clearly regarded the intransig-ence of that limitation as a necessary (or at least expedient) support for the plausibility of traditional routes through more fundamental limi-tations. However we interpret Galileo's recantation at the very end of his so-called trial, it is clear that up to that point he had been con-cerned above all to persuade the authorities that the plausibility of routes "necessary for salvation" would *not* be undermined if the Earthly viewpoint were exchanged for one more comprehensively cosmic. It has become conventional to assume that all such arguments on Galileo's part must have been mere expediencies. But it is at least possible that they were totally sincere. We cannot — or should not —

exclude *a priori* the possibility that in the construction of Galileo's own life-way the input from his religious tradition had yielded sufficient feedback in experience to sustain its plausibility, so that he felt he must remain within the boundary-conditions for God-relatedness that if defined. But this would not have prevented him from trying his utmost to persuade his old friend Barberini, in his position as Urban VIII, to accept a shift in those conditions. Indeed, only Galileo's determination to remain within his religious tradition seems an adequate explanation of why he tried so hard to persuade everyone from the Pope downwards, and why he declined all chances to escape to the safety of the Venetian republic.

In other words, Galileo's behaviour must be interpreted in the light of his attempt to use informational resources derived not only from his scientific tradition but also from his religious tradition, in the construction of his life-way — and not only his own life-way, because it is clear that he hoped to make that way open to others also. Without a glass of Momus to get inside Galileo's head, we shall of course never know for certain whether such an interpretation is correct. But it is at least compatible with the surviving evidence.[23]

VI

Conclusion

I have deliberately used Galileo as an example throughout this essay. One reason is of course that his case has become a paradigm in the mythology of the triumphalist view of science. But another reason for mentioning Galileo, however briefly and inadequately, is that in his case the relevant religious tradition, namely Counter-Reformation Catholicism, is particularly unattractive to most modern intellectuals, whether Christian or not. A plausible interpretation of Galileo's total behaviour, scientific and religious, along the lines I have suggested would therefore be particularly tough (and hence valuable) test of my general approach. Needless to say, I do not claim to have given such an interpretation here, but only to have outlined what shape it might take.

I have only been able to use the case of Galileo to suggest briefly the kind of interpretation that might be possible, if we choose to resist the cultural hegemony of those who claim that religious beliefs of the past are wholly reducible to questions of social control and that those of the present are marginal or vestigial. However important it is to try to understand historical episodes in the relation of science and religion *wie es eigentlich gewesen*, we cannot escape from their relevance to our own time. For episodes like that of Galileo, and also the broader trends of the historical relation, continue to be used as powerful myths for the support and propagation of the triumphalist view of natural science. Yet I have argued in this paper that even the 'strong programme' in the historical sociology of scientific knowledge, which openly aims to subvert the triumphalism, actually reinforces the same cultural hegemony, because of its uncritical adoption of a narrowly reductionist viewpoint. It aims to undermine the epistemological uniqueness of scientific knowledge by showing it to be a cultural product and a social construction like others. But in doing so it tends in practice to reduce the personal to the collective, and to discount the differentiating effects of externalities of any kind.

I have therefore argued that the strong programme needs to be freed from its self-imposed blinkers and to be enlarged and enriched. Firstly it must do justice to the reality of personal purposes as well as collective social interests, in the construction of human lives. Secondly it must acknowledge the differentiating effects on that construction, of inputs from the externality of the natural world. And finally it must be true to its own canons of impartiality and symmetry, by taking seriously the possible differentiating effect of claimed inputs from externality characterised in theistic terms. None of these modifications would weaken the strong programme: on the contrary they would bring it nearer its own goal of giving a fully realistic account of natural science.

This is no more than the barest outline of a possible programme for the study of the historical relation of science and religion. But I believe it could lead to a more adequate understanding of that relation, in terms of our individually and socially constructed senses of the natural world and senses of God.

REFERENCES AND NOTES

1. The reference is to two BBC television series, since shown widely in many countries: *The Ascent of Man* and *The Voyage of Charles Darwin*. Both were instructive examples of what I term the 'triumphalist' approach to science. My use of this religious term in a scientific context is closely related to Eileen Barker's notion of the 'new priesthood of science': 'Science and theology: diverse resolutions of interdisciplinary gap by the new priesthood of science', *Interdisciplinary Science Review*. 1979 (in press).
2. Bronowski, J., *The Ascent of Man* (London, B.B.C., 1973): see ch. 6, 'The starry Messenger'.

3. In contrast, the current tendency in some religious circles to dissolve traditional questions of ontology in the relation of science and religion into supposedly more 'relevant' questions of the scientist's 'sense of social responsibility' must be regarded as a sell-out to contemporary fashions. According to one journalist's report on the recent World Council of Churches conference on 'Faith, Science and the Future', the word 'God' was rarely heard except during the opening service!

4. The key work is of course Kuhn, T. S., *The Structure of Scientific Revolutions* (Chicago, Chicago U.P., 1962; reprinted with additional Postscript, 1970). His *The Essential Tension* (Chicago, Chicago U.P., 1979), reprints several important shorter essays.

5. Relevant works by the Edinburgh group include:Barnes, B., *Scientific Knowledge and Sociological Theory* (London, Routledge & Kegan Paul, 1974), and *Interests and the Growth of Knowledge* (London, Routledge & Kegan Paul, 1977); Bloor, D., *Knowledge and Social Imagery* (London, Routledge & Kegan Paul, 1976); and the collection of essays in *Natural Order: Historical Studies of Scientific Culture*, ed. Barnes, B., and Shapin, S. (Beverly Hills and London, Sage, 1979). Sharp distinctions between sociological, philosophical and historical approaches within these works would be unrealistic and misleading. German-language 'critical' philosophers have of course raised a number of problems similar to those raised by the English-language 'strong programme', but I do not deal with the German tradition here, because it seems to me to have failed to generate any significant empirical research in the *history* of the natural sciences.

6. An example is Ben-David, J., *The Scientist's Role in Society* (Englewood Cliffs (N.J.), Prentice-Hall, 1971). See Kuhn, T. S., 'Scientific Growth: reflections on Ben-David's "scientific role"', *Minerva*, 10 (1972) 166–178.

7. See the general review in Mulkay, M., *Science and the Sociology of Knowledge* (London, Allen & Unwin, 1979).

8. I prefer the word 'realistic' for what Barnes, Bloor and Shapin term 'naturalistic', because the latter word implies a philosophical 'naturalism' which in my opinion is not intrinsic to the strong programme, and which (as I argue briefly later in this paper) can actually lead it to neglect some aspects of science that a fully realistic analysis should confront. I use the word 'realistic', however, in an everyday sense, not in the strict philosophical sense, simply to convey the strong programme's 'relaxed' attitude to science, which is well summarised in the short introduction to Barnes's and Shapin's *Natural Order* (note 5).

9. See for example Laudan, L., *Progress and its Problems: Towards a Theory of Scientific Growth* (London, Routledge & Kegan Paul, 1977); and its review by Barnes, B., 'Vicissitudes of Belief', *Social Studies of Science*, 9 (1979) 247–263. Compare with the volume *Criticism and the Growth of Knowledge*, ed. Lakatos, I. and Musgrave, A. (Cambridge, Cambridge U.P., 1970) which embodies papers given at a conference held in 1965 to criticise Kuhn's work from a philosophical angle.

10. The essays in *Natural Order* (note 5) give a good sample of historical case-studies along these lines, and the references appended to them provide a useful entry into the growing body of historical literature that can be identified more or less directly with the strong programme. See also my essay-review of *Natural Order*: Rudwick, M.J.S., 'Social order and the natural world', *History of Science*, 18 (1980), in press.

11. See Rudwick, M. J. S., Cognitive styles in geology', in *Essays in the Sociology of Perception* ed. Douglas, M. and Ostrander, D (London, Routledge & Kegan Paul, 1980 (in press)).

12. An important exception is Margaret Jacob's study of *The Newtonians and the English Revolution, 1689—1720* (Hassocks, Harvester Press, 1976). This gives an implicitly Durkheimian and reductionist social interpretation of what was ostensibly a religious issue about the relation of God to the natural world.

13. See for example, Young, R. M., 'The impact of Darwin on conventional thought', in *The Victorian Crisis of Faith*, ed. Symondson, A. (London, S.P.C.K., 1970), pp. 13–35; and 'The historiographic and ideological contexts of the nineteenth-century debate on man's place in nature' in *Changing Perspectives in the History of Science*, ed. Teich, M. and Young, R. M. (London, Heinemann, 1973).

14. See for example, Turner, F. M., 'The Victorian conflict between science and religion: a professional dimension', *Isis*, 69 (1978) 356–376. Another facet of the same historical development is that the declining use of explicit natural-theological arguments in scientific publications during the nineteenth century was related not only to a loss of cognitive plausibility but also to a new *social* situation, in which the social function of natural theology, as an 'umbrella' that could unite scientists from diverse religious traditions, became less important: see Brooke, J. H., 'The natural theology of the geologists: some theological strata' in *Images of the Earth; Essays in the History of the Environmental Sciences*, ed. Jordanova, L. J. and Porter, R. S. (Chalfont St. Giles, British Society for the History of Science, 1979), pp. 39–64.

15. Shapin, S. and Barnes, B., 'Darwinism and Social Darwinism: purity and History', in *Natural Order*, pp. 125–142 (note 5).

16. See for example J. R. Jacob's studies of Boyle, which fall clearly within my definition of the strong programme but which offer a social interpretation of the work of an individual: *Robert Boyle and the English Revolution: a Study in Social and Intellectual Change* (New York, Franklin, 1977); some aspects of the argument are outlined in his earlier article 'The ideological origins of Robert Boyle's natural philosophy', *Journal of European Studies*, 2 (1971) 1–21.

17. See Gruber, H. E. and Barrett, P. H., *Darwin on Man. A Psychological Study of Scientific Creativity* (New York, Dutton, 1974), especially pp. 243–257; and Gruber, '"And the bush was not consumed": the evolving systems approach to creativity' in *Toward a Theory of Psychological Development*, ed. Modgil, C. & S. (Windsor, N.F.E.R., 1978).

18. Barnes, *Scientific Knowledge*, p.vii (note 5).

19. See Gruber and Barrett, *Darwin on Man* (note 17); also Gruber, 'The fortunes of a basic Darwinian idea:chance', *Annals of the New York Academy of Sciences*, 291 (1977) 233–245; and 'Darwin's "tree of nature" and other images of wide scope' in *On Aesthetics in Science*, ed. Wechsler, J. (Cambridge (Mass.), M.I.T. Press, 1978), pp. 121–140.

20. Bowker, J., *The Sense of God: Sociological, Anthropological and Psychological Approaches to the Origin of the Sense of God* (Oxford, Clarendon, 1973), pp. 132–3.

21. In *The Sense of God* (note 20), Bowker sets out to show that the various human sciences, by their own canons, cannot properly exclude *a priori* the possible differentiating effects of any theistic input there may be, into human constructions of a sense of God. In his second series of Wilde Lectures, published as *The Religious Imagination and the Sense of God* (Oxford, Clarendon, 1978), Bowker examines some aspects of the Jewish, Christian, Islamic and Buddhist traditions, to see what kinds of differentiating effects might count as valid evidence in this respect. For a summary of the general theory of religion underlying these works, see his article 'Information process, systems behaviour, and the study of religion', *Zygon*, 11 (1976) 361–379: this is reprinted in slightly extended form as the

Introduction (pp. 1–30) to the second book.

22. The classic modern account, and still the best, is Santillana, G. de, *The Crime of Galileo* (Chicago, Chicago U.P., 1955). Like all other accounts, however, this is a child of its time: De Santillana wrote at the height of the Cold War against Stalinist tyranny, and this to some extent structures his interpretation, although he was too good a historian not to note the contrasts, as well as the analogies, between the Inquisition and the N.K.V.D. Compare Brecht, B. *Leben des Galilei* (Berlin, Suhrkamp Verlag, 1955), which was completed shortly after Hiroshima, and which portrays Galileo as the 'pure' scientist who ultimately lacks a 'sense of social responsibility' and fails to advance 'science for the people'.

23. This interpretation does not impute to Galileo any special sanctity, piety or even morality (as Bronowski commented archly, Galileo "had rather more children than a bachelor should"). What it *does* imply is that the long-standing interpretation of Galileo as a hero of science in its struggle against religion needs very careful re-appraisal. Giorgio Spini made a fine pioneer study in this direction at the time of the last Galileo centenary, recognising the paucity of direct evidence on Galileo's personal religious belief but setting him firmly into his contemporary religious context: 'The rationale of Galileo's religiousness', in *Galileo Reappraised*, ed. Golini, C. L. (Berkeley and Los Angeles, University of California Press, 1966), pp. 44–66.

Chapter 14

SCIENCE AS THEOLOGY — THE THEOLOGICAL
FUNCTIONING OF WESTERN SCIENCE

Eileen Barker

Department of Sociology, London School of Economics & Political Science, U.K.

IN THIS PAPER I wish to look at some of the ways in which the fact that we live in what has frequently been called an age of science affects the theological beliefs of contemporary society.

Before proceeding any further one point must be made clear. When as a sociologist I talk of science and theology both terms are being employed in the reportive rather than the stipulative sense. Theology will include the general, often unsystematic, collections of religious beliefs, and perhaps even what some would term folk superstitions, which form and inform the general *Weltanschauungen* of the population. Science will cover what the members of society variously take to be science. The term encompasses a whole series of half-understood and half-digested facts, values, attitudes, theories and hypotheses and a language which frequently has more coinage in the works of science fiction than in learned journals. In short anything that is *accepted as* science by those with whom we are concerned comes under the rubric of science in this study, even if, for those of us who are more englightened, it is trumped up blasphemy, fallacious nonsense or naive scientism.

Already it will be apparent that science thus defined can cover a multitude of sins and function for a multitude of purposes. And this is indeed the subject of the present essay. Perhaps the safest generalisation that can be made, and that I wish to make, about the manner in which science is experienced and in which it affects modern religious beliefs is that one cannot generalise. There have been times in history when it has been comparatively easy to isolate one or two ways in which a society coped with differences and similarities in the subject matter, methodologies and claims of the two disciplines, but the latter half of the twentieth century is not such a time. Today we live in an age in which societies are bound together both internally and externally through heterogeneity rather than homogeneity. Increasing specialisation through the division of labour in the production of goods,

EILEEN BARKER

services and what passes for knowledge has created a world of frag-
mented experience that gives rise to assorted patterns of understanding, meaning and direction. No one theology is universally accepted.
Modern man can seek out or drift into the supermarket of socially
available religious options, trying each theology for size and seeing
how well it stands up to his experience of reality. He can seek out a
whole package — perhaps one of the New Religious Movements, a
recent import from the East or a well tried Born-Again Christianity —
or he can collect odd bits as he goes along, putting these together to
produce his own personalised theology.

It should not be thought that this is necessarily either a very
conscious or a very rational process. There are, of course, the seekers
but there are also the drifters who collect their theologies through a
sort of absent-minded accretion. Such theologies can lie dormant in
the mind, often surfacing only at points of crisis or when a curious
sociologist asks them to think about what they think. Furthermore
both personalised and institutionalised theologies can encompass the
most extraordinary ragbag of facts, opinions and beliefs which hap-
pily coexist, apparently quite oblivious of what to others are the most
glaring inconsistencies. However in the more institutionalised
theologies such contradictions may be recongnised and indeed celebrated by the believers as the mysteries of God or (in more secular
vein) the paradoxes of truth.

But it is not only in theologies that such phenomena are to be found.
As soon as we begin to contemplate the popular image of modern
science a further bewildering assortment of contradictions, mysteries
and paradox emerges. Science seeks out the immutable laws of the
universe yet reveals the universal principles of indeterminacy and
uncertainty. Science is the discovery of hard facts yet it discovers that
the table against which I bang my shin is nothing but a swarm of
atoms, nothing but bits of space in time — and it discovers that space
and time are not what we supposed them to be — extra dimensions
emerge to strain the credibility of our senses and then disappear like
the White Rabbit into a Black Hole. Everybody knows that a scientifically proved fact is unshakable. Everybody knows that Einstein has
toppled Newton from the pedestal of truth. The absolute knowledge
of science rests on everything being relative to everything else — the
only certainty is that there is no certainty. Science quantifies and
calculates yet it deals with the incalculability of the infinite and the
infinitessimal.

Science is capable of solving, but has also been responsible for
creating, some of the world's greatest problems. With science man

unleashes, and man exhausts, the resources of the world. With science he gets to the moon and he pollutes the earth. Through science man puts himself in control of our future. He raises himself to the power of God. Yet through science man is reduced to a lump of matter, programmed through natural selection and DNA into a series of stimuli and responses, determined to blow himself and the rest of creation off the face of the earth into (if science can find it) kingdon come.

Everywhere and every day science, like Big Brother both overtly or covertly reminds us of its presence and power. Even children from the most unscientifically orientated backgrounds cannot escape constant reminder that they live in the age of science. The media and the schools educate us of its achievements: new discoveries and applications accelerate in geometric progression. At every turn we become more and more hooked into helpless dependency upon its technology.

Modern science may be viewed with awe or it may be viewed as awful; it may be revered or reviled or, not infrequently, it may be both revered and reviled. But whether we understand or are mystified, whether we approve or condemn, it is universally acknowledged that for good or for evil, modern science *works*. In the supermarkets of ontologies and ethics science may have its rivals but in the supermarkets of epistemologies and technologies she reigns supreme.

It is thus not altogether surprising that the image of modern science plays its role in the packaging and even the production of the bits and pieces that go to make up the available options which comprise mid-twentieth century theologies.

At the most general level we can note a shift in language, a change in the frame of reference within which reality is defined. In the age of science journeys of mystery have been symbolically re-routed. New concepts have emerged with which to explore the beyond, and old concepts have been lost. The power of the Holy Spirit can become the force of an emanating energy. The absolute formula "I am that I am" is reduced to $E = mc^2$; Cranmer gives way to Van Daniken or Stars on Sunday and The Miracle of Lourdes is surpassed by Strange Encounters of the Third Kind.

While it is true that in the relative secularity of modern society one's beliefs may lie dormant and undisturbed so long as they are not called upon to play a conscious role in an individual's life, it is also true that modern society can provide a challenge to more consciously held beliefs, either directly or through the proffering of attractive alternatives. This it can do in both a positive and a negative way. Through a process of secondary socialisation (that is, through coming into contact with the enormous diversity of people and ideas outside the home environment), science can be experienced as either a threat or as inadequate or, it is quite likely, as both.

To take two extreme possibilities as examples: someone born into a fundamentalist Christian home, brought up with a belief in the literal truth of Genesis, can be subjected to very disturbing doubts when he learns of evolution in the biology class at school or sees Richard Attenborough on television. Alternatively someone brought up in a rational, intellectual home, believing that science can ultimately provide all the answers, may discover on, say, entering university that he is being challenged by questions that he has never even heard asked before — questions to which answers can be found in neither the science library nor the laboratory. He discovers moreover that these are questions of burning importance — possibly the only questions that are worth asking at all. Out into the supermarket he will rush, desperately grasping at anything he finds on offer with its promise to fill the gaping void newly revealed in his understanding. And it is probable that in his search he will be particularly attracted by any package which has stamped on it the scientific seal of approval.

For it is one of the curious paradoxes to be found as a consequence of the modern images of science that science is eagerly invoked to justify and legitimate those very theologies which reject its values, its uses, its methods and even its findings. While science may be viewed as a pernicious evil, it has no rival in providing a benchmark, a universally acceptable standard, by which truth can be sifted from falsehood. To *condemn* science is an effective means of inviting acceptance. to *be condemned by* science is an effective means of inviting rejection. In the age of science it takes a lot to rival the theology that is both superior to and recommended by science.

In response to such a consumer demand there has developed a whole new priesthood of scientists who, as the epistemological experts of the age, offer the necessary knowledge to sanction practically any ideological standpoint one may wish to pursue. Sitting at the feet of these most enlightened of gurus one is reassured that science can prove or, according to the guru, disprove the existence of God, the fact of evolution, the functioning of angels and evil spirits and the true sources of revelation. Science can point the way to eternal salvation and to eternal damnation. Science can make us certain that it is we who are right and they who are wrong. And it can even reassure some of us that it can do no such thing.

Of course the very diversity of the positions that are on popular display does create problems for the new priesthood and the scientists themselves are greatly concerned about the false images of science that abound. It is the duty of each priesthood to reveal a proper understanding of the true science which provides a necessary (and in some cases sufficient) pathway to the greater truth of ultimate knowledge but it is also its duty to denounce those scien*tists* who make false claims to such knowledge.

One way which I have found useful in ordering the diversity to be found among the priests of modern Christendom is to classify them according to the theological position revealed by the scientists concerning the truth or falsity of the Bible with respect to (a) its factual detail and (b) its spiritual revelation. This can produce six categories which I have called Fundamentalism, Orthodoxy, Liberalism, Modernism, Agnosticism and Atheism. (It should perhaps be pointed out here that these are examples of what the sociologist calls Ideal Types and as such are heuristic devices to be used for analytical purposes — they are ṣtipulatively rather than reportively defined and do not necessarily correspond exactly to other, possibly more familiar, uses of the terms. The familiar terms do however offer at least an inital understanding of the positions described so long as the above point is understood.)

To elaborate briefly on the types: (1) The fundamentalist scientists believe the Bible can be accepted as an historical and scientifically accurate text book. Evolutionary theory for example is the result of bad science where facts are ignored and metaphysical speculation is accepted as empirical reality. True science vindicates Genesis. (2) The orthodox scientists believe that God reveals himself equally through the Books of Nature and of Scripture and each must be interpreted in the light of the other without falling into the traps of literalism or liberalism. The theologically aware orthodox scientist has this expertise. (3) Liberal scientists play the role of the trouble shooter. It is their task to show that religion and science are concerned with two completely different universes of discourse and consequently religion is under no threat whatsoever from modern science. (4) Modernists wish to expand science to include the spiritual and qualitative instead of just the material and quantitative. The Bible is little more than part of man's historical search for truth and now modern science can illuminate the purpose of the universe, point to the direction in which we are travelling and suggest transcendental meaning. (5) Agnostic scientists, like liberals, separate the two disciplines as dealing with entirely different realms but their role is not so much to protect the spiritual truth of the Bible as to provide, through their science, knowledge of the context in which moral and political judgements should be made. The Bible may be regarded as one ethical phrase book among many. (6) Finally the atheists believe modern science can disprove religious beliefs. It can explain these away with reductionist accounts of their selective value in the evolution of man. Today however true science should take over for it alone provides hope for the future redemption of humanity.

The table on pages 278-279 summarises some of the different beliefs, practices and organisations of the various types but, having documented these in some detail elsewhere,[1] I do not wish to pursue the subject of the scientific priesthood any further in the present paper. Rather I wish to return to the attempt to depict the role which images of modern science play in the modern *Weltanschauungen* by providing a few illustrations.

One of the main points that I wish to illustrate is the diversity of uses to which science is put in informing an individual's theology. There is something of a methodological problem in this as there has been no systematic large scale study on this subject. To select some of the strange and wonderful things that people believe would be interesting but would not indicate the extent to which such uses of science are put. *Faute de mieux* I offer some illustrations from a group of just over one hundred individuals who filled in a thirty-six page questionnaire in order to create a 'control group' for the study I am carrying out into the Unification Church. Unfortunately the group is not completely representative of the population as a whole as it was selected to parallel the Unification Church membership in age and class. The most obvious 'skews' are that the majority was between the ages of 18 and 30 (although there were some older respondents), and the educational levels were well above the norm, (but again it did include respondents who had left school and gone to work without any educational qualifications). However using the control group has the methodological advantage that (a) I am restricted to using only examples from a group that was not selected for either their religious beliefs (though there was a slight over-representation of Catholics) or for their attitudes towards science, and (b) nowhere in the questionnaire was science mentioned, nor were there any questions that alluded to science in any way. Despite this well over a third invoked science to explain their theological position. From this pool are drawn the following examples of the uses of science in explaining the respondents' theological position.

In so far as straightforward competition is concerned the most extreme use to which science was put was to offer an actual alternative: "Science is my religion". More frequently science was used to

267

explain atheism, although even in such cases the direct alternative may be implied when it is considered to be sufficient reason to reject religion just to say "It is unscientific".

Although some respondents did see science as positively refuting religion, logicians would be dismayed to find how often *lack* of scientific proof for the existence of God was taken *as proof* that God did not exist. This was regretfully accepted as a necessary consequence even when the spirit was willing as in the case of one respondent who had given "no scientific proof" as her reason for not believing in God and added "I'd like to believe in an all-loving God, but supernatural forces cannot be proven".

Altogether 30% of those who admitted to having doubts over the existence of God invoked science in their explanation. A typical statement concerning the way in which doubts originated would be: "As soon as I began to ask questions it became easy to doubt. My interest in science in first year of Grammar school probably helped". Sometimes science is seen as making religion superfluous. One respondent, born into a Jewish family, wrote that she had doubted the existence of God "Ever since I read books on pre-historic animals out of interest and found that the existence of the world and the universe could be explained without the idea of God".

It was however also possible for the inadequacy of science to play its role in leading to belief, as in the case of the respondent who gave as his main reason for accepting the existence of God as the "historical, material, personal belief that not everything can be explained in purely scientific terms". And although the most frequent reason for believing in God was personal experience, a few of the respondents did couch their explanation for belief in empirical or naturalistic terms: "Seeing is believing"; "there is no way that I can look at the intricacy, efficiency and homogeneity of (the) animal kingdom and plant kingdom ... without knowing someone all powerful and good must have created them ...". Scientific explanations of the functions or "need" for religion can play their role in either direction. While one person will think that an "understanding of peoples' need to believe in an essence of goodness" will explain *away* religion, another will argue that this shows it must be true.

For some it is the consequences of science for religion or of religion for science that are considered of relevance in accepting or rejecting a theological position. It is interesting to compare the following three statements:

1. "I regard religious doctrines to be by and large (a) fake, (b) rigid,

dogmatic and unnecessarily restrictive (c) often harmful e.g. Christianity's opposition to scientific progress ..."

2. "I was brought up in a Hong Kong rural area where the Chinese gods were traditionally worshipped — also worshipped are the various Buddhas and ancestors. The variety of gods were exciting but never really quite believable ... Christianity then would mean disdaining all the Chinese traditions which somehow managed to include the discrediting of Chinese medicine which ... I was quite impressed with, so Christianity was quite distant to me."

3. "(There are a) lot of youngsters confused because of the high level of scientific development which inhibits individuals to be sentimental rather than material ... (by the year 2,000 we shall have a) Brave New World — high scientific development, materialsm at its peak, individualism highly discouraged, artificial happiness."

One of the most striking things to emerge from the control group was not just how very pessimistic the respondents were about the state that they thought the world would be in by the year 2,000, but how many of them thought there would never even *be* a year 2,000. Many prognostications for the future were informed quite explicitly by science fiction. Indeed science fiction loomed large in many of the answers for it too contributes to theologies of the respondents — in fact there were more who believed because of science fiction than because of "science-fact". (It will be noted that a distinction is being made between science fiction and fictional science). One respondent for example claimed that he believed because science fiction opened his eyes — it had really made him think — "it was the vastness of everything — (I was) frightened by the infinte dimensions of the universe — concepts deep in the subconscious ..." But then several respondents mentioned science fiction as contributing to their doubts about religion. And although the Bible was the most frequent reply to a question asking which book had most influenced the respondents' lives, many of them put down works of science fiction. One young man when asked who or what he would most like to be or do replied:

"A perfect ESPer — i.e. with the powers of telepathy, perception, telekinesis and transportation. Then I would be able to do something about this stupid state this dirt ball has got itself into through mankind."

Asked the same question another person chose "Mozart or Newton" while another respondent sorted out his priorities by declaring that "Jesus Christ is the greatest man to have ever lived, followed by Albert Einstein".

Science can also be held responsible for the *kind* of theology which is believed to be acceptable.

> "I find the idea of a Geometry God deeply attractive, but I don't think that such a God cares for souls. I feel, for instance, great sympathy with Einstein's conviction that the world is rational and therefore comprehensible."

But once again it should not be thought that there is only one theological consequence of a "scientific world view". As has been already intimated, science can be used to justify almost any kind of theological position. And here I leave the control group and turn briefly to the Unification Church and its theology for the evidence of questionnaires, interviews and participant observation at times of conversion, suggest that it is the combination of *both* the "scientificness" *and* the deep relationship with a personal, loving God that the Unification theology offers which contribute very largely to its attraction.

Over and over again Moonies will claim that one of the great achievements of the Divine Principle (the Unification Theology) is "The offering of the Theology to Science" or that it has "created a teaching which reconciles science with Christianity". Many members claim that it was exactly this reconciliation that they were unable to find in any other theology. One member, when asked to state his religion before joining the Unification Church, wrote "Scientist, Agnostic, Idealist". There was the Harvard graduate in biochemistry who testified:

> "My scientific training in university made many Christian and Eastern philosophies difficult to accept, but the (Divine) Principle fits well with a scientific orientation — uniting science and religion. I think that with my background there is no Eastern philosophy that fits well with modern science, and I could never have become a fundamentalist Christian." . . . (I found myself in) two worlds: science and the laboratory and those friends, and the counterculture, hippies, communes, mystical sense of life ..."

He became disillusioned with the communes and hippies and eventually joined the Unification Church.

As well as reconciling the scientific and theological experiences and hopes of its members' pasts the Divine Principle offers, in its millenial promise, an even greater reconciliation for science and theology in the future.[2] One member, describing his own vision of the New Age predicted:

"Man will expand his dominion to other planets and will bring science to a peak never before dreamed of. Man will live in partnership with God over creation."

And it is from a member of the Unification Church that we can take a clear illustration of the use of science as a provider of language or metaphor with which to express religious experience:

"I look upon our relationship to God as like a radio transmitter and the radio wave. Before (joining) the (Unification) Church I could only tune in for second, or a short time, often like 'blurbs' . . . now I tune in more with God . . . the 'radio transmissions' become clearer and stronger."

But the use of scientific language becomes far more than mere metaphor in the actual theology. Unification cosmology explicitly claims to rest on a scientific world view and many illustrations can be found in the Divine Principle like this extract from Chapter One of *The Principle of Creation:*

". . .Through the force of give and take action, the dual essentialities produce a reciprocal base, which in turn produces a foundation of existence in an individual self; then upon this foundation, the individual self can stand as God's object and receive all the power necessary for its own existence.

For example: an atom comes to exist through the give and take action between a proton and an electron. This is the action of fusion. A molecule comes into being through the give and take action between a positive ion and a negative ion which causes a chemical reaction. Electricity is produced through the give and take action between positive electrical charges and negative electrical charges, which causes electrical action. All plants multiply through the give and take action between stamen and pistil..."[3]

Simple, certainly — perhaps even simplistic to some — but effectively showing to an audience that wants to discover a way of knowing God in an age of science that Unification theology is able to quote the Book of Nature just as effectively as it quotes the Book of Scripture.

But the Unification Church is by no means the only new movement that espouses a scientific underpinning. Scientology claims an immediate legitimacy for its "science of the mind" through the very name under which it offers its jargon-riddled technology of dianetics.[4] Transcendental Meditation defines itself as the "Science of Creative Intelligence"[5] and produces a wealth of data proving scientifically that Transcendental Meditation really does — through, for example, changing alpha rhythms — provide the best of all possible minds.

Even movements whose theology is explicitly non-cognitive but whose members seek 'knowledge' through inner experience will still seek scientific sanctioning. In literature produced by the Divine Light Mission whose "premies" are as unscientifically orientated as one might have thought possible, one can find such statements as:

> "God (Generator, Operator and Destroyer) is Cosmic Energy. The form He exists in is Light. Science agrees to the fact that the purest form of energy is Light ... Scientists have proved that energy can neither be created nor destroyed, it can be converted from one form to another ... It is quite strange to note that if one substitutes the word 'God' for energy, we see that all the scientific laws are exactly the same as the principles or teachings on which religion is based ... In fact religion itself is a science ... Meditation, the process of bringing the mind into contact with the Cosmic Energy, is therefore a scientific study of things beyond the limits of the human mind. This experience is necessary for one who desires happiness, love and freedom."[6]

As one moves further into what Paul Heelas has called the 'Self Religions'[7] the jargon accelerates into a wild frenzy of "Psychobabble"[8] — a phenomenon that needs no documenting for those who having even the most cursory acquaintance, be it through personal or media experience, with the West Coast of America.

Concluding remarks

It might well be argued that an examination of the detailed arguments presented by the new priesthood reveals little, theologically speaking, that is essentially new. Variously attired in the new clothing that offers them the respectability of the age, one can recognise monisms and dualisms, idealisms, rationalisms, naturalisms, materialisms and mysticisms. There are deisms, theisms and atheisms; there are gnoses, prophesies and apostasies. Orthodoxy and heresy are heralded with arguments from design, with ontological proofs, with revelatory rhetoric and with scepticism. Sometimes familiar elements are packaged into unfamiliar structures, sometimes familiar structures, when unpackaged, reveal unfamiliar components. New concepts both reveal and osbcure old truths. From levels of sophisticated nicety to levels of unthinking acceptance, the language of science creates and inhibits novelty as it preserves and destroys tradition.

I would like to conclude with a few reflections arising from the phenomena with which this paper has been concerned — reflections that could be addressed to the scientist, to the theologian and to the man on the Clapham omnibus.

Perhaps it should immediately be acknowledged that if sociology is to aspire to the status of a science it is necessary (though by no means sufficient) that the sociologist preserves a position of methodolgical agnosticism. *Qua* sociologist he can claim no expertise in judging the truth or falsity of one theological position over another, nor can he claim any expertise in the natural sciences. However in documenting the range of beliefs that members of a society hold and the sort of phenomena with which such beliefs are correlated, he may notice both logical and factual inconsistencies and observe that the consequences of holding certain beliefs can lead to situations which contradict either the avowed beliefs themselves or other equally strongly held values or theologies.

To begin with a brief summary of the general situation. It has been suggested that those of us who live in contemporary Western Society are exposed to a variety of theological positions, possibly unrivalled for sheer quantity and diversity by any other period in history. Although some of us may retain a strong belief in the faith in which we were brought up, it is likely that at some time we shall find ourselves facing a challenge to many of our overtly and several of our covertly held beliefs. We cannot be assured that what made sense for our parents in the context of their world will make sense for us in the context of ours. Of course no society is ever completely static — but the pace of change and the ever increasing differentiation to be found in modern society means that we are bound to be far more exposed to the ravages of time than were our forebears. And as it is very largely science that has for the last few centuries been increasingly responsible for the increasingly rapid changes and increasingly marked differentiation, we might expect to find science — or at least her modern images — playing a role in the 'contemporary transformations of religion'. In other words it is not altogether surprising that science should contribute to forming and informing, to legitimating and rejecting modern theologies when it itself provides many of the basic

273

ingredients which go to make up the ever changing, ever diversifying social context within which life is to be given meaning and purpose and within which questions of ultimate truth are to be answered. In such circumstances it would be strange if images of modern science were *not* fed into the social construction of theological reality.

To a certain extent one can detect signs of a backlash against the idea of science *as* theology — that is there has, during the second half of the century, been a certain disillusionment with the methods, values, assumptions, and uses of modern science. But at the same time inhabitants of the space age have acquired considerable respect for the efficacy of the epistemological and technological powers of modern science. In the process of 'sorting out' and 'building up' both per-sonalised and institutionalised theologies, science has been called upon to reassure with justifications and rejections, and to recreate with conceptual frameworks that which is beyond science. And scien-tists have not been found wanting in their response. Filling the role of a new priesthood they have proved themselves ready and capable of providing contemporary symbolic resonances, scientific expressions of reassurance, for the very uncertainties that science has brought in its wake.

There are of course many types of knowledge and many ways of knowing. To try to draw a clear distinction between science and theology would be to beg many of the questions raised in the popular theologies of the day. But by their own admission most members of the new priesthood of science — and *especially* those working outside or at the margins of the prevailing paradigm — are prepared to accept at either a crude or a sophisticated level the demarcation spelled out by Sir Karl Popper: "the criterion of the scientific status of a theory is its falsifiability, or refutability, or testability".[9] Of course anyone with the slightest acquaintance with the philosophy of science knows that in practice this distinction is often extremely hard to draw, but for present purposes it is enough that a *prima facie* distinction can be made between those theories or statements which could be refuted and those which, whatever the available evidence, can always be verified.

Most people in modern society make some sort of assumption that there is a sense in which the reality of the natural world can impose itself upon us in a way that a non-scientific reality cannot. This has something to do with the potential capacity of human beings, through their five senses of sight, hearing, taste, touch and smell, to share experiences of certain external phenomena, whatever their pre-suppositions or volitions concerning the properties of the phenomena might be. Of course even this is to overarticulate quite grossly the epistemology of the vast majority which just "knows" that science "knows" in a hard way.

History has taught us that man seldom needs much excuse to exercise his more illiberal tendencies. It might be argued that the rise of modern science has made some contribution to the value and in some cases the practice of religious toleration. This is too complicated a question to consider here. What might be suggested however is that, *given* a (more or less) socially accepted belief that science has superior epistemological status to, say, divine revelation (in so far as the two are theologically separable), then the use of science to judge theological positions, be it positively or negatively, can not only lead to psychological comfort, it can also lead to social bigotry. To claim a theology can be judged by science is to claim an epistemological backing that is testable, and reliably so, by anyone who has their five senses about them. Of course the argument is rarely spelled out in detail, but the implicit assumption is that those not accepting one's own position are not just demonstrably wrong, but wilfully and stupidly so. If however, it is consistently accepted that theology and science are not epistemological equivalents, then it could also be accepted that it may be as easy and as *legitimate by the canons of science* for others to verify their position as it is to verify one's own.

This is not to argue that science should not play its role in theological pronouncements, but that, assuming they wish to preserve their epistemological expertise perhaps those who practice science should be more aware of the role that theologies play in their discipline. It has been remarked by others, and it did not require much perceptivity during my study to observe, that not only 'normal', but eminent, indeed brilliant, scientists can be remarkably ready to claim as fact what, by their own tenets of scientific practice, is patently not fact but hypothesis. What is possibly less obvious but equally insidious is not so much the claims that are made in the name of science as those which are *denied* in the name of science. One finds members of the scientific establishment refusing *a priori* to give any credence to work done — however scrupulously the researchers stick to accepted scientific procedures — on certain subjects associated with the "wrong" theological stable. Then there are the grandiose claims by scientists about some newly revealed ultimate reality. This frequently involves reductionism to a level which turns out to be arbitrarily pre-ordained by the particular discipline to which the heralding prophet owes his professional allegiance. Emergent or independent properties are allowed 'up to' the assigned 'rock bottom' but not one iota beyond. 'Real' reality stops there.[10]

This is certainly not to argue that anything goes. It is patently obvious that it does not. It is also the case that considerable psychological discomfort and social confusion can be caused by a surfeit of available options. However it is just possible that by trying to understand those with whom we theologically disagree we might not only learn greater tolerance but we might have our eyes opened to something of value in their theologies and even in their sciences that, had our eyes remained closed, we would not have dreamed of. There are, in other words, ways in which even the scientist could wish to celebrate diversity.

> Just as Durkheim suggested the pathological or the deviant can serve a positive function by defining what is 'right' and what 'wrong', so, it could be argued, those who work outside an accepted paradigm can clarify boundaries of knowledge, highlighting the distinctions between fact and interpretation of fact, between beliefs, metaphors, heuristic organising principles, theories, laws and all the other paraphernalia of categories that man employs in his search for truth. What is unkonwn and unknowable can be made clearer and the bases of what knowledge we have can be more scrupulously examined.[11]

The advantages of such an exercise do, of course, depend on the assumption that the scientist and theologian, having decided that they do not wish to ignore each other completely, would prefer to explore the potentialities of a partnership rather than those of a merger.

If it is accepted that different kinds of knowing are involved in the practices of science and theology then it can be accepted that neither can provide the *content* of the other's knowledge, but this does not mean that they will not inform the *context* within which their respective knowledge is to be constructed, accepted or rejected.

So far as the relationship between theology and a social science is concerned, I have argued elsewhere that sociology neither can[12] nor should[13] dictate to theology. However while the sociologically aware theologian need accept no limits to what his theology can teach, he must accept that there are limits to what will be accepted at any particular time. In other words, theologians can certainly argue that acceptance is not criterion of truth, but those who are anxious to share their truth with others might wish to take some cognisance of the social context within which their theology is to be lived. They may, to take an example relevant to the subject of this paper, feel it necessary to offer some explanation to account for any part of their theology which denies that which is taught by science. Such explanations do of course exist in plenty, the most common of which is the miracle. But even mircales may have to be couched in appropriate terms if they are to be given credence in modern society. It may not seem to matter too much *how* the images and symbolisms of contemporary society are employed (though the social scientist may claim to detect more socio-logic than the believers and practitioners themselves are aware of), but once such images and symbolisms are entirely ignored, a theology risks the consequence of being labelled old-fashioned, out of touch or irrelevant — or, as would seem most frequently to be the case, it will merely be ignored in ignorance. Then into the theological vacuum one will see spilling any substitute which can claim relevance, being 'with it' or which seems to touch on the experience of the individual in some kind of 'meaningful' way. Neatly filling such bills one can see many of the new religious movements and the theologies of science fiction.

None of what has been said should be taken to imply that the theologian ought to jump on any passing bandwagon — those who try to do so usually find that they have sadly misjudged the distance. Nor is it to deny the importance of tradition. David Martin has cogently argued the case for preserving the cultural heritage of Anglicanism through the historcal dimension evoked by Cranmer.[14] It is not to contradict but to complement his argument to suggest that a theology which has no contemporary resonance is as sociologically empty as one with no historical heritage. It is possible that in more cases than most of us would care to acknowledge, the medium does in fact turn out to be the message.

Ideal Typical Characterization of the Scientists' Positions *vis à vis* Christian Religious Dogma

Ideal type	Beliefs about Bible			Attitudes to Evolution	Relevance of Science to religious knowledge	Sources of true knowledge	Work to be done	Key orientations	Organization examples in UK
	Spirit	Detail	Source						
Fundamentalism (Creationists)	True	True	God	Special Creation as in Genesis account Evolution is false	Relevant: Bible verifiable (and verified) by science	Biblical Revelation (and science)	Show the Bible to be the correct textbook of science Show where false science, espcially evolutionism, is wrong Prove lack of discrepancy at all levels	Acceptance of Scriptural Truth	Evolution Protest Movement; Newton Scientific Association Biblical Creation Society
Orthodoxy (Evangelicals)	True	*(True)	God	Genesis account interpreted in the light of evolution. God is the originator and sustainer of Creation	Relevant: Bible vindicated through science and interpreted with the help of science	Biblical Revelation and Science	Reconcile science and Scripture by showing lack of discrepancy at deepest level Evangelize	Search for Scriptural truth	Research Scientists' Christian Fellowship; Victoria Institute
Liberalism	True	*(False)	*(God)	Theistic Evolution	Irrelevant: Bible and science concerned with different questions	Science or Biblical Revelation (depending on the question)	Show lack of discrepancy because of different spheres, so Bible not threatened by science Show importance of (non-scientific parts of) Bible to biological/social man	Religious Humanism	Science and Religion Forum

	*(True)	False	*(Man)						Scientific and Medical Network
Modernism	*(True)	False	*(Man)	Evolution is God's method of reaching His ultimate goal	Irrelevant: in asking different questions. Relevant: in importance of Natural Theology	Science (as the Book of Nature) and some mystical or personal revelations and Eastern philosophy	Discover direction of evolution, design, purpose, etc. through knowledge of (expanded) science and consciousness. Assist in evolutionary process towards God and/or spiritual fulfilment	Teleogical evolution, Purpose, Design	Scientific and Medical Network
Agnosticism	*(False)	False	Man	Evolution. God = Primary Cause by definition	Irrelevant: (as with Liberalism)	Science and Secular philosophies (mainly ethical and individualist with spiritual enlightenment)	Explain religious beliefs (origins, functions and persistence) through science. Find secular, but spiritual, substitute for God	Secular Humanism	British Association for the Advancement of Science
Atheism	False	False	Man	Evolution occurred by chance	Relevant: Bible refutable (and refuted) by science	Science and Secular philosophies (mainly social or political and perhaps Utopian)	Disprove God, explain away religious beliefs and behaviours and show their danger. Realize scientific ethic of the future.	Scientific Truth	British Society for Social Responsibility in Science / British Humanist Association

* Bracket indicates qualification

279

REFERENCES AND NOTES

The material in this paper is drawn from two studies, one of which, on science and religion, was supported with a grant from The Nuffield Foundation and the other, on the Unification Church, is being supported with a grant from the Social Science Research Council of Great Britain.
I would like to express my gratitude to both bodies for their assistance.

1. Barker, E., "Science and Theology: Diverse Resolutions of an Inter-disciplinary Gap by the New Priesthood of Science", *Interdisciplinary Science Reviews*, or "Thus Spake the Scientist", *Annual Review of the Social Sciences of Religion*, 3 (1979).

2. *Divine Principle*, Holy Spirit Association for the Unification of World Christianity, 2nd Edition, (London, 1973), see especially pp. 5, 8 and 9 for the destiny of science.

3. *Ibid.*, pp. 28-9.

4. Wallis, R., *The Road to Total Freedom: A Sociological Analysis of Scientology* (London, Heineman, 1976).

5. "Age of Enlightenment Newsletter", April-May, 1977 inter alia.

6. Leaflet handed out in street.

7. Heelas, P., "Californian Self-Religions and Socialising the Subjective" in Barker, E., *Society from the Perspective of New Religious Movements* (forthcoming).

8. Rosen, R. D., *Psychobabble: Fast Talk and Quick Cure in the Era of Feeling* (London, Wildwood House, 1977).

9. Popper, K., *Conjectures and Refutations: The Growth of Scientific Knowledge* (London, Routledge and Kegan Paul, 1965), p. 37.

10. Barker, E., "Apes and Angels: Reductionism, Selection and Emergence in the Study of Man", *Inquiry*, 19 (1976) 367-399.

11. Barker, E., "In the Beginning: The Battle of Creationist Science against Evolutionism" in *On the Margins of Science: The Social Construction of Rejected Knowledge*, ed-Wallis, R., Sociological Review Monograph 27 (Keele, 1979). 179-200.

12. Barker, E., "The Challenge of Social Science to Religious Faith: Can Sociological Explanation Threaten Theology?", *Sociology and Theology: Alliance and Conflict*, ed. Martin, D., Orme-Mills, J., Pickering, W.S.F., (Harvester Press, 1980). 15-23.

13. Barker, E., "Value Systems Generated by Biologists", *Contact*, 55/4 (1976) 2-13.

14. Martin, D., "Profane Habit and Sacred Usage", *Theology*, (March, 1979).

Retrospect

Mary Hesse
Department of History and Philosophy of Science, University of Cambridge, U.K.

IN HIS INTRODUCTION, Arthur Peacocke distinguishes eight types of relation currently perceived between science and theology. These range from a total separation of their realms, to the belief that the realms overlap and that theology can, and perhaps must, be formulated in terms which are consistent with or modelled on the conceptual frameworks of science. In a time when natural science still largely dominates intellectual perceptions of the world, it is not surprising to find that the dualistic view is not represented in the Symposium. What is surprising, however, is that the greatest deference towards science is to be found among the contributions of the theologians, and the greatest degree of criticism of both science and theology comes from the laymen – chiefly from the sociologists and the historians and philosophers of science.

In these concluding remarks I shall not attempt to give a detailed summary or critique of the papers, nor to pretend that clear lines of either conflict or consensus emerged from the Symposium. I shall rather try to develop an independent and highly impressionistic view of the Symposium, but nevertheless one that has been considerably educated and modified by reading the papers as a whole. My point of view can be briefly summarized in the following four points.

Firstly, as all participants argued, science and theology are both partly concerned with the common subject matter of the natural world, and hence no extreme dualism is acceptable. The natural world is not, however, identical with the subject matter of natural science. It therefore follows that theology may be concerned with aspects of that world, and may have aims in regard to it, without these necessarily being the aspects and aims that are the concern of natural science. These possible differences of aspect and aim need careful scrutiny.

Secondly, exactly what natural science implies about the natural world is at present under debate in both philosophy and sociology of science. Scientific theory cannot therefore just be taken at face value

281

as a realistic account of nature.

Thirdly, there is a hermeneutic tradition in theology which compares the subject matter and aims of theology with those of history and the human sciences rather than with those of natural science. This tradition is almost wholly absent from the Symposium. I shall discuss this absence in the light of contemporary sociological and philosophical debates about the cultural relativity of belief systems, including those of both science and theology.

Finally I shall briefly address the question as to whether, in the light of all this self-reflection, we can construct a new map of the relations between science and theology, in which they meet on the ground of different but comparable *social symbolisms* rather than of common subject matter or of method.

I

Nature as the common subject matter

In their papers, Pannenberg, Torrance, Daecke and Bowker[1] all stress, as an implication of the doctrine of creation, that nature is God's nature, and that science and theology are both concerned with understanding this nature as a whole. Nature and its regularities cannot be fully understood without reference to God, and with reference to God nature must be viewed sacramentally and as the arena of God's personal activity. In his useful historical account of one of the cruxes of the science/theology debate, McMullin explores in more detail the relations between theology of nature and natural science. He shows how Galileo makes very complex and subtle comparisons between the deliverances of Scripture and of natural demonstration, and also how he weighs not only the evidence from these two sources, but also their respective statuses as claims to truth. We should take the hint from McMullin's account, and probe somewhat more deeply than the theologians sometimes do, into the nature of this nature which is the concern of both science and theology, and into what is implied by the two sorts of study of it.

First a negative point needs to be established. If, as Daecke suggests, hermeneutic theology has in the past appeared to neglect the relation of God to *nature*, and if this balance needs to be restored, this is nevertheless not equivalent to the proposition that there is a special need for theology to come to terms with *science*. There are many features of man's relation to nature which are not the immediate concern of science. For example, however imperialistic their claims

282

about science may appear to be, most scientists would agree that it lies beyond their scope to speak of the beginning or the end of all that is, or to give an ultimate explanation of the existence of regularities in nature. They may then differ about the meaningfulness or usefulness of debating these matters, but they would generally not claim that science in itself has anything definite to say about them. They are explicitly the province of philosophy and theology. In saying this I do not at all wish to deny Torrance's claim that classical theology generated a metaphysics of contingent order within which science could develop, but I would reject some of his assertions about the metaphysical implications of particular scientific theories. There are complex questions here which I cannot go into, but let me mention an example. The theory of relativity as successful science is consistent with a metaphysics of either static determinism *or* of open process: after all Einstein himself remained a determinist even in the light of the apparent indeterminism of quantum physics. It is true that particular kinds of scientific theory do have a tendency to go along with particular kinds of metaphysics, but this is a product of local historical and social circumstances, not of logical implication, and should be stated as such.

Again, there is undoubtedly an ethical dimension to the relation between theology and nature, but this should also be distinguished carefully from the mutual implications of theology and science. Values enter scientific practice in two ways. There is the obvious fact that the *use* of science can be beneficial or destructive. This platitude has recently been given new force by the contention of those concerned with environmental problems that the very pursuit of science as such tends to have socially and ecologically damaging results. This may be true, but it does not follow that scientific *theory* as such has these implications as a matter of logic. To suppose that it does is to suppose that value can be deduced from fact, "ought" from "is".

It is, however, just this time-honoured formula that is disputed by a second way in which values are currently held to permeate science, that is that they are presupposed in the statements of theories themselves. Hefner argues in his paper that sociobiology in particular has direct value implications. The claim is that sociobiology is in principle a science which studies social needs, and can therefore discover the conditions of survival of the human species. These conditions determine systems of social value, and hence values can be derived from facts. This suggestion leads Hefner to the conclusion, about which he is admirably explicit, that "The most urgent gap experienced by humans [with regard to its value-requirements] . . . is the gap created by the possibility of not surviving. Theology, therefore, has no alternative today but to speak its truth about what is and what ought to be in terms relevant to survival".[2] But whatever facts may be discovered about the conditions of survival by sociobiology, the conclusion that survival of the human species is the most urgent *value* may itself be regarded as *morally* repugnant. This is surely a sufficient rebuttal of the claim that the facts alone permit the "ought" to be derived from the "is". The value judgment required as premiss for the argument is, moreover, one that conflicts directly with the traditional Christian judgment that the chief end of man is to glorify God. And one cannot mitigate the appearance of conflict here, as Hefner goes on to do, by speaking of the theologian's interest in the survival of "human worth, of all the conditions upon which the human spirit is dependent", for these theological virtues may *not* be the conditions which have survival value in the sociobiological sense, and they are indeed valued quite independently of its findings. God in his wisdom may have ordained values which are consistent with earthly extinction; to suppose otherwise is to embrace some form of materialism.

In this section I have made the negative point that direct concern of theology with nature does not imply the same sort of direct concern with science. In making this point I have relied on two sorts of distinction that are themselves controversial, namely those between science and metaphysics, and between fact and value. To justify these distinctions we need to look more closely at the respective domains of science and theology.

II

Science and the natural world

Since the work of Kuhn and Feyerabend there has been a long-running and detailed controversy in philosophy of science regarding theoretical realism versus relativity, and convergence versus pluralism. Is there any sense in which scientific theories should be taken as attempts to describe the real world, as attempts that converge upon the truth as science progresses? Or should we be content to regard theories as "natural myths", conditioned upon changing culture rather than nature, issuing in a potential plurality of relative representations of nature between which no question of ultimate truth arises?

No contributor to the Symposium addresses this cluster of questions directly, although some answers to them are implicit in several of the papers. I have developed my own view of the issues elsewhere[3],

284

and here I will confine myself to a consideration particularly of their influence on the papers of Pannenberg and Torrance. Both these authors *appear* to espouse a realistic view of science, but on closer inspection their arguments imply a much more subtle analysis of the relations between science and theology.

First, both Pannenberg and Torrance take the details of current science (specially physics) with such seriousness that they consider it vital for theology to come to terms with these details. It appears, therefore, that they interpret these theories realistically. On the other hand, both explicitly *limit* the capacity of science to yield full knowledge of nature. Pannenberg describes science as "knowledge that abstracts from the concreteness of physical reality", and goes on "such abstract knowledge [should not] claim full and exclusive competence regarding the explanation of nature".[4] Similarly Torrance holds that so far as theology is concerned "the material content of any scientific account of the universe is treated as a partial, provisional and revisable cosmology which can never be completed or therefore explained merely in terms of its own internal constituent relations".[5]

Both Pannenberg and Torrance go on, however, to trace very detailed correspondences and contrasts between the implications of physics and a theistic view of nature. Both hold it to be a theological requirement that natural regularities should be contingent and open-ended, and hence consistent with a dynamic view of history. Both agree that Newtonian science, with its concept of apparently self-sufficient inertia and its apparent rigid determinism, is inconsistent with this requirement. It is, incidentally, ironic that Hume, who could agree with most of what Pannenberg and Torrance say about the laws of nature as mere regularities, used this finding as a weapon *against* the deist version of theism, and concluded that it had atheistic implications. As theologians, Pannenberg and Torrance seem to be more interested in weapons against deism than against atheism.

Pannenberg goes on to make much stronger claims than Torrance for the *inconsistency* of current science with a Christian theology of nature. Whereas Torrance regards modern physics as interpretable in metaphysical terms that are highly sympathetic to a Christian view, Pannenberg isolates three concepts within the theoretical content of science that he thinks are inconsistent with that view. These are the concepts of "spirit" as the origin of life, "eternity" as the transformation of present life, and "eschatology" as the "end" of the natural world. In the last case he remarks that "scientific predictions that in some comfortably distant future the conditions for life will no longer continue on our planet, are hardly comparable to Biblical eschatol-

285

ogy",[6] and goes on to suggest that this must at present indicate an area of conflict betweeen science and theology.

It is not possible to pursue here the full implications of each of the case studies in convergence and conflict presented by Pannenberg and Torrance. Each would deserve a paper to itself. But it is necessary to ask, What exactly is going on in such case studies? If the details of the science are, as Torrance says, "partial, provisional and revisable", why do both theologians consider it so important for theology to come to terms with them? Would not a slightly less deferential view of science, such as is implied by recent epistemological and sociological critiques, suggest that such theological effort is a wrestling with shadows, and that while a Christian metaphysics of nature is being elaborated, the shadows may have slipped away and left other, perhaps radically different, kinds of theories to be contended with? I think this question must be approached on two different levels: that of the relations of metaphysics and science, and that of strategies of communication. First, whatever may be the outcome of the debate about the potential realism of scientific theories, there are certain metaphysical issues that are not going to be settled by the methods of science alone. These are such issues as determinism, the contingency or self-sufficiency of laws, the beginning and end of the natural universe, and the significance of mind and spirit in nature. No one doubts, either, that in the history of science there are many examples of mutual interactions between metaphysical views on these issues on the one hand, and developing theories of the empirical world on the other. But the history of science also suggests that it is just these metaphysical views that are "underdetermined" to the greatest degree by the science of any particular period, and are most subject to "radical revolution" when theoretical frameworks change. Science certainly exhibits progressive increase of technical control of nature through time, and it may exhibit convergence of its theoretical concepts towards "reality" in some domains, but it remains the case that, as Kant first clearly perceived, conflicting metaphysical interpretations may be given of almost any science, and almost any metaphysics may be espoused as the framework for any science.

When science is contrasted with metaphysics, and facts with values, it is science in its aspect of factual and instrumental regularity that is implied, not science in its aspect of conceptual theory and metaphysics. The conceptual frameworks of fundamental science and its metaphysics change through history and have no perennial cognitive status. So do the value judgments and norms in terms of which scientific theories are expressed and interpreted, and which, as in sociobiology, they seem to support as grounds for human practice. It is therefore not profitable to regard the arguments of Pannenberg and Torrance as contributions to a metaphysical theology of nature in the traditional sense, nor to regard the arguments of Hefner as contributions to the foundations of a Christian ethics. It is, however, possible and fruitful to regard all these as debates about an appropriate *language* for theology, and a source of appropriate *models*. It is, I think, possible to read each of the case studies in this way, as concerning *analogies* for or from science, rather than as logical implications. For example, when Pannenberg suggests that the concepts of eternity and eschatology are not comparable with physical theories of space-time, we may read him as asking how theological concepts which involve transcendence of nature may be expressed in a language accessible to those nurtured in the scientific framework. The problem is essentially not one of scientific "realism", but of communicative strategy.

This point must not be misunderstood. I do not mean to imply that theology is not concerned with truth and reality, but rather that its truth and reality should not be interpreted in the terms familiar from debates about science in the empiricist tradition. In the strategy of Pannenberg and Torrance the nature and content of theological truth is apparently not up for investigation. It is presupposed; its source is taken to be Scripture and tradition, not science or metaphysics. The problem in a scientific age is conceived to be how that truth should be presented and how it should be related to a developing science. This search for scientific models for theological truth is explicit in the papers of Bowker and Schlegel: the former addressing the problem of how to understand God's activity in the world on the analogy of an information system, and the latter on the analogy of the relation between observer and world as exhibited in quantum mechanics. Such model-building is essential apologetic strategy for theologians in the current intellectual climate, and I would not for a moment want to suggest that it is inferior to more traditional kinds of metaphysical theology. Indeed this is far from the case, since in the light of philosophical and social critique I do not believe that traditional metaphysical theology is even a possible enterprise. But this concentration on apologetics may obscure another important fact about the present status of theology, namely that its truth as justified by Scripture and tradition *itself* cannot be taken for granted. There is a problem about epistemology here that is currently more profound than the problem about metaphysics[14]. Apologetics cannot take place in a vacuum — we must have some indication as to how the theological view of nature is itself to be justified to a scientific and secular world.

287

Pannenberg and Torrance reveal an implicit position about this question also. It is clear, as also in Daecke's paper, that they are addressing themselves to a situation within theology itself which may be called the crisis of hermeneutics. Theology, they hold, must turn from the concentration on man and history in its hermeneutic phase, to the recovery of nature as created by God and as the scene of his activity. Such a turn away from hermeneutics may be read as an uncritical response to the continued prestige and influence of natural science, or, more respectably, as a programme for the most effective communication of the gospel. But is this communicative strategy sufficient? Given that scientific and theological *ontologies* of nature are sufficiently commensurable to permit mutual translations and metaphors, is it also the case that they are *epistemologically* commensurable and consistent, so that their independent criteria of truth can be taken for granted?

In Swinburne's paper this question is given an affirmative answer. He argues that there is a close epistemological analogy between theology and science, extending even to a fairly detailed theory of confirmation for arguments for the existence of God, modelled on the evidential confirmation of empirical existence hypotheses. The paper is tightly argued, and deserves a detailed critique. Here I can only venture to suggest that such appeals to religious experience (defined as those "which [seem] to the subject to be an awareness or perception of God"[7]) are not common nor intellectually persuasive nor even intelligible in the current secular climate. It is notable that at several points in his paper Swinburne puts the onus on the atheist to *dis*prove the possibility of God, rather than on the theist to prove it. This does seem to conflict with the requirements of the current intellectual scene and with the continued "triumphalism" of science, as this is described for instance in the papers of Rudwick and Barker.

Where, then, are we to look for light upon the cognitive status of theology, and for cogent epistemological strategies bearing upon its truth? Traditional theology has looked to history and hermeneutics, but this tradition has been subjected to a damaging relativistic critique from both epistemology and sociology; a critique which is represented by several of the later papers of the Symposium.

III

The relativist critique of science
The return to natural theology, as epitomised by the theological

papers already discussed, is intended to counter what their authors see as an over-emphasis on history and on the social and personal in the hermeneutic tradition. Moreover, that tradition is perceived as leading to an unacceptable relativism. In studies as diverse as Wittgensteinian philosophy, social anthropology, sociology of knowledge, comparative religion, the history of ideas, and history and philosophy of science, the emphasis has been on "internal" understanding ("*Verstehen*") of "language games", where these are regarded as self-sufficient cultural products about which no external judgments of truth or correctness are appropriate. It is only too obvious that if theology is put forward as a cognitive system, it too is subject to this relativistic critique. The return to natural theology and the metaphysics of natural science may therefore be seen as an attempt to evade cultural relativity and restore to theology the possibility of perennial truth.

I have already argued that for metaphysical and epistemological reasons this strategy does not work. We may now interpret the remaining papers of the Symposium as addressing themselves to two consequent questions:
1. Social and historical studies suggest that natural science itself as a cognitive system is subject to cultural relativity. How should we understand science in the light of this critique?
2. If the empiricist analysis of truth is a bad model for theology, what is the nature of the "truth" to which theology should aspire? Can we restore the cognitive status of theology in a way that takes account of the social and ideological critique?
I shall consider the first of these questions in this section, and the second in the next and final section.

Ravetz and Rudwick both argue on a variety of grounds for an interpretation of natural science as a social and cultural product, whose development depends on particular historical conditions, and whose justifications are traditional, ideological and evaluative as well as empirical. Both authors draw symmetrical conclusions regarding science and theology, pointing out that the arena of comparison and conflict is not that of empirical matters of fact, but of personal knowledge and wisdom, and of social tradition and values. Rudwick goes on to make a virtue of the relativity of both scientific and theological knowledge. The sociology of knowledge, he claims, "must be true to its own canons of impartiality and symmetry, by taking seriously the possible differentiating effect of claimed inputs from externality characterized in theistic terms".[8] If science and theology are in the same relativistic boat, then at least let us reject our partiality for the cognitive claims of science, and treat theology as equally deserving of cognitive consideration. Barker's paper contains a similar plea. In spite of her neutral stance as observer of the various social types of belief about science and religion, she notes how scientists manage to reinforce against criticism their image as surveyors of privileged truth, and suggests that they, like theologians, should subject their own values and unsupported hypotheses to self-scrutiny.

The tendency of such critique of science is not to deny cognitive difference but to deny privilege. Privilege has been based on the perception of science as (a) that which works practically, and (b) that which discovers natural truth. There is no reason to deny that instrumental success does constitute knowledge of a progressive sort. But science has always been regarded as more than instrumental — the question is whether its further claims ought to have cognitive privilege not accorded to other types of belief system. Social and epistemological analysis suggests that they should not. Moreover it suggests that we should regard the significance of scientific theory and metaphysics in the *same* way that we regard other cultural products, namely as reflecting social and psychological ideology and symbolism. In the past such a conclusion would have been the signal for immediate cognitive dismissal and for accusations of irrationality, and indeed echoes of such an attitude are to be found in Pannenberg's and Torrance's papers. Speaking of the New Testament affirmation of the immanent end of this world, Pannenberg asks if it is possible to understand it without reducing "the Biblical language to metaphor, or [dismissing] it as mythological".[9] And Torrance asserts that God interacts with men within physical reality, "and does not merely relate himself to men in some 'external' or 'indirect' way which could only be given mythological expression".[10] To understand the nature of theology in the light of insights coming especially from history and philosophy of science and from social anthropology, however, it is necessary to be sensitive to the question "What is the justification for such literal/metaphoric, fact/myth distinctions, which dictate cognitive privilege for the literal and factual, and hence for the methodology of science, even in the domain of theology?"

Recognition that it is new concepts of truth and reality that are needed in theology is to be found in Alves' paper. He argues that the traditional claims of science to privileged status have concealed an ideology of *contemplation* and of *givenness*. Theoretical science, however, ought rather to be understood as a game played with rules which construct a passive external nature, and which entail the exclusion of personal emotion and value. This ideology has become a therapeutic and political programme of total adjustment to given reality. It has no room for temporality, for utopia, novelty, imaginaton or action. "The man who speaks only the truth [in this sense] will become totally integrated in the system of the given, be it nature, be it society".[11] But, Alves goes on to point out, even Kant was more modest about the principles of the pure reason. He understood that they exclude practice, action, value and finality. It is just these, according to Alves, that are the province of religion, which belongs not to the game of scientific truth, but to the game of action. It concerns the absent God and a creation in travail; not givenness but utopia.

Alves's paper provides a valuable counterpoint to the papers on sociology of science, and a valuable bridgehead to the social critique of theology. But it may be suggested that its negative and pessimistic portrayal of theoretical science needs to be balanced by insight into the positive symbolic function of science in expressing the cosmology of a culture. Such insight derives from the very same social and epistemological analysis upon which Alves relies, and it is very far from the ideology of static contemplation of reality which he rejects. The fact that extra-empirical features of science are largely conditioned by the traditiohs and ideologies, and indeed the utopias, of the surrounding culture need neither be dismissed as irrationality nor as a surrender to givenness, but can be welcomed in Alves's perspective as science's own contribution to the dynamic practice without which no society nor individual can live. Such an interpretation of science can begin to heal the breach with theology on the basis of action rather than contemplation. On the other hand, Alves's account of religion as action requires to be supplemented by the sort of theological and sociological analysis provided by the remaining two papers, by Lash and Martin.

IV

The cognitive status of theology
With Alves's account we seem to return to the dualism of the hermeneutic tradition: a dualism between society and nature, history and creation, personal subjectivity and religious objectivity, theology and science. The rejection of this tradition by theologians at the Symposium is largely couched in metaphysical and theological terms, but their conclusion is nevertheless compatible with that of Alves, namely that modern science itself points to the need to revise our metaphysics towards greater dynamism, historicity and contingency. I have

argued that some of the details of this claim are inappropriate interpretations of science, but with the conclusion I have no quarrel. A radical reinterpretation of the metaphysics of science *is* required, not in the sense of a redescription of natural "reality", but in its whole methodology and cognitive status. This needs to be shifted towards a perception of theoretical science as a social symbol of nature. In such a perspective we can embrace relativity without falling into the irrationality that our natural theologians seem to fear.

Can we embrace theology similarly as social symbolism, conditional as Durkheim argued upon the collective representations of the culture? Lash addresses this question specifically in the light of the Marxist critique of theology as *ideological*, in the pejorative sense of being the illusory expression of false consciousness, or as reducible to non-religious social forms. He points out that even Marx allowed the existence of law, art and philosophy "after the revolution" as non-illusory expressions of aspects of human experience. So why not religion as the expression of experience of God? Theology as rational knowledge could, he thinks, only be excluded as illusory if it could be shown that there is no such experience, no practical transformation of life which shows forth the practical truthfulness of Christianity. Moreover, he argues that theology is *also* a critical discipline — it has its tradition of the negative as well as the positive way, and all theological statement, like all ideology, must guard against idolatry and illusion. Lash thus addresses the Marxist and Durkheimian critiques, but perhaps not the relativist one, and it is noticeable that, like Swinburne, he tends to put the onus on the *un*believer to *dis*prove the possibility of faith.

Writing as a sociologist, Martin also leaves aside the abstract problems of deterministic reduction and relativity, in favour of a concrete analysis of certain statements of Christian belief. In particular, he considers the "new man", the eucharistic unity, and the nature of hope. His standpoint requires him to adopt explicitly the interpretation of religious statements as socially symbolic, just as I have argued that theoretical science should be seen as symbolic. Martin concludes, however, that, "nothing a sociologist might tell us about the social reality of the various transitions where they come into play, whether baptism, or eucharist, or death, could conceivably bear on the realities to which the signs claim to refer".[12]

Not conceivably? Well, if this means that what the sociologist tells us cannot *in fact* influence people's belief and cause them to reject the realities to which the signs claim to refer, this is surely false. At least some of the causes of modern atheism and agnosticism lie in just such critique from social and natural science. If it means, however, that such critique does not *logically imply* the non-existence of the realities referred to, this is true, but as so often with logical implication it is relatively unimportant, since human rationality and justified belief is hardly ever determined by the canons of strict logic, nor ought it to be so. What is needed is a closer investigation of the *rational* and *cognitive* character of symbolism, by which I mean something between factual descriptions of belief on the one hand and logic on the other. Here Martin's paper gives some valuable clues. He shows how the symbols form a holistic system in which the meanings of the parts presuppose the meaning of the whole. He shows how the symbols reflect paradoxes within belief and conflicts within action. He shows how symbols combine facts with communal norms, legitimations and values. In the light of such analysis no theology or philosophy of religion can afford an atomistic or formalistic approach to statements of belief. This much at least is surely entailed by the social critique of symbols, and it has far-reaching implications for appropriate styles of theology.

What, finally, about the problem of relativity of religious belief? This question was not confronted directly by any of the Symposiasts, but some positive hints are to be found, particularly in Lash's paper, about how it might be approached. Christianity, like any religious symbol system must be judged holistically, and judged as an expression of reality permeated by value and meaning as well as of empirical fact. Moreover Christian theology always presupposes the existence of the Christian community and its practice, which is a practice partly of story-telling. "Truth" of the relevant kind for religion inheres in the stories, not primarily in their theological foundation, but in the truth found in the believer's self-involvement. As Lash puts it:

> "The Christian believer is a story-teller, and the story that he tells is of a process in which he acknowledges himself to be a participant . . . . . The task of theology, as critical reflection on religious practice, is to elucidate the truth-conditions of the tale and thus critically to assess the truthfulness of the telling". [13]

An incarnational religion has no theological language except its own stories, traditions and symbols, together with the mythologies of the science and society in which it finds itself. Lash here describes a task in which, for our culture, almost all remains to be done.

Postscript
There was once an architect who was commissioned by a vote of his

293

parish council to build a cathedral. The people promised their labour and their money for the building. They wanted it to celebrate in the most fitting way the sense of mystery and power and otherness that they experienced in their personal lives and their social community and in the world around them. They wanted to place their lives, which were often nasty, brutish and short, in a context of the meaning they dimly sensed through it all. The architect drew up his plans, and over the centuries the people laboured away, and eventually the spires reached towards heaven. But then some philosophers came along that way, and said, Look, the structure is cracking, it has not been properly put together; and they even proved this by knocking a few pieces off here and there. Then some engineers and geologists came along and peered at the foundations and the soil and said, It is built on sand; it will collapse. And indeed, in a great storm which began in about 1789 it did fall, and the people who were left to continue their celebrations had to huddle in ruined side chapels and crypts.

Then the engineers and geologists said, Look, we have prepared a firm piece of ground over here on which we have built many factories and shipyards and space-shuttle launching pads, and all these things have worked magnificently. You cannot expect your cathedral for celebrating the Otherness to stand on anything but the secure ground of what Really Is, and we are the experts about that. So certain of the leaders of the people persuaded them that there was a lot of truth in what the engineers and geologists said, and they asked the engineers to prepare some new plans. The people weren't too keen on the style of building that was now proposed, but they started to move the stones and build again on the ground prepared for them. Before they had got very far, however, some moles, mostly from the departments of sociology and history and philosophy of science in the neighbouring university, started to burrow under the ground until the foundations were no firmer than before. And the half-finished building collapsed; and the people had nowhere at all to celebrate; and the people were in despair.

When they saw what had happened some of the moles were aghast and said, We did not mean this to happen at all, we were only trying to investigate the ground in a neutral manner, as is the custom of our tribe. But other moles said Aha, it is just as we thought, there are *no* secure foundations, and even our own burrows go through the quick-sands. We can only go on burrowing according to the habits of our tribe: it is all quite meaningless. At this the philosophers got very angry indeed, and they all fell to fighting among themselves, not noticing that the people had meanwhile gone away. After a time they all got tired of fighting, and began to disperse in various directions about their own concerns. As they went, some of them passed a cave in the hillside, and looking in they saw a few of the people gathered round a stone slab. On the slab were bread and a cup of wine and some books and also the tattered plans of the original cathedral. Light shone through a hole in the roof and struck the cup, and seemed to make on it the sign of the cross. And the people were talking about how they would send someone out to study with the philosophers and the scientists and the sociologists and the historians, and then bring him back and train him as an architect.

REFERENCES*

1. For example, Pannenberg, p. 4, Torrance, p. 83, Daecke, p. 130, Bowker, p. 98.
2. Hefner, p. 76

4. Pannenberg, p. 4.
5. Torrance, p. 84.
6. Pannenberg, p. 15.
7. Swinburne, p. 182.
8. Rudwick, p. 258.
9. Pannenberg, p. 6.
10. Torrance, p. 82.
11. Alves, p. 171.
12. Martin, p. 240.
13. Lash, p. 223.
14. It should, however, be borne in mind that the two books referred to by Bowker in his final footnote (*The Sense of God* and *The Religious Imagination*) recognise the priority of the epistemological demand and its urgency for contemporary theological reflection (see, e.g., *The Sense of God* pp. 180-3, *The Religious Imagination* pp. 24-8, 300-307). Those two books in conjunction also suggest a way in which an actual response to the epistemological challenge might be constructed.

Comments

The foregoing 'Retrospect' was written by Professor Mary Hesse, at the request of members of the Oxford Symposium, as a survey of the various contributions, in the form in which they were submitted for publication. Her analysis of the papers has inevitably and properly been written from the perspective of her own particular point of view on the nature of the terms on which the dialogue between science and theology is to be engaged — a possible stance that had perhaps not been sufficiently elaborated at the Symposium itself. It was not to be expected that her viewpoint would be shared by all the contributors, so they were circulated with her 'Retrospect' and their comments were invited.

The following pages reproduce all the comments that were submitted in response to Professor Hesse's survey. They constitute an apt conclusion to the volume for, together with that survey, they focus very sharply many of the outstanding issues still to be resolved in the complex relations between the sciences and theology in the twentieth century. In our intellectual climate that is increasingly beginning to recognise, from both sides, the necessity for, or at least the desirability of, this dialogue, the 'Retrospect' and the comments it evoked serve to demonstrate what a thorough and sustained effort of clarification will be needed to continue it. So it is hoped that these final pages will provide a stimulus to similar efforts of their readers to pursue the new phase of this dialogue that is now developing — a phase clearly signalled by the 1979 Oxford Symposium itself.

A.R. Peacocke

W. Pannenberg

At the end of the Oxford Symposium it was agreed that some attempt at looking upon the whole of the conference would be desirable lest the different contributions of the participants might fall apart. The job was entrusted to Dr. Hesse, but what emerged from her pen exhibits a peculiarly personal view rather than a balanced summary of the joint efforts of the participants. The survey particularly informs everyone concerned to what degree — in the opinion of Dr. Hesse — papers were to the point or not. Most time, unfortunately, they were not. Thus, Dr. Swinburne's appeals to religious experience are just 'not common nor intellectually persuasive nor even intelligible in the current secular climate'. By and large, the theologians, — and espe-

cially those of other than English origin, — have little chance to pass
their examinations. Dr. Torrance and myself are told that it would be
'not profitable' to regard our arguments as dealing with the reality of
nature — what Dr. Hesse calls a 'metaphysical theology of nature'.
But to regard our presentations as 'debates about an appropriate
language for theology', as Dr. Hesse suggests, 'a communicative
strategy', obviously distorts the argument of my paper and equally, it
seems to me, that of Dr. Torrance's. It does not improve the situation
that in Dr. Hesse's view this may be an extremely benevolent
interpretation, since she seems to sympathise with generally viewing
theology as "social symbolism" along the line of E. Dürkheim.
Theologians can hardly be content with looking upon the Christian
tradition as a symbolic expression of something else than God and his
revelation. Certainly religious and theological language is always *also*
subjective, socially and culturally conditioned, historically relative.
In theology (in distinction from science, maybe), there is a longstand-
ing awareness of such cultural and historical conditionedness of
religious and theological language. It is difficult to become enthusiastic about it, as if it were a recent discovery. The question is whether
religion and theology have to offer anything beyond that, concerning
the reality they assert, the reality of God. Even Dr. Hesse asks for a
'closer investigation' of the 'cognitive character of symbolism'. The
question of the cognitive character of religious assertions, however,
inescapably involves the question of their truth concerning the
asserted reality of God, of his actions and of his revelation, notwithstanding the symbolic form of religious language. When everything
has been said about symbolic structure, cultural and historical relativity, the truth claims of religious assertions are still to be dealt with. I
should assume a similar situation in relation to scientific language. I
do not see how in explaining scientific language there could prevail in
the long run an extreme relativism that would evade or (culturally)
taboo the very question concerning the relation of scientific theory to
the reality of nature. To me it makes little sense to replace the
simplistic equation of theory with reality by the opposite simplification to the effect that theory had no relation to the reality it describes.
Since I dare to assume that scientific theory ('models') can tell *something* about the reality of nature and *not only* about the culture they
arise from, I may 'espouse a realistic view of science', although such
common sense assumption seems sufficient evidence to exclude me in
Dr. Hesse's view from the company of the sophisticated. And it is
only because in *some* way science is concerned with the reality of
nature, and even (in a certain sense) in a privileged way, that theology

has to be concerned with science. The question is not discussed, it is simply dismissed by Dr. Hesse. She does not even address herself to the point that cóncern for the reality of God as creator entails concern for the reality of nature and therefore (only therefore, I think), for science.

Instead of considering these reasons of theologians for being concerned for science, Dr. Hesse offers a psychological explanation. In her judgment it seems "clear" that Dr. Torrance and myself are prompted by the 'crisis of hermeneutics' in theology to seek a 'recovery of nature as created by God'. Now, as far as I am concerned, it is pure fiction to talk of a 'turn away from hermeneutics'. My book on 'Theology and the Philosophy of Science' provides sufficient evidence that I consider a hermeneutical approach to the discussion of scientific method to be fundamentally important. The critical limitation there advocated of claims to exclusive competence on behalf of the natural sciences concerning the reality of the natural world, may provoke many critical reactions. The one thing it hardly exhibits is a'deferential view of science' which Dr. Hesse attributes to me (as to Torrance) in spite of her own observation of our intentions to *'limit* the capacity of science' concerning the interpretation of reality. It is equally misleading to attribute to me the view that 'the nature and content of theological truth is apparently not up for investigation. It is presupposed'. Whoever cares to take some notice, even superficially, of my conception of theological method, cannot overlook that, quite to the contrary, I treat religious and theological assertions as hypothetical 'models'. Nobody is obliged to read books and articles of other people. But if one doesn't, one should be just a little careful in talking about their views. In any event, Dr. Hesse's survey demonstrates that in spite of the Oxford symposium a real dialogue between theology and some other disciplines concerned with science is still in a preliminary phase.

E. McMullin The Relativist Critique of Science

At the beginning of Section II of her *Retrospect*, Professor Hesse notes that the issue of scientific realism has not been addressed directly by any of the contributors to the symposium, She formulates the issue in this perspicuous way:

> Is there any sense in which scientific theories should be taken as attempts to describe the real world, as attempts that converge upon the

299

truth as science progresses? Or should we be content to regard theories as 'natural myths', conditioned upon changing culture rather than nature, issuing in a potential plurality of relative representations of nature between which no question of ultimate truth arises?

I take it that a realist would answer 'yes' to the first of these questions and 'no' to the second. I take it further that the answer given to them will be crucial to the determination of the cognitive relationship between science and theology, the topic with which so much of the symposium was concerned. In my own essay, I presupposed a realist reading of cosmology, as of natural science generally. Were I to have taken an instrumentalist approach instead, the questions I addressed would have received a quite different answer. If the theories of science are not seen as a source of insight into the structures of the natural world, there can be no question of a conflict (or for that matter of consonance) between theology and science in regard to the natural world. One can understand, then, the attraction that so many Christians from Berkeley onwards have felt for the instrumentalist account of science.

What troubles me about Professor Hesse's paper is its ambivalence in regard to the answer to the two questions she herself poses. Were this ambivalence no more than a hesitation due to the great complexity of the disputed questions and the consequent difficulty in formulating adequate answers to them in yes-no terms, I would be entirely sympathetic. But I seem to detect more of a leaning to the instrumentalist side than could, I think, be warranted by reference to the present state of the discussion among philosophers of science. This is her one concession to scientific realism:

> Science certainly exhibits progressive increase in technical control of nature through time, and it may exhibit convergence of its theoretical concepts towards 'reality' in some domains, but it remains the case that, as Kant first clearly perceived, conflicting metaphysical interpretation may be given of almost any science, and almost any metaphysics may be espoused as the framework for any science.

Here it is to metaphysics that the relativist critique is directed, and the (possible) truth-bearing of some domains of scientific theory is conceded. But elsewhere this concession appears to be withdrawn. The conclusion of the relativist critique of science (Section III) is that cognitive privilege must be denied to science if it is based on anything more than the claim that science 'works practically', specifically if it is based on the supposition that science leads to the discovery of truth about nature.

> Science has always been regarded as more than instrumental — the question is whether its further claims ought to have cognitive privilege not accorded to other sorts of belief system. Social and epistemological analysis suggests that they should not. Moreover it suggests that we should regard the significance of scientific theory and metaphysics in the *same* way that we regard other cultural products., namely as reflecting social and psychological ideology and symbolism.

Here the relativist critique is directed against both metaphysics *and* scientific theory. But I would want to argue that even though science is a social product, there is a crucial difference between it and most other cultural products. It is that the occasionally distortive influence of ideology on theory can be limited by the progressive use of the complex test-methods characteristic of science. By 'distortive', I mean something which reflects the social structures or personal interests of the knower rather than the structures of the object he or she is trying to understand. Such influences obviously affect scientific activity at all levels: the rivalries and ambitions that spark so much of the energies of research, for example. One does not have to believe in a criterion of demarcation that can clearly and instantaneously separate science from ideology in order to hold that as science progresses, the distortive effects of ideology and personal interest are gradually lessened. That is, the scientist gradually discovers which of the effects are distortive and which are not.

The metaphysical or theological presuppositions a scientist absorbs from the broader culture may or may not prove distortive in their impact upon his or her science; only time and the steady pressures of theory-extension will decide. (Think, for instance, of the influence on Newton of various theological presuppositions about the relationship between God and the natural order.) The notion of 'test' involved here is no simple matter of surviving attempts at falsification. It has to do with successful short-term prediction, of course, but much more with the guidance of theory into fruitful pathways of extension and modification.

What I am arguing, then, is that even though the mechanics of Newton and the biology of Darwin may have (in Professor Hesse's phrase) reflected the social and psychological ideology of their makers, a testing-process operated over the years to separate out what was truth-bearing in each. This is really the crucial point. The models of the organic chemist, the geneticist, the geologist, give us a positive (even though limited) insight into the structures of the real. If one were to treat them as no more than the 'cosmology of a culture', to suppose that in a different cultural setting (at a late time, or on another planet) they could be quite different, one would seriously underestimate their truth-status. One can (indeed one must) concede their metaphorical character, without for a moment suggesting that someone who takes them seriously as sources of truth is 'wrestling with shadows'.

The relativist critique of science, coming in recent years mainly from sociologists of science, has not to my mind weakened the realist claim of the natural sciences; it has not undermined their cognitive privilege in matters of natural knowledge. To say that is *not* to point to science as a unique source of truth; it is not to assume that its theories are culture-neutral. Nor does it commit the Christian necessarily to the road of natural theology. It still leaves open the hard choices involved in deciding on the epistemological relationship of theology and the sciences. Were one to suppose the relativist critique to have succeeded, it would make these choices easy, too easy.

T. F. Torrance

By way of response to Mary Hesse's comments, I would like to confine myself to two things.

Firstly she asks why theologians like Pannenberg and myself consider it important to come to terms with the details of science if they are 'partial, provisional and revisable'. Simply because, I would answer, we take seriously the fact that the universe, in which alone we know him, is *God's creation,* and acknowledge its contingent nature and intelligibility. To borrow some apt words from Meyer Abich: 'Si Dieu est Dieu, il est aussi le Dieu de la nature, ou alors il n'est pas Dieu; si le Christ est la verité, il est aussi la verité de la physique, pour autant que celle-ci soit une verité de vie'. It is because we believe in the objectivity of the reality of God and the truth of Christ that we hold that all *our* theological statements about them are contingent and revisable, just as we accept that the kind of profound objectivity with which we operate in relativity theory confers relativity and revisability upon all our conceptions and statements about the universe.

Secondly, Mary Hesse writes, 'The theory of relativity as successful science is consistent with a metaphysics of either static determinism *or* of open process: after all Einstein himself remained a determinist even in the light of the apparent indeterminism of quantum physics'. Apart from the fact that a metaphysical, or a scientific, theory of determinism fails to account for the capacities of the metaphysician, or the scientist, this statement seems to misrepresent Einstein and imply a misunderstanding of relativity theory. Einstein's rejection of the 'indeterminism' of the Göttingen form of quantum theory does not imply that he was a determinist, as Pauli showed in several letters to Max Born, but that he was a *realist*. If relativity theory were consistent with a 'static determinism', it would be consistent with the static (isotropic, necessary and unchanging) framework of absolute time and space, and thus with the idealised geometry of relations between rigid bodies independent of time, which is precisely what relativity theory completely dismantles! Nevertheless, Einstein operated, as he claimed, with a 'higher degree of uniformity of connection than is contained in our time-casuality'. The kind of casuality that static determinism operates with is artificially built up from an abstract 'cross-section of time', whereas the kind of casuality implied in relativity theory is identified with the dynamic configurations of the spatio-temporal field which characterises all empirical reality. It is precisely because relativity theory relativises the conception of time, which it will not abstract from the on-going processes of nature, that it also relativises the conception of causal connections in time, and thereby destroys the ground for a scientific or a metaphysical 'static determinism'. Mary Hesse's claim that relativity theory is consistent with static determinism *or* open process would seem to imply the very element of positivist conventionalism in the concept of science which relativity theory forced Einstein to reject in the position advocated by Ernst Mach!

It is because I am in deep agreement with Einstein's conception of science as 'grasping reality in its depth' that I do not agree that what I have tried to say about the relations of theology and science may be deflected into some kind of 'strategy of communication'.

R. G. Swinburne

Mary Hesse claims that 'appeals to religious experience . . . are not common nor intellectually persuasive nor even intelligible in the current secular climate'. The suggestion that they are not common seems just false. The history of religion is full of claims to have 'heard the voice of God'. For a recent collection of reports of 'religious experiences', some of which are religious experiences in my sense, see Timothy Beardsworth, *A Sense of Presence*, Oxford, 1977. The argument of my paper was that appeals to religious experience *ought* to be intellectually persuasive (*i.e.* to have evidential force) and that the criteria for judging perceptual claims do put the onus on the man who wishes to reject a claim. As to the claim that appeals to religious experience are not intelligible — I can only suggest that he who finds them so should familiarise himself with the literature of religion in order to see what the appeals mean.

N. Lash

There is just one brief comment that I should like to make on Professor Hesse's most interesting and illuminating *Retrospect*. According to her, I 'tend to put the onus on the *un*believer to *dis*prove the possibility of faith'. I accept this inasmuch as 'the requirements of the current intellectual scene' (to use an earlier phrase of hers) are dictated as much by custom and prejudice as they are by historical, moral or philosophical argument. There is ill-informed and intellectually incurious atheism just as there is ill-informed and intellectually incurious theism. It is a great deal more difficult appropriately to articulate the question of faith and its grounds and, above all, the question of God, than is often appreciated by believer and nonbeliever alike. Nevertheless, I am unhappy with her formulation.

In the first place, surely the 'possibility of faith' is not in question. Faith is a fact, possibly a misguided fact. What I did suggest was that the possibility of theological discourse constituting a mode of rational knowledge could only be excluded if religious faith could be shown to be in *no* sense 'experiential knowledge' of its object. Because, secondly, I do not believe that theoretical argument and reflection can ever, of themselves, decide this issue one way or the other, I further believe that the enterprise of philosophical theology is misconceived if its goals are perceived in terms of the 'proof' or 'disproof' of the reality of God. To put it another way: it seems to me that the forensic metaphor of 'locating the burden of proof' is unhelpful because its use implies that there is some single concept of 'proof' that is, and is agreed to be, appropriate in respect of any and every type of cognitive claim.

Index

Names and page references to principal contributors are shown in bold type. Page references to bibliography are given in *italics* and text references in plain type.

Gogarten, F.128
Golini, C. L. *261*
Gouldner, A. W. 218, 219, 223, *225*, 227
Gregorios, Paul 130, 132, 134, 135, 136, *140*
Gregory of Nyssa 133
Grice, H. P. *196*
Gruber, H. E. 251, 253, *260*
Gustafson, J. *78*
Gutierrez, G. *225*

Habgood, J x, *xvii*
Hadamard 204
Hall, A. R. *53*
Hannaway, Owen 205
Hare, R. M. 60, 63, 68, 70, 72, *77*, *78*
Hartshorne, C. 130, *159*
Harvey 201, 202
Hawking S. W. 41
Hebblethwaite, P. *225*, 227
Heim, Karl xiii, *xviii*
Heelas, Paul 272, *280*
Hefner, Philip 58-77 xv, 138, *140*, 156, *160*, 283, *295*
Hegel 163
Heisenberg 155
Herbert, Frank 48, 49
Hertz 91
Hesse, Professor Mary 281-295 ix, x, xvii, *297*, 298, 299, 300, 301, 302, 303, 304
Høffding, Harald 155
Holmer, P. L. *78*
Horton, R. xii, *xviii*
Hoyle, Fred 32, 33, *54*, 116
Hubble 17
Hume, David 39, 59, 73, 100, *180*, 203
Hunter, Geoffrey 60, 63, 73
Hutten, E. H. 36
Huxley, Julian 108, 242

Isham, C. J. *125*
Islam 28, 49
Is/ought 58, 59, 63, 64, 65, 66, 69, 73, 74, 76
Israel 21, 44

Jacob, Maragaret *260*
Jacob, J. R. *260*
James, William 151, 156, *159*, 197
Jammer, Max 156, *159*
Jeans, J. 34
Jensen, Ole 132, *140*
Judaism 49, 66
Jonson, Jonas 137, *140*
Johnson, P *159*
Jordanova, L. J. *260*

Kant, Immanuel 8, *15*, 38, 39, 40, 45, 90, 149, 156, 163, 165, 171, 173, *180*, 300
Katz, Solomon 69, *78*
Kaufmann, Walter *180*, *181*
Kenny, A 55
Kent, P. W. ix
Kepler x, 201, 202
Kierkegaard, Søren 155, 178, *179*, 233
Koch, Klaus 129, 130, 132, *139*
Kohlberg, L. 61
Kolawowski, L. 215, *225*
Kornhuber 104
Koyré, A. *53*
Kuhn, Thomas, S *53*, 198, 203, 219, 246, 249, *259*, 284

Lacey, J. C. 116, *124*
Laplace, P. S. 90, 142, *159*
Lakatos, I. *53*, 249
Lash, Nicholas, 209-227, 304 xvi, *227*, 291, 293, 295
Lateran Council *54*
Laudan, L *53*, *259*
Leavenworth, May 65, 67, *77*, *78*
Lecky, Prescott 170, *180*
Lefebvre, Henry 171, *180*
Leibniz 30
Lemaitre 30, 32, *53*, *54*
Libavius 205
Locke 149
Lorentz 91, 92
Longair, M. S. *56*
Lovell, Bernard 119
Luckmann, Thomas *180*
Luther 128

McDonagh, F. *57*
McKinney, R. W. A. *xviii*
McMullin, Ernan 17-57, 299-302 xv, xvi, *53*, *56*, *57*, 282
MacIntyre, Alisdair 60, 63
MacKinnon, D. M. *226*, 228
MacPherson, T. 101, 107, *123*
Mach, Ernst 90, 303
Maimonides 29
Malebranche, Nicholas de 151
Mannheim, Karl 171, *180*, 209, 210, 214, 218, *224*, *225*, 227, 247
Manichaeans 18, 19
Martin, David xvii, *229*, 277, *280*, 291, 292, *295*
Marx, Karl 166, *180*, 210, 213, 214, 215, 216, 217, 218, 219, 220, 221, 222, 224, *225*, *226*, 292
—ISM 212 213, 221
—IST 36, 60, 75, 215, 216, 217, 219
Massachusetts Institute of Technology ix